The Wild Coast

The Wild Coast
An Account of Politics in Guyana

Reynold A. Burrowes

Schenkman Publishing Company, Inc.
Cambridge, Massachusetts

Copyright © 1984

Schenkman Publishing Company, Inc.
Cambridge, MA 02138

Library of Congress Cataloging in Publication Data

Burrowes, Reynold.
   The wild coast: An account of politics in Guyana

   Bibliography: p.
   Includes index.
   1. Guyana—Politics and government—1803–1966.
2. Guyana—Politics and government—1966–
3. Political parties—Guyana—History.   I. Title
JL689.A15B87   1983   988'.103   83-7477
ISBN 0-87073-037-1

Printed in the United States of America.

*To my late father, and to my mother
Reynold and Angela Burrowes*

Table of Contents

Preface

IT is generally supposed that the split in the nationalist movement of 1953 in Guyana was a split that took place along racial lines. I believe that this is not true. The racial tendencies that began to manifest themselves in both parties were only at the leadership level. The average member of the two largest ethnic groups, it would seem, had already made a substantial adjustment toward accommodating each other at a societal level; their overwhelming support for the PPP in 1953 was an attempt to take this societal cooperation a stage further— to the political level. The PPP at that time was only the instrument through which this action was attempted. In this colonial setting, ethnic accommodation had no way of manifesting itself, but as nationalism grew, the political party was recognized as a vehicle for such an expression. The widespread support the PPP had in 1953 seems to be a good indication of this. The drop in the level of participation and voting between the 1953 election results and those of 1957 is an indication of the general disappointment with the breakup of the nationalist PPP.

Guyana, more than many other countries, provides an interesting example of colonization and decolonization. The original inhabitants, called "Amerindians" locally, have, from the beginning, had a marginal role in the country's affairs. With the importation of African slaves and indentured workers from China, Portugal and India, they quickly became a minority within the country. So that today, Indians and Africans, the largest groups within the country, are all the products of the colonial enterprise. Each group was imported to work on the sugar plantations; and in a sense the country, until recently, has remained a collection of plantations. Though other enterprises were developed, sugar remained the dominant industry right into the twentieth century.

The social and economic system was very closely linked with the plantation interests. For instance, the Portuguese, who were the first indentured laborers to be imported after the African slaves were freed, were not labelled "whites." They were given credits, however, and became established as merchants and retail shopkeepers after their indenture. Africans were denied credits and remained in coastal villages or became the urban proletariat. The Chinese, like the Portuguese, were also given credits and established themselves in the retail trade and the professions. The Indians remained, for the most part, on the sugar estates or became peasant rice farmers in the rural areas. Because the British Government and British companies were directly or indirectly responsible for keeping the systems in working order, each group, though disgruntled, abided by the rules laid down by the British. The rise of nationalism completely changed the picture.

The coming nationalism meant not only a tendency toward national character but also a change to modernity. This resulted in a total change of personality of both groups and individuals. How these groups and individuals responded to this change is the subject of this book.

In the course of my research, I discovered how much the people of Guyana identified with the leaders of their party. I then began to look more closely at the lives of the main leaders and found that the personal lives of the two main leaders, Cheddi Jagan and Forbes Burnham, reflected the disparate experience of their constituencies. Despite this, the two largest groups in Guyana seemed to want their leaders to work toward developing some sort of national unity and also toward maintaining their individual cultural identity.

This was the expectation of the Guyanese people at the local level in 1953, but their leaders had the suspicions of seasoned politicians. Their struggle was a struggle over power. How did these groups come together in the first place: Statesmen, politicians, scholars and the masses of supporters? Nationalism was becoming a more potent force all over the world, but a knowledge of the aspirations of the people and the potential of the society was important in Guyana as in any developing country. This in part made one party overwhelmingly more attractive than the others.

The two leaders, and the people, shared the same interests even though they did not necessarily completely understand each other. Those at the leadership level wanted the colonial power out because they thought themselves equipped and able to run a state and felt excluded under the colonial system. The leaders debated concepts like socialism, democracy, and power. The supporters also felt excluded under the colonial system, but they were visualizing economic and social change that would transform their lives. This made the political party an important instrument for changes envisaged and support for it total.

This was one reason why, in a few areas, party leaders found that party groups had been formed long before the leaders had penetrated them. But the main reason seemed to be in the intermediaries who understood just enough of what was going on at both levels. The intermediaries were constantly in touch with both the mass of the party and the leadership. Because of their education, never far above that of the high school level or a short course at some trade or professional school, they functioned well in their particular position.

The split of the PPP caused forces of the intermediaries to be spread too thinly, thus weakening both parties substantially. The result was that the leaders of the two parties which then emerged were able to exercise greater control over the few who remained and carefully selected those loyal to them for such positions thereafter. The leaders set out to create new parties within the old structure in order to increase their own personal power. At the same time, they eliminated all possible contenders for power within the party since the newcomers were not allowed to develop a political base on their own. This also had the effect of eliminating any formal responsibility that the leader had to the people through their intermediaries.

Despite the split, and later the expulsions from both of the main parties, apathy did not set in because race was invoked as a political tactic and was used as part of the strategy to gain power and independence. The intent of this book is to demonstrate that in Guyana, prior to the advent of the PPP and during the days of the original PPP, the two main races were united, however tenuously. In a colonial situation little more could have been expected.

Certain limits were put even on racial politics because no one racial group in Guyana had a clear majority. It meant that the parties had to give the appearance of being multi-racial in order to pick up marginal support or in order to influence each other's supporters.

The active part played by the United Force and those whom they represented—the Portuguese, upper-middle Indians, and Africans—

suggests that the main parties tended to draw nearly all of their support from the lower and middle-income groups. The same is seen when the 1953 results are analyzed. This suggests that most pre-independence parties were not as representative as they claimed to be. The claim was more a tactic used to overcome their opponents based on the number of seats won or the percentage of support received in relation to the other contending parties; their results were based on the numbers of those who were registered to vote, and not on those who were eligible to vote.

The coming of the United Force and its avowed intention to "oppose, expose and depose" the People's Progressive Party changed the rules of the political game in Guyana. There was a marked increase in the militancy of both opposition parties after that, and substantial differences in technique. The People's Progressive Party government was confronted at every turn over major decisions that it made. The PPP paid dearly for its mistake of not contesting seats in the urban and city areas in 1961. They caused the United Force to be over-represented in Parliament and weakened their own percentage standing *vis-à-vis* the opposition parties. The breakdown of order that followed, and the lack of resources to contain the decaying economic situation did not help the survival of the PPP against two determined opposition parties. The PPP's weakness at home gave those long opposed to its radical ideology the chance to align themselves with the domestic parties, all in order to oust the PPP.

One interesting feature of this process related to the leader within his party and the uniformity of his position, whether in opposition or in government. He is accustomed to being director within his own party because of his entry from the top, and so does not develop a spirit of compromise or of alliances. His position does not encourage him to develop sympathy for individuals or groups within the political process; he is distanced from the ways of political infighting and cannot appreciate it. This may be one reason why third world leaders cling to colleagues of similar view and discourage dissent of any type. This reinforces the hold that most leaders already have on their parties and consequently gives a party a lopsided structure.

Because of this hold, the structure is generally weak. The party becomes a destructive rather than a creative force helping to build a political and administrative structure. For its own survival, it finds it has to destroy or stifle all other organizations into submission.

The material here allows the reader an insight into the personality of most of the major leaders of Guyana. This was especially difficult to do since many of the speeches made by politicians in Guyana were not recorded. Care was taken during interviews to decipher provided information, and to differentiate fact from rumor.

The book traces the involvements of the parties before the United Nations and with the United States and Great Britain in their attempts to gain power or to retain it. It also looks at the external motivation for changing the electoral system. With the People's National Congress and United Force coalition in office, we look briefly at their first years in office and the steps they seemed to be taking toward uniting the country and toward dealing with the desperate economic position. The last chapter deals with what has taken place over the years since independence.

Acknowledgments

GROWING up in a world in which so much political change was taking place caused me to become passionately interested in politics and government. I could barely understand fully the ramifications of the simultaneous breakup of several European empires, and the birth of new nations, but I knew I was living through historical times. It is with such an eye that I watched and noted events as they unfolded in Guyana. Several people were always willing to share their views with me even while I was a high school student and even afterwards. I acknowledge with gratitude the encouragement that George DePeana, Lloyd Searwar, Miles Fitzpatrick, Victor Forsythe and Victor O'Connell gave me at difficult and different stages of my development. George DePeana, when head of the then Critchlow Labor Institute, allowed me to participate in his second one month seminar for trade unionists; this was an exercise of immense value to me.

I would also like to thank Frank Pilgrim, David De Groot and Daisy Lancaster for help and advice. Though I was a junior member of the staff, Frank and David often included me in many of their high level activities which provided me quite early with a view of the inner workings of Government. To them I am most grateful. I would also like to thank Prime Minister Forbes Burnham for the interest he showed in me while I was his employee.

Professor Arpad von Lazar, my thesis adviser at the Fletcher School of Law and Diplomacy, encouraged me to do this research: for this I am most grateful. Also at Fletcher, Professor Rosemary Rogers and W. Scott Thompson gave me much appreciated assistance. Dean Charles Shane supported me in committees and Mary Van Bibber Harris was always very helpful as a foreign students adviser.

My first two years at Fletcher were supported by a Fulbright-Hayes fellowship. Ms. Kay Ray of the USIA was convinced of my potential and made a personal effort to help me obtain the Fulbright; I thank her for helping me realize my dream. My subsequent years were financed by my mother, Mrs. Angela Burrowes, and I must formally thank her not only for her kindness but for the immense significance of this help.

When I arrived in Boston, Mary Boyd Troy was the one person I knew in the city. She became a great source of friendship and support. I would like to acknowledge the following friends I made while at Fletcher: Maurice Ngou, Charles Odidi Okidi, Shukri Ghanem, Nihal Goonwardene, Peter Thomas, Sewanyana Kironde, Robert Hill, Charles Ebinger, Henry Philips Williams, Osei Tutu Poku and Osei Owusu. Cholchineepan Patumanonda (Pao) and I shared a special friendship, this I recall here with fondness.

Many friends aided me in improving my manuscript. Mary Haynes and Cynthia Massey Nurse read the first draft; they suggested several changes and improvements. Nancy Amy did a superb job of helping to transform a rough piece of research into a readable book. The revisions she put me through turned out to be an education in itself; working with her was a most profitable experience.

Mrs. Penny Gosdigian who typed for me from the inception of my days as a graduate student and who typed Part 1 of this book is dearly remembered. Helen Wohl typed several drafts of Part 2 and Ann Marche who corrected and retyped several chapters is also remembered.

Several people at Morgan Guaranty have been very kind and assisted me over the last few years. Among them I would like to thank Durant A. (Andy) Hunter, Unn Boucher, William Setterstrom and Douglas A. (Sandy) Warner III. The help and encouragement of those whom time does not permit me to mention is also appreciated. Finally, I thank my wife Rosanne for understanding, and more.

But having written all this, it must also be stated that I alone bear responsibility for the views presented here.

Reynold A. Burrowes, III

New York
May 1983

Chronology

1950	January	Announcement of the formation of the PPP (out of the Political Affairs Committee)
1950–51	Colonial 280 (1951)	British Guiana Constitutional Commission (Waddington Commission)
1953	April 27	First Elections under adult sufferage; PPP victory
	May 18	House of Assembly sworn in
	October 9 Cmnd 8980	Constitution suspended
1953–57		Interim Government composed of nominated and ex-officio members replaced the elected government.
1954	Cmnd 9274	British Guiana Constitutional Commission (Robertson Commission)
1955	February 13	PPP split
1957	August 12	National elections; PPP victory
	October	PPP Burnhamite changes its name to People's National Congress (PNC)
1960	October	United Force (UF) formed
	March 7–31 Cmnd 988	British Guiana Constitutional Conference
1961	August 21	National elections; PPP victory; full internal self-government
1962	Cmnd 1870	British Guiana Constitutional Conference
1963	April 20	TUC general strike begins
	July 7	End of TUC's 80-day general strike
	Cmnd 2203	British Guiana Constitutional Conference

1963–64		GAWU strike; escalation in bombings and African-Indian hostilities
1964	December 7	First elections under the new system of Proportional Representation (PR) PNC—UF coalition
1964	Colonial 359	Report by the Commonwealth Team of Observers on the Election in December 1964
1965	Cmnd 2849	Report of the British Guiana Independence Conference, 1965
1966	May 26	Independent nation of Guyana is born; LFS Burnham, first Prime Minister
1970	February 23	Guyana becomes a Republic; Arthur Chung becomes first President.
1971	July 15	Guyana Nationalized the Canadian owned Demerara Bauxite Company (Denba) and established the Guyana Bauxite Company in its place
1973	July 16	National Elections held. PNC victory
1975	January 1	Guyana Nationalized the U.S. owned Reynolds (Guyana) Mines Limited and launched in its place the Berbice Mining Enterprises
1976	May 26	Guyana Nationalized the British owned Booker holdings in Guyana
1978	July 10	Referendum on a Constitution Amendment Bill 1978 to approve the writing of a new Constitution
1980	December 15	National Elections held. PNC Victory

Main Parties and Organizations

BRITISH Guiana changed its name to Guyana when it achieved independence, on May 26, 1966. The country's new name is used throughout the text. However, the original name is used in quotations and when referring to books, articles, and organizations existing before this time.

BGEIA   British Guiana East Indian Association. Indian sectional organization to which most Indian professionals and business elite belonged.

FUGE   Federated Union of Government Employees. Represented nonadministrative government workers.

GAWU   Guyana Agricultural Workers Union.

GIWU   Guyana Industrial Workers Union. GIWU sought to represent sugar workers from 1948. It finally did so after a pool in 1975, and changed its name to Guyana Agricultural Workers Union.

LCP   League of Coloured People. Organization to which most of the black professionals belonged. The organization was the main force behind the NDP, then the UDP.

MPCA   Man Power Citizens Association. The union that represented most sugar unions.

NDP   National Democratic Party

NLF   National Labour Front—Lionel Luckhoo, leader

PAC   Political Affairs Committee. The group formed for political education as the forerunner to the PPP.

PAC   Organ of the Political Affairs Committee
Bulletin

PNC   People's National Congress—Forbes Burnham, leader

PPP — People's Progressive Party (orig. Jaganite PPP)—Dr. Cheddi Jagan, leader. From 1955 to 1957 there existed two PPPs, one led by Forbes Burnham and one by Cheddi Jagan. The Burnhamite PPP changed its name to People's National Congress in 1958.

PYO — Progressive Youth Organization. The PPP's youth arm.

SPA — Sugar Producers Association

TUC — Trade Union Council. The federated body of most active trade unions.

UDP — United Democratic Party—John Carter, leader

UF — United Force—Peter D'Aguiar, leader

WPO — Women's Progressive Organization

YSM — Young Socialist Movement. The PNC's youth arm.

PART 1

Pre-Independence Politics

CHAPTER 1

Historical Background

GUYANA, as the country has been called since Independence, is the part of South America formerly known as the Wild Coast. This stretch of coast between Brazil and Venezuela was named by early European explorers. The territory was wrested from Spain by the Dutch in the seventeenth century, but was only recognized as Dutch with the signing of the Treaty of Munster in 1648. Essequibo and Demerara were settled and administered by the Dutch West India Company while Berbice was settled by the mercantile house of Abraham van Pere. The territory changed hands several times among the Dutch, French, and British as European powers sought to establish their own empires or, after a war, sought to enhance their bargaining positions by exchanging captured countries.[1]

The Dutch penetrated deep into the interior to establish their first settlements, but shifted these settlements to the coastal areas as the economic emphasis changed from trading with the indigenous Indians to plantation agriculture. By the beginning of the eighteenth century, cultivation was spreading along the banks of the Essequibo and Demerara Rivers. The settlement of the colony was greatly accelerated when the energetic Laurens Storm van Gravesande took up duties as the Dutch West India's secretary in Essequibo in 1738.[2] Subsequently, as the Governor, he threw open the Demerara and Essequibo region to planters of any nationality, thus beginning a period of rapid growth and prosperity for the colonies. At that time, the planters in the British Islands in the West Indies, realizing that the soil of the islands on which they planted was nearly exhausted, took up the offer. They settled particularly in the Demerara area, and soon the Demerara settlement had more Englishmen than Dutch.[3] The Demerara settlements spread along the coast to the low lying areas requiring that dikes be built to keep the river out and to control irrigation. Though sugar remained the main crop in both counties, increasing quantities of cotton, coffee, and cocoa began to be grown.

The British took the colonies during the French Revolution in 1796, and held it until 1802. During this time, British financial interests became closely tied with the planters in the colony. However, the colony was restored to the Dutch in 1802, only to be retaken by the British in 1803.[4] From that time onwards, the colony remained in the hands of the British, although it was not formally ceded to them until 1814. The British kept the Dutch structure and institutions intact except for a few minor alterations. The union of Essequibo, Demerara, and Berbice, previously administered as separate colonies, was created in 1831 and called British Guiana. The Dutch constitution was changed in 1928 after a series of disagreements between the representatives and the Government, which precipitated a number of financial crises.

Not long after the British assumed full control of the colony, slavery was abolished in all British colonies. At the time of emancipation, 1834, the colony had only two villages, "one at Mahaica and the other at plantation Aberdeen on the Essequibo Coast."[5] Since no preparation was made for their welfare after emancipation, the slaves had little choice but to remain on the plantations as paid employees. An economic crisis in the sugar industry caused the planters to make many demands on the freed Africans. Rather than accept the demands, the Africans left the estates. They pooled the money they had saved from sales of provisions at the Sunday market and bought out whole estates, thus establishing themselves as villagers and peasant farmers. They began what came to be known as the village movement. At the end of the movement, the number of slaves who lived on the estates numbered only 19,939 versus 44,456 persons who lived in villages. In the process, "twenty-five communal villages had been established over 9,049.5 acres of land, purchased at a cost of $400,000. In the proprietary villages more than 7,000 villagers held freehold title to plots of land with an aggregate area of 6,413 acres and an aggregate value of $631,000."[6] It was estimated that the cost of erecting the 10,544 houses was another one to two million dollars. The village movement lasted only ten years before it began to decline. It brought with it, however, a resentment on the part of the Africans that remains present in the

African psyche—that of having had to expend large sums of money for their settlement. Plantation owners were then faced with a shortage of labor for the estates and it had to begin to adjust to dealing with a free society.

With the movement of the slaves off the estates, indentured labor was sought elsewhere. Chinese were brought from China and Portuguese were brought from Madeira, but soon after their indenture, these groups moved away from the estates and into the retail trade as shopkeepers in the villages set up by the former slaves and into other businesses. From 1844 to 1917, indentured labor was brought from India. During that time, almost 240,000 Indian immigrants arrived in the colony. Though many Indians returned to India as the terms of their indenture stipulated, the majority remained in the colony. As a group, most remained on the estates until the beginning of this century. Apart from being bound to the estates by contract, they were regarded as "coolies" and as economically subservient. Further, because they were generally illiterate and retained their Hindu and Muslim religion, they were not part of the Western culture and, therefore, not accepted in Guyana where the emphasis was on Western culture.

However, as is traditional in the history of nations, ethnic groups blend and adjust. In the pages that follow, we will look at the adjustment the separate groups made to become a nation in the twentieth century.

NOTES

1. The Colonies were captured by Britain in 1781, lost to France in 1782, and restored to the Dutch in 1783. In 1796 they were taken by Britain, and restored to the Dutch in 1802, retaken by Britain in 1803.
2. Sir Cecil Clementi, *A Constitutional History of British Guiana* (New York: Macmillan, 1939), p. 28, 31.
3. Ibid., p. 28, 31.
4. Ibid., p. 51, 56, 57.
5. Allan Young, *The Approaches to Local Self-Government in British Guiana* (London: Longman, Green, 1958), p. 6.
6. Ibid., p. 23.

CHAPTER 2

Political Activities in Guyana
Prior to the PPP, 1945–1950

IN studying this period of Guyanese political movement, it is necessary to study the personalities as carefully as the events themselves.
There were a number of organizations, and the public impression
made by individuals at different times made a significant difference in a
candidate's ability to manipulate the system and command political
support. Also important is the way the Guyanese people perceived
events in the light of their own unique historical experience. It would
be fair to say that, until the formation of the People's Progressive Party
(PPP), leadership positions in social and political organizations in Guyana were usually sought by individuals because of the prestige conferred on them and not because of the service they thought they could
render to the organization or its members.[1] When these leaders were
cooperative toward British policy, by keeping the rank and file in check
and by not making serious demands on the system, they were coopted
into the system. They were rewarded with British declarations—Order
of the British Empire (OBE), Member of the British Empire (MBE), or
even knighted "Sir." In other words, they were used as instruments of
British policy. Leadership seemed to be based on 1. profession and
education; 2. position in the society; 3. ethnic origin. Thus, leadership
in an organization was an invitation to increase prestige and, at times,
financial standing.

This was sometimes done by voting themselves and their executives
large expense allowances (WT, 88). After World War II, several new
organizations were formed for political activity of one type or another.

There were a number of new unions representing nearly every category of worker. In addition, there were the cultural organizations like the League of Coloured People (LCP) and the British Guiana East Indian Association (BGEIA). Most of the organizations were quite active, but limited in their outlook because of their narrow ethnic concentration. 1945 was an important year for Guyana because it was the year that the labor leaders of the Caribbean gathered in Guyana for a conference. Out of this conference, the Caribbean Labour Congress was born. In 1946, the radical Political Affairs Committee was formed and its pamphlet, the *PAC Bulletin*, began to be published. Many people sensed the activity and questioning going on throughout the country (WT, 89–90).

When India became independent on August 15, 1947, it was an occasion for rejoicing among the Indian people. Though celebration of the occasion was more on a personal or immediate group level, it was sufficiently widespread for other ethnic groups to take notice.[2] The Indians of Guyana were glad and proud that their old country was finally free of British rule.

Changes on the Estates Between the Wars

To the social observer, it was clear in 1950 that living standards which had deteriorated during the depression of 1929 had not recovered; instead the general poverty level had increased. As a result of worsening housing and economic conditions, there were industrial disturbances on the estates and in the cities in Guyana and throughout the Caribbean. These disturbances reached such a scale that the British Government appointed a commission to investigate social and economic conditions existing in the West Indian colonies. The result was the West Indian Royal Commission Report 1945.

Major Disturbances in the Caribbean

May–July 1934	Disturbances on sugar estates in Trinidad
January 1935	Disturbances in St. Kitts
May 1935	Strike of wharf labor at Falmouth, Jamaica, followed by disturbances
September–October 1935	Disturbances at various estates in British Guiana

October 1935	Rioting in Kingstown and Camden Park, St. Vincent
June 1937	General disturbances in Trinidad
July 1937	Disturbances on the From Estate, Jamaica
May–June 1938	General disturbances in Jamaica
February 1939	Disturbances at Leonoro Plantation and neighboring areas in British Guiana.*

During WWII, German interruption of shipping in the Caribbean led to severe shortages in Guyana. In turn, pressure was put on the Guyanese for self-reliance and ingenuity. This self-reliance restored some confidence to the people in themselves as productive forces—the lack of imported goods meant that people bought more local substitutes, and it also hastened the social development already taking place.

From Sugar to Rice

Sugar production began to stabilize around 1911 after suffering from the competition of beet sugar on the international market, for there were already as many Indians living off the estates as on the estates in Guyana. There were 60,707 Indians residents on sugar estates and 65,810 living elsewhere. The number of urban dwellers was still quite small at 7,310. Some of the Indians who moved off the estates went to live in land settlement schemes, which they were granted in lieu of return passage to India. Others formed village communities.[3] Those who were not close to the sugar estates, where occasional work could be found, turned to the cultivation of rice as a staple for themselves and their immediate communities. "It was the development of the rice industry and the acquisition of the overseas markets for rice, mainly in the other West Indian territories, that gave the Indians their opportunity to become established on the land."[4] In order to have an abundant supply of labor present on the estates, the planters had approved of Indian squatters on estate lands; but it was "the First World War which gave a tremendous impetus to the industry and the value of exports of rice rose from $310,000 in 1910 to $1,423,000 in 1917."[5]

If World War I gave the rice industry the impetus it needed to

---

*From: West Indian Royal Commission Report, Cmd. 6607, 1945, p. 196.

become viable, at least for domestic use, World War II made it a
permanent industry and a source of revenue for the country. The
establishment of rice as a permanent commercial crop in Guyana provided the springboard for a different type of Indian personality—that of
the independent peasant. With a certain degree of prosperity in the
countryside, and depression and unemployment in the city, the country was swept with the tide of nationalism. The two main leaders of the
movement in Guyana were Cheddi Jagan of Indian descent, and
Forbes Burnham of African descent.

The New and Old: Early Experience

Dr. Cheddi Jagan returned to Guyana from the U.S., where he had
been attending dental school, in October 1943. His American wife,
Janet, joined him in December of that year. His absence had left him
practically a stranger in Georgetown (WT, 86). To establish himself, he
set up his dentistry clinic and went about building a practice. Most
such professionals at that time concentrated on building a successful
practice and a comfortable life in a suburb while doing some charitable
work in their spare time. But Jagan, and the other Guyanese returning
from overseas at that time, were different. They were the first to have
benefited from what was to be a tremendous new movement throughout the world. Cheddi Jagan and his colleagues opted for public service
instead of following the normal route.

After establishing his practice, Cheddi Jagan began to enjoy some of
the superficial "spoils" of being a professional man in Georgetown. But,
"this was a period of searching and frustration, I wanted to identify
myself with the real hard world around me" (WT, 87). The working
people were poor, ill-housed, badly educated, and in poor health. The
middle class had high aspirations, a better education, and a knowledge
of the changes taking place outside Guyana. At the same time they
were prejudiced and very concerned with their status before anything
else. They were not ready to assume their role as modernizing vanguard. They did not have such positive ambitions for themselves.
Cheddi Jagan tried at first to join the League of Coloured People and
the British Guiana East Indian Association, but found that their outlook was too narrow for what he thought needed to be done. He turned
his attention to the unions and other groups, where people seemed to
want to take a more positive stand against the colonial government and

where people felt that they could use their influence and organization to bring about worthwhile changes within the society.

In 1945, Cheddi Jagan became Treasurer of the Man Power Citizens Association (MPCA)(WT, 88), the union responsible for representing the sugar workers in the country. Soon after his election to office, Jagan disagreed with the leadership of the union. He felt the leaders compromised too easily and defended the management's position too often. "I objected to what I considered to be the high level of expense allowances from the funds of a poor union, and the tendency of the union leaders to collaborate with the sugar planters" (WT, 88). One year later, because of his extreme and consistent disagreement with the executive over matters of policy, Jagan was ousted from his position as treasurer. While Treasurer of the MPCA, he had used his position to further his contacts with other union leaders. At the meeting of Caribbean Unionists held in Georgetown, he took the opportunity of meeting the many top leaders of the other Caribbean labor movements and of discovering how they were using their unions to bring about change in their countries.

One of the other groups Cheddi Jagan joined was the Carnegie Library Discussion Circle. "Here one was able to speak freely. My wife and I began to make our impact and to gather around us a group of young radicals and intellectuals" (WT, 89). In this group, Dr. Jagan came into contact with radical, urban, middle-class Guyana, mostly mulattoes and blacks with some social standing. This group included young men who were interested in new ideas, new experiments, changes in the world and their relation to Guyana, and most of all, their role in bringing about those changes. Another forum for Cheddi Jagan's political views was the press; he, and those who had become his close friends, constantly wrote letters to the editor in order to get a wider audience for their views (WT, 89). In urban, conservative Guyana, Dr. Jagan's views were controversial,[6] but among the lower-middle-class and rural Guyana, Cheddi Jagan and his friends echoed a note of great hope. Their voices were raised for a change long overdue.

The PAC

In 1946, having become convinced of a need for a forum for discussion and exchange of ideas, Cheddi Jagan, Janet Jagan, Ashton Chase, and Jocelyn Hubbard[7] founded the Political Affairs Committee (PAC) and the *PAC Bulletin*. "I had become convinced of the necessity for having a theoretical organ and political platform. The people were on the move." The name Political Affairs Committee was adopted "from the Political Action Committee of the Congress of Industrial Organization" (CIO) of the USA (WT, 90).

The aims of the Political Affairs Committee were: to assist the growth and development of the Labour and Progressive Movements of British Guiana in order to establish a strong, disciplined, and enlightened party, equipped with the theory of Scientific Socialism; to provide information, and to present scientific political analyses on current affairs, both local and international; and to foster and assist discussion groups, through the circulation of bulletins, booklets and other printed matter.[8] The organization began to make its views known by issuing a six-page, mimeograph newsletter to influential and politically conscious Guyanese. The *Bulletin* became what it set out to be, a forum for expression for the views of progressive Guyanese. Within a short time, the *Bulletin* became such a popular forum that one legislator, in a speech to the House, suggested that it be banned. Along with the PAC, Jagan also had a hand in the formation of the Women's Political and Economic Organization (WPEO) in 1946. Its leadership included Winifred Gaskin, Frances Stafford, and Janet Jagan as Secretary (WT, 90–91). The Political Affairs Committee kept up its constant political activism until November 1947, when General Elections were held.

Just before these elections, a new party appeared on the scene—the Labour Party. Headed by Dr. J. B. Singh, the party was formed in June 1946 and represented an attempt to form a coalition of different interest groups and various unions to sponsor candidates for the election.[9] The PAC at this time was still a small, relatively unimportant body.[10] The two Jagans and J. Hubbard of the PAC fought the election as Independents. Jagan stood for the East Demerara constituency, an area which included several sugar estate areas along with the East Coast. He won his seat running against John D'Aguivar, a man who had had tremendous influence among the business and plantation elite and in the government. In his election campaign, Jagan had the energetic help of school teacher Sidney King of Buxton and civil servant Balram Singh Rai of Beterwagting, two men who eventually became very prominent in his party. As far as the election went, it was a year of upsets (WT, 91–93). The politicians who traditionally represented the business interests and sectional interests lost their seats.

The Labour Party won six of the fourteen seats contested. Those in the new group were all of the same school; they represented either business or some sort of narrow sectional interest.

Two points must be raised about the November 1947 election: 1. Why did the Jagans contest their seats as Independents when they already had the nucleus of a party functioning; and 2. Why did they not lend active support to the newly formed Labour Party? Peter Simms, in his *Trouble in Guyana* (p. 83), thinks that because the PAC was only a group of people of divergent views, it suited everyone that they did not fight the election as a party but as a collection of individuals. It would seem by his action that Jagan did not have very high regard for the politics of the Labour Party, and was himself ambitious to become its leader, something he could not realize in a party dominated by much more established men than himself.

The PAC and the Labour Party

When Cheddi Jagan won the election to the Legislature, it must have been clear to him that he would be leader of whatever movement was to spring from the PAC. In the legislature Jagan saw his role as the role of politics of protest (WT, 95). He joined forces with the elected members of the Labour Party, the Party that had won six of the fourteen seats in the election. But more than that, Jagan officially joined the Labour Party. "I applied for membership of the Labour Party and was admitted to its charmed circle. But the alliance was short-lived—shorter than I had expected" (WT, 95–96). There was much disagreement between Dr. Jagan and the Labour Party members on tactics. One of the major points of dispute in the Labour Party occurred over the nomination of Frederick Seaford by the Government. Of the incident Jagan (WT, 96) says:

> He had been the local head of Booker Bros., McConnel and Co., Ltd. He had been defeated in the North Georgetown constituency by Nicholson but had been nominated by the governor to the Legislative and Executive Councils. The whole country was angry at this total disregard of the elementary rules of the democracy. Although the appointment was opposed by the executive of the Labour Party in a strongly-worded statement of protest, many of its legislative members were unenthusiastic; consequently, the appointment was confirmed. The Labour Party Executive prepared a reply which attacked the government, but

no one of its legislative members would read the statement in the Legislative Council. It fell on me to "bell the cat."

This incident gives a clear indication of the way Her Majesty's representative in British Guiana, the Governor, thought democracy ought to be interpreted in a colony. It was also the type of action which bred disrespect by the emerging young politicians for the rules set up by the British and for democratic government. It also points out how much the Governor thought that British business interests was to be taken into account in administering the colony. Bookers, the largest British firm operating in the colony, was such a dominant part of the agricultural and industrial economy that some people referred to the colony as Bookers Guyana rather than British Guiana. The episode also illustrates how different the legislative leadership of the Labour Party was from the party's executive, which was drawn from a broader cross-section of the population, even though there was a property qualification in order to become a voter. Their willingness to cooperate with the governor, in voting to seat a man who had been rejected in the election, was typical of the leadership at that time. It is one reason why the more radical parties succeeded once adult suffrage was granted in Guyana and in so many other former colonies.

The Labour party, with its legislators prepared to support the governor almost automatically, did not have very wide support in the country and very soon after lost the support of any of the progressive forces it had managed to attract. While it continued to function, the party was a good foil with which the PAC could emphasize a difference in political tactics. To do this, Mrs. Jagan as editor of the PAC Bulletin used the difference in the position taken by Labour party legislators and Dr. Jagan. Whenever a bill came up before the legislature that could be presented as one of major importance to the lives of her readers, she described its advantages and disadvantages in the clearest and strongest terms. It was important that the issues be clear-cut even if they were sometimes over-simplified. She then listed how the different members voted. She not only proved that Dr. Jagan consistently voted for the people, but also showed that the Labour Party was hopelessly split, a group who repeatedly appeared as frightened, sycophantic followers of the ruling class.[11]

With the belligerent PAC *Bulletin* on its back and with divisions within, the Labour Party soon disintegrated. From the start the party was not a very popular party. It was a party built on the image of a few men, mainly on that of Dr. Singh and Hubert N. Critchlow, and had no real political base. Most of its support came from the urban areas and its environs where the unions were strong and where the candidates were known personalities. They seem to have made little attempt to canvas the countryside and had no clear program of reform to present to the people or to the government.

The PAC and GIWU

Cheddi Jagan's real break to establish himself as a national political figure came in 1948. Because of the charges by some of the members that the MPCA had become a company union, the newly-formed Guiana Industrial Workers Union (GIWU), headed by Dr. Latchmansingh, sought to challenge the MPCA to represent the sugar workers. In February 1948 the MPCA decided, at a conference with representatives from every estate, that its membership did favor "cut and load," but wanted to be paid $1.00 a ton instead of 60 cents. ($1 US = $.50 Guyana).

"The Sugar Producers Association finally agreed on 85 cents on April 15th. In the last week of April the GIWU called a strike."[4] Because of the inter-union dispute, there was much confusion among the workers on the estates, especially on the estates along the East Coast area. Some workers were willing to return to work, realizing that the management was in a stronger position than they were. Others felt stronger and decided to make the issue a *cause cèlébre* to force the hand of the estate managements. Encouraged by the GIWU, the strikers' slogan became "sit and starve rather than work and starve" (WT, 109). A state of uneasiness dragged on in the industry for more than two weeks, when isolated incidents of violence began to occur along the East Coast. On June 16, 1948, after days of demonstrations by a number of workers, the police shot and killed five and injured twelve persons on Plantation Enmore along the East Coast of Demerar.

The funeral of the five Indian estate workers was used as a platform by the PAC and the GIWU for their political identification with the workers' cause and their opposition to the plantation and colonial system.

"The Enmore tragedy affected me greatly," wrote Jagan. "I had personally known the young men who were killed and injured. My wife and I, Dr. Latchmansingh, and other leaders led the funeral procession on the morning of June 17. It became a tremendous protest demonstration. We left Enmore on foot and marched to the city 16 miles away, taking the bodies there for burial. As the procession progressed strikers, workers and villagers joined in. Nearing Georgetown, we were told that we could not proceed to the Public Hospital where we were to pick up the body of Dookhie. The police had conveniently escorted his coffin to the cemetery. Armed police guarded the streets in the city, and meetings, assemblies and processions were banned in Georgetown.[12] At the graveside the emotional outbursts of the widows and relatives of the deceased were intensely distressing, and I could not restrain my tears. There was to be no turning back. There and then I made a silent pledge—I would dedicate my entire life to the cause of the struggle of the Guianese people against bondage and exploitation" (WT, 109).

Even before the funeral Jagan knew that the incident would put him in the limelight for leadership among the Indian people of Guyana. His presence and show of concern at the funeral confirmed upon him a dominance and leadership that he had been working to establish for about two years. He had become a national leader. The funeral itself was so well attended that a special train was laid on to supplement the normal service for the area. Peter Simms, commenting on Jagan's position after the incident, says: "After Enmore, Dr. and Mrs. Jagan were a power in the land. The Indian vote was solidly behind them and they could start to plan for their party,"[13] which would be called the PPP, the People's Progressive Party.

What is most interesting about the events of the strike and the shootings is the irony of the whole episode in its super-colonial overtones. Here the stratifications and occupation patterns of the racial groups clashed. The estates management was all white. The police who were defending the property and who fired on the protesters were all black and the protesters and those killed were all Indian. The strict occupational grouping of races in Guyana which manifested itself at Enmore has been a factor with which every political organization in Guyana has had to grapple in trying to organize any mass movement. However, this fact was not to become pronounced until later. At that time, Cheddi Jagan was still basking in the sunshine of the breakthrough that he had scored with the Indian people. Janet Jagan in a private conversation summed it up: "Enmore made us."[14]

NOTES

1. Cheddi Jagan, *The West on Trial* (London: Michael Joseph, 1966), p. 127. Hereafter referred to in the text as WT, followed by the page reference.
2. The Constitutional Commission of 1950–51 notices and refers to the strong loyalty Indians still had with the subcontinent. See British Guiana, *Report of the Constitutional Commission 1950–51*, HMSO 1951, Colonial 280, p. 14.
3. Raymond Smith, *British Guiana*, London: Oxford University Press, 1962.
4. Ibid., p. 50.
5. Ibid., p. 50.
6. "One controversy which brought severe criticism on my wife was her advocacy of birth control. The Catholics and the newspapers which they controlled were angry and never forgot or forgave her for this. They expressed their opposition in anti-communist terms, but their bitterness, I believe, was due more to their fanatical opposition to birth control" (Ibid., p. 89).
7. Chase and Hubbard were leaders in the Trade Union Movement.
8. Peter Simms, *Trouble in Guyana* (London: Allen & Unwin), p. 80–81).
9. Smith, *British Guiana*, p. 167.
10. Simms, *Trouble in Guyana*, p. 81.
11. Simms, *Trouble in Guyana*, p. 85.
12. On April 5, 1948, out of 30,000 sugar workers (including maximum seasonal labour) the MPCA had a registered membership of 6,000 while the GIWU had only 60. Simms, *Trouble in Guyana*, p. 89–90.
13. The PAC and GIWU, which had planned the funeral procession, had planned to hold massive demonstrations in the capital city afterwards. The governor declared a ban to forestall these demonstrations; Simms, *Trouble in Guyana*, p. 94.
14. Simms, *Trouble in Guyana*, p. 95.

CHAPTER 3

Leadership in the People's Progressive Party, 1950–1955

MOST people would agree that the modern political life of Guyana began with the formation of the People's Progressive Party in January 1950. The party evolved from the Political Affairs Committee which Dr. Jagan, Janet Jagan, Ashton Chase, and Joslyn Hubbard had formed four years earlier mainly for the purpose of political education.[1] Dr. Jagan himself had stood for and won a seat in the legislature in 1947 to represent the constituency of the East Demerara, and he was an already known political figure when the PPP was launched. Jagan knew that any serious successful political movement had to rely on the broadest support possible. He therefore took great pains to put together a coalition that became the PPP.[2] According to Janet Jagan, the Political Affairs Committee was trying to seek out all Guyanese who felt strongly enough about some sort of change for the colony in order to recruit them into their organization. One contact in London recommended Linden Forbes Sampson Burnham.[3] Burnham had come to the attention of these London-based friends of the Jagans through his political activism and his academic record. The Jagans contacted Burnham, then a law student at London University, and arranged for him to visit Jamaica on his way back to Guyana in 1948 in order to study the organization of the People's National Party of that island. On his return to Guyana, Burnham took some time making his decision whether to join the Jagans or The League of Coloured People, which tried to recruit him after his arrival.[4]

Upon formation of the PPP, two men rose to leadership and popular-

19

ity very quickly—Cheddi Jagan and Forbes Burnham. Jagan's rise
could have been predicted. He had been making his views known
through the PAC's monthly news sheet; he had attended and participated in the Public Library and other quasi-political discussion
groups; and he had, most of all, established himself as a leader of the
workers since the Enmore riots. Burnham's rise was less predictable.
He was a bright Guyanese who had gone to London to study with
much fanfare after having won the country's most coveted academic
prize.[5] On immediate observation, it might be noted that he was one of
a few of the Guyana scholars who, until that time, even bothered to
return to Guyana.

Background of the Two PPP Leaders in 1950

Cheddi Jagan

Cheddi B. Jagan was born in Guyana at Plantation Port Mourant on
March 22, 1918, to immigrant Indian parents. They both began life as
child laborers. At the time of his birth, most of the Indians entering
Guyana as indentured servants seemed to have made a decision to
make Guyana their home and, as a result, an Indian culture began to
evolve. In 1870, a visiting Royal Commission reported seeing only two
temples in Guyana; by 1917 there were 46 Muslim mosques and 43
Hindu temples.[6] Dr. Jagan, a Hindu, was a product of that culture; but
he was also a product of the Estate Culture that caused him to perceive
the world differently than urban Guyanese society.

At this time, during Jagan's youth, another social movement was also
going on within Indian society. Indians began to leave the estates in
large numbers:

> The main avenue of achievement for those who moved off the estates
> was through farming or trading. Like the Portuguese and the Chinese,
> the Indians took to trading and shopkeeping wherever they could and by
> 1917 Indians held licences for 10 spirit shops, 363 provisions shops, 49
> stores and 14 butcher shops. They still lagged behind the Chinese in a
> number of these trading licences, but by this time the Chinese had
> practically given up the huckster trade and were soon to dwindle from
> the ranks of the shopkeepers as their children began to get higher educa-
> tion and enter the civil service and the professions. As they and the
> Portuguese moved onward and upward from the ranks of the small
> shopkeepers the Indians moved in, and a new class of Indians began to
> develop. This was composed of men with money. Perhaps they were not

very rich but they were rich enough to command respect within the local communities. There is a good deal of evidence to show that they have been the prime movers in the process of resurgence of "Indian culture." Whereas the educated Indians who went into the middle class tended to shed all trace of that "coolie" behaviour that was so looked down upon by other ethnic groups. This other Indian elite *sought prestige within the Indian group itself*, particularly through observance of Indian religions and performance of proper rituals, and later on they tried to claim recognition for the value of "Indian Culture" within a wider social context.[7]

Another important influence during Jagan's youth was his estate experience. There had been little change on the estates since the slaves had vacated them and sugar prices were beginning a precipitous slide down from the mild boom they had enjoyed during the war years.

On the estates themselves, living conditions and wages were bad. Wages had increased only a little and were barely enough to keep a family at subsistence level. The Moyne Commission, reporting on their investigation of the West Indies (Cmd 6607, 1945, P. 32) said, "In some parts of the West Indies, notably the smaller and poorer islands, rates for agricultural labourers have advanced little beyond the shilling a day introduced after emancipation. In the larger and more prosperous colonies, wages, starting from this basic level, have shown some advances." (In British Guiana, wages were 2s 2d or 26 cents per day for men and 1s 6½d or 13 cents for women.)

The Commission recognized that the main reason for the discontent, manifested in a series of industrial conflicts, was the problem of intermittent employment both in towns and in the country. "The plight of the unemployed, aggravated as it is by the seasonal character of employment, is serious to the point of desperation." Even during the sugar season, employment was scarce. In 1938 it was found that throughout the whole year, "there were available no more than 3.66 days work per week for male employees, who nevertheless actually worked on the average of only 2.3 days in the case of residents and for approximately 3 days in that of non-residents."[8]

But Jagan's family reminiscences of earlier years are a bit different. "My mother relates that she had to work from 7 A.M. to 6 P.M., manuring sugarcane in the fields for 8 cents (4d) per day, and also three times per week from midnight to 6 A.M. fetching fine bajasse into the factory for 4 cents (2d) for the 6-hour period. Her total take-home pay was about 60 cents (2s 6d) per week (WT, 16).

"At about the age of fourteen my father moved to the cane-cutting gang and my mother to the moulding gang. The cleaning of trenches were allotted as an additional duty, particularly to women. My mother's earnings increased to 20 cents (10d) per day, and my father's were 36 cents (1s 6d). But the hours continued to be just as long. The normal practice for workers in this category was to wake up about 4 o'clock in the morning and trek from three to five miles on foot for task assignment" (WT, 15).

In addition to a condition of estate labor, life at that time was very uncertain. Because of the extremely poor housing and sanitary conditions, most of the estates were infested with disease, malaria in particular: death was a common sight. There was also social and economic discrimination. Cheddi Jagan relates his having to scamper from a social meeting point on the bridge when the estate manager was seen approaching, and tells of visiting the "world of exploiters," "the world of whites" with its well-kept roads, lawns and electrically lit mansions, where the manager's wife threw coins from her window for which the workers' children scrambled (WT, 18–19).

Closer to home, his father took to the bottle sometimes out of frustration and, at other times, out of contempt. He saw his father, an able laborer, suffer upon reaching the height of his job at the age of thirty and being unable to advance further because of a vicious system of colonial discrimination. He heard his father complain of having to train newly recruited estate managers to distinguish between young sugar-cane plants and grass. He saw these same men later use their positions in the estate hierarchy to amuse themselves with the women of the estate (WT, 17–20).

But Jagan was fortunate in the world of sugar estate. His father moved up to the position of driver, "the lowest level of the middle stratum" (WT, 19). Cheddi was respected, as a result, in Indian estate society because of his father's position of authority. His father, realizing the impossibility of the estate system, was determined that his son should not have to be trapped likewise. He sent his son to primary school, and then to secondary school at Port Mourant.[9]

At fifteen, Cheddi Jagan was sent to Queens College, the government secondary school for boys in Georgetown, the capital city. This was a major decision for Cheddi's father. In Guyana in 1933, sending one's son to Queens College was the equivalent of sending one's son to university. And if one wanted to have a secure place in the sought-after

civil service in Guyanese colonial society, high school was essential.
For only the very best was university a possibility. The decision shows
that Cheddi Jagan's father was determined that his son should break
with the estate culture, even if at great cost.

Leaving home for Queens College (High School) meant several
things for Cheddi Jagan. It meant leaving the estate, a world of its
own—a society within a society. It was his first protracted contact with
urban western commercial society with its divisions, interest groups,
and hostilities. He had been relatively privileged while on the estate;
while in the city, he was just a cane-cutter's son from the country.
Cheddi Jagan describes his predicament thus: My self-confidence was
to receive a sharp blow on my arrival in Georgetown. At Port Mourant
I had been a big fish in a small pond, a king in my own kingdom.
Georgetown was different. There I was a country boy in a big city, a
tiny minnow in a big pond. At home I had felt the social distance
between my parents and even shopkeepers. Here I was personally and
suddenly thrown among the sons of "famous" people (WT, 21).

While Jagan seems to have been able to cope with the prejudices of
the wider urban society and at school, he resented the treatment he
received in the three households in which he stayed. Here he was
treated and used like hired help (WT, 23–24). While at home he had
helped to cultivate the family's five acres of rice and helped tend cattle;
but he resented the implications of going to market, washing his guard-
ian's car, cutting grass for the goat, and sleeping on the floor: that he
could not appreciate the advanced ways of urban dwellers, and was to
be used for menial work.

Having completed his secondary education, young Jagan returned to
Port Mourant. Since his father would not even entertain the thought of
his working even in a "white collar" job on the estate, he began a long
hunt for a job in Georgetown. Despite his qualifications, he could not
find a job in the civil service, and teaching meant that he would possibly have to change his religion, from Hindu to some Christian religion, something he would not do, nor would his parents allow (WT,
46). Faced with the possibility of a long unemployment, Jagan was
encouraged by his Queens College friends to go to the United States to
study dentistry.

He chose the U.S. because it represented the possibility of being
able to work and study. In the metropolitan worlds of New York,
Washington, and Chicago, Cheddi Jagan gained new and wider experi-

ences of western society. As a poor student, he had to work to pay his bills. He was discriminated against and exploited. He was separated from his friend and roommate because of his friend's color; in addition, he contracted tuberculosis because of his poor living conditions. Notwithstanding, Cheddi Jagan received his D.D.S. from Northwestern University in 1942. After qualifying as a dentist, he tried to take the state board examination in Illinois but was excluded from doing so because he was categorized as oriental and so came under the Oriental Exclusion Act (WT, 62). Some time later, Dr. Jagan married his American girlfriend, Janet Rosenberg. He probably would have settled down in the United States and begun to practice his profession, but the U.S. Army drafted him as a private just then; because of his qualifications, he felt that he should be recruited at a higher rank, as an officer. Rather than going into the U.S. army as a private, young Dr. Jagan returned home to Guyana, where he would soon begin a new career in politics.

Forbes Burnham

Linden Forbes Sampson Burnham was born on February 10, 1923. He was the only son of a family of three children. His father, an African, was headmaster of Kitty Methodist Primary School in a Black village just outside of the city of Georgetown. The world of Forbes Burnham was very different from that of most other boys of his time. He was a teacher's son. Teachers then were among the "educated" in Guyanese colonial society. Though poorly paid and badly trained, they used their education to articulate their views on every subject with authority. The job of headmaster was often combined with that of catechist or some such function within the Christian church that administered their school or that was attached to their school.

In Forbes Burnham's youth, Guyana, like the rest of the world, was in a depression (see Table 1). The depression was probably felt hardest in the towns and urban areas because they tended to be more integrated with the metropole. For the Afro-Guyanese, it was a period of marking time after nearly a century of slow and deliberate progress. A number of societal problems began to appear in greater proportion than ever before and the colonial machinery had no clear way of dealing with them. A new order was waiting to come into being—everyone felt it but there was great uncertainty how it would happen.

TABLE 1
Prices of Colonial Export Sugar During the Period 1921–40
(average prices per ton refining sugar 96° f.o.b. Trinidad)

1921	$111.80	1931	$ 43.90
1922	71.20	1932	46.60
1923	132.00	1933	45.60
1924	123.60	1934	40.00
1925	71.20	1935	36.60
1926	66.00	1936	37.10
1927	82.20	1937	43.60
1928	72.80	1938	37.10
1929	56.70	1939	46.10
1930	49.00	1940	49.20

Figures f.o.b. Trinidad are not available from 1940. The following tables are c.i.f. and excluded the Special Certified Preference and Canadian Benefit Pool.

1940	$ 54.00	1944	$ 73.20
1941	60.60	1945	82.80
1942	66.00	1946	93.60
1943	68.40	*1947	116.40
		*1948	130.80

*These prices include the allocations to the Reserve Funds as follows:

Labour Welfare Fund	$2.40
Rehabilitation Fund	4.80
Price Stabilization Fund	6.00

Source: Table taken from Report of A Commission of Inquiry into the Sugar Industry of British Guiana, Col. No. 249, 1949, P. 181.

The Urban Environment

Since slavery had been abolished, two generations had passed. Those generations had served their apprenticeship to the British and had done well. A new generation stood ready for change. But there were many societal constraints to this yearning for change. Though social forces were hankering for progress, the controls were still in the relatively strong hands of the British colonial government, and the rigid stratification of urban Guyanese society could not bring itself to link forces with the workers.

Basically the society was divided as follows: Most whites were either government leaders or estate managers, the top level of society. The next level was the professionals, businessmen, and upper-level civil servants, which comprised some whites, some Africans and Indians, but mostly Portugese, Chinese, and mulattoes. Next came teachers; the lower-level civil servants, government employees, and professionals; and small shopkeepers, made up of Portugese, Chinese, Africans, and Indians. At the bottom were the African and Indian laborers (estate field hands and villagers).

Over the years, more and more people had escaped the social barriers and had gotten an education, only to find that the situation was unchanged. The historic development of Guyana brought with it a certain type of societal development that must be understood in order to assess the action of this segment of the Guyanese society. Though slavery was abolished a century earlier in 1838, the blacks of Guyana continued to feel alienated from the mainstream of society. To begin with they lived in villages and had very little opportunity for regular work. This fact is difficult to discern. Most foreign scholars tend to disregard it even when it manifests itself. Indeed, the transition from slavery to freedom was "so traumatic that present day Guyanese, like Barbadians or Jamaicans, continue to refer to a slave past abolished over a century ago as if it were a continuing factor in their present discontent."[10]

Most Africans seem to feel that they were never given the opportunity to realize the freedom they were supposed to have gained over a hundred years before; many can cite several obstacles deliberately placed in the path of Black progress over the years by either the colonial government or the local legislature and plantation interests. The Africans seem never to have recovered from what they see as these societal injustices. At the same time, very little mention is ever made by their detractors of the progress made by Afro-Guyanese from abolition onwards. One reason for this might have been because the professionals who emerged from this group preferred to move out of their communities from which they came and to adopt the mores of the colonial power. On the other hand, the lower-middle-classes, upon gaining some skill or knowledge necessary for becoming functional in a western economy, preferred to emigrate, so there was always a vacuum within the black community.[11]

There existed a large gap between the black professionals and the black working classes. The result of the 1928 elections[12] and the 1953 elections, in which the National Democratic Party was sponsored by the League of Coloured People, show that blacks did not vote in large numbers for organizations and individuals on the basis of their ethnic background or for those who claimed to be able to advance black interests. This might well be because the majority of the population did not like the devaluation of the folk culture and the growing emphasis on the value of anything "English" by the political leadership.[13] This created a situation in which the working people formed an alliance with those professionals who were willing to articulate their grievances but would not trust them with the most serious duty of political leadership. It would seem that the difference stemmed from their environment: in all schools throughout the country, children learned about the English countryside, English history, and read English literature; the urban and professional group, however, could not identify themselves as English, but neither could they see their immediate surroundings as interesting, valuable, or potentially creative.[14] In other words, many of these professionals were strangers to their own people because of the foreign culture they had embraced so totally. It is this incongruity of the professional classes that caused the Moyne Commission to observe: "Most West Indians have always looked to English for their model, and have opposed any attempts to treat the West Indies differently from England as a design to keep them in an inferior position. In fact, the England which many West Indians keep before their eyes is dead."[15] Among this group, mulatto professionals conjured up several distinctions among blacks so as to obscure their own cultural insecurities, and also to secure a higher place in colonial society. This fitted in quite comfortably with the British policy of playing one group off against the other.

The world of Forbes Burnham was one of discrimination by blacks against blacks on a racial and social plane, and also one of discrimination by British against blacks. The bleak economic situation at the time exacerbated this situation. As the Moyne Commission said in its Report (p. 8), "serious discontent was often widespread in West Indian colonies during the nineteenth century, as is indicated by the occasional uprisings that occurred, leading sometimes to considerable loss of life. But the discontent that underlies the disturbances of recent years is a phenomenon of different character, representing no longer a mere blind protest against a worsening of conditions, but a positive

FIGURE 1
Social Stratification in Guyana

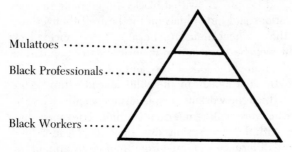

demand for the creation of new conditions that will render possible a better and less restricted life. It is the co-existence of this new demand for better conditions with the unfavourable economic trend that is the crux of the West Indian problem of the day."

It further reported (p. 197) the speech of Mr. Malcolm MacDonald, then Secretary of State, which summarized the situation on June 4, 1938: "These feelings of unrest are a protest against the economic distress of the colonies themselves, a protest against some of the consequences of that economic distress: uncertainty of employment, low rates of wages, bad housing conditions in many cases and. . . ." At that time, the Moyne Commission says (p. 195) unemployment was "rife among the products of secondary schools, owing to the lack of suitable white collar jobs and the disinclination of the pupils to take employment in agriculture as at present organized." Even though it was generally recognized that the urban youths (mostly black and mulatto) did not like the idea of working in agriculture, there were no jobs in agriculture to turn to either. The Commission recognized this when it said of the workers in agriculture (p. 99), "the plight of the unemployed, aggravated as it is by the seasonal character of employment, is serious to the point of desperation." Evidence was submitted to the Commission that:

> gambling was rife in certain of the large towns, and that quite an appreciable portion of the exiguous earnings of many labourers disappeared through this channel. It is easy to condemn, and no one can but regret the futility of such expenditure; but it is impossible not to recognize it as the result of a natural craving for excitement in lives whose

amusements are few, and an expression of the dream of pennies from heaven so appealing to those whose best efforts fail to provide them with a tolerable competence. Another problem of causalisation, consequent on a large surplus of labour over the supply of work. (p. 34)

The situation within the government bureaucracy at this time was just as depressing.

> The organization and machinery of colonial governments everywhere were originally designed to perform certain elementary functions, such as the preservation of law and order, which were essentially negative in character. This conception of the function of government was popular during the nineteenth century and all over the world it was preached by the political philosophers of that age, and accepted by most thoughtful people, as the true and sufficient object of the state. By a process of evolution of which both the starting time and the rate of progress varied widely from country to country, this theory has lost favour among the more advanced peoples and has been replaced by a political philosophy which involves an ever-increasing intervention and participation by government in most spheres of life and work. The effect of this change on the scale and complexity of public administration (in England) needs no emphasis here. During the early stages of this period of transition in Europe the old doctrine continued to dominate the field of colonial administration. (Moyne Commission Report, p. 363)

The local effect of the failure of the colonial civil service of Guyana to respond to societal needs was one of mistrust and racial discrimination. "The chief weakness of the Crown Colony system of government widespread in the West Indies is that the unofficial element, precluded from the exercise of complete administrative control, tends to adopt a consistently hostile attitude towards government and government officials. Associated with this problem is the regrettable fact that colour prejudice, although universally depreciated, is generally on the increase" (p. 451). In analyzing the evidence, we might come to the conclusion that, where a predominantly black and Indian labor force is directed by white expatriates, the resultant conflict could be a confusing one of labor troubles or economic trouble—this seemed to be the case in Guyana. "Be that as it may, there is ample evidence, in the form of press articles, memoranda of evidence submitted to us by unofficials and information received from governments, that in all responsible quarters in the West Indies, there is a widespread feeling that colour prejudice is seriously on the increase. The causes of this are economic, social and political" (p. 59).

Even though the Moyne Commission did not make the explicit link between racial discrimination and appointments in the Guyanese civil service, they did recognize it as a sore point: "Reference has been made above to the resentment frequently caused by the appointment of officials from elsewhere to the public service in the West Indies. Even the most hostile opponents of such appointments will usually admit that in present circumstances governors, colonial secretaries and other senior administrative staffs must generally be found from outside the group. Their claim is that with these few exceptions, all official posts in the West Indies can be filled satisfactorily by local candidates who should have priority of claim to all vacancies for which they are qualified" (p. 60). In short, the Afro-Guyanese and mixed community who made up the bulk of the service at that time suffered from discrimination within and from colonial office employment practices and policy.

The world of Forbes Burnham's boyhood could be fairly described by this excerpt from the Moyne Commission Report (p. 242): "Behind the various economic and social defects that have been described, the rapid increase of population is to be found, sometimes as a major cause, and almost always as an aggravating factor. It has contributed more than any other single influence to the formidible increase of intermittent employment in the towns and of under-employment in the country, and thus has gone far to nullify the effects of wage advances in improving the standard of living."

World War II provided a breathing space for what was already a social problem. Many young men, mostly from the towns and villages, volunteered for the services just to have an opportunity to get out of Guyana and with that the extreme hope of getting an education, skill or simply some exposure.[16] The end of the war saw a return to the same social situation that existed before 1939.

NOTES

1. Raymond Smith, *British Guiana* (Oxford: Oxford University Press, 1962), pp. 167–168. Janet Jagan, *History of the People's Progressive Party* (New Guiana Printing, n.d.).

2. The initial announcement of the formation of the People's Progressive Party is very interesting and is worth reproducing. The front page announcement was headed: "B.G. to have People's Progressive Party." The announcement went on to state: "Preliminary moves to form a People's Progressive Party along the lines of PNP of

Jamaica have been made since the year opened and a provisional committee is likely to be appointed in another week or two. Dr. C. B. Jagan is reported to be one of the key figures in the moves and it is hoped that, when formed, the party would include representatives of every trade union, the TUC, LCP and the two major race groups. Several barristers and other big names likely to run for seats at the next General Election are reported to be interested. It is understood that provisional party plans include the printing of a monthly bulletin to educate the people of the colony as to their political rights and the need for constitutional reform. After the provisional committee is elected, details of party strategy will be mapped and office-bearers elected. It was stressed that the party is unlikely to veer to the extreme left but half-way left of centre." *Chronicle,* January 12, 1950.

3. Personal interview with Janet Jagan.
4. Personal interview with Janet Jagan.
5. Burnham had won the then much coveted Guyana Scholarship. The Guyana Scholarship was given to the high school student who was rated first in the GCE advanced level examinations. It entitled the winner to study at any university at the Government's expense. The enormous popularity and prestige accorded the winner was due to the fact that most of those who aspired to university education were poor, so it was in many cases the only way to get higher education. The absence of a local or regional university made this even harder. The Guyana Scholarship was the only scholarship offered to Guyanese by the Government at that time to pursue studies at university. At London University he won the Best Speaker's cup and became President of the West Indies Student Union. For an account of the early school leaver's position in Guyana, see West Indian Royal Commission Report, Cmd. 6607, 1945, . 215. Also, *The West on Trial*, p. 15.
6. Smith, *British Guiana*, p. 108.
7. Ibid., pp. 108–109.
8. Ibid., p. 32, 195, 76.
9. Primary school was free, but secondary school had to be paid for. In those days only the well-off or the determined sent their children to secondary schools; it cost money and the children could have been more useful working on the estates.
10. Gordon Lewis, "The Growth of the Modern West Indies," *Monthly Review*, New York, 1968, P. 259; see also R. Smith, *British Guiana*, p. 204.
11. Many Guyanese pan-boilers emigrated to other parts of the West Indies and sometimes to Africa under contract. Many others also went to help in the construction of the Panama Canal, and to the oil fields in Venezuela, Aruba, Trinidad, and countless others emigrated to the U.S. in most cases never to return. *Moyne Commission Report*, p. 60.
12. See Clementi, Appendix.
13. Smith, *British Guiana*, pp. 203–204.
14. West India Royal Commission Cmd. 6607, p. 119.
15. Ibid. p. 119.
16. Many tell the story of arriving in England and being laughed at by Englishmen when they told them that they had volunteered to serve. Of those who served only a few managed to get an education. Some got a skill but the bulk of them returned home and were eventually absorbed in services like the Police Force and Public Works Department.

CHAPTER 4

The Nationalist PPP, 1950–1955

THE People's Progressive Party (PPP) was formed in January 1950; Cheddi Jagan was the only established politician within the group. He was a legislator and had been articulating the grievances of the people for five years. He had further identified himself with the workers in the Enmore strike and was known to a certain segment of the population. Furthermore, in 1949 he had become President of the Sawmill and Forest Workers Union. "This union organized workers in sawmills, stone quarries and wood grants in Georgetown and the interior" (WT, 116). He had made his leadership felt in the Indian community, which at that time was mainly rural and estate bound. As president of the mostly black Sawmill and Forest Workers Union, it would seem that he was attempting to build a base within the black community. But more than this, he realized the need to combine political action with industrial action when opposing the colonial government. "Early in my apprenticeship, therefore, it became clear to me that the struggle must be joined at the industrial and political level outside the legislature."

The People's Progressive Party took its name from "the Progressive Party formed by Henry Wallace in the United States" (WT, 116–117). Originally the Political Affairs Committee, the political discussion group transformed itself into the People's Progressive Party, the political party. The PAC's literary arm, the PAC *Bulletin*, changed its name at the same time to *Thunder*, taken from William Morris's poem:

> Hark the rolling Thunder
> Lo the Sun! and lo thereunder
> Riseth wrath, and hope and wonder.

"In place of a duplicated bulletin, we now had a printed paper," wrote
Jagan.

"My dental surgery at 199 Charlotte Street became the headquarters
of the Party. This arrangement was most realistic since we had no paid
personnel, and my wife Janet was provisional general secretary. Other
officers were L. F. S. Burnham, as chairman, and myself as leader.
Actually, Ashton Chase should have been chairman, but he gave way
to Burnham who had an impressive scholastic record" (WT, 117). The
ethnic composition of the leadership of the newly formed People's
Progressive Party tells an interesting story. Cheddi Jagan as leader
seems automatic because of the stature he had already attained locally,
regionally in the Caribbean, and internationally. He became leader of
the PPP's parliamentary group, comprised of himself and Teopholus
Lee, a Chinese. As a matter of fact, the Jagans were recognized as such
a threat to the colonial system that as early as February 1949 Janet and
Cheddi Jagan were humiliated by the immigration authorities in St.
Vincent. His passport was seized and she was declared a prohibited
immigrant and allowed to stay for only fourteen days on condition that
she address no public meetings (WT, 122).[1]

It was predictable that Janet Jagan should become provisional secretary of the new party, since she was already doing most of the secre-
tarial duties of the PAC. In addition she was editor of the PAC *Bulletin*
and later *Thunder*.

It is most interesting that Ashton Chase, an original member of the
PAC and Unionist, should step down so that the chairmanship of the
new party would go to the scholarly Forbes Burnham. Ashton Chase
was a man seasoned in the political and industrial affairs of his country,
a man who had done much organizing for his union, who had at that
time held high office in the union, and who later became the union's
General Secretary. The decision to step down for a total unknown
might have been due to a lack of confidence on his part, which is likely;
but it also reflects the Guyanese preference of giving primacy to the
lettered man, the university trained person. It was a part of the
"Crown Prince" syndrome that so many politicians and students from
developing countries enjoyed, having been the first to go off to university.

The inheritance by Forbes Burnham of the chairmanship of the PPP
also emphasizes Dr. Jagan's absolute desire to have an Afro-Guyanese
of some prominence in the African community within the PPP's leader-

ship. At this time, however, Forbes Burnham's prominence was based solely on his scholastic record and his association with the church group to which he belonged in his village just outside Georgetown. Cheddi Jagan describes his motives for accepting Burnham: "In London, he became President of the West Indies Student's Union, and was closely associated with the left wing and communist movements. He attended conferences in Eastern Europe and stopped off in Jamaica on his return journey home in late 1949. The trip to Jamaica was organized by me in collaboration with Billy Stracham, who was secretary of the London Branch of the Caribbean Labour Congress. This had been done to give him the opportunity of studying the constitution, structure and organization of the People's National Party (PNP), led by Norman Manley. The PNP largely influenced us in framing the constitution of the PPP and in organizing its work" (WT, 117). Burnham's influence then was mainly among lower-middle-class Afro-Guyanese who saw him as a symbol of "local boy makes good." He was looked at as a symbol of what was possible within a difficult colonial system if one tried hard enough. In 1949 Burnham became president of the British Guiana Labour Union, a union made up mainly of black waterfront workers; in doing so, he began to build a political base of his own.

The PPP was a very special type of political movement coming into existence in many parts of the world. Two commentators analyze their impact in this way:

> The early PPP filled a vacuum in our political life which will never again exist. This experience was not peculiar to Guyanese. Indeed, the political movements of Jamaica (PNP) and Trinidad (PNM) had inherited, at different times, the same political possibilities; and in different ways they rendered a similar service to those territories. These opportunities had been created by two closely related factors: the accumulated dissatisfaction of the mass of the population with the old colonial society, and the introduction of universal adult suffrage (in 1953).[2]

The birth of the PPP led to an increase of political action within the country. Its coordinated action in the legislature and on the industrial fronts led to the government's raising of the minimum wage from $1.52 to $1.68 per day.

The PPP's first cooperative activity came with the municipal elections of 1950. The party contested three of the nine wards in which the elections were being held. L. F. Sampson Burnham, Janet Jagan, and

Cheddi Jagan were the Party's candidates.[3] If the chairmanship was handed to Burnham, he certainly had shown that he was worth the confidence placed in him in the 1950 municipal campaign. Burnham treated the public to his reputed oratory at several meetings and endeared himself to the black urban workers. According to many activists, he was able to combine a brilliant oratory with biblical jargon and so reach the African masses in a very direct way: "Like Sampson I shall slay them with the jawbone of an ass,"[4] he said at one meeting.

Burnham made an impression on all who heard him and although both Jagan and Burnham lost their elections for seats in the Georgetown Municipality, Janet Jagan was successful. A few months later the Jagans took off on a Caribbean tour: "Our principal purpose was to spend two weeks in Jamaica as guests of the People's National Party. We had drawn inspiration from the leaders of the PNP— Norman Manley, Ken Hill, Richard Hart and others—and were anxious to meet them and study at firsthand how the party was organized" (WT, 121).

Toward the end of 1950 the British Government, through the Secretary of State for the colonies, appointed a commission "to review the franchise, the composition of the Legislature and of the Executive Council, and any other related matters, in the light of the economic and political development of the colony, and to make recommendations."[5] The Commission held its first session in Georgetown on December 19, 1950. A number of people and organizations, representing every aspect of the political spectrum of Guyanese society, gave depositions before the Commission. The arguments for constitutional change were wide ranging. The Commission's report made some very perceptive observations about the society and its institutions. They recommended that the country be given an advanced constitution but not quite full internal self-government as some people, especially the PPP, had hoped for. They recommended universal adult suffrage and the ministerial system but retained extensive power for the Government and for the executive branch. The Commissioner gave these reasons for its recommendations: "We subscribe wholeheartedly to the belief that the preponderant voice in any deliberative assembly should be that of the elected representatives of the people, but we are convinced that a community in which these checks do not exist or are of illusory power is not truly democratic, and we dismiss at once from our consideration all proposals for a legislative which does not in some way

or other embody these safeguards. Having said this, there is little need
to elaborate the point that the reserved powers of the governor, acting
upon the deliberations of a wholly elected single chamber, do not
accord with democratic experience, and do not offer a practicable alternative to a system of checks and balances embedded in the structure of
the legislature itself. The governor's powers of suspension, veto, and
certification are intended to be exercised only on rare occasions of
grave public consequence, and to ensure that 'public faith, public
order, and other essentials of good government are preserved.'"[6] The
recommendations of the Commission had a mixed reception in Guyana. Some hailed it as a revolutionary step forward; some, including
the PPP, thought that little had been gained. The decision to adopt the
universal adult suffrage in voting was the only decision hailed by the
majority.

Meanwhile, the popularity and activities of the Jagans and the PPP
were becoming so well known throughout the region that in February
1952 they were deemed prohibited immigrants in Trinidad and
Grenada (FF, 122–123). "The bans created quite a stir throughout the
Caribbean. Caribbean leaders and interested individuals intervened,
protesting the bans as violations of the civil rights of British subjects.
The British Guiana Trades Union Council (TUC) cabled protests to the
Secretary of State for the Colonies as well as to labour organizations in
the West Indies. A special meeting to consider joint action was summoned by Caribbean labour organizations; the ban on us was recognized by them as a serious violation of civil liberty and as an attack on
the progressive political and trade union movements" (WT, 123). Dr.
Jagan was able to use his union affiliation to encourage protests by local
and regional organizations against the ban imposed on him. This had
the effect of making the leadership of other organizations acquainted
with Jagan and his political ideals. As he himself says of the ban,
"Indeed we regarded them as badges of honour" (WT, 123).

The People's Progressive Party seemed to be gaining more and more
attention from the general public. The Party became such a moving
force among the progressive youth of the country that the established
colonial interests began to feel uneasy. The People's Progressive Party
was openly hostile to capitalism, and in politicking, it was beginning to
convince the attentive public that some form of socialism was necessary
in building a modern Guyana. In 1952, the legislature passed an "Undesirable Publications Bill." The motion, dubbed the "dunce" motion,

was introduced by the newly nominated head of the Man Power Citizens Association (MPCA), lawyer Lionel Luckhoo, and was aimed at prohibiting the importation of literature, publications, propaganda, or films that were subversive or contrary to the "public interest" (WT, 125).[7] The bill was clearly aimed at the PPP. Given the high literacy rate of the Guyanese people, the PPP found that their job was one of supplying the raw material; the people were eager to rally on their own to the banner of the PPP.[8] The mass involvement and mood the PPP was able to bring about is illustrated by this poem written by one of its leaders:

> This I have learnt
> Today a speck
> Tomorrow a hero
> Hero or monster
> You are consumed
> Like the jig
> Shakes the loom
> Like the web
> Is spun the pattern
> All are involved:
> All are consumed.[9]

By 1953, when the political campaigns began to get rolling, the People's Progressive Party was organized to launch an effective campaign. Its leadership was known, especially to opinion leaders throughout the country, and its philosophy suited people's interests. The Party members and supporters were to be found among the following groups:

Small farmers
Sugar workers
Industrial workers
Small shopkeepers and independent artisans
Domestic workers, miscellaneous laborers
Government workers
A percentage of the young professional middle class
Some support (mainly clandestine) from local businessmen
Young members of the civil service and other clerical workers and
    unemployed workers.[10]

In other words, the party's support was rather broad with a solid base but in the main they belonged to a group which had a lot to gain by changing the old order. As Dr. Jagan himself observed, "For the first time in the history of British Guiana the people were really involved" (WT, 127).

But, we might ask, "involved in what?" The people of Guyana in the People's Progressive Party were for the first time "involved" in using their creative talents to do something. What is more interesting was that many of them knew that they were making history. The party needed everyone and anyone. The junior civil servant was needed to pass government information to the leadership of the party and to help in other party organizational matters, and the sugar worker was needed because he had to go on strike when the party was ready to protest and take industrial action, as were the waterfront workers and industrial workers. The young professional and civil service workers were necessary to assist in group organization in leading discussions, and assisting in group strategy. All were involved. "Racially, the party represented a step towards the unification of the African and Indian workers and intellectuals who shared in the common desire to remove the imperial presence and initiate a programme of social reform."

Economically, the party represented a coalition of the peasant, the "rural proleterian," and the city worker: all in different ways affected by the social structure of colonial rule, and all eager for change. Geographically, the PPP linked the cities (Georgetown, New Amsterdam, and Mackenzie) with the rural areas in the drive for independence and reform.[11] Prior to the formation of the PPP these groups had all shared the same experience of having worked on the estates, then relocating to villages or cities at different times. With a common background of economic exploitation, colonial discrimination, and lack of opportunity, the two major races came together formally for the first time in the PPP. In other words, the party was made up of a coalition of interests. The supporters of the PPP had from the inception realized that the PPP was dominated by Socialists, but they were convinced that only some type of radical change could bring about some betterment in their own economic position. Even though the colonial government was then initiating programs to hasten the pace of change within the country, most of the people, having become familiar with the changes then occurring in the outside world, saw the gradual introduction of new programs as "too little too late." Thus, when the conservative press labelled the PPP as "communist," its supporters construed this as opposition to the radicalism of the party.

Within the party, however, the Jagans were already beginning to have reservations about having given Forbes Burnham the chairmanship of the PPP. He could not be bothered with the drudgery of party organization, whereas the Jagans felt that the total leadership of the PPP should be involved in this very important aspect of party business. Burnham was occupied with building his law practice and with socializing. His political activity was restricted to those times when he addressed and captivated great audiences. He gained the plaudits of tumultuous crowds, but these were the show occasions, where ardent supporters were marshalled in overwhelming strength. They were very different from the bustling experience of a party organizer or coordinator, with its disorderly gatherings, its organized oppositions, its hostile little meetings, its stream of disagreeable and often silly questions.[12]

Even with what the Jagans considered Burnham's many shortcomings as a member of the party's leadership, they were willing to put up with him. Burnham was a valuable asset to the party; his flamboyant personality and oratorical style complemented Dr. and Janet Jagan's managerial skills and passionate ideological persuasion. In the absence of any disagreement, it was a perfect combination of personalities and the Jagans were quick to notice this. Burnham, on the other hand, also knew his strength. He knew the party relied on him so he behaved continuously as a *prima donna*, though within limits.

Campaign and Elections 1953

The PPP campaign of 1953 solidified the inclinations that had already developed within the leadership of the PPP. Dr. Jagan explained the distribution of the work: "My wife was in charge of Essequibo and West Demerara. I was responsible for the East Coast of Demerara and Berbice while Burnham conducted the campaign in Georgetown. This division was forced upon us for we had soon discovered that Burnham was not one of those who was prepared to undertake arduous work. He never ventured very far away from Georgetown and he made very few contributions to the Party newspaper" (WT, 132–133). The fact was that Georgetown did not need much organization. The Jagans and the PPP had been working and operating in Georgetown for a long time and it was an area accustomed to organizations and politics—unions and social organizations had been based and were operating in the city for a long time.

The election was fought around very few issues. It took the form of the old style politicians coming together or individually fighting against the PPP.[13] "Our opponents were numerous but weak" (WT, 127). One writer described the opposition in this way: "The opposition merely seized upon the word 'communism' and attempted to equate it with evil, so that words such as 'red,' 'communist,' 'imperialist,' and 'exploitation' became weapons hurled back and forth until they tended to obscure the real issues and to make rational action less easy for anyone."[14]

NDP's Cultural Challenge

The National Democratic Party (NDP) and two other splinter parties, the United Farmers' and Workers' Party, and the United National Party, fought the elections. The National Democratic Party was the only party with any semblance of effective organization. The party, though it tried to present a national front, was mainly comprised of members of the League of Coloured People; predominantly African in its make-up, it had a few Portuguese and East Indians in its hierarchy (WT, 127–128). In December 1950 the League of Coloured People had invited a Nigerian studying in the U.S. to visit the country as the League's guest so as "to stimulate interest in the League and its work and to advertise to the country as a whole the significance of the African share in the nation's present and future."[15] Even though the organization was registered as a "friendly" society, most observers remained convinced that the League had strong political motives for inviting the young African. The executives of the League knew from experience that the black population tended not to vote for candidates based on their ethnic background and attributed this to a lack of cultural pride. Eze Ogueri II's visit was their attempt to stimulate this cultural pride.

Over the years the Africans in Guyana had tried their best to maintain some of their cultural links with their original homeland. Because of their historical experience they had lost most of that culture; succeeding generations were even urged to despise it. On the other hand, the immigrant groups that arrived in the country later were encouraged to keep their culture. This meant nothing when the colonial government was in control but it counted once nationalism began to emerge. In the case of the other ethnic groups, they could point to their individual countries of China, Portugal, and India, with their documented histories and cultures for all to read. The Africans could only explain that they came from West Africa, none could say where specifically, and though not recognized they did possess a culture, even though it was not written down. As a result, in an era of growing nationalism, they were looked upon by other groups as "lost children," even though their economic and political positions were the same.

Despite this cultural gulf, Africans, especially those in the lower income groups, were quite secure. All along their faith in their past was expressed in the names of organizations like "African S. Church Albonystown," "African Nationalist League," and in the names of many friendly and burial societies. The independence of India brought the cultural rivalry of the two major groups into the open. The Indians, the largest cultural group, felt proud; they felt that they belonged and could identify with a home. This feeling was reinforced with the appointment of an Indian Commissioner to the West Indies and British Guiana in 1948. On his first visit to the country he was given an enthusiastic welcome by the Indian people. In their enthusiasm they treated him as a political representative rather than as a diplomat and began to complain about some of the problems they faced in Guyana.[16] Subsequent visits to the country by the Pakistan High Commissioner in 1948 and Indian Congress Party officials thereafter strengthened the confidence of the Indian people in themselves.

The visit to Guyana by the Our Lady of Fatima Statue on August 31, 1950, aroused the cultural sentiments of another cultural group—the Portuguese.[17] As has been pointed out before, the Portuguese were not treated as whites in colonial Guyana, though European in background, they were treated as a sort of poor cousin. If their inferior position within the society as merchants and shopkeepers stemmed from the fact that they arrived as indentured laborers and were originally part of the laborers classes, they differed from the ruling group in their religion. They were mostly Catholics. The coming of the Our Lady of Fatima Statue from Portugal, the homeland, brought the Portuguese into the streets in large numbers. For nearly three months the statue travelled up and down the country to different communities and Catholic churches. Every day the newspapers carried an itinerary of where the statue would be and sometimes an account of its reception.[18]

The victory of Mao Tse-Tung in China in 1949, the independence of India, and other acts of nationalism around the world by different groups were a source of pride to their natives in other parts of the world. These events had the Africans in Guyana feeling left out. The League of Coloured People knew this and tried to fill this void while at the same time gaining some points politically. When it was first announced that Ogueri had been invited by the LCP to Guyana, the Governor let it be known that Eze Anyanwa Ogueri II was not an African king as had been suggested, nor was he a royal personage. "He was a Nigerian, but only the son of a farmer."[19] As a result, the visit was cancelled. But there was such an outcry from the African population that shortly afterwards the League's President and Secretary went to the U.S., where Ogueri was studying, to see him. They returned announcing that they were convinced that Eze was indeed a king.[20] The Governor and Executive Council refrained from taking part in the controversy after it was agreed that "its motives would immediately be suspect."[21]

Eze was taken, over a seven-day period, to almost every African village in the country, where he was given a royal welcome.[22] It was clear that the reasons for Eze's visit were more political than cultural. However, the organization's concentration on representing the African interest hampered any prospect of the NDP becoming a national party. The main support of the NDP was in Georgetown and New Amsterdam, both predominantly African, and in some of the more conservative rural African villages.[23] The other parties contesting the elections lacked any cohesion and were more based on the aspirations and ambitions of their leaders. Consequently, their impact on the electorate was negligible, as the results show.

Unofficial Opposition

The PPP's unofficial opposition was the subsidiaries of the many British firms in the country that saw their interest threatened, the few established local businesses, the churches, and the press, which was then heavily controlled by the expatriate businesses.[24] One researcher wrote of the opposition to the PPP in this way:

> Shortly before the elections in 1953 the anti-PPP campaign intensified by the daily newspapers (all of them controlled by the sugar and commercial interests and by the president of the MPCA, which was by now the main union enjoying the confidence and cooperation of the sugar producers and the bauxite companies. Mr. Luckhoo's final piece of (indi-

rect) assistance to the party took the form of a four page supplement to the Sunday newspapers published a week before the elections, enlarging on the dangers of communism, the horrors of slave camps in Russia, the evil designs of the PPP on peasants' land, and urging the electorate to vote for any candidate other than a PPP candidate. Since it was widely believed that this supplement must have been paid for by the sugar producers, the general reaction was—"if they are so much against the PPP, it must be good for us."[25]

Dr. Jagan himself described the role of the churches in this way:

> The churches, too, played a role in opposition against the PPP. This was so because in our colonial society, the hierarchy of the Anglican Church was closely identified with the rulers. The planters and their supporters and high Anglicanism were inseparable and so the Anglican Church was deeply committed to the preservation of the *status quo*. A similar role was played by the powerful Roman Catholic Church, controlled by the small but wealthy Portuguese group who, next to the ruling British-European group, dominated the social and economic life of the country. (WT, 134)

The reasons as seen by Dr. Jagan for some of the church's attitudes were as follows:

> The church's hostility to us was mainly due to our policy with respect to the control of schools. We had stated categorically that we were in favour of the abolition of the system of dual control (church-state schools.[26] We Guianese were in the anomalous position of having our primary schools run and managed by the Christian denominations which employed, dismissed and promoted teachers while the Government had to foot the bill. We accepted religious education in the schools. We wanted more secondary school scholarships, and the provision of more nursery schools. (FF, 47)

Not only did the Christian churches come out in opposition to the PPP, but other religions did also:

> Opposition, however, did not come mainly from the Christian church. The organized Hindu and Muslim groups—the Hindu Maha Sagha, the Pandits' Council, the Sad'r Islamic Anjuman and the Muslim League—although for different reasons, also joined in attacks against us. (WT, 134)

One of the charges levelled against the PPP during the campaign was that their election expenses were being paid for by money they were getting from Moscow. Dr. Jagan denies this:

The fact was that our campaign was run on a shoestring. The Party election manifesto was our major expense, candidates had to carry out their work on a very limited budget, and some of them conducted their campaign on foot or bicycle. We had neither enough cars nor public address systems. What we did have, however, were volunteers; people who believed in what they were doing and who were prepared to give free service. We have learned from experience that this is the most reliable type of service. (WT, 133)

The election of Monday, April 27, 1953, was the first election to be based on universal adult suffrage; it resulted in a resounding victory for the People's Progressive Party. The Party gained 51 percent of the vote and won 18 out of the 24 seats up for election. The field had consisted of no less than 130 candidates, 79 of which were independents. Of the total number who contested, 78 candidates lost their deposits. The main opposition party, the National Democratic Party, won two seats. The other four seats were won by independents.[27]

TABLE 2
Election Results[27]

	Votes	Seats	Number of Seats Contested
People's Progressive Party	77,695	18	22
National Democratic Party	20,032	2	16
United Guianese Party	5,961	0	7
People's National Party	3,000	0	6
United Farmers and Workers Party	1,623	0	2

The campaign and election went off smoothly. There was no violence or disturbance as some had predicted, despite the great public interest and enthusiasm: "The country felt itself to be on the eve of a revolution."[28] Of the eighteen seats won by the PPP, nine could clearly be called estate constituencies. The People's Progressive Party won them all. "Nine of the twenty-four constituencies in the colony were sugar constituencies—and we won all with overwhelming majorities" (FF, 52).

Analysis of PPP Victory

The election victory of the People's Progressive Party and the advent of a mass nationalist party has been the subject of investigation by many scholars. Most agree that it was a unique period in Guyanese politics. From the evidence it would seem that a number of reasons could account for the extreme excitement of the election. First, it was the first election held under universal adult suffrage system; second, it was suffrage for a highly literate population that had, for nearly half a century, been excluded from any type of political participation because of property qualifications. In addition, it was the conclusion of a century-long struggle for the Guyanese Africans to establish their civil rights; for the Indians, who had long since decided to make the country their home, it was a confirmation of their rights as citizens. The PPP was successful insofar as it harnessed the energies of the different racial groups and helped them realize the dreams which they all shared. More than that the PPP was able to bring together the two major racial groups, Indian and African, in the same organization for the first time. Even though both groups had had the same background of working on the sugar estates they had never really met. The Africans had left the estates when the Indians arrived, so the two groups never really had an opportunity to work together or share a common organization. The PPP provided the opportunity for the two groups to work together for a common dream.

The leadership of the party was given greater legitimacy because they were comparatively young and had not been involved in the politics of "co-option" played by the British with local interest groups. The different ethnic groups had been working to create the PPP leaders for a number of years. The PPP leaders were a group of men proud of their group culture even after they had left it. Unlike many of their predecessors, they were men who were sufficiently rooted in their own group culture to be proud of it, even though they had certain aspects of western culture and had done well both academically and professionally. As has been shown, this culture developed in opposition to the colonial culture, which only dominated cities and towns where Europeans were more numerous and where only a certain few felt accepted and involved. Thus, the problem of the PPP identifying with the people and the people with the party took only a short time. They recognized each other.[29]

This is one reason why, as some researchers have discovered, party leaders, upon "visiting areas where they had hoped to establish the party found an already established party."[30] One party worker claimed that, in many areas of West Coast Berbice, groups were organized and functioning and that it was only after some time that they bothered to inform the party's head office. These facts seem to negate some of the assertions made by some scholars that give the politicians total credit for great organizational ability. The truth, it would seem, was that the PPP of 1953 was a people's movement and that its supporters at every level had a strong hand in forming and running it. Later the poor showing of both the main political parties in the 1957 election after a split and the disillusionment of its supporters seems, in terms of the number who turned out to vote, to bear this out. Another writer's view of a similar situation is that "among the many groups which appeared in West Africa shortly after World War II were some headed by leaders who were better able than other men to capture the spirit of widespread aspirations, who were quicker than others to learn the value of organization and of communications, who were willing to engage in mass action, and who were bolder in attacking the *status quo* defined by the colonial administration."[31]

Who were these people then who made up the nationalist PPP? Who organized the nationalist movement? The PPP membership can be broken down into four parts: members, sympathizers, activists, and leaders.

1. Members were those who paid regular dues to the party and were given a card but, because of an occupation, were not necessarily active in party affairs at a regional or group level.

2. Sympathizers were those who did not care to become active in politics but were prepared on occasion to make monetary contributions or volunteer their services.

3. Activists were those who, because of philosophy and/or conviction, were willing to work for the promotion of the Party by organizing groups or in any other type of organization work. They may or may not have been a card-carrying member.

4. The Party's leadership was comprised of those who were activists working for the party and who were elected to regional and national party positions.

Thus, the leaders, apart from having the structure, credibility, and confidence of a large group of people, had the best and most enthusiastic groups behind them. In other words, the situation was ready for change.

"The new leaders benefited from two major changes in the political situation. First, the many cultural, social and economic changes that began during the 1920s were accelerated by the effects of World War II and its aftermath; they resulted in a growing stratum of 'transitionals,' individuals no longer fully in the traditional society but not yet modern, who were available for mobilization."[32] It was these "transitionals" who were recognized by the Moyne Commission of 1938–1939 and who, because of the lack of employment, were able to devote all of their time to building and organizing a party. If for no other reason than lack of employment, it would be wrong to look at figures of party membership as an indication of the popularity of the PPP or any nationalist movement in most developing countries.

The movement itself embodied two spirits, one to which people were willing to pay lip service and strive for, and another that was cultural. It was recognized by the leadership of the PPP from the inception that race was a force in the social order of colonial Guyana. This was a historical fact. But most forward-looking people knew that it would be necessary to overcome this, in order for the country to progress. The PPP of 1953 made a conscious effort to overcome the problem. This is why Dr. Jagan was intent on having as broad an ethnic representation as possible when constructing the PPP leadership. Culturally, the two major ethnic groups in the PPP, Indian and African, were very much apart. The Africans had become creolized while the Indians had managed to preserve much of their original culture. The difference in culture, though tending to be divisive, was not bound to have this effect, but the lack of economic opportunity that was a permanent colonial feature, failed to bring about the blending of a Guyanese culture. One writer summarized the 1953 PPP victory in this way: "Anyone who was in touch with the ordinary people of British Guiana in April 1953 knows that they had accepted the PPP as the instrument of a new deal for the country, and they voted for it as a party that would work for a better future for them and their children. For a brief moment sentiments of a national unity transcending race or class or religious affiliation predominated. It was a time of excitement and hope containing the promise of a release of new energy and purpose for the building of a better future."[33]

Though the PPP was successful, its victory looked better when compared with the poor showing of its main rival, the National Democratic Party, and the other parties and independents who had not realized the extent of the change which had finally reached the country. The NDP represented the older generation of nationalists who considered the PPPs a bunch of "kangalangs" (rowdies) who were damaging the respectability they had fought for and built up over many years with the British.

PPP in Office and Suspension of the Constitution

Upon winning the 1953 elections, the tensions of the coalition that made up the PPP began to surface almost immediately. A struggle over the distribution of ministerial and parliamentary responsibility developed within the party. This struggle brought many personal and sectional rivalries to the forefront and revealed the outlines of the future split.[34] In accordance with the constitution, the party had to select its ministers and submit their names to the governor. At the first meeting of the joint session of the new PPP parliamentary group and the party's General Council, the Chairman of the Party, Forbes Burnham, refused to get to the selection of ministers. He wanted the leadership question settled first, and let it be known that he wanted to be "leader or nothing" (WT, 137).

There was an immediate panic among the leadership of the party. The surprise of the members of the executive shows the naivete that existed among the party's leadership. They did not seem to understand the desire for power once victory was attained. To most of them leadership was never an issue to be discussed; first, they were too busy most of the time, and secondly, prior to the election, leadership was "collective."[35] Burnham's demand put a damper on the euphoric spirit that had enveloped the party. For almost a week no word was released by the party's secretariat about ministerial selection and this caused great suspense among the party's rank and file. The demands put forward by Burnham caused executive members within the PPP to think seriously for the first time about their own personal alignments and the structure of the party. Prior to that it was quite easy for the leadership of the party to oppose colonialism, big business, and other tottering interest groups. Their commitment was more on a group level. The leadership question asked that everyone identify themselves.

Forbes Burnham had had his eye on the leader's position long before his 1953 ultimatum. Prior to that, at the March 1952 Congress held in Georgetown, he had suggested that the following Congress be a "members" and not an open party congress. He had hoped, with the aid of his supporters, to pack the General Council with his supporters, then have them elect the party's leader after the parliamentary elections, but he failed. Sidney King (now called Eusi Kwayana), in an impassioned speech to the delegates, had the motion thrown out (WT, 137). At that Congress several positions were voted on:

Cheddi Jagan	Leader
Forbes Burnham	Chairman
Janet Jagan	Secretary
Sidney King	Assistant General Secretary
B. Ram Karran	Treasurer

The crisis of "leader or nothing" only died after a compromise had been reached between the two parties involved in the leadership struggle—Forbes Burnham and Cheddi Jagan. At a meeting held at Jai Narine Singh's house it was agreed that the original names agreed upon for ministerial positions would be modified to accommodate Burnham's demands. He put forward for inclusion as ministers the names of Jai Narine Singh and Dr. Hanoman-Singh, and they were accepted with George Robertson and W. H. Thomas as State Councillors. The PPP was then ready to take its place as part of the country's administration.[36]

The legislature was opened on May 30, 1953. The PPP parliamentarians were determined to make the opening of the Parliament another spectacle for their "politics of opposition." The women dressed in white dresses and the men in white suits with red ties. They gathered at the party's office on Regent Street and marched as a group to the legislature a few blocks away (WT, 139). Some seized upon the dress of the PPP legislators to confirm that they were indeed communists and to raise a greater communist scare in the country; this writer prefers to view it as merely an act of defiance designed to upset those who were indeed upset at the PPP clear victory and to show their contempt for the constitution with which they were supposed to work: "We told our supporters that even though we had won the election, we were really Her Majesty's Government's Loyal Opposition" (WT, 139). Dr. Jagan's first speech in the legislature gives a view of the course the PPP was going to pursue while in office. After paying the usual Parliamentary respects, he said:

> The House observes with favor the initiative recently shown by Her Majesty's Prime Minister, the Right Honourable Sir Winston Churchill, in attempting to ease the present tense world situation and hopes that

the same initiative will be shown in bringing about the end of racial discrimination and ruthless oppression of, and aggression against, colonial and native peoples, particularly in South Africa, Malaya and Kenya. In such efforts he can be assured of the full and enthusiastic support of the people whom this house represents.

Your Excellency's optimistic views about the new Constitution and in particular the State Council have been marked. We, however, harbour no illusions about the nominated State Council which can only serve the purpose of curbing the will of the people—a reactionary and undemocratic purpose.

The presence of three Civil Servants in the House and their control of the three key ministries in the Government and the Governor's veto are an anomaly and contrary to the professed democratic principles of Her Majesty's Government. We shall continue to struggle for a democratic Constitution for British Guiana.

The House is fully conscious of the role which private capital is playing and will play in the development of British Guiana. We will take such steps as will encourage and attract private capital for the development of the country and above all, will guarantee that the Government will honour and fulfill all its obligations and undertakings.

The House notes Your Excellency's observations on the need for the development of a spirit of cooperation between 'capital' and 'labour.' The relationship of capital and labour must not be based as hitherto on the whims of the capitalist but on the recognized rights of workers to organize and bargain through the trade unions of their own choice and to take an active part in the running of the industries in which they are engaged.[37]

The speech in no way suggests that Dr. Jagan or the PPP was a communist or intended to pursue a Marxist or Communist line but at the height of the cold war many took such a view. It seems more anticolonial and nationalist. But the speech was unorthodox as far as the British colonial experience was concerned. The PPP was not about to "play ball" as other colonial politicians had done. First of all, they were far younger than most colonial politicians and took their ideology more seriously, even while their party was in its formative stages. The PPP's style contrasted sharply against that of other colonial politicians of the time. "One might think that the willingness of such leaders (Kwame Nkrumah and Houphouet-Boigny) to cooperate with the colonial power after the first major victory might be interpreted as a sell-out that would cost them popular support. But the fact that rather the opposite took place suggests another advantage which accrued to the victorious mass movement."[38] The pattern set by leaders more popular than the PPP leaders gave the British Colonial Office a precedent that it expected the PPP to follow in 1953. Instead, the leaders of the PPP, seeing themselves as a different group and in a unique position, were intent on a different course. They did not, as Dr. Jagan's first speech to the legislature suggests, intend to legitimize the partial turnover of internal government in exchange for their total cooperation with the British. On the other hand, the British were accustomed to a period of tutelage where their civil servants guided the new leaders in the affairs of government and the ways of democracy.

The PPP embarked on a program of trying to modernize the structure with which they had to work.

> The changes we began to introduce now seem quite modest—to bring all schools under the supervision of government and local education committees; to reform local government so that on this level, too, there would be universal adult suffrage without property limitations, to appoint working people to government boards and committees; to revise the fees of government medical officers in order to make medical care possible for the poor; to curtail unnecessary expenditure of public funds; to provide more scholarships; to bring about social security and workmen's compensation; to improve drainage and irrigation; to make available and usable large tracts of land then uncultivated; and to review and act on the recommendations of the Central Housing and Planning Authority. Increased rates were prescribed for certain categories of workers, primarily the sawmill workers, employees in cinemas and hired car chauffeurs. An eight hour day was approved for factory watchmen. And the Minister of Labour prescribed a $13 weekly minimum wage for employees at drug, hardware, grocery and dry goods stores. (WT, 139–140)

Even though these and the other reforms attempted by the early PPP were quite modest, they were met with the greatest hostility. The PPP felt sincere in its program and naively expected everyone to recognize this sincerity. Their overwhelming victory at the polls made them overconfident and, at times, arrogant. They formulated their programs of reform and then attempted to execute them without taking into account the interest of entrenched and opposed interest groups. They made little attempt to persuade reluctant groups to cooperate in trying to achieve their goals. Another source of conflict was that they could not work with the Governor and many other top colonial civil servants, who were accustomed to implementing projects at a measured pace. The colonial civil servants were reluctant to cooperate, knowing that it meant a lessening of their own power; furthermore, to cooperate in the implementation of projects labelled socialist did not evoke an enthusiastic response from them.

Because of the structure of the 1953 Government with its limited autonomy, the PPP leaders saw no reason why they should give up their important leadership positions in the unions that they had earlier used as a power base to pressure the British Government into instituting some changes within the country. Of the six PPP ministers, no less than four remained active trade union leaders and, in addition, a number of backbenchers were in union leadership positions.

In October 1953, the PPP introduced to the legislature a Labour Relations Bill. The bill, which was similar to legislation in many parts of the world, drew much criticism and objection from many interest groups, particularly those connected with the sugar industry. Aimed at minimizing interunion rivalry, the bill was an attempt by the PPP to get rid of the suspect company union, the MPCA. More particularly, it was aimed at the MPCA-GIWU conflict that began with the Enmore riots and had been dragging on ever since. The MPCA, the union representing the sugar workers, had been closely identified with the status quo and its leaders were openly opposed to the PPP. The GIWU, on the other hand, was closely wedded to the PPP and its leaders were PPP legislators. On the day that the Labour Relations Bill was introduced into the House, the GIWU called a 25-day strike, paralyzing the sugar industry. The strike had the support and sympathy of many other branches of the trade union movement. It was the last of a series of measures the PPP was to undertake. The British Government was puzzled by the continuous affront and unorthodox methods of the PPP, and decided to call a halt to the PPP government.

Raymond Smith saw the PPP predicament in this way:

In British Guiana the leaders of the People's Progressive Party did not accept, perhaps did not understand, these unwritten clauses in the Colonial Office-drafted contract. Whether it be to their credit or their shame they tended to mean what they said in their election manifesto and attempted to implement their declared policies. To begin with they did not accept the Waddington Constitution as the proper instrument for the independent government of the country, and therefore never ceased to oppose what they considered to be the real locus of power. They did not feel themselves to be the government of the country; their aim was complete self-government for British Guiana, and much of the action of the elected members between April and October of 1953 must be viewed in the light of these facts. Such powers as they had, they often used to embarrass the "government," meaning the representatives of the Crown, and to try to further the progress of the party as an instrument uniting Guyanese in an opposition to outside forces. This had been recognized and deplored by all critics of the party. The alleged participation of ministers in trade union disputes, including the fomentation of strikes must also be viewed in the light of these facts. This might be an improper course for a minister of the British Crown but not necessarily improper for a man who feels himself to be fighting on a broad front for freedom from foreign domination.[39]

On Friday, October 9, 1953, the British Government suspended the Constitution. The Nationalist PPP was put out of office.

Constitutional Suspension and After

A few days prior to the suspension of the Constitution, it became clear both in London and in Guyana that some move by the British Government was afoot. The People's Progressive Party leadership dismissed the threat, confident that their overwhelming majority at the polls and the fragmented nature of the official opposition precluded any move by the British. On Sunday, October 4, after an extraordinary visit by the Home Secretary, the Colonial Secretary and other high officials to the Queen, the British press questioned the significance of the visit. "On their return the Home Secretary told newsmen that there was no special significance in the visit, that it was a normal visit for members of the Privy Council" (WT, 145). But quite soon after, British warships and troops from the Caribbean and Britain itself began making their way to Guyana; when questioned, the Admiralty spokesman denied that the movement of five ships had anything to do with events in Guyana.

However, on Tuesday, October 6, when it was known that the ships were definitely en route to Guyana, the Colonial Office released this statement:

> It has been evident that the intrigues of Communists and their associates, some in Ministerial posts, threaten the welfare and good administration of the colony. If these processes were to continue unchecked, an attempt might be made by methods which are familiar in some other parts of the world to set up a Communist dominated state. This would lead to bloodshed. In view of the latest development, Her Majesty's Government have felt it necessary to send naval and military forces to Georgetown (capital of British Guiana) with the utmost

despatch, in order to preserve peace and the safety of all classes. Any reinforcements that may be necessary will be sent from the United Kingdom. (WT, 146)

In Guyana there was much excitement. PPP leaders were in the dark for news, as were their supporters. All were relying on the BBC world service for their information. At meetings PPP leaders confessed that they did not know what course events were taking but they urged their supporters to remain calm. In private they assured their party activists that the British could not possibly suspend the constitution. They felt that the world had long passed that stage of colonial government.

On Friday, October 9, 1953, what many had suspected for some time was made official. The British Government had decided to suspend the constitution of Guyana. The announcement was made in Guyana by the Chief Secretary, John Gutch, in a radio broadcast. He said:

> Her majesty's Government has decided that the Constitution of British Guiana must be suspended to prevent Communist subversion of the Government and a dangerous crisis both in public order and in economic affairs. . . . The faction in power have shown by their acts and their speeches that they are prepared to go to any lengths, including violence, to turn British Guiana into a communist state. The Governor has therefore been given emergency powers and has removed the portfolios of the Party Ministers. Armed forces have landed to support the police and to prevent any public disorder which might be fomented by communist supporters.[40]

Upon arrival in Georgetown, British troops and the international press were surprised to find no disorder of any sort. As a matter of fact, the troops asked citizens continuously that they be shown the site of the disorders, and from accounts were surprised to hear that there were none. The international press was also quite surprised, after the build-up from Whitehall, to find that there was no civil war, no disorder in Guyana on their arrival. It became obvious to almost everyone concerned that the whole crisis was the result of an overreaction of the colonial civil servants stationed in Guyana and, in turn, of the British Government itself. In the context of the cold war it is quite easy to see how such a muddle could come about.

Several organizations in Guyana, including those which had contested and lost the election, cabled their support and approval for the actions taken by the British Government. In Britain the official explanation for the suspension of the constitution[41] was so woolly that there was a clamor by the opposition and the press for a parliamentary debate on the subject. The official explanation stated:

   (i) Fomenting of strikes for political ends;
   (ii) Attempting to oust established trade unions by legislative action;
   (iii) Removal of the ban on the entry of West Indian communists;
   (iv) Introduction of a bill to repeal the Undesirable Publication Ordinance and the flooding of the territory with communist literature;
   (v) Misuse of rights to appoint to Boards and Committees;
   (vi) Spreading of racial hatred;
   (vii) Plan to secularize Church, schools and to rewrite textbooks to give them a political bias;
   (viii) Neglect of their administrative duties;
   (ix) Undermining the loyalty of the Police;
   (x) Attempts to gain control of the Public Service;
   (xi) Threats of violence.

Each one of these acts judged separately was serious enough, and the cumulative effect was disastrous. Viewed in the light of Communist connections of Ministers, their aim was unmistakable.[42]

If there was any crisis in Guyana in October 1953, it was at the most a crisis of confidence. The allegations made in the British Government's white paper were spurious[43] and certainly did not demand the harsh response of suspending the constitution.

As a result of mounting criticism of the handling of the whole affair, the British Government fixed October 22 for the beginning of a debate, in London, on the subject. The PPP leadership decided to send Dr. Jagan and Forbes Burnham to put their case to the British people and to brief their sympathizers (WT, 148). But as the two PPP leaders prepared to leave Guyana, the opposition in Guyana tried to frustrate their departure. On the other hand those who supported the action of the British government were not hindered in trying to get to London.

Once it was known that the Jagan-Burnham visit was to coincide with the Parliamentary Debates, every effort was made to delay their journey. The Governments of Trinidad, Barbados, Jamaica, and the United States refused the two leaders rights to pass in transit through their territories. Neither the American Pan Am, the British BOAC, nor France's Air France would accept Dr. Jagan and Forbes Burnham as passengers. The Dutch KLM agreed to take them, but this meant an overnight stop in Surinam—which the Surinam Government would not grant. It was prepared to grant only an in-transit permit. The party was thus forced to charter a local DC-3 plane to Surinam. "The cost was almost prohibitive—$800 just for two of us" (WT, 149).[44]

The PPP leaders were well received by student groups on their in-transit stops in Holland and in France. In England, too, Jagan and Burnham were welcomed, especially in anticolonial groups and among student organizations. The two leaders addressed some members of the parliamentary Labour Party and attended the debate in the Commons seeking approval for the Government's action against Guyana. In the British Parliament itself the PPP did not get the support it had hoped for or the support it was led to believe it would get. The principal labor speakers chided the PPP while disagreeing with the action of the Secretary of State. Only a few obscure backbenchers spoke up for the PPP. "That the Labour Party had no intention of putting up a vigorous fight against the British Government became clear a few days after the debate. We had decided to put our case to the British public and planned a series of meetings throughout the United Kingdom (England and Scotland) and Ireland. The Labour Party, to which we appealed for help, not only rebuffed us but blacklisted us. It threatened its affiliates with prosecution if they associated with us" (WT, 153). The Labour Party's action was very embarrassing to some of its supporters, especially the socialists within the party. The weekly periodical, *New Statesman*, came out against the Labour Party and TUC action. The article said:

> The National Executive of Labour Party, after having interviewed Dr. Jagan and Mr. Burnham, published a statement condemning them and virtually forbidding its members to organize or speak on Dr. Jagan's platform. Nothing illustrates better the change in climate of Labour Party opinion towards colonial nationalism.

The article then went on to give an account of a meeting between the PPP leaders and the TUC where they were chided for their conduct. It continued:

> Dr. Jagan had himself, naturally and properly asked to have the opportunity of putting his case to the Commonwealth Sub-committee of Labour's National Executive. Reports of this meeting suggest that it resembled the proceedings of a criminal court rather than a conversation between fellow socialists.

In conclusion, the article says:

> It is not as a Communist but as a Nationalist that Dr. Jagan is the
> freely elected champion of the people of Guiana. And if, when he speaks
> to put their case in Britain, he is insulted and rebuffed, the insult will be
> held to be directed, not against a small cell of communists which may or
> may not exist inside the PPP, but against the people of Guiana and their
> struggle against exploitation.[45]

Among the Caribbean leaders, also, the PPP lost most of its friends.
It would seem that the PPP did not quite understand the international
ramifications of its own actions, or the inability of a colonial government to coerce even some of their seemingly independent friends.

International Actions—External Reactions

Interest in cross-national organizational contact and cooperation has
always been a phenomenon of European organizations.[46] In the case of
Guyana and most other former colonies this phenomenon is more
pronounced. The population of Guyana for the most part comprised
the sweepings of different continents down to the last indentured servants. Because the country was always a colony, the connection with
the metropole was always of paramount importance. Since advanced
education could only be pursued abroad, this made the link between
Guyana and Britain even stronger. The habit of always looking outward
makes it seem natural then that the PPP should have looked outside of
Guyana in setting up its party. In doing so, the rhetoric of the communist states seems to have appealed to them as a framework for opposing
the colonial government and heightening the confidence of their supporters. However, none of their economic programs suggested that
they were anything but nationalists. If we can make a distinction, then,
between communist rhetoric and PPP party actions, the politics of the
PPP assume different proportions.

The exposure of PPP leaders to external political influences began
with Dr. Jagan in the United States. His politics then were limited to
political science courses, discussions with other students, and his experience doing odd jobs (WT, 62–65). In Guyana, Dr. Jagan's first contacts with external politicians came on his return to Guyana, and at the
meeting of Caribbean labor leaders in 1945 (WT, 89). For some time
after, Jagan's personal external contacts were limited to contacts with

other West Indian Unionists and informally through letters to radical organizations in London. The importation of communist literature from Britain was for Dr. Jagan a continuous source of support for the feelings he had possessed. Not having been trained as a socialist thinker, Jagan could find easy answers and cliches within this literature that suited his purpose of attacking the colonial government and its capitalistic structure.

On the other hand, Forbes Burnham had taken a keen interest in politics when he was a student in London. He was elected president of the West Indian Students' Union and attended the meetings of communist and other left-wing organizations quite regularly. In his capacity as head of the West Indian Students' Union he led a delegation to do voluntary work in Eastern Europe. However, Burnham claims he never joined any of the organizations he frequented. None of the PPP leadership had any personal external contacts with foreign dominated communist organizations, except for these superficial contacts. The informal contacts of Dr. Jagan and the PPP were limited to letters to "Billy Stracham, who was Secretary of the London Branch of the Caribbean Labour Congress" (WT, 117).[47] It could also be supported that Mrs. Jagan, editor of the party's paper, had some contact with the British Communist Party newspaper since quite a few articles from that paper were reproduced in the PPP organ.

Much of the official accusation of communist inclination in the PPP resulted from visits paid by high PPP officials to conferences of communist organizations outside the country between 1950 and 1953.[48] But the particular branch of communism that the PPP had in store for the country was never anticipated by the party or investigated by their detractors. Instead of gradual approach to communistic change, with a local flavor, their speeches suggest a strong desire for complete independence from the British and a desire to raise the standard of living of the people of Guyana.

Because of the nature of the economy and the society that the colonial government operated in Guyana, the PPP felt it had no alternative but to tackle the economic structure in a dramatic fashion, hoping at the same time to raise the political consciousness of its detractors while reversing the trend of the economy. But the constitution as it had been understood by colonial administrations did not allow for any innovation. It was merely to be a period of learning and familiarization on the part of the politicians who would eventually take over from the British.

"They were expected not to tamper with British economic interests in the country and preferably to pursue a policy of attracting foreign capital for private investment. The principal task of government was felt to be the creation of a favourable climate for investment, the provision of social services, and the development of basic capital assets such as roads, drainage and irrigation, and so forth."[49] This was certainly not the PPP's idea of running a government on behalf of the people they were elected to represent.

Local Perceptions

According to the evidence, the first time any People's Progressive Party leader was accused of being communist was before the PPP or its forerunner, the PAC, even existed. While Dr. and Mrs. Jagan were beginning their political careers, they came into conflict with the Catholic Church while advocating abortion, and were labelled communist as a result. The incident, though minor, is very important in terms of understanding the accusations against the PPP. In most metropolitan countries there is a distinct separation between the Church and the State. In the colonial countries, however, where the Church had a larger role to play, it became an integral part of the government mechanism and wielded significant political influence. The composition of Guyanese political and social society made this even more possible. The planters, or their local representatives who were nearly always British, were predominantly Anglican. In addition, most of the colonial administrators beginning with the Governor were also Anglican. The Portuguese community in the country was strongly Catholic. Because the Catholic Church had great influence with the merchants who controlled much of the retail trade (the Portuguese) and wielded considerable political influence within the Civil Service and in local government, especially in the municipality of Georgetown, the Church had an important influence on certain sections of Guyanese opinion. In addition, the churches had a say in managing the primary schools and was responsible for making all appointments within the schools they managed, even though the government paid the teachers' salaries. Such was the power of the Church to direct popular opinion. Its denouncement of the Jagans as communist must not be either underestimated or undervalued.

Other points that caused the PPP to be labelled communist might seem trivial, but even trivial matters can contribute weight beyond their own individual importance. The use of the term "comrade" as a friendly salutation had at that time been clearly identified with communist parties. The PPP use of the term, though appreciated by its supporters, seems to have alienated some of the more conservative elements in the country. Though the term has been long accepted now, it did cause a stir then and was one of the points some people held onto in categorizing the PPP. Apart from the socialist rhetoric of the PPP leaders, stressing the need to make far-reaching economic and social changes, the majority of complaints seem to stem from the social behavior of the PPP's leadership. The PPP was most daring in its "politics of protest" even by today's standards. In some cases their behavior was construed as plain rude.

This type of politics, coupled with the behavior of some members of the party, frightened many moderates who took the easy way out by charging the PPP with being communist. They felt both threatened and insecure. One of the official charges by the British Government against the PPP was that of appointing party supporters and unsuitable people to boards. "Ministers' appointments to Statutory Boards and Committees showed their determination to put these Committees under party control without regard for members' suitability and experience. They appointed four PPP supporters, three of whom were primary school teachers, to the Education Committee while the representatives previously on the Committee of the denominational governing bodies which control 260 out of 277 primary schools in British Guiana were excluded."[50]

The difference of opinion between the PPP's idea of control of the primary schools and that of the churches has already been mentioned. Given this, we can begin to understand the PPP's reasons for excluding representatives of the denominations from the committee. To charge, however, that the people appointed were not qualified is a bit far-fetched. Those appointed were teachers within that same system and were technically competent and sufficiently intelligent to be able to make recommendations for changes. The denominational representatives were usually clergymen who had no experience in education administration or teaching in public primary schools but sat on such boards mainly to make sure that the church's view was represented. The appointments then were an attempt to professionalize the department using the talent then available. Any difference in appointment would have had the effect of a difference in the views of the board, which was probably also hoped for by the minister, when making the appointments.

On a more personal level, some critics charge that some PPP ministers were provocative in their manner of dress and their use of language. One person remembered an official party given in New Amsterdam in honor of one minister. As the story was told, the guests were all dressed formally; the Minister walked in, wearing an open-neck sports shirt, with two friends similarly attired. The guests at the party were quite disturbed at the Minister's dress and considered it in very bad taste. Even though such dress is acceptable in Guyana today even for official occasions, it was regarded as extremely radical then; the behavior of a "kangalang." In addition, the response of the Minister of Works to the intransigence of the Governor, Sir Alfred Savage, in dealing with the PPP is remembered by many: "This confounded nonsense must stop."[51] On Sunday, October 4, 1953, the PPP held a meeting outside the residence of the Governor. The main speaker at the meeting was Forbes Burnham. Because there were already speculations in Britain by the press that some action against the radical government in Guyana was imminent, the meeting was well attended. Burnham's famous quote, "Her Majesty's Government will suspend this constitution over my dead body," was remembered for its daring and is always cited in reference to the 1953 PPP radicalism.

The PPP, the Unions, and Communism, 1953

From the inception of their political agitation, the leading PPP politicians realized that the unions were an important political force that had to be brought into their overall plan if their eventual goal was going to be independence and not just reform. Unions were important, too, because of the positions they occupied in the society. The colonial and exploitative nature of the dominant group meant that unions had to assume an anticolonial posture, whether they wanted to or not. This made it easy for the unions in Guyana, like the unions in countless other colonial countries and in the nearby Caribbean, to nominally ally themselves with the PPP in opposing colonialism. In addition, "The politics of trade unions in the colonies were often centered on the issue of national independence."[52] It was natural for the trade unions to be political because only political changes could have brought about a change in the relation of the employers to the worker or a difference in employment practices that they sought in the country.

Trade Union Foreign Policy

As early as 1926 the Guyana Labour Union, then the only union in the country, held and hosted the British Guiana and West Indies Labour Conference. "The Conference was originally convened by the British Guyana Labour Union (BGLU) and met in Georgetown, British Guiana in 1926."[53] The Conference, it would seem, dealt mainly with political and social issues. The Conference "accepted proposals for federation and passed other resolutions of a regional rather than an insular nature. It urged the development of a private telegraphic code which would allow secret labour communications in case of attempts to break strikes by inter-territorial transfer of workers, up-keep of a Labour Commissioner in England, compulsory education for the masses, industrial and social legislation, prison reform and a series of resolutions referring specifically to the situation in British Guiana." In addition, it was, as far as has been recorded, the union's first physical contact with trade unionists from outside the Caribbean region. At the Conference, the British Trade Union Council was represented.[54] The subsequent 1938 and 1944 conferences passed similar resolutions. "At the third and last meeting of the British Guiana and West Indian Labour Conference in 1944, the resolutions tended to be nationalist rather than labour-oriented and federation was, as in 1926, the main issue. Anti-British feelings were evident in the newer leaders but Cipriani and the older leaders held their pro-British and anti-American position."[55] As the older unionists moved out of office, they were replaced by younger, more aggressive leaders. The older leaders were prepared to negotiate incremental change in the country over a period of time. The new leaders felt the pressure and support of a more impetuous, well trained, and sophisticated generation. In 1945 the TUC began to become more international. "H. J. M. Hubbard and D. M. Harper, Secretary and President of the TUC, attended the founding Congress of the World Federation of Trade Unions in Paris in 1945" (WT, 89).[56] In the same year the West Indies Labour Conference held a meeting in Georgetown where even more new faces with an interest in both politics and the unions were present.

The end of the war marked not only a turning point in the leadership of the Guyanese and West Indian Unions and political movements, but also a turning point in European and North American relations, which were to affect the Caribbean and Guyanese political and trade union movements seriously. The trade union movement, like the political movement, had proceeded in Guyana without thinking much about the rapidly changing international situation, or thinking that their independence as international actors was guaranteed by the strength of their domestic support. The suspension of the constitution changed all of that.

The Cold War

The Guyanese political movement had come full circle. The Political Affairs Committee, the People's Progressive Party, and some of the unions, which had attracted the brightest elements in Guyanese society in the late 1940s and early 1950s because of their forward-looking posture, became engulfed in a situation over which they had no control—the cold war. The party that had staked its reputation on its ability to cope with the international maneuverings of Western society had fallen victim to it. The Western powers, because of their concern about communism and communist gains in Europe and Asia, were not about to give the PPP the chance they might have had if circumstances were different.

The claim of a communist threat in Guyana seems to have had little or no basis whatsoever. Most writers would agree that the PPP was surely socialistic and that some of its leaders may have been communists. They publicly professed their admiration of the Soviet Union, China, North Korea, and all those countries that opposed colonialism and exploitation. They also admired the rapid pace at which these countries were able to modernize their societies and perhaps would have followed many of their programs; but these were not sufficient reasons for automatically assuming that they would have fallen under complete Soviet control.

NOTES

1. Mrs. Jagan's passport was not seized probably because at that time she was still a U.S. citizen.
2. David DeCaries and Miles Fitzpatrick, *Twenty Years of Politics in Our Land*, *New World Independence Issue*, George Lamming and Martin Carter, n.d. (eds.)

3. Ibid.
4. Personal interview with party activist.
5. British Guiana, *Report of the Constitutional Commission, 1950–1951*, London, HMSO, 1951, Colonial No. 280, p. iv.
6. Ibid.
7. As new head of the MPCA, the largest union, Mr. Luckhoo was nominated to fill the seat for a labour representative.
8. According to the 1946 Census Report, the literacy rate was as follows: White, 98%; Negro, 96.7%; Mixed, 96.3%; Portuguese, 96.4%; Chinese, 92.7%; Indian, 55%. See Report of the British Guiana Commission of Inquiry, Constituted by the International Commission of Jurists, October 1965, Memorandum by G. S. Roberts with the assistance of J. A. Byrne, pp. 145–461.
9. Martin Carter, *Poems of Resistance from British Guiana* (London: Lawrence and Wishart, 1958).
10. David Decaries and Miles Fitzpatrick, *Twenty Years of Politics in Our Land*, New World Independence Issue, p. 39.
11. Ibid.
12. W. Churchill, *Great Contemporaries*, London: Fontana Books, 1937, p. 16.
13. For a good account of the 1953 Elections, see Colin A. Hughes, *The British Guiana, General Election 1953—Parliamentary Affairs*, Vol. VII, 1953–54, pp. 213–220.
14. Smith, *British Guiana*, p. 169.
15. Eze. A. Ogueri II, *Seven Amazing Days* (Boston: House of Edinboro Publishers, 1954), p. 13.
16. *Argosy*, August 23, 1948
17. *Chronicle*, August 31, 1950.
18. For a detailed account of the history of the statue and of the visit to Guyana see *Cariba*, The Annual of the Caribbean, 1950. B. A. Litographic, Georgetown, pp. 77–82.
19. *Minute 610:* Minutes of the Executive Council of British Guiana held on Tuesday, 5th of September 1950.
20. *Chronicle*, November 5, 1950.
21. *Minute 799*, Minutes of November 14, 1950.
22. Eze A. Ogueri II, *Seven Amazing Days* (Boston: House of Edinboro Publishers, 1954). Eze means king only insofar as it suggests that one is the head of one's own clan.
23. Smith, *British Guiana*, p. 171.
24. *Chronicle*, April 12, 1953; also, April 15, 1953.
25. Smith, *British Guiana*, p. 170.
26. 252 of the 269 state-aided primary schools were administered by one or another religious denominations.
27. Colin A. Hughes, *The British Guiana*, General Election, 1953, Parliamentary Affairs, Vol. VII, 1953–1954, p. 218. Also, *Report on the General Election 1953*, prepared by H. R. Harewood, Government Printing, Georgetown, 1970.
28. Smith, *British Guiana*, p. 171.
29. Most of the nationalist parties were somewhat surprised at the numbers of seats they captured very soon after their formation in the 1950's both in Africa and in the Commonwealth Caribbean.
30. See Dennis Austin, *Politics in Ghana*, London: Oxford University Press, 1964, p. 114. Interview with Gwendlyn Grant Greenidge, former party worker, 1953, PPP Rosignol.
31. Aristide R. Zolberg, *Creating Political Order* (Chicago: Rand McNally), p. 12.
32. Ibid.
33. Smith, *British Guiana*, pp. 171–172.

34. DeCaries and Fitzpatrick, *Twenty Years of Politics in Our Land*, p. 39.
35. Personal interview with former PPP General Council member.
36. See Appendix I for composition of the Government.
37. See full text in *The West on Trial*, pp. 461–462; see also *Hansard*, June 17, 1953.
38. Zolberg, *Creating Political Order*, p. 17.
39. *British Guiana*, pp. 183–194.
40. The Constitution Suspension Ordered on October 8, 1953—Statement by Her Majesty's Government. White Paper Reprinted by Command (The Bureau of Public Information).
41. See *British Guiana Suspension of the Constitution*, HMSO, 1953, Cmd. 8980.
42. Ibid., pp. 3–4.
43. For a full account of the allegations levelled against the PPP see Cmd 8980, pp. 4–8.
44. This event demonstrates the ability of a colonial government to get the cooperation of business and other governments in executing its policies in third countries.
45. *New Statesman and Nation*—The Weekend Review, Saturday, November 14, 1953, Vol. XLVI, No. 1184 (London: New Statesman and Nation Publishing Co.), p. 588.
46. Jeffrey Harrod, *Trade Union Foreign Policy* (New York: Anchor Books, Doubleday, 1972), p. 35.
47. Billy Stracham was labelled "a Jamaican Communist resident in London" by the British White Paper suspending the 1953 Constitution. See Cmd. 8980, Appendix A, p. 13.
48. For a full account of the conferences attended and the PPP participation, see Cmd. 8980, Appendix A, pp. 13–15.
49. Smith, *British Guiana*, pp. 172–173.
50. Cmd 8980, 1953, p22.
51. Personal interview with party activist.
52. Harrod, *Trade Union Foreign Policy*, p. 111.
53. Ibid., p. 235.
54. L. Braithwaite, "Federal Association in Institutions in the West Indies," p. 298; as quoted in Harrod, *Trade Union Foreign Policy*, p. 236.
55. Harrod, *Trade Union Foreign Policy*, p. 237.
56. See also Ashton Chase, *A History of Trade Unionism in Guyana, 1900 to 1961* (New Guyana Company Ltd., n.d.).

CHAPTER 5

The Interim Government and Political Division, 1953–1957

THE British Government nearly "lost" Guyana because of lack of attention and discriminatory colonial practices, then got a chance to correct it. The suspension of the Constitution was a clever move on the part of the British. It bought time for everyone. It bought time for the Colonial Office, which did not know in which direction the new leaderships in the colonies in Africa and the Caribbean were going once independence was granted; it bought time for British business interests in Guyana, which began recruiting more local managerial staff and reorganizing itself to meet the changing times; it bought time also for the local elite and conservatives to make some adjustments to the new realities that had by-passed them earlier. In Guyana it was a signal to all interest groups that a new political race was about to begin. Or rather, the 1953 race was going to be rerun. When the PPP was formed, it gathered around it the intelligent, articulate young—men and women who by training and disposition were very middle class. The new movements did not seem to be able to accomplish the same.

The organizations that emerged after the suspension of the Constitution were more ethnic in their make up. A further reason for the almost total collapse of the nationalist PPP was the smallness of the Guyanese society. In a society where the educated elite and the middle class are both small, their refusal to participate in the political process has a serious effect on the quality of the organizations which eventually emerge. The suspension of the Constitution frightened many members of this group. Fearing for their security and not being able to tell what

reprisals would be taken, many Guyanese political activists returned to
a state of inactivity. Many government servants lived with the guilt
that they had violated the ethics of political impartiality and neutrality
patiently taught to them by the British.[1] The arbitrary arrest, detention and restriction of PPP activists and leaders and the general policy
of the government harassment frightened most PPP sympathizers.
This is more easily understood when it is remembered that the government was the biggest employer in Guyana outside the sugar estates.
But more than that, there was a general feeling among the PPP followers that something had gone desperately wrong. The experiment they
had supported and in which they had such high hopes had collapsed.
Their young leaders had blundered badly. They had gambled and lost.
Once the few progressives were out of the body politic, those who
remained were spread too thin to make any significant impact on the
political life of the country. After this fragmentation in the Nationalist
movement began, the parties which emerged were built more or less
around a single person, thus becoming more of a personal vehicle for
power than a party with the spontaneity of the early PPP. In other
words, the parties became brokers in their bid for power. The simplicity which was a feature of the politics of 1953 was lost when the Constitution was suspended.

The politics of Guyana from the suspension of the Constitution onwards is one of a steady decline. In London, Jagan and Burnham,
though given the cold shoulder by the British Labour Party and the
British Trades Union Congress, were well-received by most Guyanese
and West Indian residents and by student groups. The two leaders left
Britain and proceeded to India, arriving November 21, 1953, to "inform the government and people there about developments at home"
(WT, 188). In India, Jagan and Burnham's tour was organized by the
Congress Party, which had them speak in several of the main cities.
"The highlight of our two-month visit was an address in New Delhi to
an informal assembly of the members of both Houses of Parliament
with Prime Minister Jawaharlal Nehru in the chair. We were warmly
received wherever we went, sometimes with great pomp and cere-
mony" (WT, 189). But even though the Congress Party went all out to
give the PPP leaders a hearing and an audience, both the Indian
Government and the Congress Party were at that time under increasing pressure from the Western powers, especially the U.S., for the

non-aligned and anticolonial posture it had adopted in international affairs. "The Government of India seemed hesitant to give us official sponsorship. I was carefully made to understand that India was in trouble with the United States over Pakistan and Korea and thus needed the support of the British Government. Moreover, the Indian Government, preoccupied with its own communists in Kerala, Hyderabad, and elsewhere, was somewhat influenced by British Government anti-communist propaganda against us" (WT, 189).

Meanwhile, new developments were taking place in Guyana. The British Government, rather than revert to a direct colonial type government with direction coming from the colonial office, implemented an intermediate stage of government. The new government and legislature were headed by the Governor and included politicians, businessmen, civil servants, and unionists, many of whom had been rejected by the populace at the April 1953 election. "Five of the six non-PPP elected members on the old legislative were nominated to serve in the Interim Legislature . . . and some who had lost at the elections even their deposits (WT, 185). It would seem that the Colonial Office was intent on demonstrating to the people that the moderates could better represent and achieve what the Guyanese people had hoped for. This obvious attempt by the Colonial Office to offer the moderates as an alternative, leadership in Guyana, was probably suspected by other politicians and was crystallized when the National Democratic Party merged with a number of splinter groups to form the United Democratic Party (WT, 185).

One of the first acts of the new interim government was to suspend the civil liberties of the people by declaring a state of emergency. Following this, a number of PPP militants were detained. Atkinson Field Air Base[2] was the site of the detention camp where Sidney King, Rory Westmaas, Martin Carter, Ajodia Singh, and Bally Latchmansingh were detained (WT, 188). Other high-ranking PPP leaders were placed under restriction and were made to report to the police in their areas at regular intervals. One detainee, Bally Latchmansingh, was released quite soon after being detained because of ill health, but the others were not released until January 12, 1954. Their release was precipitated when the detainees went on a much publicized hunger strike on December 27, 1953. They had done so to dramatize their protest against their arbitrary imprisonment. Almost every form of political activity in which the PPP engaged was banned by the Government. All forms of assemblies, public and group meetings, even film shows were banned.[3]

To take care of the added duties that were assigned to the police, and also the frustration that led large numbers of Guyanese to support the PPP, the interim government embarked on a scheme of promotions and expansions within the whole Government service. "The police force, which the British Government claimed we had tried to subvert, was rapidly expanded and the upper ranks encouraged with rapid promotions. The numbers of the ordinary commissioned ranks were increased by nearly 50 percent and 100 percent respectively, and expenditure on the force doubled almost overnight" (FF, 189). In the civil service, too, the same accelerated pace of promotion and training was noticeable, though not at quite as rapid a pace as in the police force. As time went on, police harassment increased. Dr. Jagan recollects:

> Apart from those detained, other party leaders and activists were hounded and persecuted. Their houses were constantly raided by the police. They were restricted and could not move out of their limited areas without police permission. Brindley Benn, Secretary of the Pioneer Youth League and executive member of the P.P.P., could not leave New Amsterdam; Ram Karran, treasurer of the Party, was restricted to Bel Air, East Coast Denerara; Sidney King, on his release from detention, to Buxton; Janet Jagan, Chrisna Ramsarran, Eric Huntley and others to Georgetown. Many were placed under police surveillance. Several of those restricted were forced to report daily to the police and some had to serve prison terms for failure to do so. Many went to jail for refusal to pay court fines for minor offences. Refusal to pay court fines was part of our campaign to embarrass the government. Nazrudeen and Fred Bowman were charged with sedition, but the case was struck out by the trial judge on the brilliant submissions of D. N. Pitt, the famous English barrister who came in March 1954 to defend them. (WT, 190).

It would not be far-fetched to say that the state of emergency and the bans imposed were meant almost exclusively for the PPP (WT, 190). Despite the ban, some PPP leaders did travel outside their restricted areas and even held meetings, if only in the rural areas. In some areas, party meetings were conducted under the camouflage of a house party. While members were dancing, they would discuss proposed group activities or information received would be passed on.[4] At this time a strain in relations began to develop between the party's chairman,

Forbes Burnham, and the General Secretary, Janet Jagan. Burnham returned to rebuilding his legal practice and began giving less and less time to party affairs. The party secretary directed supporters who had been harassed and charged to party lawyers who would represent them in court. Burnham seldom made himself available and let it be known that he was a professional lawyer, implying that he should be paid for his advice. Mrs. Jagan thought that the suggestion lacked sympathy for the party's poor membership and showed an unwillingness of the Party's chairman to make any sacrifice for the party.

In mid-1954 more PPP activists were arrested and detained without explanation. On April 3, Cheddi Jagan, who had been placed under restriction shortly after his return from India, broke his restriction and was arrested when he was found some distance outside his restricted area (WT, 193).

> In keeping with our declared policy of civil disobedience, I broke the restriction order on April 3 by travelling 35 miles away to Mahaicony on the East Coast of Demerara where I had established a branch dental surgery. This was after the Governor had refused me permission to travel to Mahaicony. The police arrested me and brought me to Georgetown for trial. Some of our supporters who demonstrated in protest were also arrested. This was the beginning of demonstrations and arrests throughout the country.[5]

Rather than granting Jagan a trial by jury, the government empowered the Magistrate's Court to hear the case. Jagan was placed on bail and released. The crowd that had waited outside to hear the verdict gathered around him and spoke with him as he walked to his office a few blocks away. For this he was rearrested, along with some of his supporters. The Magistrate refused to grant Jagan and his comrades the usual bail, so he and fifteen supporters spent the night in custody. The next day in court the Magistrate sentenced Dr. Jagan to six months imprisonment with hard labor (WT, 194). Even though there was protest about the severity of the sentence, Jagan was kept in prison and held to the letter of the law. He came into conflict with the authorities in the Camp Street Georgetown prison where he was held for some time for trying to influence the regular inmates. Then he led a number of prisoners on a hunger strike in protest against the poor diet served at the institution. Soon after this conflict he was transferred to the distant Mazaruni Penal Settlement in Essequibo.[6] Cheddi Jagan served five months in prison, and while he was there the Interim Government outside was keeping up its reign of terror, intimidating and harassing innocent citizens merely for their political beliefs, or because of their political affiliation. At every turn PPP sympathizers, supporters, and activists were harassed, arrested, and, in many cases, imprisoned. Just as Dr. Jagan himself was about to be released, Janet Jagan, Secretary of the PPP and Editor of the Party's newspaper, was about to enter prison.

> After five months in prison I was finally released. One month was remitted, as is normally done for most prisoners for good behavior. On the appointed day, September 11, of my release, the prison authorities decided to release me at 4 A.M. instead of the normal time at 6 A.M. This was done to frustrate the huge crowd which was expected. I refused to be tumbled out at that hour; by the time I got to the Superintendent's office, it was 6 A.M. I was put on a charge of disobeying an order and fined one day's loss of remission. All this maneuvering did not prevent a large crowd from welcoming me on my discharge the following morning (WT, 197).

A few days before, Mrs. Jagan had been sent to prison for six months on two counts: "One for being in possession of a secret Police Riot Manual and the other for holding a public meeting" (WT, 197). So the two Jagans, the Party's leader and secretary, were out of Party affairs for a total of ten months between them. It was not until January 18, 1955, that Janet Jagan was released from prison. The restriction of executive members and party activists paralyzed the PPP. The black-listing of PPP supporters had the further effect of creating a crisis within the Party. Many could not find work and so became more dependent on the Party, and the professionals had to return to try and rebuild a practice in a very hostile environment.

One of the matters of serious discontent and one that caused a very serious strain among party leaders was the fact that Forbes Burnham was not restricted during 1954; then, when restricted and under obligation to report to the police at regular intervals, he utterly refused to do so, yet the police failed to prosecute him (WT, 198). The rumors ran the gamut among the radicals in the party. There were rumors of Burnham being in private conference with the governor; of his acquiescing to the British Government for information; and of his trying to maneuver for leadership of the party with the help of the British administration. Burnham's explanation of trying to build his law practice and his general snobbish and austere attitude toward the party's rank and file and some executive members did not help his image. His actions regarding the welfare of the Party were those of a man who had gone into a party, had been handed the chairmanship primarily because of his reputation as an intellect, had made a name for himself very quickly, and inevitably because of his education, had not concerned himself with much more.

The fact that Burnham was never arrested and imprisoned should not be underestimated in terms of the influence it had on subsequent events with the PPP. For the "generation of '53," it seems from the interviews I conducted that this was an extremely crucial point in deciding legitimacy in the people's perceptions of leadership in Guyana. One activist termed being arrested and imprisoned the "supreme sacrifice" for leadership within the Party. And not only that, Jagan's arrest and imprisonment put him in the big league. From then on, he was put in the same category with leaders like Nehru, Nkrumah, Kenyatta, and all of the other anti-colonial leaders who were being imprisoned by the British and other colonial powers around the same time in other parts of the world. If Enmore won Cheddi Jagan national prominence in Guyana, then his six-month prison sentence won him an international reputation. It established Jagan as a radical among political commentators and among students and scholars, a standing which Forbes Burnham craved throughout his political life. It also gave Dr. Jagan the legitimacy that helped him to dominate Guyanese politics for more than a decade after. In the nationalist movement of 1950–1955 Burnham played a part very much that of the British Gentleman politician. He had sought the palm without the dust. This was not true in the sense in which the phrase is often used—that of avoiding hard work. On the contrary, Burnham was very capable of hard work and of long hours of daily concentration both on politics and on his legal practice. He had indeed sought the palm, but the dust had never come his way.[7] Thus, throughout the modern political life of Guyana, Burnham and Jagan had lived continuously in each other's shadow and Burnham has lived since then continuously trying to overcome the image of Jagan the radical. One commentator, writing some time later, observed: "My own conclusion, for which I can offer no evidence, is that between these men, who have shared an important Guiana experience, there remains a mutual sympathy and respect stronger than either suspects, each perhaps regretting the other for what he was."[8] This is a precise summation of the two main actors and rivals in Guyanese politics since the war.

The 1954 "Robertson" Commission

After the suspension of the constitution, the Colonial Secretary appointed a Commission on December 2, 1953. The terms of reference of the Commission were "in the light of the circumstances which made it necessary to suspend the Constitution of British Guiana to consider and to recommend what changes are required in it."[9] The report of the Commission, which was published in September, 1954, caused quite a stir among the different factions in Guyana, especially those embroiled in the power struggle taking place within the PPP. It is also used as one of the signposts in analyzing the 1955 split of the PPP. Indeed, some commentators tend to see the report as the main source of the split. The report probably did have some influence on the events as they were being played out, but it is my belief that it had little effect on the final outcome.

The Commission's report showed little sympathy for the People's Progressive Party Government; its sympathy lay with the colonial administration and the locals who supported it. In some areas, it was just plain discriminatory. In dealing with the Labour Relations Bill, the Commission looked at the CIWU's charge that the MPCA was "weak and inefficient and entirely subservient to the employers."[10] The Commission sought to excuse these allegations by observing that "these are charges easily made against any trade union anywhere which carries the day-to-day responsibility for trade union policy and administration."[11] But the Commission found nothing unusual about the union's activity when it said, "it has, we believe, on occasion accepted money from sugar companies for some special purpose."[12] In a thorough analysis of the situation at that time, the Commission wished that events in Guyana had proceeded in a more planned way, i.e., that more moderate and compatible leadership had emerged. In looking at the other ethnic groups from which such leadership could have come, the commission said:

> The other elements in the community—of Portuguese, Chinese and United Kingdom origin—are much smaller in numbers, though their influence is great. Members of the last named community are anxious at the way in which the Indian and African sections have now obtained virtual domination through universal adult sufferage. In common with the Portuguese and Chinese, they have no particular enthusiasm for socialist policies, but many members of all three communities have a

real understanding of the aspirations of the poorer people. They realize the folly of trying to resist the trend of the times, but they are not unnaturally fearful of the more extreme policies of the People's Progressive Party. We are convinced that, in a country where leaders are needed, they could play a more valuable part than they do."[13]

It does not seem quite true that these groups, including the colonial administration, had as deep an understanding of the aspirations of the common people as was supposed. If they did, they never showed it and did nothing tangible to convince anyone of their concern. The British Government had published two reports of conditions in the country and little was done or said about this until the PPP came along.[14] One dealt especially with conditions˙ on the sugar estates, yet it was not until November of 1953, after the suspension of the Constitution, that the local Colonial Administrators were stirred to act: "The Sugar Producers Association agreed in November last, at the suggestion of the Governor, to the diversion to the Welfare Fund of $2½ million (Guyana dollars) from the Sugar Industry Price Stabilization Fund in order to expedite the rehousing of sugar workers living in obsolete ranges."[15]

The Commission failed to say explicitly that the Colonial Civil Service structure was very inefficient and not conducive to development; this the PPP Ministers and the public knew well. The Commission noted, however: "In the past the administration of colonial territories was very largely a matter of preserving law and order and had little to do positively with securing the development of resources and the improvement of social and economic conditions. In a comparatively short time, however, all this has changed. Governments have assumed more and more responsibility for the provision of medical and welfare services, for housing and education and generally for the economic and social development of the territories. In British Guiana, as elsewhere, this has thrown new and heavy burdens on the administration, and it is perhaps not surprising that without the spur of experienced ministers responsible to the electorate the machine has laboured under the strain."[16] That the colonial civil servants were no more "experienced" than the politicians themselves, and could not really offer the PPP Ministers the help they needed in order to implement their election promises caused a greater distrust between the new government and the civil service than may have been the case under ordinary circumstances. Rather, the PPP Ministers felt that senior civil servants were more of a hindrance when trying to implement their projects. Coupled with the attitudes of some other influential groups, it is quite easy to see why the PPP was particularly distrustful of the colonial civil servants.

> With the reputation that the P.P.P. has created for itself it would have been surprising if the Party's success at the election had not created some alarm and despondence among the better off sections of the population in British Guiana. But some of our witnesses went very much further and urged us to believe that there were many—particularly among those who were concerned with the management of the larger agricultural and commercial undertakings of the colony—who had been determined from the beginning that the elected Ministers should not be allowed to implement the P.P.P.'s election promises; and who were influential enough and quite prepared, if necessary, to provoke a constitutional crisis in order to get rid not only of P.P.P. Government but also of the Waddington Constitution to which they had always objected as being much too liberal for a country like British Guiana.[17]

The statement is self-explanatory and shows the strong and entrenched opposition operating in Guyana at that time which the PPP felt they had to combat so that they could become effective. The accusations that PPP Ministers were abrasive in their rhetoric only suggests that they were more naive and less discreet than the interest groups working against them.

The Commission, in turning its attention to communist influence within the People's Progressive Party, said: "On the evidence as a whole, we have no doubt that there was a very powerful communist influence with the P.P.P. At the time of the elections at least six of the Party's most prominent leaders—specifically Dr. Jagan (Leader of the Legislative Group), Mrs. Jagan (General Secretary and Editor of *Thunder*), Mr. Sidney King (Assistant Secretary), Mr. Rory Westmaas (Juror Vice Chairman), Mr. B. H. Benn (Executive Committee member and Secretary of the Pioneer Youth League) and Mr. Martin Carter (Executive Committee member)—accepted unreservedly the 'classical' communist doctrines of Marx and of Lenin: were enthusiastic supporters of the policies and practices of modern communist movements; and were contemptuous of European social democratic parties, including the British Labour Party."[18] But in analyzing the other wing of the Party, the Commission said: "Even among those of our witnesses who were keen supporters of the P.P.P. there were many who thought that as the recognized leader of the socialists in the Party, Mr. Burnham ought to have taken a much stronger line than he did in opposition to the more blatantly communist activities of the Jagans and their supporters, we come to the conclusion that, besides the ambiguous Mr. Burnham, at least two of the more prominent leaders of the party—specifically Mr. Ashton Chase (Executive Committee Member) and Mr. Clinton Wong (Senior Vice Chairman)—and a number of its less prominent leaders were socialist. They were as bitterly opposed as their communist colleagues to British colonial rule, but they were not communists."[19] It had been known that some leaders were more ideologically left than others, but this has hardly been a basis for disagreement in any political party. As a matter of fact, in other parties different wings seem to become more influential at different times. In some countries this is known as the "democratic" process. In the case of Guyana, however, the Commission felt forced to conclude: "We have, therefore, come reluctantly, but quite firmly to the conclusion that in present circumstances in British Guiana we must recommend a period of marking time in the advance towards self-government. We would hope that in this period plans for social and economic development would be energetically pursued and that the gradual improvement of social and economic conditions would help to bring about a change in the political outlook of the electorate. We would also hope that the contrast presented by the rapid progress towards self-government elsewhere could lead the people of British Guiana to realize that, notwithstanding the exceptional difficulties of their country, the extremist leaders of the P.P.P. and the policies for which they stand are the sole barriers to constitutional progress."[20]

Though subtle, the message was quite clear. The British Government was not about to give any more autonomy to the government, as long as it was likely to fall into the hands of the "extremist" leaders. In addition, they intended to do everything in their power to bring about a "change in the political outlook of the electorate."[21] Soon after the suspension of the Constitution, the British Government extended so much money in the form of gifts and loans to the country that the government could not spend much of it because of a lack of plans and the necessary expertise (WT, 199).[22] The result was that more studies were prepared for projects than had been undertaken throughout the history of the country. "Experts were stepping on each other's toes" (WT, 193).

In assessing the overall situation and the possibility of restoring a measure of representative government in the country, the Commission had said: "We have subjected this analysis to most careful examination but we can find no escape from the logical conclusion that so long as the present leadership and policies of the People's Progressive Party continue, there is no way in which any real measure of self-government can be restored in British Guiana without the certainty that the country will again be subjected to constitutional crisis."[23] It is this statement that some scholars and commentators seized upon and cited as an indirect signal by the British for PPP Chairman, Forbes Burham, to break away and lead a party of his own. "While we are willing to concede that the statement could have had some influence on any decision by Burnham to lead an independent party, we are not willing to concede as much importance to it as others."[24] The Commission did, however, succeed in leaving the impression that those whom they labelled "socialist" had a more convincing commitment to democratic socialism than those who were labelled communist and would be more acceptable to the British Government. However, from the evidence presented it is clear that Burnham had for some time prior to the publication of the report had his designs on the Party's leadership.

As a matter of fact, from the time the PPP was formed in 1950, Burnham was under constant pressure from admirers and from supporters, especially in Georgetown, to assume leadership of the Party.[25] Though extremely popular throughout the country as a PPP leader, Burnham's much touted academic achievements made him appealing to the upwardly mobile urban middle class, whence came his power in the Party. In addition, he was able not only to master a brief within minutes, but also to articulate it with an amazing clarity that would cause even its author to see greater wisdom than he had thought it embodied. But he lacked the warmth that endeared Jagan to even those who dismissed him as a demagogue or an angry young man. Jagan's warmth seemed to at least convince poeple of his honesty and well-meaning so that even when he became excited and often lost his point or line when debating, supporters felt very close to him. The Commission closed its report by summing up its recommendations.

> We are satisfied that the setback to orderly constitutional progress in British Guiana was due not to defects in the Constitution but to the fact that those in control of the People's Progressive Party proved themselves to be relentless and unscrupulous in their determination to prevent the authority of government to their own disruptive and undemocratic ends.

We are, therefore, driven to the conclusion that so long as the P.P.P. retains its present leadership and policies there is no way in which any real measure of responsible government can be restored without the certainty that the country will again be subjected to constitutional crisis.

We have no doubt that British Guiana, with its precarious economy, cannot afford another crisis of the kind that developed in 1953 and we can, therefore, see no alternative but to recommend a period of marking time in the advance towards self-government.

We cannot estimate the length of the period which should elapse before the advance towards self-government is resumed. Everything will depend upon the extent to which the people of British Guiana, including the leaders of the P.P.P. themselves, can be brought to the realization that the futile and deliberately disruptive policies for which the P.P.P. at present stands are no basis for the future constitutional progress of their country.[26]

This activity and debate continued within the PPP and in the country until well into 1955. It was then that Forbes Burnham made another attempt to capture the leadership of the People's Progressive Party.

The Split: Pamphlets and Conferences

"From the time of their return in 1954 and the imposition of restrictions by the British Government the split began to reveal itself in the form of an internal struggle for power, though this was overlain and complicated by ideological disputes and differences involving the 'left wing' in the Party, among whom Martin Carter, Sidney King and Rory Westmaas were prominent. The imprisonment of Dr. Jagan for a breach of the restrictions (allegedly unauthorized by the Party) strengthened urban conservatism and provoked racially tinged accusations against those who were not jailed."[27] Forbes Burnham made his first move to try to wrest the Party's leadership at a meeting of the Executive Committee held in November 1954. The more radical wing of the Party were not in attendance because they were either in prison or under restriction. With their absence, the Executive Committee passed a decision to hold the Party's Congress on February 12 and 13, 1955 (WT, 202). At a subsequent meeting it was decided that the Congress would be held in Georgetown. This was a reversal of a decision which had been made at the prior Congress, selecting Berbice as the venue for the next Congress. Even though the decision was ques-

tioned by the Secretary, the Chairman (Burnham) used the power
vested in him to have the decision pushed through and sustained.
Present at the meeting were seven persons, an official quorum. When
it was apparent that Chairman Forbes Burnham was going to have the
majority of votes, Cheddi Jagan left the meeting and claimed subsequently that the decision was unconstitutional as a result (WT, 203).

On January 18, 1955, Janet Jagan was released from prison. The
same day an Executive Committee meeting was held. At the meeting,
"a motion for recommital of the question of the holding of Congress was
moved but was not allowed for discussion by Burnham the Chairman.
At that stage an attempt was made to convene a meeting of the General
Council of the Party as a previous meeting fixed for December 27,
1954, had fallen through for lack of a quorum. At the meeting of the
General Council on January 23, 1955, only ten members attended; four
Georgetown members, including Latchmansingh, boycotted the meeting" (WT, 203). It was then clear to both Cheddi and Janet Jagan that
they were being outmaneuvered in a political struggle for the leadership within the Party. As a matter of fact, the Party was already split.
Each had made up his mind to fight for the leadership of the Party.
Jagan, however, had one thing in his favor: his wife had been the
General Secretary of the Party from its inception and, in addition, she
was editor of the Party's newspaper, *Thunder*. This was no mean job
for one person; it reveals her amazing capacity and dedication to hard
work; Jagan knew he could rely on his wife's support. "Faced with the
failure of the General Council to meet, and with the refusal of the
Chairman to allow a recommittal, the General Secretary at the next
Executive Committee meeting pointed out that the Chairman would
be obliged to issue a statement that there would be no Congress unless
it was ratified by the General Council and fixed for the month of March
in accordance with the Party constitution, with the venue in Berbice as
had been decided at the previous Congress and published in the May
1953 issue of *Thunder*. At that point, when it appeared that there
would be an open rift in the Party, it was agreed by the majority of
members to hold especially summoned meetings of the Executive to
resolve the problem" (WT, 204).

After a number of meetings where the issue of the "Congress" was
discussed, no agreement acceptable to both sides was reached. Cheddi
Jagan proposed that a "Special Conference" with a fixed agenda should
be summoned for the same dates in February (WT, 205).[28] "However,

it was pointed out that 'Members' Motions' and 'Any Other Business' would offer a snag to a fixed agenda, and since at that time the Chairman was not prepared to exclude completely 'Members' Motions' and 'Any Other Business' from a limited agenda, discussions broke down again" (WT, 205).

From that time until the Conference, when the split became official, there began an open struggle among the Party's executives and a battle of pamphlets ensued.

Since there was an apparent impasse arriving at a negotiated agreement, Janet Jagan preempted anything Burnham might do by issuing the following statement in *Thunder* on February 5, 1955:

No Congress on February 12 and 13

An announcement has appeared in the press that the People's Progressive Party will hold an annual Congress on February 12th and 13th in the city of Georgetown.

This statement is incorrect for the following reasons:

The supreme authority of the Party shall be the Annual Conference which shall be held at such time and place in the month of March as the General Council shall decide.

No decision has been taken by the General Council.

The meeting of the General Council, fixed for January 23rd, fell through for the want of a quorum. Four non-restricted members did not attend, only ten members attended but twelve are required for a quorum.

With respect to the venue of the Congress, it was specifically resolved at the last party Congress that

Whereas the last three annual meetings of the PPP have been held in Georgetown;

And whereas many members of the Party who live in the country do not find it possible to attend meetings in Georgetown;

Be it resolved that the next Congress shall be a Congress of delegates from different groups and that the next Congress be held in Berbice.[29]

On the same day Burnham issued a handbill saying:

The PPP Chairman Confirms Party Congress

The PPP Congress will be held as previously announced on 12th and 13th February. The sessions begin at 2 P.M. on Saturday 12th at the Auditorium, Charlotte Street, on Sunday 13th, the session will be at the Metropole Cinema, commencing at 9 A.M.

Sidney King, Assistant Secretary, then issued the following leaflet:

Hold People's Congress, Not Police Congress

A leaflet headed "PPP Chairman Confirms Congress" was recently circulated. In it the PPP Chairman claims that a decision to hold a Congress in February 1955 was taken at an Executive meeting "early in December." This was at a time when five Executive members were in prison and three others not allowed to attend Executive meetings owing to restrictions and no police permission.

In his leaflet the Chairman states:

"There has been no Congress of the Party since 1953. In February 1954 the General Council decided to post-pone the 1954 Congress because of the existing conditions in the colony at that time . . . No one, however, can deny its wisdom at the time it was made . . . The circumstances of our Party at the moment demand that our members have an opportunity to express their views and receive an explanation and advice from their leaders."

But the circumstances today have, in fact, worsened since last year. Since the unanimous decision not to hold Congress was made last year more members have been restricted, new repressive laws have been passed, arrests, imprisonments and detentions have occurred. Why then the urgency to hold Congress now? PPP groups all over the country are not allowed to meet. Certain members are not allowed to attend Executive meetings. Is it not clear that the Government has given permission for a Congress only because the Government hopes to win at this Congress?

No Comrades! They can kick us out of the Government. They can jail us, make us report daily to the police, but can we allow them to carry out their designs? This will be surrender.

In his pamphlet the Chairman says:

"There seems to be an unwillingness on the part of some individuals to face a Congress and hear its views. This is strange in the context of our Party, which claims to be democratic."

The Chairman says that other Party members are responsible for killing Party democracy. But it is the Emergency Order and the police that prevent the Party groups and organs from working. Hence, it is the State that is killing Party democracy. To say that it is possible to have Party Democracy now, when group meetings throughout the country are banned is to deceive the people, to hide the crimes of the State, to paint the Emergency Order in beautiful colours to blame one's comrades for the sins of the State and hence to walk into the trap set by the enemy.

Let all true comrades demand the lifting of the Emergency Order. Then we will hold a People's Congress and not a Police Congress. (WT, 205–206)

Even though both factions were claiming legality for their actions, their public protestations and statements suggest that they were uneasy about the decisions they had made. They did not seem to have confidence in themselves.

On February 7, the General Secretary circulated a statement for the signature of the members of the General Council. The statement read: "In view of the conflicting statements by the General Secretary and the Chairman of our Party on the questions of holding of an Annual Congress on the 12th and 13th February at Georgetown, we, the members of the General Council, declare that according to our constitution any such Congress is illegal and unconstitutional. Accordingly, we wish to point out to members of the party that we will neither take part in the deliberations of this unconstitutional meeting nor recognize any of its findings" (WT, 207). Fourteen members signed the statement and five did not. The statement was a loyalty test by Cheddi Jagan to try to identify his support so that in the event of a showdown he knew where his support lay, and how much he could depend upon it. Jagan and the Executive were quite surprised when on February 8, the day after the statement of support by the General Council was issued, Burnham and those members of the Executive who had refused to sign the statement turned up for the normal statutory meeting of the Executive Committee (WT, 207).

Inevitably, the discussion drifted to the rift which was developing among the executives in the party and the possibility of the leaders mending their differences. "It was finally decided that Burnham and I should meet and see whether a solution to the problem could be found and to report back to the Executive Committee on Thursday, February 10" (WT, 207). Their first meeting ended in deadlock. On their second meeting the two leaders agreed that Dr. Jagan's original demand for a Special Conference with a fixed agenda excluding members' motions should be convened on the dates originally selected by Burnham of February 12 and 13. For some reason Dr. Jagan changed his mind and relented to the Chairman's demand that a conference be held in Georgetown. Perhaps he did not want to run the risk of losing an element of the Party that he considered important. So on Friday, February 11, the day before the Conference was to be held, the compromise was announced by the Chairman and the General Secretary.

Party Unity Forged—Party Chairman and Secretary Clarify Situation

In view of the conflicting statements issued by the Chairman and Secretary of the People's Progressive Party with respect to the conven-

ing of an Annual Congress of February 12th and 13th and the necessity
of maintaining unity at this critical period of our country's history, it has
been agreed by the Executive Committee that what will be convened on
the above dates will be a Special Conference of members under Rule 9 of
the Constitution and not an annual Congress.

At this Special Conference on the 12th and 13th February the Executive Committee has decided that the following agenda be discussed
exclusively:

1. Chairman's opening address.
2. Reports of Party Members on their visits abroad.
3. Resume of the Party's activities since 1953.
4. The role of Trade Unions in the National Movement.
5. The role of Youth in the National Movement.
6. The role of Women in the National Movement.
7. The Party and Race.
8. The amendment of rules to provide for the election of officers and
   members of the General Council by ballot of members in each
   constituency at such places as the General Council shall decide.

L. F. S. Burnham
Chairman PPP

Janet Jagan
General Secretary PPP[30]

A few hours after the agreement was reached an unauthorized pamphlet appeared in the streets:

Rally the People at Congress

Congress will be held at 2 P.M. on Saturday, 12th February 1955 at
the Auditorium Charlotte Street, Georgetown and on Sunday, 13th February, at the Metropole Cinema, from 9 A.M. (WT, 209)

Upon inquiry by Dr. Jagan to Burnham, authorship of the pamphlet
was attributed to Jai Narine Singh. Burnham agreed with Jagan that he
would call a "Special Executive Committee" meeting at noon on the
day of the Conference to discipline Jai Narine Singh for his anti-party
activity. "Then shortly before mid-day the Chairman intimated that he
would not go ahead with the Special Executive Committee meeting"
(WT, 209). Dr. Jagan, having made the earlier agreement to attend
public, was then trapped into going along with the other proceedings.
First, he acquiesced and allowed a Conference to be held; regardless of
what it was called, it was held one month before the date stipulated in
the Constitution for "Congress." He had received what amounted to a
pledge of loyalty from two thirds of the General Council; yet, armed
with such security, he acquiesced to a conference that Burnham had

planned and wanted badly and was doing his best to control. It would seem that Cheddi Jagan as party leader, with most of his Executive and General Council behind him, lacked the ability to make a firm decision and stick to it. Instead, he allowed the Party, including the General Secretary and himself, to be dragged through one meeting after another with the Chairman who, on the other hand, seemed to be more determined to get what he had long wanted—the leadership of the Party. Because of the unauthorized leaflets appearing on the day before and on the day of the conference, terming the agreed "Conference" a "Congress," and because the Chairman had arbitrarily cancelled the executive meeting to discipline the executive member responsible for these actions, Dr. Jagan, some of the Executive Committee and General Council members refused to attend the Saturday session of the Conference. "In the light of these circumstances, Janet Jagan, Rory Westmaas, Fred Bowman, Martin Carter, George Robertson, Naipaul Jagan, Lionel Jeffrey and I decided to boycott the session on Saturday. But after issuing a leaflet explaining our position in relation to the boycott, we attended the Sunday morning session at the Metropole Cinema" (WT, 209). Jagan had fallen into the careful web which Burnham had been weaving for almost four months.

On Sunday, February 13, 1955, at the Metropole Cinema the Party gathered for the second day of its Conference. Forbes Burnham gave his agreed opening address, then called for discussion on the reports of the three members who had gone abroad. At that point Clinton Wong rose and moved a motion to suspend the standing orders.[31] "The Chairman said that he was not disposed to allow the motion unless he knew what the motion was all about. Clinton Wong then said that he wanted to move a motion of 'No Confidence' in the present Executive Committee" (WT, 210). As though to caution him, Janet Jagan then said to the Chairman, "It is all in your hands now, Forbes."[32] Burnham allowed the motion for the suspension of the standing orders. Immediately Cheddi Jagan and those who had boycotted the Conference the day before walked out. In examining the whole leadership struggle one commentator said: "One must admire the fine legal distinction with which the Chairman's mind had looked ahead at the time he agreed to there being neither 'Members' Motions' nor 'Any Other Business'—a vote of 'No Confidence' is something different."[33] Those present were in a state of total confusion. With calm restored, new elections were held and the new officers elected were:

Forbes Burnham	Leader
Dr. J. P. Latchmansingh	Chairman
Cheddi Jagan	Senior Vice Chairman
Clinton Wong	Junior Vice Chairman
Jai Narine Singh	Secretary
Jessie Burnham	Assistant Secretary
Janet Jagan	Treasurer

The other office holders were relegated to the General Council and Executive; but a number of the militants were not included in the top brass at all. Dr. Jagan allowed himself to be trapped into going through all the motions leading up to the split and was a party to it. Jagan denounced the election as unconstitutional and refused to recognize any of the changes. Burnham denounced the Jaganites and claimed his was the legitimate PPP. From that time in February 1955 until 1958 there remained two PPPs in existence, each with a weekly newspaper named *Thunder* and each claiming legitimacy.

Neither leader knew what reaction to expect from the Party's rank and file; and both were confused. The Burnhamite PPP sent out a circular to party groups asking them to continue as before, adding that they would be brought up-to-date later with the developments by letter and by a personal visit.[34] The Jaganites PPP sent out a similar letter but it explained that the Congress held was illegal and that the always ambitious Mr. Burnham had sought to take over the Party. However, since a majority of the Executives and General Council remained with Dr. Jagan, they were told that it would be appreciated if they would continue to support Dr. Jagan and the old PPP. Subsequently, there were visits paid to the groups from the representatives from both parties. In her visits to these groups, Mrs. Jagan gave a detailed explanation of the events, as she saw them. Forbes Burnham, in his visits, gave as callous an explanation as his earlier letter had, while seated in his car on the roadside.[35] The Rosignol group, and we suspect many other groups, gave their support to the Jaganite PPP because of this simple lack of courtesy on the part of the Burnhamites.

According to Dr. Jagan, Burnham's reason for splitting the Party was his feeling that a party led by him could win an election. "The basis of the split was the prospect of new elections and the calculations that the splinters would take away majority support from us. Burnham felt that he would carry with him the five seats in Georgetown and Latchmansingh the eight seats in the sugar belt, thus gaining between them a majority of 13 seats out of 24" (WT, 202). Later they found out that this was not as easily accomplished as they had anticipated.

After the dust had settled, the Jaganite PPP published a pamphlet entitled "The Great Betrayal." The pamphlet reflected the Jaganite PPP's official view of the split, and was meant to show Burnham as an ambitious opportunist who would split the nationalist movement for his own ends. The pamphlet made much of an article by Mr. R. B. O. Hart, a senior member of the United Democratic Party. Writing in his paper, the *Clarion*, (just after the split), he said:

> On July 25, 1954, I sold Burnham an idea which he is now putting into practice. I quote the *Clarion* of that date: You owe a duty to the people of this country who have followed you blindly. So far you have been lucky. You have done nothing to merit their blind support and idolatry. How can you, a young man of any character and decency, lead them astray again? You and Dr. J. P. Latchmansingh would make a very effective team; if you stood hand in hand you would be able to keep the Party together while kicking the extremists out. Latchmansingh is no spring chicken himself, but is one of the few men in your Party of whom I would say, he is not a Communist.[36]

It is hardly likely that Mr. Hart really gave Burnham the idea of splitting the Party when all the evidence of Burnham's continuous maneuvering is considered. What the pamphlet seemed to be designed to do was to associate Burnham with the bankrupt politicians of the United Democratic Party and, at the same time, to show that his ambitiousness had misled him.

One ironic result of the split that is often overlooked was that most of the influential Indians in the PPP's top leadership positions went with Burnham after the split, while the Africans stayed with Jagan. Both groups recognized the need to have adequate representation from each of the major racial groups. What they did not know was how much rank and file support these leaders would bring along with them. Jagan's way of viewing the split was: "The Party leadership saw the split in the Party in ideological terms. That was why, of the eleven non-Indian 'members of the General Council,' only three joined with Burnham and this was mainly for family and personal considerations" (WT, 211).

With the split in the PPP into two factions a similar reorganization occurred in the Trade Union movement. Many of those who resented the former PPP's image before now had a choice. But if choice was widened, it also left the door open for opportunists, and for manipulation by the politicians themselves. Politics in Guyana took on a new personality. A more personal leadership was adopted: the collective leadership of the nationalist PPP was abandoned by both parties.

When on a visit to Jamiaca a year later, Burnham analyzed the split in this way:

> The People's Progressive Party is now two parties which once was one. Our differences are ideological and tactical. I for one have no power over a man who says he is a Communist and who thinks that every gyration of Stalin when he is in office was inspired by genius. That is his business! I have no power over a man who because Stalin abuses Tito thinks in British Guiana he should abuse Tito.
>
> What I say is although a man is free to follow any ideology he wants, he must not jeopardize a national movement. It is my conviction that the People's Progressive Party was not a Communist dictatorship; what I say is that the British Government used certain isolated incidents and certain people's declarations that they were Communists as an excuse to the world to isolate British Guiana when her constitution was suspended.
>
> A national movement cannot afford to be sectarian, and you cannot behave in such a way as to give the impression that your party is a Communist party; for the national movement as the one in our area, it is nothing short of suicide under the peculiar geographical conditions to be shouting to the world that you are a Communist.[37]

Burnhams's statement reflected the sharp disagreement between himself and Dr. Jagan. He seemed to have had a much greater awareness of the external influences and their repercussions within the country and so was much more willing to vary his tactics to achieve his ends.

At the end of October 1955, the British Government prematurely replaced the Governor, Sir Alfred Savage, with Sir Patrick Renison.[38] Other changes in the colonial hierarchy were the replacement of Colonial Secretary, John Gutch, by Derek Jakeway and the promotion of Attorney General Frank Holder to Chief Justice (WT, 214).

With the population growing and no new investments being made, the interim government was finding it increasingly difficult to provide work. Unemployment was growing fast. The *Daily Chronicle* (November 27, 1955) put the problem this way: "Two years have gone by and we are no better off than we were before the political debacle. We have had more houses built, we have had a few self-aided schemes, a little of this and a little of that, but the population is increasing faster than ever, unemployment is increasing and the cost of living continues to rise. We submit to marking time politically, and even here we expect the time where the economic development of the country is concerned. Must we continue to live as we are living or should we say existing? Let there be an end to this nonsense."

An "All-Party Conference" comprising all political parties was held on April 5, 1956. The object was to try to bring about some unity between the nationalist forces in one party or organization. However, the group could only agree that their collective pressure was needed for the emergency to be lifted and that elections should be held (WT 216–217). The group also agreed to meet again. Before another meeting of these groups could be held, the Governor preempted them by announcing on April 25, 1956, what became known as the "Renison" constitution. The proposal offered a single-chambered legislature with twelve elected members, balanced by eight nominated and four ex-officio (colonial service) members. In addition, the Executive Council would comprise five elected Ministers with four ex-officio and one nominated member. With the Governor's announcement some saw no further need for an all-party conference. Dr. Jagan did. He went ahead and organized a second conference. Again, the two PPPs and a few other splinter organizations attended. Conspicuously absent was the newly formed National Labour Front (NLF) headed by Lionel Luckhoo. It was agreed that the body would use their collective efforts to try to have the emergency lifted and to press for a restoration of the suspended Waddington Constitution (WT, 217). The Constitution had then become a political issue because the Governor had announced a new constitution that was more limiting in the power it gave to the politician, more so than the former suspended Waddington Constitution. It would seem that although the British were quite willing to have some sort of representative government, the possibility of the PPP, and especially Dr. Jagan, returning t office was uppermost in their minds, which precluded having a more liberal constitution.

For some time, the All-Party Conference failed to gain an audience with the Governor. Eventually, when the All-Party Conference was able to get a meeting on July 28, 1956, the Governor let it be clearly known that he strongly disapproved of their request. In October, after a trip to London for consultations with the Colonial Office, the Governor announced a few changes in his earlier proposed constitution. Instead of twelve, the legislature would have fourteen elected seats, with three rather than four ex-officio members and eleven rather than eight nominated members (WT, 218). It seems that the British Government by this time was quite certain that Cheddi Jagan would be back in office come the next election. They were therefore making sure constitutionally that he would have to take a moderate road. Of the new political parties and interest groups, "nobody however, except the P.P.P. (Jaganites), was prepared to go out into the countryside and win votes. The P.P.P. (Burnhamites) and the United Democratic Party (U.D.P.) did not mind going out on a Sunday afternoon to hold a meeting. But they had no organization and would have been shocked had anyone suggested that they stayed out overnight and build up personal contact and got to know the people's problems."[39] The Jaganites, led by Dr. and Mrs. Jagan, were doing what they did naturally, frequently travelling the length and breadth of the country. Later in the year the All-Party Conference was disbanded. The politicians and the country were ready for another general election.

But if Burnham was at that time fighting for his political life, Jagan was too. In his 1956 speech to his Party's Congress, Jagan initiated a period of self-criticism within the Party and signaled that a new tactic was about to be undertaken. In his criticism he attacked some members of the Party's left wing of which he himself was leader, for actions they had taken so long as three years before: "Up to October 1953, we committed deviations to the left. We definitely overrated the revolutionary possibilities of our party . . . we became bombastic . . . We were attacking everybody at the same time . . . We tended towards what Mao Tse Tung called all struggle and no unity."[40] One writer summed up the perceptions of the new strategy in this way:

Since King, Carter and Westmaas were among the most "bombastic" of Marxists, they immediately interpreted Jagan's remarks as personal criticism. In fact, they interpreted them as an effort to clear himself of any responsibility for the constitutional suspension by projecting the blame entirely upon left wing "dogmatists."

Because of the special circumstances associated with the Guyanese political situation, King, Westmaas, and Carter began to suspect Jagan of sectional politics. The right wing elements which they had helped to remove from the party were mainly Africans. And now they also appeared to be under attack. Their suspicions were further reinforced by Jagan's analysis of the position which the P.P.P. had to adopt with respect to the Caribbean Federation and by the Strategy he outlined for the P.P.P. with respect to the nationalist movement. In the first instance, it appeared that Jagan was so much opposed to the federation on the grounds that it would alienate his East Indian support as he was on the grounds that it would make Guiana's nationalist movement a domestic affair. In the second instance, Jagan's proposed strategy appeared to be opportunistic in the sense that it relied rather heavily on the political integration of the East Indian cultural section. Although Jagan suggested the possibility of developing an alliance between the P.P.P. and the Burnham forces, it was clear that he did not expect such an alliance to materialize or, if it should materialize, to be more than a temporary affair.[41]

Shortly after, Sidney King, Martin Carter and Rory Westmaas resigned from the Jaganite PPP. One writer gave this interpretation to their resignations:

Since these three individuals represented the pillars of Jagan's remaining African support, their resignation came not only as a shock but also as an extreme blow to Jagan's plans for a truly integrated nationalist movement. From the very beginning of the movement, these three were the most idealistic of the Marxists. They were completely loyal to Jagan's leadership.[42]

But Cheddi Jagan viewed the situation a little differently. He says:

Soon after the party split of 1955, there occurred an "ultra left" split within our ranks. Roray Westmaas, Martin Carter, Lionel Jeffrey and a few other youths virtually seceeded from the Party in 1956 after disciplinary action was taken against Keith Carter for flouting Party instructions, and after I had criticized them in a paper I had submitted to the 1956 Party Congress. These comrades, through the Demerara Youth League and the B.G. Peace Committee, had taken some "ultra left" positions which opened the party to unnecessary criticisms and attacks both from the opposition and from the right wing of the party. In 1953, they had taken part in May Day demonstrations displaying banners of Stalin, and, contrary to the advice of the party, had picketed Princess Alice on her visit in 1952 with anti-British slogans such as "limey go home."

But far more harmful was their sniping at the Party leadership and at me personally. From late 1954 they began to attack the Party on two ·points. Firstly, they declared that the Party's line of non-violence and civil disobedience was un-Marxist and non-revolutionary . . . Secondly, and more fundamentally, this small group advocated the abandonment of the Party's stand on the West Indies Federation, and urged unconditional support for it (WT, 212).[43]

The shift in Dr. Jagan's rhetoric and his willingness to take a more moderate line suggests that at this time he was trying to make himself and the Party more attractive to the general electorate in view of the anticipated elections, and the more idealistic left no longer suited his plans. It had probably become clear to him then also that the British Government, far from taking a more enlightened and more positive view about events in Guyana, was determined not to have an "extremist" government in the colony. Furthermore, the international environment, rather than becoming more liberal because of the intensity of the cold war, was becoming much more rigid. Given Guyana's position as part of the Western hemisphere then, he probably felt he had to make some ideological adjustments.

In assessing the PPP's Jagan-Burnham leadership split and the Jagan-Carter-King-Westmaas "ultra-left" split, one has to wonder to what extent the two splits were based on differences in cultural experience and as a consequence political priorities. Jagan and the PPP, in its actions from 1950–1953, showed an abnormal preoccupation with the rural areas: with the sugar and rice industry and drainage and irrigation. Little attention seems to have been given to the towns and cities or to the attraction of other industries from any source at all. But even the sugar workers whom Jagan seemed to be preoccupied with during the short period when the PPP was in office in 1953 were not of any help to any of his revolutionary goals when the time came for him to show his strength: "Our call for a general strike after the suspension of the constitution had not been very successful" (WT, 212). So that the PPP in the end had little to show but the revolutionary fervor of its leaders and even that could not be contained in a cohesive fashion.

From 1956 onwards, the politics in Guyana took on different characteristics. Unlike the 1950–1955 period when ideology and nationalism were the dominant forces in politics, the next decade saw expedience, racism, and personal ambition gain the upper hand. To a certain extent, it was the "Politics of Recurrence": nearly every event which had taken place was replayed and the actors had an opportunity to choose once again with hindsight. The parties prepared for another election.

The 1957 Election and the Politics of "Recurrence"

The elections were held in August 1957. Unlike the previous elections of 1953, the electorate did not become excited about this event. As a matter of fact, many people claimed not to have known about an election. It was the politicians who were more excited about the election, and it was in large part they who attached great importance to it. The factions of the PPP contested the electorate: PPP-Burnhamite and PPP-Jaganite; among the other parties there were the United Democratic Party (UDP), the National Labour Front (NLF), the Guyana National Party and a few independents. The only new party worthy of comment was the National Labour Front. It was headed by Mr. Lionel Luckhoo, who had become head of the Man Power Citizens Association in 1949 and, shortly after, was nominated to fill a labor seat in the Legislature. The son of a wealthy Indian lawyer and a lawyer himself, he always worked closely with the colonial government. From the start he was opposed to the Nationalist PPP. Ideologically he and Dr. Jagan were most incompatible and exchanged harsh words both in and outside the legislature. Luckhoo proposed and was the moving force behind the Undesirable Publications motion in 1952 which prohibited the importation of books, literature, and films deemed subversive and contrary to the national interest. In 1953, as head of the MPCA and as an executive of the National Democratic Party, he did not contest a seat, but wrote a critique of the PPP and its communist intentions that appeared in all of the national papers. After the suspension of the constitution in 1953, he was again nominated to the legislature. He remained in the legislature while carrying on a lucrative legal practice in his family's firm. His formation of the National Labour Front was another in a series of attempts to gain national office.[44]

The politicians continued to make slogans among themselves in the face of an ambivalent electorate: None knew what the outcome of the election would be. As they stood then, they had all lost support and did not really know how it would affect the number of seats they would obtain. "When the election results were announced the Jaganite PPP came romping home with nine seats out of fourteen. The PPP (Burnhamites) won only the three Georgetown seats. The NLF contested every seat and won only one which was the North-West because its candidate was Mr. Stephen Campbell, who always wins regardless of party. The UDP only contested eight seats but their fate was identical: while there is a New Amsterdam constituency and a Mr. W. O. R. Kendall, he will be elected. He is known as the 'favorite son' but by reputation he has seen himself as something other than this."[45]

The election settled quite a few arguments. First of all, it settled the two PPP's issues. The name People's Progressive Party had belonged to Cheddi Jagan and he won the right to keep it. It settled the question of mushroom parties that had the tacit sponsorship of the colonial government. Except for W. O. R. Kendall, all of those who had served in the interim government lost.[46] Thus, Britain's attempts to give legitimacy to the moderates by having them share the government from 1954–1957 completely backfired; the people rejected them.

The apathy of the 1957 elections has several explanations. First of all, because of restrictions imposed earlier, none of the parties were well organized, people's homes were still being searched for subversive literature, and this made many activists hesitate to do much campaigning. In addition, many people were fearful of the harassment experienced by those in leadership positions.

The election report of 1957 gives other reasons for the small election turnout:

> In all but one constituency (Eastern Berbice) there was heavy rain in the forenoon and in two (Eastern Demerara and Western Essequibo) the returning officers described the weather as very bad. Conditions underfoot in the Rupununi were "exceedingly difficult." In the extensive Essequibo River electoral district (51,290 sq. mi.) a light poll is ordinarily to be expected in August not only in the Rupununi Division (for reasons of weather) but also in the Mazaruni and Potaro where August is traditionally the holiday period, to be spent with friends and relatives on the coastlands.
>
> The weather doubtless contributed to the lightness of the poll, but another factor of importance was the evident failure of very many persons to avail themselves of the opportunity offered by revising courts in 1956, to have their names added to the register of their addresses corrected. Apathy and indecision were apparent in the body politic at the time of the revision in 1956, and public interest began to show itself only after the various political parties announced in turn their intention to present candidates. By that time the period specified for additions and deletions from the list had expired. Short of a further revision, there was no way of saving electors from the consequence of their own negligence. It came as a surprise to many that the categories of elector permitted to vote by proxy were limited in number and there was no provision in the Ordinance for postal voting.[47]

The popular saying around the country at this time, especially among the civil servants, was "we working with de government." This meant that everyone was prepared to cooperate with the newly elected PPP government even though they did not agree with its philosophy. This attitude was especially important because the PPP was very weak in the urban areas, and needed to have the civil service and urban population cooperate in order to govern effectively.

External Influences and Internal Adjustments

Many commentators see the severe British Government reaction to events in Guyana as a result of the anticommunist hysteria of the McCarthy years.[48] Perhaps it was, but it was also a little more than that. The tenuous relations that had existed between the East and West prior to World War II were shattered by the maneuvers of the Russians in Eastern Europe at the close of the War. "It was not until the end of World War II that the issue of communism-in-government began to gather momentum. The attendant causes were no doubt the anxiety and frustration of the cold war and revelations of Russian espionage in Canada, Great Britain and the United States."[49]

With the realization that the Soviets were penetrating with success, the principal western democracies gave way within the U.S. to latent fears of communism. Joseph McCarthy, who entered the Senate in early 1947 to become the standard bearer of the anticommunist movement, was only one in a long line who had gone before him.[50] The loss of the unquestionable American and Western military supremacy with the Russian explosion of an A-Bomb on the third of December 1947 deepened the pessimism of the West in its ability to withstand communist infiltration.

However, because of the economic arrangements governing international relations, the British, U.S., and French governments were not in a position to play the role they thought would be a natural result of their decision to grant independence to their colonies. Not having been a colonial power and possessing an ideology compatible with that of Third World Leaders, the Soviets were in a better position to assume a supportive role for the newly independent countries. This they tried to do. The image of the Soviet Union among many colonial politicians at that time was "that of the socialist fatherland, the bastion of world peace, mighty yet benevolent St. George slaying the imperialist dragon in the defence of the oppressed peoples. In this imagery, colonies and dependencies derive inspiration as well as moral and political support from the Soviet Union where exploitation of man by man has ceased and the State belongs to the toilers."[51] The U.S.S.R.'s willingness to supply large amounts of anticolonial propaganda and to sponsor international conferences, where colonial questions were always discussed, made many nationalist leaders sympathetic to the communist cause.

The Unions' Communist Influence and Domestic Adjustments

As has already been mentioned, H. J. M. Hubbard, Secretary of the TUC at the time, and D. M. Harper, President, attended the founding meeting of the Congress of the World Federation of Trade Unions in 1945. However, shortly after the organization was founded, the communists gained control of its executive positions and encouraged them to be used as a platform for encouraging anticolonial and cold war activities.[52] The Americans were willing to allow the organization to be used as a platform for anticolonialist expression, but seemed to resent communist control of the organization. However, all unions use their international affiliations as a means of achieving certain ends and this is so even though "much trade union international activity is ascribed to idealistic reasons, even by groups not usually inclined to credit trade unions' leaders with such sentiments."[53] The west, with the U.S. in the lead, then moved to isolate the Soviets and their allies by creating a new international organization, the International Confederation of Free Trade Union, the ICFTU.

Over the years the influence of foreign unions in Guyana brought about the same changes within the union as had been brought about in government, in the face of what was perceived to be a communist threat. Though the "threat" was mainly in the dominant political party—the PPP—there was great concern by the British and U.S. governments about the unions as well, as a number of PPP leaders held positions in unions and because the PPP received wide support from union members. Thus, the interest of the British TUC and the American AFL-CIO focused on Guyana. Not being able to penetrate the militancy and solidarity of the British Guiana TUC in the early 1950's, attention was turned to a union disenchanted with the PPP and the TUC, the MPCA. Between 1951 and 1953, when the British Guiana TUC had taken a militant, anti-imperialist, pro-PPP line, it was affiliated with the WFTU.

The MPCA (under the leadership of Lionel Luckhoo) became, by contrast, the main pillar of the ICFTU and its regional body, ORIT. It received £3,000 from the British TUC and was advised by its Assistant General Secretary George Woodcock, and Andrew Dalgleish, who had spent some time in British Guiana (WT, 179). ORIT provided the MPCA with a motor car, a projector and films to "educate workers," and other materials to help the union boost its strength among sugar workers. Shortly after the constitution was suspended in 1953 the TUC affiliated with the WFTU was disbanded. Later a new TUC was formed, this time affiliated with the ICFTU, so that the political and main interest groups in the country reflected the sentiments of the cold war struggle which was then going on between east and west.

NOTES

1. The British Government accused the PPP government of encouraging "junior officers to act as informers on department activities" and having sought more views regarding the efficiency and conduct of their senior officers. British Guiana; Suspension of the Constitution Report, Cmd. 8980, 1953, p. 5. They also accused the PPP of undermining the loyalty of the police, p. 4, and other boards, p. 5. See Appendix.
2. Then on lease to the U.S. Government for a military base, now Timehri International Airport.
3. "The reign of terror resulted even in the banning by the police of a film showing the arrival in India of Burnham and myself and our placing of writs at Mahatma Gandhi's Sanadhi at Rajghat, New Delhi" (WT, 188).
4. Interview with party activist.
5. Ibid., p. 193.
6. See *Chronicle*, September 10, 1954.
7. Winston S. Churchill, *Great Contemporaries*, p. 15.
8. V. S. Naipaul, *The Middle Passage* (London: Andre Deutsch, 1962), p. 132.
9. Report of the British Guiana Constitutional Commission, 1954, Cmd., 9274, p. 5.
10. Ibid., p. 59.
11. Ibid.
12. Ibid. This seems to be a reference to payment by the Sugar Producers Association for the supplement in the national press by the President of the MPCA, Mr. Lionel Luckhoo, attacking the PPP two Sundays before the election. See Jagan, *The West on Trial*, pp. 133–134; Smith, *British Guiana*, p. 170.
13. Report of the British Guiana Constitutional Commission 1954, Cmd. 9274, p. 16.
14. West Indian Royal Commission Report, 1938–1938 (London: HMSO, 1945), Cmd 6607.
15. Report of the British Guiana Constitution Commission 1954, Cmd. 9274, p. 19.
16. Ibid., p. 21.
17. Ibid., pp. 38–39.
18. Ibid., p. 36.
19. Ibid., p. 37.
20. Ibid., p. 70.
21. Ibid., p. 70.
22. "In November 1953, after Oliver Lyttelton, Secretary of State for the Colonies, had declared in the House of Commons that as much money as was required would be found so long as worthwhile schemes were available, a sum of $44 million was voted as development expenditure for 1954 and 1955. This was in marked contrast to the planned expenditure of $26 million agreed to in 1949 for a ten-year plan (1949–1959). Its annual target expenditure was also larger than that proposed under the $66 million five-year development plan which the World Bank Mission had formulated in 1952" (WT, 192–193).

23. Report of the British Guiana Constitutional Commission 1954, Cmd. 9274, p. 70.
24. Jagan sees the statement as the main reason for the eventual split of the PPP.
25. Interview with party activist (Kitty). Smith says in his analysis, "Many of the professional men and government employees who had joined the party when it was formed or when they had returned from studies overseas, found that the over-enthusiasm of some of the party members for the cruder forms of communist propaganda was becoming a source of embarrassment to them and they began to be worried about the Communist label that was being ever more firmly attached to the Party. Many of them resigned and attempted to persuade Mr. Burnham to do the same. The majority of these men were Negro or Coloured and they would have liked to see a political party in British Guiana taking the path that was being followed by moderate socialists in other colonies . . . They did not fear the left-wing element in the party as a group organizing to secure power and establish a totalitarian state; they considered that the actions of the extremists were stupid and ill-informed." Smith, *British Guiana*, p. 178.
26. Report of the British Guiana Constitutional Commission 1954, Cmd. 9274, pp. 74–75.
27. David Decaries and Miles Fitzpatrick, *Twenty Years of Politics in Our Land* (New World Independence Issue, 1966), p. 40.
28. A Conference is usually held for discussion of Party business and tactics. A Congress is held for informing Party supporters and delegates of the Party's activity over the year, to elect officers and to make policy.
29. *Thunder*, February 5, 1955; see also, *The Great Betrayal* (Georgetown: Arcade Printery, n.d.), pp. 10–11.
30. As quoted in Jagan, *The West on Trial*, p. 208; also *Thunder*, February 12, 1955; *Argosy*, February 12, 1955.
31. Simms, *Trouble in Guyana*, p. 130; also Jagan, *The West on Trial*, p. 210.
32. Interview with activist.
33. Simms, *Trouble in Guyana*, p. 130.
34. One activist said she did not like the callousness of the Burnhamite PPP letter. The inference was that they did not have anything to do with the changes at the leadership level. Interview with party activist.
35. Interview with activist (Rosignol); the activist said that it was on the basis of these letters and Mrs. Jagan's visit that they continued to support Dr. Jagan.
36. *The Great Betrayal*, p. 4.
37. *Daily Gleaner*, as quoted in Simms, *Trouble in Guyana*, pp. 131–132.
38. Simms, *Trouble in Guyana*, p. 133.
39. Simms, *Trouble in Guyana*, p. 134.
40. As quoted in Leo Despres, *Cultural Pluralism and Nationalist Politics in British Guiana* (Chicago: Rand McNally, 1967), p. 218.
41. Ibid.
42. Ibid., p. 217.
43. But Jagan explains Sidney King's exit from the Party this way: ". . . his personal loyalty to Rory Westmaas and his friends whom I had criticized in my early 1956 P.P.P. Congress paper for ultra-left, deviationist tendencies, King would have become chairman of the Party at the Congress in September 1956, but he declined nomination because I had disagreed with his proposal to sponsor Westmaas *et al*, on an agreed list" (WT, 222).
44. In 1965, Lionel Luckhoo was finally appointed Guyana's High Commissioner to Britain; he held the post from 1966–1971.
45. Simms, *Trouble in Guyana*, p. 140.

46. See Smith, *British Guiana*, p. 180.
47. Report on General Elections 1957 by Chief Elections Officer (Georgetown: Government Printery, 1957).
48. See Peter Newman, *British Guiana* (Oxford University Press, 1964), p. 80.
49. Robert Griffith, *The Politics of Fear, Joseph R. McCarthy and the Senate* (Lexington: The University Press of Kentucky, 1970), p. 34.
50. Ibid., pp. 30–48.
51. Paul Katona, *Soviet Propaganda in the Colonial World* (New York: Praeger, The Year Book of World Affairs, 1955), p. 162.
52. See Jeffrey Harrod, *Trade Union Foreign Policy*, p. 111.
53. Ibid., p. 37.

CHAPTER 6

The Politics of Recurrence, 1957–1962

The PPP in Office, 1957

UPON assuming office as Premier in 1957, Dr. Cheddi Jagan was faced with a task that would have tested the ablest statesman. First, the country had been tremendously set back by the suspension of its constitution and by the subsequent loss of its constitutional gains of 1953. Second, the nationalist movement was split; and third, the country's population was increasing rapidly. The interim government did not so much as dent the high unemployment that it found upon assuming office, nor did it do much toward motivating the civil service to take on the new responsibilities of economic development.

By 1957, those people who were not caught up in the fever of nationalism realized that British policy had changed toward its colonies. The independence of Ghana (in 1957) helped to dramatize this point, as it caused many Guyanese to take a different view of their own future. Some decided to become politically active, others decided that to gain a university degree and become a professional was going to be their way of becoming involved. Whatever the means, by this time people had become much more mature politically and interest groups began to become a much more potent factor in the body politic. The local civil servants especially saw before them the possibility, for the first time, of reaching the top of their departments and at the same time increasing their economic and social positions. The progressive middle class, having gone into the nationalist movement, and having helped to give it support and direction since 1950, had then withdrawn and was beginning to seek its own interests.

The two mass parties had to adjust to the changes taking place rather

quickly around them. Professor Leo Despres interprets the dilemma of
the parties in this way:

> Before the disintegration of the nationalist movement, mass support
> could be mobilized primarily by appealing to the frustrations that most
> Guianese shared as a result of colonial domination. After its disinte-
> gration, this approach continued to be useful, but it was no longer
> sufficient. The new political alignments which emerged from the col-
> lapse of the nationalist movement required a more specific appeal. Thus,
> the change in Guiana's political situation necessitated a change in the
> organization strategy of the nationalist parties.
>   To state the problems more precisely, by 1958 the East Indian and
> Afro-Guianese cultural sections appeared to represent the only bases of
> mass power accessible, respectively, to the People's National Congress.
> In order to integrate these cultural sections politically, however, adjust-
> ments in organizational strategies were needed. Specifically, particular-
> istic appeals had to be made to the groups contained within each cultural
> section.[1]

Within months after the 1957 election, the major political parties
began to campaign in an effort to extend their political bases. The PPP
(Jaganites), being in government, was able to use its position as incumbent to travel up and down the country. For the opposition PPP (Burnhamites) and the other splinter parties, it was more difficult.

One group which the PPP made an earnest effort to cultivate for
both financial and strategic reasons was the Indian businessman.
Despres describes three categories:

> One type of Indian businessman is comprised of those individuals who
> moved into Georgetown twenty to thirty years ago. As a result of the
> boom in the rice industry during the First World War, these individuals
> accumulated large landholdings in rural areas. The capital which derived
> from these holdings was used to finance medium-sized shops in Water
> Street, Georgetown's main business district. As these enterprises ex-
> panded, their owners tended to buy up residences in the old, prestigious
> suburbs (e.g., Brickdam and Kingston), where most of the expatriates
> once lived. Since the end of the Second World War, businessmen of this
> type have been closing in on the European business houses from both
> ends of Water Street. Because these Indian businessmen have never
> been allowed to compete directly with the well-established European
> firms, their economic growth has been restricted. As a consequence,
> they continue to maintain their rural enterprises.
>   A second type of Indian businessman found in Georgetown does not
> comprise a very large group, but it is a group which has recently become
> extremely influential in commercial circles. The members of this group

consist of a few overseas immigrants who have come mainly from Trinidad and Surinam. For the most part, these men are well established in the business world. Their presence in Guiana marks an effort on their part to expand already flourishing enterprises by penetrating the Guyanese market. Members of this group, most notably Thani and Kirpalani, own large retail houses in the heart of the Georgetown business district. These retail houses are potentially highly competitive with the old European and Portuguese-controlled firms.

The third type of Indian businessman found in Georgetown is also a recent migrant. The members of this group, however, predominantly come from the rural areas surrounding the city. Generally, these individuals are the sons of small rice farmers or sugar workers. Their capital is extremely limited. Some of them are attracted to the city because they need wage employment. Others have moved to the city as a result of having spent years carrying produce to the urban marketplaces. Subsequently, these individuals establish themselves in small shops or market stalls. They sell food, cakes, soft drinks or dry goods. If they own shops, the shops are usually located in peripheral business districts (e.g., Regent and Lombard Streets) or urban neighborhoods. Often, these shops may be found beneath the homes in which the owners reside.

Businessmen of this third type are "penny" capitalists, and they are hard pressed to survive. Their shops do not compete with the European firms. They are strictly family affairs, and most of their competition derives from similar kinds of shops owned by Africans or other Indians. If such enterprises manage to grow, structural modifications are made in the home, and the shop expands by adding a new line of goods. Canned goods may be added, and the cake shop becomes a small grocery store. Or dry goods may be added to the grocery store and it becomes a general store. Frequently, these shops are maintained by women and children, while the men of the household earn wages.[2]

The grievances and the strategic location of this group as a whole suited the PPP's (Jaganites) purpose. By wooing this group, Cheddi Jagan and his PPP could kill several birds with the same stone: They would have ready finance through contributions to the Party, and they would also have a much needed foothold in the city. At the same time, they would have support for their ideological battle with the capitalists and their local business representatives.

As the People's Progressive Party settled into government and began to consolidate and woo different segments of the community, the outlook of the opposition and other political parties was extremely dim. In his capacity as Minister of Trade and Industry, Dr. Jagan maintained an influential position with respect to the businessmen. To flex his power, he removed all quota restrictions and did away with the

Commodity Control Commission, which gave British businesses located in the country an automatic advantage over the local businessman. The result was that more goods could be imported by individual businessmen themselves. Japanese and other cheaper European goods began to flood the market; naturally, East Indian businesses became the major outlets for these products.[3]

This move by Jagan erased the fears some Indian businessmen had about his being a communist and endeared him to others. Within a few years, Indian businesses managed to corner a sizable portion of the market by underselling their main competitors in many areas, especially the retail market.[4] But as Jagan was consolidating his political power at home, he was still being ignored by the colonial government.

The Search for Aid

As he saw it, there was much wrong with the country's development plan that he had inherited. Jagan and his ministerial colleagues felt that the plan was not geared to solving what they saw as the two most urgent problems then affecting the country: unemployment and crime and delinquency. Dr. Jagan recalls his objections in this way:

> I urged that apart from enlarging the plan for providing more work, we must reshape it to place greater emphasis on agriculture and industry, so as to lay the basis for future diversification and self-sustaining growth. I advocated the scrapping of the $91 million five year plan and the implementation of a new $200 million development plan. But the Colonial Office would not move. The Colonial Secretary, using delaying tactics, decided that we must come back in a year wth detailed plans. . . .
> I then contacted officials of the Swiss Bank in London, who were prepared to offer us a loan of between £6 million and £8 million with the proviso that the British Government should guarantee the loan. However, this the British Government was not prepared to do, for it claimed that the only loans it would guarantee were those of the World Bank. I thereupon proposed that we should immediately make a direct approach to the World Bank and the U.S. Government. Again, delaying tactics were adopted; I was advised to go home and make a proper application. I decided, however, to remain in London and work out a preliminary application to the World Bank. Having done this, I flew off to Washington for talks. (WT, 226)

In Washington, Dr. Jagan was given the runaround and was finally ignored by both the U.S. Government and the World Bank.

Prior to leaving Guyana, accompanied by the Governor, Sir Patrick

Renison, and his minister of Natural Resources, Mr. Edward Beharry, Dr. Jagan had gone on record as saying "that his government might resign if not given forty million pounds. Or else . . . he will look elsewhere."[5] If the Premier was beginning to reassure skeptics by his performance in government thus far, his failure to get the aid the country required was a severe setback. Thought to be the best person to represent a majority of the electorates, he was beginning to become a liability by not being able to make good his promises. One reason given for the treatment Dr. Jagan had received in London and in Washington was the imprecision and incohesive plans he had submitted for funding. They gave an unmistakable appearance of having been hurriedly conceived and thrown together (WT, 226).

Soon after his return from a frustrating search for development loans, Dr. Jagan and the PPP had to deal with their first scandal. During his absence several questions were raised about the way concessions were handled by the Minister of Natural Resources, Mr. Beharry. Shortly after that, in the midst of accusations of corruption, Mr. Beharry was fired.[6] It is said that Minister Beharry was guilty of awarding his company a lucrative contract to distribute British cigarettes on the East Coast (WT, 242). Mr. Benn then replaced Mr. Beharry and Mr. Balram Sing Rai became Minister of Education in his place.

Then in November 1957, the Government, in an effort to save funds, announced that since most of the Civil Service were by then Guyanese, "it would stop paying fares to the U.K. for Civil Service families on long leave."[7] Needless to say, many of the Guyanese Civil Servants who had for years aspired to fill the posts vacated by expatriate British Civil Servants, because of their attractive fringe benefits, balked at the idea of losing these benefits. Even though they were not "going home," they felt this was a privilege worth maintaining. As a result of what they perceived to be a threat to their job security, the Civil Service Association then applied to and joined the Trade Union Council.

On October 6, 1959, the PPP Burnhamite faction announced that it had merged with the United Democratic Party. The two came together to form the People's National Congress (PNC).[8] This added one vote, that of W. O. R. Kendall, to the main opposition. But when Jai Narine Singh left the Party shortly after to form his own Guyana Independence Movement (GIM), the PNC parliamentary vote was back where it had begun.

In the summer of 1959, Dr. Jagan left the country once again to try to seek loans and grants for development. His travels to Britain and several West European countries were not as fruitful as he had hoped. The British provided him with loan guarantees, but no other country would make a commitment.

The year came to an end with a strike by the lower echelons of the Government Service for increased salaries and better working conditions. A complete strike by the entire Civil Service was averted only after the acting governor asked Premier Jagan to seek a compromise.

Change of Tactics

Suspecting that the British Government was dragging its feet on the questions of loans and grants to the country, perhaps so that the PPP would prove itself incapable of meeting its campaign pledges and managing the economy, Dr. Jagan changed his strategy. "I realized that there could be no real economic and social benefits without a change in our constitutional status" (WT, 230). A little more than a year before, the Legislative Council had unanimously passed a resolution calling for a change to complete self-government for the colony. Resolution No. XXIX read:

> Resolved, That this Honourable Council affirming its belief in the principle of the basic right of the peoples to governments of their own choice as enunciated in the Atlantic Charter, the United Nations Declaration of Human Rights and the Washington Declaration signed on February 1st, 1956, by the Rt. Honourable Anthony Eden, then Prime Minister of the United Kingdom Government and President Eisenhower, President of the United States of America, requests Her Majesty's Secretary of State for the Colonies to receive a representative delegation chosen by and from this Council to discuss:
>
> (i) Constitutional reform with a view to the granting to British Guiana of the status of a fully self-governing territory within the Commonwealth; and
>
> (ii) The working out of an agreement between the British Guiana Government and the United Kingdom Government for a transitional period whereby the United Kingdom Government would exercise control over defence and give guidance in foreign relations other than trade and commerce.[9]

Premier Jagan had raised the subject of Constitutional advance with the British Secretary of State for the Colonies on his visit to London in 1958. The Secretary of State in turn had asked the British Governor in Guyana as titular head of the government "to set up a Committee to

SCHENKMAN PUBLISHING COMPANY, INC.
P.O. Box 349 1570
Cambridge, MA 02139

$18.45 CLOTH
$11.95 PAPER

recommend what form of constitutional advance the new arrangements should take. . . . With the agreement of the Secretary of State, the Governor appointed a Constitutional Committee comprising the Speaker as Chairman and all unofficial members of the Legislative Council, with the official members as advisors without vote. The Committee was set up in November 1958, and presented its reports to the Governor in August 1959."[10]

Scheduled to meet in London in late 1959 to discuss the committee's report, the conference was suddenly postponed when Governor Sir Patrick Renison was transferred. Renison, who had arrived in the colony with both a reputation as a skilled negotiator and a specialty for dealing with conflicts, was transferred to Kenya and replaced by Sir Ralph Grey. The postponement of the conference was to allow the new Governor time to adjust to his new situation.[11]

1960 Constitutional Conference

The conference at Lancaster House began on March 7, 1960. Those taking part in the Conference were:

British Guiana Delegation

Delegates

The Hon. Dr. C. B. Jagan, Minister of Trade and Industry, PPP
The Hon. Mr. B. H. Benn, Minister of Natural Resources, PPP
The Hon. Mr. B. S. Rai, Minister of Community Development and
  Education, PPP
Mr. L. F. S. Burnham, PNC
Mr. W. O. R. Kendall, PNC
Mr. Jai Narine Singh, GIM
Mr. R. B. Gajraj, Nominated Member of the Legislative Council
Mr. R. E. Davis, Nominated Member of the Legislative Council

Adviser

Mr. B. A. Abrams (adviser to Mr. Burnham)

Governor of British Guiana

Sir Ralph Grey, K.C.M.G., K.C.V.O., O.B.E

Official Advisers

Mr. A. M. I. Austin, Q.C.	Attorney-General
Mr. F. W. Essex, C.M.G.	Financial Secretary
Mr. M. S. Porcher, O.B.E.	Deputy Chief Secretary

United Kingdom Delegation
Delegates

The Rt. Hon. Ian Macleod, M.P.	Secretary of State for the Colonies
The Rt. Hon. The Earl of Perth	Minister of State for Colonial Affairs
Mr. A. R. Thomas, C.M.G.	Colonial Office
Sir Hilton Pynton, K.C.M.G.	Colonial Office
Mr. A. M. MacKintosh, C.M.G.	Colonial Office[12]

At the conference all of the parties present called for a new constitution with full internal self-government for the colony, and with independence as the eventual goal.

Dr. Jagan and the PPP delegation favored an immediate change of constitution to full internal self-government, and requested that "independence within the Commonwealth" should be granted by August 1961, when the normal four year life of the current legislature expired.

"The British Guiana delegation with one exception proposed, and the Conference accepted, the principle of independence, within the Commonwealth for British Guiana. The Member (Singh) who differed wished for immediate independence but not within the Commonwealth."[13]

Dr. Jagan and his delegation left the Conference "far from satisfied." He had expected that a date would be set for independence. "We came here with a mandate for independence. We are going back still as Colonials with a Crown Colony status."[14]

Though Dr. Jagan and his PPP had not campaigned in 1957 on a platform for independence, it was uppermost in the minds of most progressive politicians. But Jagan's experience in office convinced him that only full independence would give him the flexibility he needed for governing the country. He had seen that his style and desire for quick success in social and economic reform was not what the Colonial Office was accustomed to, and he was impatient with it.

The Secretary of State's opening remarks, calling for an "orderly and progressive transfer of responsibility and power," must have struck a good note with the PNC delegation.[15] Somehow, Burnham and his PNC became convinced at the conference that some change would take place that would give them a chance at governing the country. Most political observers at the time thought their hope was optimistic, if possible at all. Their reasons for so thinking were because of Dr. Jagan's preeminence as an international revolutionary, his defiance of the Colonial Office and his popularity as a colonial leader, and his ability nevertheless to transfer any disadvantage into successive election victories in 1953 and 1957. In the light of their low popularity at home and almost complete anonymity abroad, the PNC delegation favored a progression to independence "by stages and not in one step."[16] The PNC and Burnham were hoping that time would in some way change their fortune.

Under the normal circumstances of colonial constitutional advancement, the British Government should have showed some willingness to set a date or give a tacit agreement to a later conference where independence would be discussed. But the case of British Guiana and Dr. Jagan was apparently different. The British Government seemed willing to wait and see what developed before committing themselves. Dr. Jagan, his PPP, the opposition, and most others concerned in the Guyanese process of political development recognized this. At the end of the conference, Forbes Burnham was attacked by several Guyanese and West Indian student groups for advocating a "step by step" approach to independence. Many suggested that he had put his ambitions before the principle of independence for the country.

The denunciation of Burnham and the PNC by the different student groups in London was a severe blow to his pride and his political standing among academics and because he had always seen himself as one of them and had been one of their leaders ten years earlier.

The delegations left with a new constitution that gave the country a little more internal power, yet not quite full internal self-government. The new Constitution provided:

Legislature

The new Constitution would provide for a bicameral Legislature which would consist of an elected chamber to be called the "Legislative Assembly" and a nominated chamber to be called the "Senate."

The life of the Legislature, as hitherto, would be four years. The sessions of the two chambers would be coterminous.

The Legislative Assembly would consist of not less than thirty-two members and not more than thirty-five members, the precise number to be determined by the advice of a Boundary Commission to be set up to delimit new constituency boundaries in time for the next general election. . . .

The Senate would consist of thirteen members, of whom eight would be appointed by the (British) Governor in accordance with the advice of the (Guyanese) Premier, three by the Governor after consultation with such persons as, in his opinion, could speak for the differing political points of view of opposition groups represented in the Legislative Assembly, and two by the Governor in his discretion.

The Speaker of the Legislative Assembly would be selected by the Assembly from amongst its members or from outside the Assembly. If chosen from among the members of the Assembly, the Speaker would have a casting vote but not an original vote; if selected from outside the Assembly, the Speaker would have no vote at all.

The President of the Senate would be chosen by the members from amongst their number and would have only a casting vote.

The Governor would prorogue the Legislature on the advice of the Premier.

The Governor's power to dissolve the Legislature would be exercised in accordance with the conventions applicable to the exercise of the like power by the Queen in the United Kingdom.

. . . it was recognized that the institution of a Senate would provide the opportunity for persons of wisdom and experience, who might be unwilling to stand for election, to participate in the government of the country. Nevertheless, the Senate should be so constituted as to membership and powers as not to be in a position to thwart the will of the Legislative Assembly. As to membership, the appointment of eight members by the Governor on the advice of the Premier would ensure a majority in the Senate for the party in office. As to powers, the Senate's functions would be restricted as follows:

Money Bills

(i) no Money Bill should be introduced in the Senate;

(ii) if a Money Bill, having been passed by the Legislative Assembly and sent to the Senate at least one month before the end of the session, is not passed by the Senate without amendment within one month after it has been sent to the Senate, it should, unless the Legislative Assembly otherwise resolves, be presented to the Governor for assent;

(iii) if by the end of a period of six months from the date when a Bill other than a Money Bill is sent to it, the Senate has failed to pass the Bill either with or without amendments the Bill should unless the Legislative Assembly otherwise resolved be presented to the Governor for assent;

(iv) if within the said period of six months the Bill is passed by the Senate with amendments it will be returned to the Assembly and the Assembly may

(a) resolve either that the Bill be presented for assent in the form in which it was sent to the Senate or that it be presented for assent with such of the amendments made by the Senate as agreed to by the Assembly; or

(b) resolve that the Bill be not presented for assent.

Legislative Powers

The Governor would assent or refuse to assent to Bills in accordance to the advice of the Minister. However, unless he were authorized by the Secretary of State to assent thereto, the Governor would be required to reserve for the signification of Her Majesty's pleasure any Bill which, in his opinion, affected defence, external affairs or the Royal Prerogative or was inconsistent with the Constitution.

The Executive

The Executive Council would be replaced by a Council of Ministers consisting of a Premier and a maximum of nine other Ministers, one of whom would be Attorney-General.

The Governor would appoint as Premier the member of the Legislative Assembly who, in his judgment, was best able to command the confidence of a majority of the members of that chamber. He would appoint the other Ministers in accordance with the advice of the Premier, not less than one and not more than three being members of the Senate and the remainder being members of the Legislative Assembly.

Electoral System

It was agreed that the election to the Legislative Assembly should be by the "first past the post" system in single-member constituencies.[17]

> The British Guiana Delegation preferred the title of "Prime Minister" but the Secretary of State considered this inappropriate to the Constitutional Status of the Colony. . . .

The Road to Racial Politics

The delegations left London knowing that elections would be held sometime in August 1961 or thereafter, and that in all likelihood it would be the last before full independence was granted to the colony.

Throughout Jagan's period in government, the newspapers had given prominence to the projects, feasibility studies, negotiations, and general activities of the Government. The rejections Dr. Jagan received in his attempts to get aid and his sometimes impetuous outbursts were seen in a sympathetic manner by the press and the people, even those who did not support him at election. There was a general resignation to the fact that Dr. Jagan would run the country for some time to come.

The PYO (Early Beginnings)

The PPP was constantly building its Party structure to insure successive Party victories. The Party's youth organization, the Progressive Youth Organization (PYO), had successfully organized a substantial number of young people through the country, especially in traditional PPP areas. This organizational effort was begun at the end of October 1957 with a call by its General Secretary, Mr. Nevill Annibourne, for a "youth conference for November 9th and 10th to unite the youth of all races between the ages of 16 and 35."[18] The PYO effort in organizing the youth was very successful not only in the PPP areas, but also in many opposition strongholds as well. The organization acquired a strong following among teachers especially; also, a number of young civil servants could have been counted among their ranks. With the unemployed also within their ranks, the PYO not only seemed to be cutting across the racial barrier but was also becoming a powerful force within the PPP itself.

One reason for the PYO's success among these unlikely groups was the patronage they were perceived to be able to influence. From the time it first entered office, the PPP began increasing the number of scholarships the government gave for students to go off to university. In addition the PYO also solicited and obtained scholarships to Eastern European universities through its international friends and affiliates. These scholarships, though few in number, were a magnetic enticement to young people who could see the future status of the professional man in an independent country, but were too poor to finance their own university education. In 1960 there was a dramatic increase in the number of students the government sponsored to attend the University of the West Indies in Jamaica, making the PYO even more attractive to qualified young people. Prior to the rise of nationalism many of this group would have been content to remain minor functionaries in the civil service or become head teachers if they were selected by the Church, with only a high school education. Many now saw the PYO as an opportunity to escape this uninspiring future.

The PPP Dual Control and the United Force

The election campaigns got off to an early start with the two main parties, the PPP and PNC, busily organizing and building support.

However, talks between Burnham and Peter D'Aguiar, the head of the newly organized conservative party, the United Force (UF), launched in October 1960, broke down after an agreement could not be reached on the composition and the management.

While most parties were campaigning on promises of social and economic reform, Cheddi Jagan and his PPP could point to projects they had initiated and seen through. In November 1960, the Minister of Education provided a cause for the hitherto mild campaign. He announced that the Government had decided to assume control of 51 denominational schools that had been built on church land with public funds. The announcement brought instant public outcry from all sections of the opposition, both active and passive, and suddenly there was a bright side to the campaign for the opposition. Because the non-Indian population was all Christian while most of the Indian population was not, the government's action was construed as a further attempt by the PPP to gain control over a vital institution. But why would Dr. Jagan, an experienced politician, wait until such an inopportune time to make such an announcement?

One explanation is that "Indian teachers had been putting considerable pressure on Jagan since 1957 to do something about the injustices associated with the system of dual control (state and church). The teachers were concerned particularly about their inability to win promotions in denominational schools and were also concerned about unfair treatment from African head teachers in government schools . . . many teachers had been notified through party channels that the government would take action to improve their situation. As of 1959, no action had been taken, and considerable unrest existed among Indian teachers because of unfulfilled promises. In 1960, when there was talk about a new political party being formed under the leadership of Peter D'Aguiar, some Indian teachers threatened to quit the PPP and join the opposition."[19] It is true that Jagan's announcement came one month after the formation of the United Force, but it seems unlikely that Jagan felt that the support of some 3000 teachers would be worth the general alienation which this action was likely to cause and did cause.

It is more likely that Jagan just had a bad sense of timing, though by no means should we rule out completely the influence of the young teachers within the PYO, which could have been a strong contributing factor to the bad timing of the bill. The PPP's record of bad timing from

1953 onwards and until it left office in 1964 seems fairly consistent with the pre-election announcement.

The Education Amendment Bill, more than any other single factor, changed what had thus far been a straightforward fight between the PPP and PNC. The ecumenical movement had just formed the Christian Social Council. The Council mounted mass rallies that were announced and supported from nearly every pulpit around the country. The most conspicuous group at the Bourda Green rallies were the Portuguese, most of whom were Catholics. During the whole process of political development, which it is agreed began in 1950 with the formation of the PPP, the Portuguese, as an ethnic group, had remained very much in the background. Because they tended to be merchants and shopkeepers they considered themselves upper middle-class and part of the status quo, and took no part in the radical politics of opposing British rule. Even when Peter D'Aguiar had arranged his "Axe the Tax" campaign in 1959 against the increased tax on beer, it was the Africans who were most supportive. Dual control or the take over of the Church-controlled schools by the government brought the Portuguese into the streets in large numbers as a pressure group for the first time.

Other groups were also involved in the rallies, especially the conservative mulattoes and the more conservative elements who did not like the radical nature of the politics of the PPP and the PNC. Peter D'Aguiar, seeing an opportunity for his new party, appointed himself spokesman for the Catholics in particular. This meant that he became spokesman for a large percentage of Portuguese, the predominant group in the Catholic Church. Thus, the activism of the churches in the Dual Control issue caused a whole group of new people to become actively involved in the political process. The close identification of the UF with this issue caused it to be labelled the Portuguese Party. The Portuguese and Chinese tended to be well-educated professionals, and the main merchants of the country from the turn of the century; the Portuguese especially were very prominent in the retail trade and the liquor business. Together with the mulattoes who occupied higher positions in the civil service, these groups felt a certain closeness because they had been more accepted into colonial society. On the basis of his Catholic background and conservative political opinion, Peter D'Aguiar, along with his United Force, was a natural leader of this group. In 1953 this group of people supported the UDP and a number of independent candidates, all of whom had lost their election. In 1957 they chose not to participate. Had the United Force not become a factor, the competition between the PNC and PPP for the support of these groups would have been interesting. Instead the groups for which the PPP and PNC competed were relatively poor and lacked influence within the society. The United Force membership, however, though substantially smaller, was very influential. This realignment of interest groups hurt both the PNC and the PPP financially. This was especially so for the PNC, whose supporters tended to be urban wage earners and from the coastal villages. For them, obtaining funds for mounting an effective political campaign became a problem.

The PNC took up the cause of the Christian Social Council in the Legislature, the United Force did so on the road, and the press was sympathetic to the UF which excited more opposition to the PPP bill. It seemed then that Dr. Jagan had encountered greater opposition than he'd foreseen. But the PPP leaders were able to turn the situation partly to their advantage. "During the course of these discussions, an unusual opportunity was presented to the PPP leaders to demonstrate their interest in the Indian cultural section. Rai, for example, declared that religious 'apartheid' was being practiced in Guianese schools to the detriment of East Indians. Ram Karran, Jagan's Minister of Communications and Works, accused the churches of trying to bully the Government on the issue. Jagan announced that the bill was designed to correct the injustices that were being imposed upon the non-Christians. When Burnham opposed the bill, apparently in contradiction to his position in 1953, he was described as a racist. When the churches labelled the bill as communist inspired, Rahman Gajraj, a nominated member of the Legislative Council, accused the churches of practicing facism. By the time the bill became law, practically every East Indian in the country was convinced that only the PPP was interested in their education."[20] Considering that almost half of the country's population is non-Christian, the fact that the Portuguese and other middle-class groups could so influence the issue was a tribute to its still remaining power.

PNC-UF Merger Talks

In July 1961, the on-again-off-again talks between Forbes Burnham and Peter D'Aguiar about a merger of the PNC and UF was officially terminated.[21] Of the failure of the two parties to merge, "the official mimeographed history of the UF says the PNC began 'as an African organization when they split from the Jagans in 1955 and they adamantly refused to consider accepting Indians on their Executive in any reasonable proportion to Africans. Valuable time was wasted while some form of compromise was sought with Burnham.' Valuable time was a euphemism; when Burnham finally turned them down, there were only six weeks to go before the elections. It looked very much as though he had wiped out their chances of winning any seats at all."[22] During the interim the United Force, on the lookout for support, began to organize the long neglected vote of the American Indian in Guyana. The established political parties, always short of money, never bothered to pay much attention to this hard-to-reach vote. The areas where they lived were distant, with a population scattered miles apart; transportation was expensive, and there was never a certainty of obtaining the two seats. It was a bit easier for the UF to organize these areas because they needed the support as an untried party, and in addition they had the cooperation of the Catholic missionaries and ranchers who worked in the area, and they were better financed. The formation of the UF severely hampered the chance of either of the two major political parties to broaden its base.

Party Perceptions

The United Force, from the inception of the campaign, tried to sell itself as the party of "balance." They saw themselves as the party that would be able to influence either of the two mass parties into taking some sort of moderate approach in government. The leadership of the Party was comprised of several wealthy Indian and Portuguese businessmen and the new leadership of the MPCA—its President, Mr. Richard Ishmael, and its Secretary, Mr. Cleveland Charran. These men, though influential in business and unions, controlled no real political support and did not have any vote-getting ability, hence their efforts to form an alliance with Burnham and the PNC.

In those days the Indian community was seen as the more stable section of the community. Everyone accepted that they were capitalists at heart, and the belief was that one day they would come to their senses and recognize that their personal interests demanded that they should stop voting for Jagan and communism.

The Negro, on the other hand, was seen as the unstable element who was not really interested in the creation of a modern and viable society, but only in power and its immediate enjoyment. It was thought that he would be quite content to see Guyana disintegrate into a voodoo state similar to Haiti. The "black man" represented violence and rape and the worst forms of disorder.[23]

Despite their incompatibility, an alliance with some group was necessary for the survival of the United Force and the PNC was the lesser of the two evils. The PPP was totally unattractive to them because of the United Force's anti-communist stand, and because of a difference of ideology that did not accommodate the United Force's commitment to a free enterprise system. But in order for the United Force to exist, the PNC knew that they, the UF, would have to rely on the support the PNC was already expecting to pick up. Hence, the PNC's first tactic was to negotiate with the United Force, then after being unable to reach an agreement, to try to prolong the discussion and so outmaneuver the UF from participating in the election by delaying the "no" answer as long as possible. Negotiations between the parties finally broke down because of what the PNC considered to be D'Aguiar's impossible demands:

In effect, D'Aguiar proposed the following package to the PNC's Executive Committee. D'Aguiar and his associates would join the PNC and make their membership public. In addition, they would provide the PNC with all the financial backing it needed to organize a massive campaign against Jagan and the PPP. In exchange for this support, the PNC would give D'Aguiar's group nine of the fifteen seats on its Executive Committee and Burnham would remain the party leader. In the event of victory, Burnham would become Prime Minister, and D'Aguiar would become the Minister of Trade and Industry. In other words, the Portuguese business community, along with a few Indian labour leaders of little consequence, offered to purchase the People's National Congress. The offer did not even involve a question of merger, because D'Aguiar and his group did not represent an organized political party.
Needless to say, the leaders of the PNC were insulted by D'Aguiar's offer. As Burnham stated, "He wanted to buy the party as though it were a box of empties being returned to his brewery." Nevertheless, in view of the support which D'Aguiar claimed to have, Burnham was instructed by his Executive Committee to make a counter offer. Specifically, the PNC offered to give D'Aguiar six seats on its Executive Committee, providing he could fill four of these seats with the East Indian supporters he claimed to have among the members of the Rice Producers' Associa-

tion. D'Aguiar accepted the offer. However, when he returned his list of nominees for the Executive Committee, it included himself, two members of the Rice Producers' Association, and three Portuguese businessmen of no political status. The PNC rejected D'Aguiar's list of candidates. Burnham's Executive Committee reasoned that unless D'Aguiar were able to bring into the party Indian leaders of political status, men capable of mustering support in areas where the PPP was strong, he could contribute very little to the party's strength except by way of financial support. Moreover, if the PNC accepted D'Aguiar's list of candidates, it would not only provide Jagan with substantial evidence that the party had sold out to "imperialist" capitalists, but it might also serve to alienate the support of important Afro-Guianese labor leaders. Consequently, the PNC decided that it was better off proceeding without D'Aguiar's support. Considering the fact that the Portuguese had no choice but to vote for the PNC or the PPP and considering that they were not very likely to vote for the latter, this appeared to be a wise course of action.[24]

The rejection of the alliance or merger by the PNC set off a struggle between both the PNC and the United Force. So severe was the struggle that in the end the parties were both concentrating entirely on reducing each other, thus freeing their real opponent, the PPP, to take a completely free and easy course. Moreover, the PNC at that point was struggling for its life in another way. Most of the possible sources of funding for its campaign were then either with the PPP or with the United Force.[25] The PNC, which had thought it had a very real chance of winning the elections after the 1960 Constitutional Conference a year before, saw its position eroded within a few months; then the situation among the Afro-Guyanese began to change. One writer described the change in this way:

> With the emergence of the United Force, a change in attitude began to develop among the Afro-Guyanese. They began to feel that they were caught up in a racial war for political survival. In the rural areas of the country, the Afro-Guyanese were up against the apanjaht ("vote for your own kind") politics of the Jagan government and the East Indian masses. And now, in the urban areas, they were opposed by the economic power of the white Portuguese community.[26]

But if Peter D'Aguiar and his United Force were causing problems for Forbes Burnham and his PNC with their electoral support, he showed that he was also capable of disrupting the PNC's executive:

An effort was made by the UF to split the Afro-Guyanese middle class away from the PNC. The UF leaked a rumor to the Guiana Graphic that John Carter and other members of the PNC who once belonged to the United Democratic Party were about to dissociate themselves from Burnham and join forces with D'Aguiar. Although this proved to be nothing more than a rumor, it fell sufficiently within the realm of possibility to be taken seriously by many PNC supporters. Thus, as a PNC meeting scheduled early in October, a motion was passed requesting the former members of the UDP to reaffirm their loyalty to the party. In response to this motion, John Carter delivered a speech in which he asserted that it was not his intention or the intention of any of his old UDP associates, to join the United Force in opposition to the PNC.[27]

The change in the political thinking among Africans in the country strengthened the PNC in its ability to influence their vote, especially in rural areas where that vote tended to be split.

In effect, between October 1960 and August 1961, the PNC employed a strategy of reverse racialism combined with a program of anti-communism. In other words, PNC leaders did not openly and publicly call for an African vote. Instead they devoted most of their campaign efforts to informing the African people how the PPP was practicing apanjaht politics in order to mobilize the Indian community for the purpose of bringing British Guiana under Communist rule. The purpose of this strategy was to impress upon the African people the idea of their voting as a block in opposition to the PPP and East Indian population.[28]

Sugar Estates in Transition

This form of propaganda could be most effective within the African population because of the developments going on within the Indian community at about the same time. The sugar estates' management had for some time been undertaking a program of mechanization of the industry, and of revising their paternalistic role within the estate culture. This was being done under the pressure of increased cost of production and because of the rapidly rising Indian population living on the estates. For the first time, twice as many people lived on the estates as were needed. Indeed the figures of the overall rise in population is rather staggering, but shows the rapid rate at which things were changing demographically and, consequently, politically.

The high rates of unemployment on the estates, especially among young people, caused them to be able to devote more time to politics

TABLE 3
Vital Statistics for Guyana, 1931–1961[a]

Period	Col. (1) Population at end of year	Col. (2) Number of registered live births	Col. (3) Number of registered deaths	Col. (4) Natural increase of population	Col. (5) Net immigration (+) or emigration (−)	Crude birthrate per 1000 population	Crude death rate per 1000 population	Rate of natural increase per 1000	Infant mortality rate per 1000 live births
Avg. 1931–1935	320,816	10,	7226	3114	+ 509	32.2	22.5	9.7	141
" 1936–1940	339,135	10,922	7199	3723	+ 30	32.2	21.2	11.0	119
" 1941–1945	364,294	12,525	7087	5438	− 115	34.4	19.4	15.0	112
" 1946–1951	395,018	15,835	5560	10,275	+ 13	40.5	14.3	26.2	81
" 1952–1956	460,692	19,737	5644	14,113	−1140	43.5	12.5	31.0	75
" 1957–1961	535,438	23,056	5297	17,759	−1857	43.5	10.0	33.5	60

Note: Data for 1931–45 include the registered Amerindian population (about 8000–16,000 during this period), while post-war data do not.

Sources: 1931–45: R. R. Kuczynski: *A Demographic Survey of the British Colonial Empire, Volume II* (London, Oxford University Press for the Royal Institute of International Affairs, 1953), Chapter XXI, Tables on pp. 151 and 178.

1946–58: *Annual Report of the Registrar General, 1958* (Georgetown, Government Printer, 1962), Tables 2, 23 and 25.
1959–61: Columns (2) to (4) from *Quarterly Statistical Digest*, September 1962 (Georgetown, Government Printer, 1963), Tables 6 and 7).
Columns (5) to (9) from *United Nations Demographic Yearbook* 1962 (New York, 1963), Tables 25, 26, 14, 18 and 17.
Column (1) calculated from Columns (2), (3) and (5). All figures for 1960 and 1961 are provisional.

(a) Taken from Peter Newman, *British Guiana* (Oxford University Press, 1964), p. 35.

and so made them more susceptible to party persuasion. This was also true of the urban areas, but here there was more distraction: "the sudden on-rush of population had a disorganizing effect on the society and economy that until recently was geared to the opposite situation."[29] The PPP, being in control of the government, could deal with the rural overpopulation situation in such a way as to give them a significant political advantage. The enlargement of the land development schemes enabled the government to attract some of these workers into the rice industry.

On the estates in 1960 the Sugar Producers Association began to sell house lots in the extra-nuclear areas in an effort to get the growing numbers of people off the estates. The growing cost of providing facilities, and the prospect of having to provide additional housing, did not appear likely to be met in the light of the new political consciousness on the estates. By selling the lots cheap, the Association thought all sides would be satisfied. The people would be glad to own their own homes, and management would be rid of the most talked about aspect of estate life—estate housing. "It was expected that by alienating these lands to the people who lived on them, the estate population would eventually be organized under local authorities. In this way, the estate population would be forced to become responsible for the management of its own affairs. As part of this policy, the SPA also offered the Government the opportunity to take over the ownership and management of the estate medical centres. In place of the medical centres, the SPA planned to continued to provide workers with first-aid facilities and to expand its program of industrial accident insurance."[30]

But the estate workers never wanted to be organized or included in local authorities, for "as long as they lived on estate land, they received a variety of services, perhaps a greater variety than any local authority could provide, and they did not have to pay taxes to support these services. Similarly, the health centres operated by the estates provided better medical treatment than could be obtained in many government-operated health centres."[31] The increase in population, together with the mechanization and the resultant loss of jobs by many on the estates, made the PPP more popular in the estates. The sympathy that these groups received from the PPP caused them, as the 1961 election progressed, to call for apanjaht. The slogan was used openly and deliberately to heighten the racial feelings of the other ethnic groups. This further polarized the society along racial lines. The slogan brought to

light the worst fears of most of the Guyanese people, who had all along
realized that race could become a force in the society, but always
pledged to fight any attempt to encourage it.

The situation on the estates made more credible the PPP contention
that it was the only party willing to attack the "imperialist exploiters"
for not doing enough for its people while reaping high profits from
their labour. The PPP accused the PNC and the United Force of being
in league with Bookers (the leading English firm in Guyana) and with
other exploitative forces in the country. "During the 1961 election
campaign, apanjaht politics among Indian sugar workers was focused
most sharply on the People's National Congress. Throughout the campaign, the PPP made a concerted effort to link the PNC with sugar
industry. At political rallies, for example, PPP speakers outlined what
appeared to be a warm relationship between Burnham's party and
Bookers. They noted that the PNC publication, *New Nation*, was seldom critical of the sugar industry. They also noted that the PNC received much less critical attention in the business-controlled press
than the PPP and the Jagan Government. The most substantial evidence that the PPP offered in support of these accusations was based
on the fact that the Chairman of the PNC, Winifred Gaskin, also
happened to be the editor of *Booker News*, a company newspaper
widely circulated on the estates."[32]

So complete was the PPP's campaign and influence, especially on
the estate areas, that neither of the opposition parties, in particular the
PNC, could hold a political meeting in the area.[33] By attacking and
isolating the PNC, the PPP seemed to hope to get what little rural
support the PNC might have had. At the same time they knew that
D'Aguiar's UF was waging total war against the PNC in their traditional stronghold, the urban areas. With the PNC being attacked on
two fronts, it was probably hoped that their electoral and parliamentary vote would be substantially reduced. Should this have happened,
the PPP probably would have been able to deal with a more vulnerable
D'Aguiar and the United Force successfully, since the Guyanese were
not likely to support the United Force in mass.

Politics and Rice

If the PPP had a fortunate situation on the estates, fate also seemed
to be with them in their attempts to influence the rice farmers. The

interim government (1953–1957) had set up a number of projects geared to help the peasant rice farmer. Apart from the fact that the crop had become a very important export, it was hoped that by making the Indian peasantry more independent of landlords and the estates, their grievance would be submerged and they would be less likely to support the PPP.

In the election, one of the main points used by the opposition to show the blatant discrimination against other ethnic groups by the PPP Government was a project called the Black Bush Polder: "Located on the Corentyne Coast, the polder was one of the Jagan Government's most publicized projects during the 1961 election campaign. The project involved the reclamation of 31,000 acres of swampland. Upon completion, it was to provide for the settlements of 1586 families. Each family was to be given a twenty-one-year lease on fifteen acres of land to be used for the cultivation of rice. In addition, each family was to be given two acres of land for house lots and garden plots. Some idea of the magnitude of the project can be had from available statistics. It required the construction of approximately twenty miles of road, two hundred miles of drain embankments, three hundred miles of drainage and irrigation canals, the clearing of 20,000 acres of jungle bush, and the construction of numerous sluices and access bridges. Expenditures were estimated at approximately $18.67 millions. This represents a capital investment of $11,800 per family."[34] Most of the land allocated went only to PPP supporters, mostly Indians.

As the project started, the PPP realized its tremendous pull for votes. The dislocation in the sugar and rice industry, which was being mechanized, coupled with the growing young population, meant that there were more than enough people eager to take up the places. Table 4 gives an indication of the youth of the population.

"When the polder was first conceived, prior to Jagan's election in 1957, it was to be organized as a local authority under the Department of Local Government. The families that were to be settled in polder were to be selected on the basis of need and previous agricultural experience. However, when the polder was nearing completion, it was suggested by Jagan that it be organized as a land society under the supervision of the Department of Cooperatives, a department included in his portfolio as Minister of Trade and Industry."[35] This enabled the Government to exercise more direct political control over the selection of those who would be granted land in the area.

TABLE 4
Age Distribution of the Population, 1921–1960

Age Group	1921 Census	1931 Census	1946 Census	1960 Census
Over 0 and under 5	30,754	45,077	62,732	98,195
Over 5 and under 13	64,613	66,369	84,338	161,075
Over 15 and under 45	148,448	146,563	162,241	215,255
Over 45 and under 64	42,666	43,607	47,597	67,072
Over 65	9,136	8,459	12,422	18,809
Age not stated	2,074	858	348	—
Total	297,691	310,933	369,678	360,406

Percentage Distribution

	1921	1931	1946	1960
Over 0 and under 5	10.4	14.5	17.0	17.5
Over 5 and under 15	21.9	21.4	22.8	28.7
Over 15 and under 45	50.2	47.3	43.9	38.4
Over 45 and under 64	14.4	14.1	12.9	12.0
Over 65	3.1	2.7	3.4	3.4
Total	100.0	100.0	100.0	100.0
Number of dependents per person of working age (15 to 64)	0.55	0.63	0.76	0.98

Sources: 1921 and 1931, R. R. Kuczynski, *op. cit.*, Table on p. 158,
1946, R. R. Kuczynski, *op. cit.*, Table 4, p. 160.
1960, Census Bulletins No. 1 and No. 12, *Population Census 1960, Series D, British Guiana* (Port of Spain, Population Census Division, 1963).

As cited in Peter Newman, *British Guiana* (Oxford University Press, 1964).

"According to informants, most of whom were government officers directly involved with the settlement program, it was virtually impossible for an applicant to receive land in the polder unless the PPP wanted him to receive land. As of the October 1960, the Commissioner of Lands and Mines had received more than 3300 applicants for land. Of these, less than 200 had been received from Afro-Guyanese. As of February 1961, one hundred and fifty families had been settled in the polder. Of these, 147 were East Indian families. Only three families were Afro-Guyanese, and informants were certain that the heads of all three were financial members of the PPP."[36]

In this way, the PPP was able to demonstrate to its supporters, who were mainly Indian, that by having a party of their choice as the government, they could indirectly use it to serve their own interest. It was easy for the PNC to stress the same point throughout the 1961 election campaign in relation to the African in their election campaign.

Party Strategy in Election Campaign: 1961

The election campaign was in full swing with the PPP supporters shouting *Apanjaht* in the countryside, and with the PNC and UF locked in a serious battle with each other in the urban areas. The PPP only put up candidates in those constituencies where it thought it stood a good chance of winning. In this case, it put up candidates only in the rural areas. To its few supporters in the urban areas, it openly suggested that they vote UF. This leads some commentators to conclude that the UF and PPP had struck a deal, but it seems doubtful. The PPP's strategy all along had been to contain the PNC and this was an adequate way of so doing. Of the thirty-five constituencies to be contested, the PPP put up 29 candidates; the PNC and the UF both put up 35. The six seats that the PPP did not contest were the Rupununi, District New Amsterdam, and the four Georgetown seats. The four urban seats were traditionally PNC strongholds and the interior seats were more favorable to the UF.

In the campaign the PNC and the PPP came out strongly in favor of independence; the UF did not. The churches, especially the Catholic Church, supported the UF. This further alienated and polarized the African Catholics who, as the campaign rolled on, began to stay away from the church in large numbers. The Christian Social Council as a whole was strongly against the communism of the PPP and was skeptical about the socialism of the PNC. The UF's platform of "economic dynamism" seemed more to their liking.

Before the election, Burnham dismissed any possibility of forming a coalition either before or after the election with any of the other two political parties. He stressed that the people had to make up their minds as to which party they wanted to lead them to independence (WT, 246). But Jagan saw Burnham's strong call for independence an act of necessity:

> The People's National Congress came out strongly in the campaign for independence. It also claimed that it was in favour of socialism. It had become politically necessary for the PNC to take such a position because

from the time it was formed in 1958 (by the merger of Burnham's PPP and the United Democratic Party) the PNC had become more and more conservative and race-minded. The result was loss of support particularly among the Negro youth, students and intelligentsia. This was clearly evident at a meeting in London in the House of Commons at the time of the 1960 Constitutional Talks. Then, the majority of students, mainly Negroes from British Guiana, the West Indies and Africa had attacked Burnham for his opposition to independence. The People's National Congress realized that in order to get the votes of the Negro workers, students and intellectuals, it would have to take a more progressive line. Thus it made strong statements in favour of independence and socialism (WT, 245).

As has been pointed out before, Burnham's political position was always compared with the more radical positions taken by Dr. Jagan and the PPP. Even though the political situation was developing into one where race was the deciding factor, Burnham still could not muster certain small but influential groups to his side. He could not bridge his credibility gap. Burnham after 1953 had probably thought that by modifying his ideology he would be more acceptable, but this was not the case: "Although this middle-of-the-road ideology may appear attractive in an economically developed society, it is a difficult perspective for a nationalist party to maintain, particularly in an underdeveloped country. On the one hand, the PNC wanted to mobilize the support of the Portuguese and other economically conservative elements. On the other hand, it had to maintain the support of the Afro-Guyanese labour movement. To accomplish the latter, the PNC had to present itself primarily as a working-class party. This necessity, as Jagan predicted in 1956, required Burnham to employ leftist phraseology. He had to be critical of colonialism, of colonial institutions, of ascribed status, and of economic exploitation. At the same time, however, it was precisely this leftist phraseology that would make the more conservative elements suspicious of Burnham's intentions. In other words, the PNC's strategy contained certain ambiguities that would make it extremely difficult to implement."[37]

The merger of the PPP (Burnhamites) with the UDP in March 1959 had produced a mixed bunch at the executive level of the PNC that the leader, Forbes Burnham, was finding difficult to reconcile.

Some of its members were strongly inclined toward some form of socialism, while others favoured an opposite view. At political meetings, PNC speakers often displayed a remarkable variety of conflicting views, even on relatively specific topics. John Carter, for example, might deliver a talk on how the PNC intended to attract private capital and build up many new industries. The following speaker, perhaps A. L. Jackson or Jane Phillips-Gay, would emphasize the party's plans for controlling private enterprise and putting an end to the exploitation of Guianese workers. This range of views made it extremely difficult for the Executive Committee to reach an agreement on the party's official policy statement. In fact, such an agreement was not reached until only a few months before the 1961 elections, and it might not have been reached even then if Rawle Farley, a Guyanese economist from the University College of the West Indies, had not been brought in by Burnham to mediate the situation and help draft a policy statement.[38]

One month before the election, Sidney King (who after having left the PPP had joined the PNC and become its General Secretary) was thrown out of the PNC. After King left the PPP, where he was labelled an extremist and a communist, his views became more black nationalist. Probably it was this change of view that led him to join the PNC in 1958. Shortly after Burnham's acceptance of King into the Party, Jai Narine Singh left the PNC and set up the Guianese Independence Movement. Jai Narine Singh's departure put Burnham's parliamentary vote at two. Originally Burnham had wooed Jai Narine Singh and Latchmansingh to his party, hoping they would bring along an Indian following over to his party, but this never happened. As a matter of fact, Jai Narine Singh had stood for and won a seat in Georgetown where he had relied on the urban African vote.

On the other hand, Sidney King had once before in 1953 won the East Coast seat. He had, in the 1957 election, stood as an independent and lost by a narrow margin in a three-way race. Burnham probably thought he needed Sidney King in his drive to acquire the extra seat. King disagreed with the PNC's executive in 1961 because of Burnham's announced unequivocal support for independence no matter who won the election. The newspapers reported: "Mr. Sidney King, still named Secretary of the PNC, threw a bombshell into the General Elections scene yesterday. Copies of a publication over his signature stated that he withdrew as a candidate for the PNC in protest against Mr. Forbes Burnham's statement on immediate independence for British Guiana and his support for Dr. Jagan on this issue. If Dr. Jagan wins . . . I am sure that Burnham's statement is dangerous to the African people—I cannot be any part of Burnham's plans" (WT, 247).

A few days after this stirring press release, the papers carried another: this time it was a release by the PNC Executive announcing the expulsion of Mr. King, its General Secretary.

> With respect to the ground upon which Mr. King has declared his intention not to run as a candidate for the people's National Congress, the Executive Committee declares that it is unequivocally committed to independence for British Guiana and will not swerve from its present policy which has been accepted by the Congress and the Executive Committee of the Party of which Mr. King was a party.
>
> It was advocated by the Party's representatives at the London Constitutional Talks in 1960. Independence is the inalienable right of Guiana, and the People's National Congress. Though it will always strive to protect the interests of all groups it will never stand in the way of independence regardless of the party in office. (WT, 247–248)

The official PNC statement gives the impression of a party trying to set the record straight. It gives some confirmation to the argument that Burnham, by supporting independence, was trying to appeal to certain interest groups, especially the university students and academics, for support. Perhaps this was one reason why he recruited Dr. Rawle Farley, a well-known Guyanese academician, to the Party. Apart from using him as a conciliator for the disagreement within the PNC Executive, it may have also been his hope that Farley would attract a few of the black academics to the PNC.

Nevertheless, even with its many problems with both the PPP as an incumbent and front-runner, and the UF, which could split its votes, the PNC maintained that it had an excellent chance of winning the elections, or at least of gaining sufficient seats so as to make the British Government and Dr. Jagan take it seriously. That was the way the parties lined up as election day approached.

> For the election each party had chosen a symbol: the PPP a cup; the UF a sun; and the PNC a broom (a besom). Burnham has always maintained that the besom was chosen to show that though one could break each single individual twig quite easily, when they were all bound together they could not be broken. His followers however took up the slogan: "A broom to sweep them out and keep them out."[39]

The elections were held on Monday, August 21, 1961. On Sunday, PNC supporters came out into the streets of Georgetown armed with brooms. They began chanting their slogan, "Sweep them out and keep them out," and sweeping dust into the faces of any Indian and Portuguese they met. They surrounded houses, and told the people they had better vote PNC; otherwise, they would come for their wives and daughters. By the end of the day some 51,000 people were roaming the streets and the news swept along the coastline, "If the PNC wins, no one is going to be safe." The Negro was confirming the image that everyone had of him. In July, Burnham had called the PPP the "greatest communists of the century," but after the Sunday demonstrations, communist government, inefficiency, and everything else became insignificant and when the people went to the polls, they voted race.[40]

Results and Analysis

When the results came in, the PPP had won 20 seats with 42.6 percent of the vote; the PNC, 11 seats with 41 percent; and the UF, 4 seats with 16.3 percent. Under the new constitution, Dr. Jagan was designated Premier and was asked to form a new government.

The immediate reaction of the supporters of the PPP was euphoria. Cheddi Jagan led a mammoth motorcade into the city with a number of his supporters from the Corentyne and along the coast, and Janet Jagan held several celebrations along the Essequibo Coast; they were extremely pleased with their victory. The UF was also pleased with their result. They had never claimed to be able to form a government, and as far as they were concerned, they were doing fine by holding the "balance of power."

The PNC, on the other hand, was extremely bitter at the outcome of the elections, for a number of reasons. The most important was the feeling that the UF cheated them of what could have been their election victory. Two of the four seats that the UF won were in the urban areas and were traditionally PNC seats. PNC reasoning was that if some of the other constituencies had not been a three-way race, their candidates could have carried a few marginal seats as well. The PPP victory rallies were so large and partisan that Africans in many parts who had voted for the PPP or the UF began to have second thoughts and regrets within a few days of the election. Among the Indians in some areas the chant was "a we pon top" (we are on top).

Rather than the result affirming the PPP dominance, the campaign more than any other factor in the intervening period heightened tension between the different ethnic groups. Prior to 1961 this tension generated by the indirect actions of the PPP and PNC put the Indian against the Afro-Guyanese. At this election a new group was brought into the political rivalry, the commercially strong Catholic UF.

The thought that the election result would allow Dr. Jagan and the PPP to be the government in office when independence was granted to the country by the British was a frightful one to everyone opposed to the PPP. Suddenly the attention of all of those opposed to independence was on Forbes Burnham and the PNC. Would they support Dr. Jagan in his fight for independence as he had promised? But Burnham was still sore at losing the election by default.

> Burnham held a monster meeting on Bourda Green. One of the reporters was so carried away that he wrote "it would appear that every person in Georgetown attended, so vast was the gathering." Burnham spoke for nearly two hours denouncing D'Aguiar, the UF and the leaders of the Christian Churches as traitors who had caused the PNC to lose the election by their short-sighted policies.[41]

As well as blaming the UF for their loss of the election, some PNC executives were blaming themselves, too. They blamed themselves for choosing the broom as their symbol and they blamed their supporters for overenthusiasm in the name of loyalty to the PNC.

The PNC also felt that had they won their eleven seats plus the four UF seats and so had fallen short of the majority, they would have been exceedingly pleased to have gained a greater percentage of votes at the polls than the PPP. However, the quibblings of the PNC and UF did not affect the PPP. They went ahead and began settling down to their second term in office. Dr. Jagan, appointed Premier, presented his cabinet for running the country for the next four years.[42]

NOTES

1. Despres, *Cultural Pluralism and Nationalist Politics in British Guiana*, pp. 221–222.
2. Ibid., pp. 230–231.
3. Ibid., p. 233.
4. Ibid., pp. 230–231.
5. Simms, *Trouble in Guyana*, p. 143.
6. Simms, *Trouble in Guyana*, pp. 143–145.
7. Ibid., p. 143.
8. *Chronicle*, October 7, 1959.
9. Report of the British Guiana Constitutional Conference, London, Cmd. 998, p. 4.
10. Ibid., 998, p. 4.

11. Ibid., p. 304.
12. Ibid., p. 15.
13. Ibid., p. 5.
14. Ibid., p. 16.
15. Ibid., p. 15.
16. Ibid., p. 5.
17. Ibid., pp. 6–9.
18. Simms, *Trouble in Guyana*, p. 142.
19. Despres, *Cultural Pluralism and National Politics in British Guiana*, p. 237.
20. Ibid., pp. 237–238.
21. Simms, *Trouble in Guyana*, p. 149.
22. Ibid., p. 149.
23. Ibid., p. 148.
24. Despres, *Cultural Pluralism and National Politics in British Guiana*, pp. 257–258.
25. Ibid., p. 258.
26. Ibid., pp. 257–258.
27. Ibid. p. 259.
28. Ibid., pp. 260–261.
29. Newman, *British Guiana*, p. 39.
30. Despres, *Cultural Pluralism and Nationalist Politics in British Guiana*, pp. 239–240.
31. Ibid., p. 240.
32. Ibid., pp. 243–244.
33. Ibid. p. 244.
34. Ibid., pp. 246–247.
35. Ibid., p. 247.
36. Ibid., p. 248. This information was confirmed in an interview with the former Parliamentary Secretary for Agriculture.
37. Ibid., p. 255.
38. Ibid., pp. 255–256.
39. Simms, *Trouble in Guyana*, p. 151.
40. Ibid., p. 151.
41. Simms, *Trouble in Guyana*, p. 151.
42. See Appendix IV for composition of 1961 legislature.

CHAPTER 7

Disorder and Riots, 1961–1964

New Tactics

NOW that Dr. Jagan was in office with a clear majority, the UF sought very early to try to influence the PPP, but the PPP brushed the UF aside. The PPP had an open pledge of support from the PNC, and since it knew that the PNC could in no way back out of its stated commitment, they had no need for the UF. "The UF discovered that although the PPP had been willing to engage in a little electoral support in the battle against the PNC, they were certainly not in the slightest interested in UF views or opinions.

"This became apparent when the UF tried to discuss the government's taking control of the denominational schools, a number of them Catholic; these were all heavily subsidized by the tax-payer. Nobody in the PPP cared at all about what D'Aguiar of the UF or anyone thought of their actions."[1]

Slowly the UF began to realize that holding the balance of power meant nothing when dealing with the PPP, so that they felt out on both sides, ignored by the PPP and at odds with the PNC.

Their pledge to support the PPP in seeking independence had effectively limited the PNC's options in dealing with the government. Burnham tried criticizing and objecting to PPP policy at every opportunity in an effort to retain the attention of his supporters. One of the first protests undertaken by the PNC was over the allocation of senate seats. According to the constitution, the senate was to have eight seats, three of which were to be given to the opposition. Burnham felt that as the main opposition party the PNC should get the three seats, and was annoyed when Governor Sir Ralph Grey in his discretion gave the

PNC two seats and the UF one. Over this, Burnham launched such a campaign and tirade against the Governor and the UF that for a time it seemed as though opposing them was his main goal, rather than making efforts to rally his supporters. "At a meeting held on the Parade Ground, he attacked the Governor, using uncomplimentary language. His party soon after passed a resolution for the Governor's recall. On the day of the formal opening of the Legislature, Burnham and the other People's National Congress legislators squatted in front of the two gates of the Public Buildings in Brickdam and had to be lifted bodily out of the way before the Governor could make his entry and exit" (WT, 249).

The campaign launched by the PNC, "Grey must go," was somewhat naive to say the least. Apart from the fact that the PNC did feel entitled to the three senate seats, it was known that within the PNC executive, so many people were in competition for the seats that Burnham welcomed not having to nominate anyone. One writer summed up Burnham's political prospects at this time thus:

> In 1953, after the British Guiana Constitution had been suspended, I heard both Mr. Burnham and Dr. Jagan speak at Oxford. Though power and responsibility have brought about certain changes, Dr. Jagan remains what he then was. The same cannot be said of Mr. Burnham. In 1953, he spoke, however uncertainly, like a man with a case. In 1961 I felt he had none.[2]

With the same enthusiasm, the PNC mounted a "Boycott D.I.H." products campaign against the D'Aguiar family firm. The idea is indicative of the then lack of direction of the PNC: D.I.H. products were closely tied to Bank Breweries, Ltd., a public company in which many PNC members had shares. Because of the interlocking management of the Brewery, which was public, and D.I.H., which was private, the campaign met with only marginal success.

The most successful of all their attempts to fill the void and insure publicity was the bringing of several election petitions by the PNC against the PPP. Executive members of PNC admitted that the petitions were brought merely for the publicity. They charged several PPP legislators with election misdemeanors, and resulted in one PPP legislator being unseated. Much more than the results of the trials, the PNC was interested in the spectacle it provided. Two lawyers were brought from Britain at great expense to try the cases, not because they could not find local lawyers of competence or even regional lawyers, but because they wanted to dramatize to their supporters the importance of the cases. In addition the PNC knew that the local judges would have to be more tolerant and more objective with an English lawyer who could take his story to the British press.

While this was going on, Premier Jagan was getting on with the business of government. The election campaign over, a modicum of impartiality returned to both the press and the public toward the government. Dr. Jagan appointed as his Private Secretary and Public Relations Officer Mr. Jack Kelshall. Mr. Kelshall was a Trinidadian lawyer with a good practice, money, and a Marxist philosophy. He had known the Jagans for many years and in coming to Georgetown, he made very considerable personal sacrifices.[3]

Premier Jagan and U.S. Aid—1961

In October 1961, Premier Cheddi Jagan left Guyana on an official visit to the United States and Canada. His intention was to seek aid for the country's development program and sagging economy. Arthur Schlesinger, Jr., recorded Jagan's appearance in Washington and some U.S. reactions:

An election in September 1961 brought the Indian party, the People's Progressive Party, and its leader Dr. Cheddi Jagan into office. Jagan was unquestionably some sort of Marxist. His wife, an American girl whom he had met while studying dentistry in Chicago, had once been a member of the Young Communist League. His party lived by the cliches of an impassioned, quasi-Marxist, anti-colonialist socialism.

Jagan was plainly the most popular leader in British Guiana. The question was whether he was recoverable for democracy. Senator Dodd of Connecticut had pronounced him a communist agent, but then he had said the same thing about Sekou Toure. The British, on the other hand, were not unsympathetic toward Jagan. Though they had earlier imprisoned him more than once, they now claimed it was possible to work with him and that he was more responsible than his rival, the Negro leader, Forbes Burnham. Their view, as communicated at the highest level, was that if Jagan's party were the choice of the people, London and Washington should do their best to keep him on the side of the West by cooperating fully with him and giving his regime economic support. Otherwise he would turn to the communist bloc, which would only guarantee Soviet influence in an independent British Guiana.

This was the situation when Jagan, after his election, expressed a desire to come to Washington and talk about assistance for his development program. At that point the State Department saw no real alternative to the British policy. The aid budget made tentative provision for assistance in the magnitude of $5 million. Then in late October 1961 Jagan arrived. He made his American debut, like so many other visiting statesmen, on Meet the Press, where he resolutely declined to say anything critical of the Soviet Union and left an impression of either wooliness or fellow-traveling. This appearance instantly diminished the enthusiasm for helping his government. The President who caught the last half of the show, called for a re-examination of all aspects of the problem, saying he wanted no commitments made until he had seen Jagan himself.

Jagan talked with the President on the morning of October 25. He turned out to be a personable and fluent East Indian but endowed, it seemed to those of us present, with an unconquerable romanticism or naivete. He began by outlining the economic circumstances of British Guiana and his own development plans. When he explained that, as a socialist, he felt that only state planning could break the bottlenecks, Kennedy said, "I want to make one thing perfectly clear. We are not engaged in a crusade to force private enterprise on parts of the world where it is not relevant. If we are engaged in a crusade for anything, it is national independence. That is the primary purpose of our aid. The secondary purpose is to encourage individual freedom and political freedom. But we cannot always get that; and we have often helped countries which have little personal freedom, like Yugoslavia, if they maintain their national independence. This is the basic thing. So long as you do that, we don't care whether you are socialist, capitalist, pragmatist, or whatever. We regard ourselves as pragmatists." As for nationalization, the President said that we would, of course, expect compensation, but that we had lived with countries like Mexico and Bolivia which had carried out nationalization programs.

He then began to draw out his visitor's political ideas. Recalling Jagan's words of admiration for Harold Laski on Meet the Press, Kennedy observed that he himself had studied for a term under Laski at the London School of Economics and that his older brother had visited the Soviet Union with him. Jagan replied that the first book of Laski's he had read was The American Presidency; he considered himself, he added, a Bevanite. We all responded agreeably to this, citing Bevan's faith in personal freedom and recalling his belief that the struggle of the future would be between democratic socialism and communism.

Jagan, after avowing his commitment to parliamentary government, went on to say that he also admired the Monthly Review and the rather pro-communist writings of Paul Sweezy, and Leo Huberman and Paul Baran. George Ball and I pressed him on this point, declaring there was a large difference between Bevan and the Sweezy group. Jagan finally said, "Well, Bevanism, Sweezyism, Hubermanism, Baranism—I really don't get those ideological subleties." Kennedy observed later that this was the one time when his exposition rang false.

For the rest Jagan spoke as a nationalist committed to parliamentary methods. When Kennedy asked how he conceived his relations with the communist bloc, Jagan inquired whether the United States would regard a trade agreement with the Soviet Union as an unfriendly act. Kennedy responded that a simple trading relationship was one thing; a relationship which brought a country into a condition of economic dependence was another. Ball described the case of Sekou Toure who in order to recover his independence was now disengaging himself from the Soviet embrace.

The President avoided any discussion of aid figures. There were special problems here because Jagan was requesting $40 million—a figure all out of proportion to the size of his country, especially in relation to the competing needs of Latin American nations with much larger populations and closer bonds to the United States. For this and other reasons, it was decided after the meeting that no concrete commitments could be made to Jagan and that each project would have to be examined on its merits. Jagan was considerably upset on learning this and asked to see the President again. Taking advantage of the President's usually free half-hour before luncheon, I reported these developments. Kennedy wholly agreed with the staff's recommendation that he not receive Jagan a second time but instructed me to see him myself in view of the great British concern that Jagan not return disgruntled to British Guiana; perhaps a statement could be worked out which would give Jagan something to take home and satisfy the British without committing us to immediate action. Sitting down at his desk, he dashed off a longhand letter to Jagan, explaining that I came with his confidence, and asked Evelyn Lincoln to type it. When he looked at it again, he decided that it was a little cold, told me to "warm it up" and signed the warmed-up letter. The President went on to express doubt whether Jagan would be able to sustain his position as a parliamentary democrat. "I have a feeling," he said, "that in a couple of years he will find ways to suspend his constitutional provisions and will cut his opposition off at the knees. . . . Parliamentary democracy is going to be damn difficult in a country at this stage of development. With all the political jockeying and all the racial tensions, it's going to be almost impossible for Jagan to concentrate the energies of his country on development through a parliamentary system."

With William Burdett, a careful and intelligent Foreign Service officer, I saw Jagan that afternoon at the Dupont Plaza. He was in a desperate mood at the thought of going home empty-handed but brightened at the prospect of a statement.[4]

The statement was no more than an attempt to placate Dr. Jagan. It read:

> During talks with the President and other United States Government Officials, Dr. Cheddi Jagan, Premier of British Guiana and his colleagues described at length his country's program and aspirations for economic and social development. These talks resulted in a fuller understanding of British Guiana's problems.
>
> United States representatives expressed sympathy with the desire of the people of British Guiana to develop their economy, and looked forward to closer association between a free and democratic British Guiana and the nations and organizations of the Hemisphere. Premier Jagan reiterated his determination to uphold the political freedoms and defend the parliamentary democracy which is his country's fundamental heritage.
>
> In response to Premier Jagan's request for aid the United States undertook to take the following steps:
>
> 1. to provide as early as possible in consultation with the British Guiana Government, and unilaterally or in cooperation with hemisphere organizations, economic and other experts to assist the Government of British Guiana to bring the most modern economic experience to bear upon the reappraisal of the development program;
>
> 2. to provide technical assistance for feasibility, engineering and other studies concerning specific development projects;
>
> 3. to determine as soon as possible after the steps mentioned in paragraphs one and two and on the submission of suitable projects within the context of the British Guiana Development Plan, what assistance the United States can give in financing such projects, taking into account other United States commitments, available financial resources and criteria established by applicable legislation;
>
> 4. to expand its existing technical assistance. (WT, 249-250)

U.S. Interests in Guyana

By 1961, it had become clear to Cuba watchers that Cuba had drifted toward the communist bloc. Though it was the intent of the U.S. at that time to support the African colonies in their independence drive and to assist the Latin American countries economically, it was their "absolute determination to prevent any new state from going down the Castro road and so giving the Soviet Union a second bridgehead in the hemisphere."[5] It was in this context that the U.S. viewed its relations with Guyana in 1961. Though skeptical, the U.S. had had an open view toward Premier Jagan when he arrived in Washington in October 1961. But from the one recorded account, Jagan seemed to have been his own worst enemy. On the other hand, Forbes Burnham seemed to have impressed those officials whom he met on his visit to Washington a few months later. The record is helpful because it gives an important insight into British thinking at the time and American influence on subsequent British policy.

On the question of aid to Guyana, the President and his executives felt that they were damned if they did give Jagan aid and damned if they didn't. Nevertheless, even when they did consider giving help, they thought that the problems this would cause in the Congress would in Schlesinger's words, "injure the whole aid program." Despite these reservations, the President thought very highly of the British recommendations that there was "no alternative" in Guyana. The Americans, however, came to interpret the British view as an attempt by them to get out of Guyana "as quickly as possible," especially in the light of the U.S. policy contradiction of support for early independence for African states. But the official U.S. impression was based mainly on British recommendations and their own domestic constraints; later they got an opportunity to assess opposition leader Forbes Burnham for themselves. Schlesinger continues:

> Thus far our policy had been based on the assumption that Forbes Burnham was, as the British described him, an opportunist, racist and demagogue intent only on personal power. One wondered about this, though, because the AFL-CIO people in British Guiana thought well of him; and Hugh Gaitskell told me that Burnham had impressed him more than Jagan when the two visited Labour party leaders in London. Then in May 1962 Burnham came to Washington. He appeared an intelligent self-possessed, reasonable man, insisting quite firmly on his "socialism" and "neutralism" but stoutly anti-communist. He also seemed well aware that British Guiana had no future at all unless its political leaders tried to temper the racial animosities and unless he in particular gave his party, now predominantly African, a bi-racial flavor. In the meantime, events had convinced us that Jagan, though perhaps not a disciplined communist, had that kind of deep procommunist emotion which only sustained experience with communism could cure; and the United States could not afford the Sekou Toure therapy when it involved a quasi-communist regime on the mainland of Latin America. Burnham's visit left the feeling as I reported to the President, that "an independent

British Guiana under Burnham (if Burnham will commit himself to a multi-racial policy) would cause us many fewer problems than an independent British Guiana under Jagan." And the way was open to bring it about, because Jagan's parliamentary strength was larger than his popular strength: he had won 57 percent of the seats on the basis of 42.7 percent of the vote. An obvious solution would be to establish a system of proportional representatives. This, after prolonged discussion, the British government finally did in October 1963; and elections held finally at the end of 1964 produced a coalition government under Burnham.[6]

Local Reactions

The failure of Premier Jagan to get any aid from the United States after his mission in 1961 ended his honeymoon with the country that followed his election in 1961. The problem of the increase in population was very apparent; unemployment, underemployment, and a steadily rising cost of living were also clear to most people. Some people interpreted Jagan's inability to obtain aid from the U.S. as due to its lack of confidence in him. With the expectation for economic progress rising, people were not about to make any useless sacrifices for the sake of an ideology that they did not necessarily believe in, and that was not contributing to their welfare or the development of the country.

The opposition parties felt this way: "As they looked back on the election they began to wonder whether they had allowed their last chance to pass by them. If the PPP had the patience and skill to sit out the next four years, they were virtually certain, with the rapidly increasing Indian population, to win that election and every election afterwards. The Jagans were building up a reputation for invulnerability: they could take any number of splits, any numer of defections, and still go on to win elections."[7]

Dr. Jagan, in the meantime, saw early independence for Guyana as his only way out of the whole situation. The regional situation made this a very easy proposition, at least so Dr. Jagan thought. The British Government had already set a date for the independence of the West Indies Federation—May 31, 1962. Dr. Jagan probably felt that this being the case, the Guyanese people would support immediate independence so as not to be outdone by their neighbors. In November 1961, the House of Assembly passed a resolution requesting the Secretary of State for the Colonies to fix a date during 1962 for the full

Independence of Guyana within the Commonwealth of Nations. The resolution was passed in the Legislative Assembly by a majority of twenty-six to four, and in the Senate by a majority of nine to one. All the People's Progressive Party and People's National Congress members supported the resolution. Only the one United Force nominated member of the Senate and the four elected members of the Legislative Assembly opposed the motion. Realizing that the PNC had to officially support the parliamentary motions for independence, the UF launched its own campaign. Its slogan was "no independence under Jagan."

The UF's opposition to independence under Dr. Jagan was not taken seriously for sometime. After all, the performance of the UF at the election, though impressive, was not so impressive as to make them opinion leaders on such an important subject. Furthermore, the nature of support the UF represented would not have been satisfied with independence under either the PPP or the PNC.

The UF, however, was busy behind the scenes. They began to import an array of anticommunist propaganda from anticommunist organizations in the United States. These they distributed up and down the country, especially in the urban areas. They then sent a few of their cadre to the U.S. for anticommunist training and became heavily involved with the Christian Anti-Communist Crusade of the United States. The UF's anticommunist campaign was not only intensive but thorough.

In the meantime Dr. Jagan approached the British Government about independence for Guyana on the basis of the tacit British promise at the Constitutional Conference in 1960, and on the basis of the motion in the Guyana legislature in November 1961. He was brushed aside by the colonial secretary when he asked the secretary to either set a date for independence or call for a conference to discuss the granting of independence. Suspecting that the British government was probably coming more under U.S. State Department influence, Dr. Jagan decided to take his case to a more public and international forum—the United Nations.

At the UN

Premier Jagan, while still in London, dashed off a cable to the Chairman of the Fourth Committee of the United Nations, "Requesting permission to address Fourth Committee, 18 December on British Guiana Independence."⁸ The United Kingdom delegate was a little surprised at the urgency of the request. At first he suggested that the request be put off for consideration at the following meeting until Dr. Jagan was contacted, "in order to ascertain the exact purpose of the request."⁹ The delegates of India and Guinea saw no reason why a decision should not have been made then, since the request had been made to the committee itself. Realizing that the general opinion of the Committee was to allow Dr. Jagan to address the Committee, the British delegate then suggested that "the Premier of British Guiana would perhaps wish to make his statement under the aegis of the United Kingdom delegation, in which case the latter would like to be informed in advance. If the Committee was going to grant the Premier a hearing as a petitioner, that would raise a question of principle for the United Kingdom delegation, which would be obliged to register a formal objection."¹⁰ With U.K. acquiescence, it was decided "in principle" to hear Dr. Jagan on the date requested.

Jagan arrived and addressed the meeting on December 18, 1961. Prior to Dr. Jagan's speech, the Committee wrangled over his status before the committee. Dr. Jagan had decided that he wanted to be heard by the Committee as a "petitioner." In the interim the British had been pursuing its own strategy: "The British delegation, realizing that its attempts to stop me from being heard had been unsuccessful, then tried another maneuver. It suggested to me that I should address the Committee from its chair. I refused, pointing out that it would be improper for me to speak from the British Chair when I had intended to attack the British Government" (WT, 251–252). The British delegation, along with the French and U.S. delegates, raised some procedural objections about having a petitioner speak before the committee. Nevertheless, Dr. Jagan insisted on being heard as such. A vote was taken and the motion to have him speak as a petitioner was carried 33 to 21 with 21 abstentions.

Dr. Jagan first outlined his conflicts with the Colonial Office from 1953. He then outlined his more recent experience with the Colonial Office, which took place despite the fact that even the main opposition was willing to support independence. He said "On 13 December 1961 he had spoken to Mr. Maudling, Secretary of State for the Colonies, who had categorically refused to fix 31 May 1962 or any other date for British Guiana's independence. The date of 31 May 1962, which was the date fixed for the independence of the Federation of the West Indies, had been proposed during the election campaign by the main opposition party: the People's National Congress had polled 83 percent of the votes. Mr. Maudling had even refused to fix a date for a Conference to discuss the question of independence; he had simply promised to consult the cabinet and to inform him of the decision early in 1962. Experience had taught him not to place much faith in such promises and he saw in Mr. Maudling's delaying tactics a threat to peace and a threat to his people's belief in the parliamentary system of Government, since an honestly elected Government would be prevented by some extraterritorial power from carrying out its promise."[11] Dr. Jagan then went on to give the Committee a view of Guyana's economy and its ability to sustain itself as an independent nation. He saw independence for Guyana as "the right of peoples and nations to self determination and independence (which is) inalienable and must be enjoyed by all. Only independence could give a country the necessary dynamism for rapid economic development."[12] The Premier compared Guyana's struggle for freedom and development to that of Ghana, India and Israel.[13]

A resolution sponsored by a number of Third World countries asking the "two governments concerned to resume negotiations immediately"[14] was put off for consideration after the Christmas recess. But the British Government stalled the Committee's action when, on January 14, 1962, it announced its decision to hold a conference in May 1962. No doubt Dr. Jagan's appearance before the Committee played some part in embarrassing the British Government into action. More importantly, however, was that each side got an insight into the change of tactics by the other. And with the UF leading, domestic pressure was also being built up against the PPP Government.

The 1962 Budget: Riots

By 1962, Guyana's treasury was nearly empty. Premier Jagan had failed in his attempt to get additional aid from either the USA or Britain; because of the need to save money, temporary workers in government departments were retrenched by the hundreds to join the ranks of the unemployed, especially workers from the service ministries. Many skilled Guyanese, frightened by the United Force's anti-communist propaganda and the country's racial tension, migrated to the United Kingdom, to North America, and to other parts of the Caribbean. The cost of living was up 10 percent which in turn fueled widespread demands for higher salaries.

Naturally, the first people to feel the pinch of rising prices were those who lived in the urban areas, and who generally supported the two main opposition parties. In an attempt to meet these demands, the Jagan government introduced on January 31, 1962, an austerity budget prepared by Nicholas Kaldor, a Professor of Economics at Cambridge University. Dr. Jagan explained the need for the budget: "Soon after our assumption of office in September, 1961, we were faced with a grave financial crisis. A huge deficit was anticipated in the 1962 recurrent budget. This was principally due to a large amount which was payable to civil servants, teachers and policemen in fulfillment of the recommendations of the Guilleband Salaries Commission. Payments were to be made for the increases in salaries not only for 1962 but also for 1961. These alone totalled nearly $4,000,000; and there were other incidental increases. There was also the problem of rising budgetary surpluses at home to finance a bigger capital development programme, particularly industrialization, for the solution of the ever-pressing urban unemployment" (WT, 252).

More precisely "the finance Minister was faced with the immediate need for $15 million for certain extraordinary expenses and to meet increases in the cost of certain service. The government had agreed to increase the salaries of civil servants and for this purpose an additional sum of $3.5 million was required. The Government also needed $2.5 million for the repayment of certain loans, and $1.5 million for extra expenditure on sea defences, the maintenance of roads and improvements of the aerodrome which was long overdue."[15]

Basically the budget was sound. It was realistic in terms of what both the government and the people hoped to see in the way of development in the country. The Minister of Finance proposed some new taxes, "the burden of which was to fall on the higher income groups only. He proposed a capital gains tax, an annual tax on property and a tax on gifts. In addition to these, he proposed certain measures for preventing the evasion and avoidance of taxes. He also proposed a new mode of assessing the minimum measure of income tax in respect to commercial transactions. He proposed that the minimum income of a businessman should be deemed to be 2 percent of his annual turnover irrespective of whether his business had shown a profit or a loss, but wherever there was a loss it was to be set off against profits in the subsequent years. Obviously, this measure was aimed at dishonest businessmen who reported a loss year after year although their business continued to flourish. Another unusual provision in the bill was a reduction of the advertising allowance to one-quarter of one percent of the total turnover. This was intended to prevent unnecessary waste on prestige advertising and the consequent reduction in the income tax payable. In order to increase the flow of resources for development purposes a scheme of compulsory savings was also to be introduced. This scheme contemplated a deduction at source equivalent to a contribution of 5 percent of wage and salary income in excess of $100 a month and 10 percent of other income in lieu of Government bonds redeemable after a period of seven years.

"These measures were not calculated to yield the full additional amount of $15 million required; the balance had still to be raised. The Minister of Finance therefore proposed an increase in the import duty on certain goods which he considered were not necessities of life. . . . He pointed out that these duties and taxes would not impose any hardship on the people of the lower income groups and that the increase in the urban consumer price index would be only one percent."[16] Immediately upon the first reading of the budget, the press came out vehemently against it, and the inflammatory articles helped generate much anxiety among an already restless anti-government urban population. The *Graphic* headline of January 31 described it as a "Budget of Tears." The *Chronicle* headline of February 1 proclaimed: "Government to Squeeze Dollars from Workers." Subsequent headlines announced: "Tax Avalanche Will Crush Working Class," "Slave-whip Budget," "Budget Exposes New Dangers Under Jagan."[17]

The restlessness of the population was so obvious that as early as January 14, the editor of the Sunday *Graphic* had predicted that there would be demonstrations during the three-day visit by the Duke of Edinburgh to be held in February. This is not to say that Dr. Jagan and the PPP government did not recognize the potential for civil disturbance, but they could do nothing to take advantage of the situation. To make matters worse, on the very day the budget was read in the Legislature, shopkeepers throughout the city raised their prices to cover the new taxes, and in many cases raised them far beyond the stipulated limits. Ironically, these shopkeepers seemed mainly to be recent Indian migrants to the city who were eager to make a quick dollar and who would have tended to support the PPP. However, with so many repressed grievances, the opposition groups were waiting for an excuse to confront the government.

There was a general feeling of apprehension about the Premier; when he was unable to obtain aid for development, panic resulted in both the business sector and among the people. So that on February 6, the Chamber of Commerce came out publicly against the budget. The Government's attempts to check the trend produced a more widespread feeling of helplessness among the people. The Commission, which visited the country subsequently, summed up the situation:

> The internal resources of the country were extremely small and wholly inadequate to meet the increasing needs of the development programmes. Foreign aid . . . was not forthcoming. The growing suspicion that Dr. Jagan's failure to arouse international sympathy was due to his communist leanings made the commercial classes of British Guiana apprehensive of the country's future and of their own prospects. They began to look elsewhere for opportunities to set up and expand their businesses. Thus, a flight of capital from British Guiana started. At first, this was gradual, but soon more and more financiers were transferring their money and assets to other countries. Dr. Jagan, in the course of his statement before us, could not give the exact figure of the assets which were removed from the country. He was himself not in British Guiana at the time, but he was informed that the flight of capital was substantial and his Government was faced with the prospect of a country depleted of its present resources and unable either to replenish its losses or to restore its economy by external aid.
>
> So in December 1961, the Government introduced stringent currency restrictions, prohibiting the export of liquid assets from the country. British Guiana forms part of the sterling area and is also a member of the Eastern Caribbean Currency Board. The Currency is therefore a regional one and up to December, 1961, the holders of Eastern Caribbean dollars in British Guiana could only change them into foreign currencies in accordance with the exchange control regulations then in force in the Colony. The new regulations suspended their convertibility into sterling. Financial restrictions have been imposed and do indeed exist 'in many other countries, and have come to be accepted as a necessary feature of the present-day complexity of international economics. Nevertheless, the action of Dr. Jagan's Government in suspending convertibility into sterling without, it may be added, prior consultation with the Eastern Caribbean Currency Board, gave rise to considerable alarm and resentment.[18]

Not only did the Eastern Caribbean governments and local businessmen resent these new measures but all those who hoped to travel abroad saw them as curtailing their flexibility.

The first visible signs of organized mass opposition to the People's Progressive Party Government took place on Wednesday, February 7, 1962. The Duke of Edinburgh, who began a state visit to Guyana on that day, was met at the airport by Dr. Jagan and members of his Cabinet. As the procession approached Georgetown, it was greeted by a hostile crowd whose placards read: "Resign Now"; "Jack (Kelshall) go back"; "Anti-working class budget."[19] Hundreds of placards had been painted by the United Force and were handed out wherever crowds had gathered to welcome the Duke, and as the PPP ministers drove past the crowds, they were heckled and abused.

On Friday, February 9, the meeting of the legislature commenced with an announcement by the Minister of Finance that "in order that the government may give careful consideration to all of the representations received, it is proposed to defer consideration of the Second Reading of the Appropriation Bill to a date to be announced. Discussion will be held immediately with all persons and organizations so that the Budget may be debated in the House without undue delay."[20] The government had decided on this tactic to try to take the steam out of the opposition. But those opposition forces responsible for inciting the people could not be appeased. They were not willing to settle for anything less than total embarrassment of the government, or in a few cases, a total collapse of the government.

Then Premier Jagan made a motion for the establishment of a committee to consider a draft constitution that the People's National Congress leader Mr. Burnham, greeted as a matter of great importance, describing it as "the cornerstone of the constitutional edifice which we hope to erect for an independent Guyana."[21] He announced that the People's National Congress had already fixed May 31, 1962, as Independence Day, but Burnham then accused the government of representing only a minority and of preparing the Constitution without consulting the opposition. He quoted the Attorney General, Dr. Fenton Ranshoye, as saying at a public meeting: "Even if I die tonight, the draft constitution prepared by me as British Guiana's first political Attorney General, is the constitution that will definitely rule this country. It is the only constitution you will have—the only constitution Maudling (Colonial Secretary) will give you, whether you wish to accept or not." "How," Burnham asked, "could the Parliament ratify

Jagan's motion under such circumstances?"[22] Burnham's tactic of refusing to support the PPP on the issue of independence because he was not consulted on the draft constitution was a clever way of extracting himself from his earlier promise, while at the same time not appearing to change his position.

After Burnham had spoken, he and the other PNC Parliamentarians left. That session of the Legislature had already begun in an uproar. Earlier on, about four hundred people had crowded in to find seats in the public gallery, which normally seated only one hundred and eighteen people. Those who could not find seats had remained standing outside throughout the session. All departed noisily with Burnham and the rest of the PNC parliamentary group.[23] The PNC legislators were greeted by a large group of supporters assembled outside as they emerged from the House. Peter D'Aguiar also spoke opposing the motion and left immediately after. Once outside, he was also cheered by PNC supporters. Of this event, the subsequent investigating commission wrote: "The simultaneous emptying of the seats occupied by a major section of the opposition and public must have given the appearance of a pre-planned and somewhat histrionic demonstration designed to shock and humiliate the government. . . . This reduced the proceedings in the Chamber to the force of a unilateral debate solely conducted by the party in power."[24]

So, to the empty opposition benches, Dr. Jagan made a statement on the domestic situation:

> It has come to the knowledge of the Government that violence is actually being planned on a general scale by certain elements acting for a minority group. In addition, it is understood that attempts against the Premier's life and the lives of certain of his Ministers and supporters are contemplated.
>
> These acts of violence are intended to secure the overthrow of the legally elected Government by force and the tax proposals in the budget are being used as a screen for the general strike for Monday, February 12. Since there is no likelihood of this strike call being widely supported by the workers, certain elements of the business community plan to shut down their business houses. The intention is in effect to stage a general lockout on the excuse that the strike has created conditions which prevent continued business operations. Every step possible is being taken to bring the Civil Service in on this strike and if these designs are successful, the total result will be to cause widespread dislocation of the colony's economy.
>
> Such a course of action will be very likely to end in riot and violence.

The people who plan this operation must be aware of this. It seems that they are seeking to cause turmoil and unrest in order to halt our march to independence and economic well-being for all. This small clique is determined to preserve their positions of privilege. They want to create another Congo here. They talk about freedom and democracy but are determined to use unconstitutional means to achieve these ends. They feel that they can depend on foreign support.

In the circumstances, the government intends to take energetic steps to forestall this plan and I am now appealing to all reasonable public-minded citizens not to allow themselves to be persuaded or fooled into taking part in what can only be a disastrous and futile effort on the part of a small misguided and selfish element in the community to turn back the clock of history. (WT, 258)

After making the statement Premier Jagan withdrew the motion he had proposed earlier, "since it was clear that the opposition did not intend to cooperate" (WT, 258).

As Dr. Jagan and members of his cabinet attempted to leave the Parliament building, they were booed and picketed. If Jagan knew of a plot to overthrow the government as he claimed, why did he not issue an order for the plotters to be arrested? The simple answer is, he just did not have the power. Furthermore, he could not, even if he had the power, without provoking a crisis beyond his control. The opposition politicians knew of Dr. Jagan's predicament, and were prepared from then on to systematically undermine the government for their own political advantage.

The opposition parties, especially the PNC, felt that they had to make a stand after the Attorney General's statement referring to his draft constitution. The PNC felt that after it had publicly committed itself to independence, there was no need for the PPP to weaken it publicly. The Attorney General's statement at a public meeting in a PNC stronghold was totally uncalled for, but was typical of the uncompromising arrogance of the PPP in dealing with others. The PPP then lost the support of the PNC on the independence issue, though it is probably doubtful whether the PNC ever really meant to support the PPP in its independence bid at all.

Dr. Jagan's fear of violence and civil disorder was well founded. What took place the following week fulfilled his predictions. The Trade Union Council had already made a decision to go on strike. However, "the strike action was scheduled to take place at a time when it would be most effective."[25] This decision to strike by the TUC must be seen in two ways. There were those in the TUC who had always maintained that trade unionism and politics do not mix, and there were those who maintained that it did. The decision to strike was agreed to by all, but for different reasons. The pure trade-unionists felt that the government had delayed the salary increases of government workers for too long, while not giving any reasonable explanation or acting in a way to gain the sympathy of its workers. As far as they were concerned, it was a straight industrial dispute, which was being reinforced by a strike. For the others, it was a political decision. It was either an opportunity to embarrass the government or an attempt to gain more political leverage with the government.

Week of Demonstrations: Riots

On Sunday, February 11, the Civil Service Association and the Government Workers Unions summoned their members and held a march to demonstrate in favor of the salary increases they were to have received. (This dispute will be examined further in another section.)

The general knowledge among the politicians that the TUC was set to call a strike caused some problems and confusion since each party hoped to give the strike some direction in the hope of increasing their own political strength. This was true especially within the United Force. At first, the TUC was said to have decided to call the strike for Monday, the 12th. In the meantime, on the evening of Sunday, the 11th, the UF held a meeting at Bourda Green, and the word went around calling for the cooperation of the business sector to coordinate a strike as well. It was felt that this, with a general TUC strike including the government sectors, would paralyze the Government.

Not knowing that the TUC had not given the final go-ahead on the strike, the UF swung into action in the commercial area on Monday, the 12th. "Early in the morning. . . . it was noticed that small groups of shopworkers of Water Street were collecting at various points. The employees of Messrs. Fogarty were prominent among them. Some of them were carrying placards. There was a certain amount of confusion at the other stores. At J. P. Santos the workers were inside the store, but they were not attending to their business. The workers of Bettencourt had been locked out."[26] UF Senator, Miss Anne Jardim, tried to bring the workers together for an effective demonstration, but only succeeded in marshalling a small group who marched up and down the streets demonstrating:

Groups of men had also collected and begun to agitate in other parts of the town. Small and unorganized processions were moving from one street to another and intimidating shopworkers to come out and join them. There were, however, very few defections from work and most of the shops and stores carried on in their normal manner.[27]

When UF leader Peter D'Aguiar arrived at his office opposite the Public Building at midmorning, he was met by a group of unorganized people. He spoke to the gathering, then led a procession through the streets of Georgetown, "passing deliberately in front of Mr. Kelshall's house and then past the Premier's house." The march ended at the Parade Ground where members of the UF addressed the gathering. While the meeting was in progress, "someone from the crowd shouted 'Radio Moscow.' This was rightly interpreted to mean 'Radio Demerara' against which frequent complaints appear to have been made on account of Dr. Jagan's Marxist views having been propagated through its machinery."[28] For some time the opposition political parties had been asking that they should be given access to this media to make their views on several issues, including the budget, known, but they were refused. However, Dr. Jagan, as Premier, could and did use the radio on several occasions to communicate the government's views to the people on the same issues; this the opposition resented. On his way to the radio station at the head of the demonstration, Mr. D'Aguiar was stopped by the police who observed that D'Aguiar had no permission to lead a demonstration. D'Aguiar's excuse was that it was a spontaneous procession and, thus, was not illegal. Realizing the tenseness of the situation, the police did not arrest anyone. After demonstrating in front of Radio Demerara, the crowd was led back to Mr. D'Aguiar's office where he again addressed them.

The next day, Tuesday the 13th, there was much excitement throughout the city in anticipation of the TUC's announcement of a general strike. "The majority of shop employees absented themselves from work in anticipation of the strike. There were several instances of groups of strikers calling upon the businessmen to close their premises and let the employees join the strikers. The demonstration in the afternoon was a very large one and was entirely successful from the point of views of the strikers and agitators."[29]

The Civil Service Association gave the government notice that it would go on strike at 1:00 p.m. on that day. The demonstration was organized by the TUC to express support for the Civil Servants and to explain to their members the objections they intended to lay before the

Minister of Finance with regard to the Government's Budget proposals. While the demonstration was in progress, a messenger brought
word that the Premier had gone on the air and had threatened to
dismiss any Civil Servant who absented himself from his post.

After receiving the news that the government workers would be
fired for going on strike, the union bosses decided that the time was
ripe to implement their previous decision to call a general strike. In
turn, each union leader mounted the rostrum and called for his union
to go on strike. "The enthusiasm of the crowd had risen to a pitch of
frenzy and the declaration of a strike by the various union leaders
appears to have given complete satisfaction to everyone. A sense of
triumph prevailed after the announcement had been made."[30] There
can be no doubt that the crowds, throughout the weeks of agitation,
wanted some action, much more than most leaders were willing to take
responsibility for. It could be argued that the people were to some
extent programmed to respond this way. The politicians in the preceding weeks had had large audiences, not because they had anything to
say but because politics was the only attraction in town; through
rumor, they had led the people to believe that they were about to take
some action against the government.

In checking on the facts after they had called the General Strike, the
trade union leaders were confronted with a series of half truths. No one
could be found who had actually heard Dr. Jagan make the remarks
that striking government servants would be fired, attributed to him,
and in the end the union bosses were given clear proof that Dr. Jagan
was completely innocent of the accusations. The leaders were remorse-
ful but the deed was already done.[31]

The government, at the Commission of Inquiry, suggested that "the
broadcast may have been made by a private radio which was later
discovered," and was willing to accept the incident as a misunderstand-
ing.[32] Even though this was so, it could be assumed that the trade
union leaders, subject to the pressures of politicization over a protracted period of time, and due to the frustrations of dealing with a
government that seemed to require sympathy without showing any,
were caught up in the general euphoria of trying to have the government recognize their strength as representatives of a certain interest
group. They knew a general strike would harm the country but felt it
would reassert their position with a seemingly unresponsive government.

On Wednesday, February 14, the strike had its full and serious effects as some of the essential services began to be affected. At the Georgetown hospital all personnel remained on their jobs on Monday and Tuesday; "on Wednesday, however, only 89 out of 181 nurses reported in the morning and out of 36 orderlies only 8 reported."[33] At the Waterworks and the Electricity Corporation a skeleton staff was left on duty. The other essential services, however, were not affected.

The Governor, by proclamation, declared the area around the Public Buildings (the Legislative Council, the Treasury, and the Premier's office) a restricted area. The obvious reason for doing so was that it was a focal point of attention for many demonstrations, but it was always chosen as a point of protest because that was where most of the important decisions were made.

On Wednesday, "Mr. D'Aguiar told his supporters that there would be a surprise in store for them and that they should be available in the afternoon. Mr. D'Aguiar, who had a special predilection for the spectacular and the flamboyant, had arranged a parade of his trucks bearing slogans through the streets of Georgetown. The parade did take place and we have no doubt that the population was duly impressed."[34]

In the morning the TUC, which included Civil Service Association representatives, had the meeting that had been scheduled days before with the Minister of Finance. The meeting was arranged for the Minister to hear the TUC's objections to the budget and the grievances of the Civil Servants and government employees. "Mr. Chase, one of the representatives at the meeting (pointed out the impropriety of the decision to go on strike before discussions) and Mr. Stoll came to the rescue by saying that even though there was no threat to dismiss civil servants, the strike had in fact been declared and should continue because it was in the fitness of things that the Civil Service Association and the Trade Unions make common cause against their common adversary." The Commission thought this action by the trade unions "amounted to a breach of faith and a display of irresponsibility to bang the door of negotiations, as it were, in the very face of the Minister and declare a general strike."[35] While this was true, it was also true that experience had taught the unions that the government had sometimes acted irresponsibly or inconsiderately. The unions felt that the only way of dealing with the government was from a position of absolute power.

"Agitation had continued to increase and a large number of the shop

employees were on strike . . . There was a partial closure of the
electricity plant and a temporary cessation of the water supply."[36] That
evening Premier Jagan went on the radio to announce some
modifications in the budget: "Because the PNC claimed that it was
opposed only to the indirect taxes, we decided to withdraw tax increases on all imported commodities except motor cars, spirits, tobacco, coffee extracts and concentrates. I also declared that the lower
limit of the compulsory savings scheme would be fixed at $3,600 per
annum instead of $1,200 per annum. This was agreed to after discus-
sions with the TUC. It was my hope in taking these decisions to satisfy
the PNC and TUC and thus split them from the extreme right UF.
Unfortunately my hope was in vain" (WT, 261–262). The Premier
hoped that a modification in the budget proposals would bring an end
to the strike, but this did not happen. The trade unionists and the
politicians knew that the government was at its weakest and were
prepared to keep it there in order to force their demands on it.

On Thursday, February 15, 1962, the strike continued. "The strike
on this day was almost complete and business in Georgetown had come
to a complete standstill. Messrs. Bookers had announced their decision
that employees absenting themselves from work would not be paid
their wages with effect from Thursday morning. There was a number of
employees who did not attend."[37]

Until this day the PNC's official role had been limited to political
meetings; the agitation and political confrontations were mainly under
the direction of the UF and the TUC. On February 15, Burnham, at
the head of a large crowd, defied the proclamation and led a group of
demonstrators to the Public Buildings. D'Aguiar then arrived and was
asked to join Burnham at the head of the march, and this he did. The
two leaders, leading a large crowd, then marched around the Public
Buildings three times in order to show their disregard for the proclamation (WT, 262). They then led the march away to the headquarters
of the PNC where Peter D'Aguiar was asked to take out membership
by paying the usual fee. He paid but did not accept the party's card.
The two leaders shook hands and departed, but according to one PNC
executive member,[38] it had been hoped that making D'Aguiar a member would have been the first step toward a merger of the two parties.
Unfortunately for them, D'Aguiar wasn't taking his membership seriously.

Both the TUC and the PNC had applied for permission to hold a

public meeting that evening. The police granted permission to the
TUC to hold a meeting from 6:00 p.m. to 10:00 p.m., but refused the
PNC's application. However, the TUC arranged with the PNC that it
could use two hours—8:00 p.m. to 10:00 p.m.—as the TUC did not
anticipate needing all of the time provided. For this concession the
PNC agreed to lend the TUC its public address system. At the TUC
meeting, the President of the TUC, Mr. Ishmael, announced that a
PNC meeting would follow. This was a questionable act for a TUC
president who was supposed to be concerned with industrial disputes.
At the meeting Burnham addressed the crowd:

> He began by congratulating his listeners on the splendid performance
> of the morning when there had been a wholesale breach of the proclama-
> tion. Exhilarated and carried forward by the flow of his rhetoric, he
> criticized the unsympathetic attitude of the Volunteer Force and of the
> police. In his peroration he declared that a government could not be got
> rid of by merely saying "Resign" or "Down with Jagan." "Those are
> useful and helpful slogans, but much more than slogans are required in
> the present circumstances. Comrades, first of all, let me say this, that
> the People's National Congress sees the way clearly, step by step and
> phase by phase. All I can tell you is this, that it is no sense taking part in
> this explosion which has happened at this moment if you are going to
> peter out or turn back half-way. You have to see it through . . . I believe
> that the PNC knows what we all want and knows how we will seek to
> achieve what we all want; but one thing I know you do not want, one
> thing I know the PNC will not countenance, and that is violence. Com-
> rades, violence we shall never start because we are a peaceful people. If
> there is to be violence, let others start it, not the People's National
> Congress; but comrades, they shall not pass." After this, Mr. Burnham
> advised his audience to take a rest on the following day, but he had by
> now worked them up into such a state of frenzy that they declared their
> firm determination to continue the agitation in the morning. There was
> an ominous foreboding in the promise which Mr. Burnham made in
> reply to the reaction of the audience to his exhortation for rest.

> "I have heard what you have had to say, and I have noted very carefully
> what you prefer and want, and therefore, Comrades, you will be in-
> formed what exercises may be necessary tomorrow. Comrades, you will
> be informed I do not want to make any suggestions here tonight what
> that exercise should be. You will be informed through the usual channel
> which has proved effective in spite of the fact that our comrades, the
> Post Office workers, are on strike, and tomorrow we shall meet again
> some place, somewhere, somehow."[39]

Mr. Burnham's speech illustrates the extent to which the opposition

was prepared to go in its protest. It also marked a change of tactics by
the PNC in its role as opposition. By then they wanted nothing short of
the downfall of the PPP government. Because of its lack of tactics the
PNC was by then maneuvered into a situation which was largely dictated by the United Force. Originally it was the declared intention of
the United Force to "oppose, expose and depose the government." But
events after the presentation of the budget, especially in the month of
February, had made the PNC part of the same movement. As we have
seen before this, the PNC was continually struggling for its political life
against the dominance of the PPP and later became involved in a
serious battle over political support with the UF. In February 1962,
however, Burnham said, "the PNC sees the way clearly, step by step
and phase by phase." His esoteric communications suggested that the
PNC had developed a number of signals all their own. This enabled the
followers to understand its leader without being understood by members of other groups.[40] For instance, Burnham's play on his party's
rejection of violence was ended with "but comrades they shall not
pass." This phrase was perfectly familiar to most PNC followers: With
the growing unrest in the city and its threat to the stability of the
government, there had been a rumor that Dr. Jagan intended to bring
a number of supporters from the rural areas to support and protect
their party and the government.[41] The PNC had heard the rumor and
vowed that such an excursion would not pass two noted PNC strongholds on the East Coast. They were prepared to stop them, hence
Burnham's remark.

Black Friday

Black Friday got its name because historically most of Guyana's
tragedies, especially large fires, have occurred on Fridays. Friday,
February 16, 1962, was the most memorable Friday in recent times.
Crowds were active at an early hour. The store clerks gathered outside
their stores at 7:30 a.m. Senator Ann Jardim exhorted the workers to
form a procession and march to the Parade Ground. In the meantime,
further down Water Street, another crowd had gathered outside the
Electricity Corporation's power house. The plant, at that time operating with a skeleton staff, was being guarded by two members of the
volunteer force. It was singled out because it was the only essential
service not to have completely shut down its service, even for a few

hours. When the police arrived at 8:55 a.m., a crowd of about 400 people was shouting, demanding that the scabs come out and that the plant be closed.[42] The appearance of reinforcements made the crowd angrier, so that appeals from the police fell on deaf ears. Eventually the police succeeded in placating the crowd; after a while, most of them left.

At the Parade Ground a meeting was held for those who had gone there. Among the speakers were Ann Jardim and Peter D'Aguiar.[43] As the meeting ended someone announced that there were "scabs" working at the Electricity Corporation's Power House, and that voluntary pickets were needed there. Soon a crowd gathered there and began throwing bottles and stones at the windows. The riot squad was sent for. One policeman assessed the crowd at about 1000 persons but it soon afterwards swelled to about 3000. The officer in charge asked the crowd to disperse, warning that tear smoke would be used if they did not. "No, no, use, use, smoke," some members of the crowd retorted. As the tear smoke was fired, the crowd ran into nearby alleys and yards, only to emerge shortly after, once again hailing stones at the windows of the Power House. From a house nearby a woman emerged carrying a small child in her arms. The child, suffering from gas inhalation, appeared lifeless. The crowd began to chant, "They killed a child, they killed a child." Though the child had only been slightly affected by the fumes, news of the child's death travelled through the city quickly. At another meeting, this one outside his office, Mr. D'Aguiar again spoke to another crowd.

Another crowd had gathered at the Parade Ground sometime later when a police van passed by; the crowd stoned the van; the police responded with a tear smoke grenade. The crowd converged on Freedom House, the PPP Headquarters. When the police arrived they found that the angry crowd had thrown stones and other missiles at the building. With the rumor of the child having been killed fresh in their minds, the crowds showed greater opposition to the police. Missiles were thrown at the officers and tear gas shells were of no avail. The crowd responded, "We are going to murder you, we are going to eat you, we are not going to disperse."[44] Suddenly someone fired a shot and Superintendent McLeod was hit. The police returned fire. Soon a full battle ensued. In all, six police officers, including McLeod who later died, were wounded on the spot.

The disturbances then extended to several parts of the city. Fires were set to business places, and wholesale looting of shops started. The fire service as it responded was faced with burning electric poles, live electric wires, and no water in the mains. In addition, there was considerable interference from the crowd who hindered the firemen as they attempted to work. This, coupled with the fact that Georgetown is a city with most of its buildings of wood, caused extensive damage.[45]

In the end, the disorder was put down by the regular forces assisted by the British Army. At the end of the day, 56 stores were destroyed by fire and 87 were damaged, of which 66 were also looted. The total loss has been assessed at $11,405,236.

One policeman was shot and killed by the rioters and 39 more were injured. Of the rioters and looters, 4 men lost their lives as a result of shooting, and 41 were injured.[46] During the riots, the Governor called both opposition leaders and appealed to them to use their influence to advise the crowds "to desist from acts of violence," but neither Mr. Burnham nor Mr. D'Aguiar responded. "The Governor asked the PNC leader to employ his loud-speaker system and ask the crowds to leave the streets. Mr. Burnham, however, replied that he would consult his executive. Strangely enough, the executive could not see his way to accede to the Governor's request. In his statement before the Commission investigating the riots, Mr. Burnham explained his actions this way:

> We could not help. There were two main obstacles, one was that we were very short of petrol and we felt that if we went all around Georgetown using up this petrol at the Governor's request, we would have no petrol for the vehicles to carry out Party work. We also considered it ill-advised to go and tell people to desist from what they were doing when we had nothing to do with the start up of it. The man who calls off the dog owns the dog.[47]

The Commission summed up its attitude to Mr. Burnham's statement thus: "This callous and remorseless attitude is reminiscent of Marc Anthony's observation, 'Mischief thou art afoot. Take thou what course thou wilt.'"

As regards Mr. D'Aguiar, the commission said all he could think of was to ask the Governor to give protection to his wife and family. He telephoned the Governor and said that he could not see his way to make an appeal for peace to the riotous crowds of Georgetown.[48]

Analysis of the Riots and Party Involvement

Of the riot itself, the Commission concluded: "We find no substance whatever in the contention made on behalf of the government that the disturbances of Black Friday were the culmination of a deliberate plan to overthrow the Government by the use of force."[49] Indeed, it seems the real reason for the riots and tensions prior to the riots was an attempt by the opposition parties and the unions to try to influence the PPP to consult them in making major decisions. The statement attributed to the Attorney General and quoted by Mr. Burnham is one example of this. In addition, the government was unable to deal with the more fundamental problems of unemployment and underemployment. Each time the Premier failed to receive aid while on one of his missions, his ideology came under more and more criticism within the country. Although the PPP was criticized by both the urban middle-class and an elite, conscious of its growing role as a stabilizing force within the society, they were gaining more influence among the Indian groups who saw them more as their hope and escape from economic backwardness and construed the ideological criticisms as racial attacks on "a we boy," our leader, Dr. Jagan.

Dr. Jagan and the opposition parties recognized the forces at work and did wrestle with them for a time, but in the end they were all overtaken by events. For instance, Dr. Jagan realized the repercussions that would follow his receiving no aid from the U.S., hence his anxiety even for a statement of intent by the U.S. government. However, by this time the grievances of the government workers, the civil servants, and the rise in the cost of living, coupled with the PPP policies that did nothing for the urban masses, did not make for a spirit of compromise and sympathy on either side.

At the same time the PNC did not take action against the government until they saw that action was being undertaken by the UF and that they stood to be left out. Again, it would seem that PNC fear of total UF control of a protest movement was uppermost in spurring the PNC to action. The predicament of the PNC leadership is best told by Mrs. Jagan, General Secretary of the PPP in her analysis of the events:

> (They were) pulled along with the hysteria which was building up in Georgetown, and still feeling a sense of injustice over their loss at the polls. Many of Burnham's supporters joined with the D'Aguiar demon-

strations in their search for any positive action against the PPP, Mr. Burnham found himself in the awkward position of not being part of the United Force demonstrations against the government, but with a large section of his following participating. He was therefore forced to declare his position. He could not risk ordering his members to pull out, as they had become, by then, emotionally part of the anti-PPP hysteria in the city. Even though his party had been in pitched battle with the United Force in contesting the city seats, he was now obliged to join hands with D'Aguiar in efforts to bring down the government.[50]

The Commission summed up its investigation of the riots in this way:

> A careful reading of the evidence . . . shows that although there was a certain element of racial consciousness which promoted the tension among the different political parties, the disturbances were not racial riots in the sense that members of one race strove to do injury to the personal property of the members of the other race. The real origin of the riots lay in political rivalries and jealousies which finally found expression in the criminal acts of a few groups of hooligans.[51]

But the PPP government must accept some responsiblity for the whole affair, for they, knowing the domestic situation, still provided the pretext that the opposition needed to gain recognition. The PPP did not secure the environment for the budget that they were about to launch. "It would not have been an easy budget for a government that had the confidence, or was accepted, by the majority of the people. Unfortunately for the PPP, it was neither of these. PPP supporters were spread along a straggling coast road, but the opposition was firmly consolidated in the capital and had on its side the control and leadership of both the Civil Service and the trade unions."[52]

As has already been pointed out, some of the trade union leaders had political motives for calling the strike, but they could have succeeded only with the cooperation of the people. Dr. Jagan and his government were aware of this, yet they did nothing to separate the politicians and unionists from the people prior to the budget. In addition, the PPP seriously underestimated the strength of the UF and its constituency. The prominent businessmen and influential supporters of the UF had been caught off guard in 1953 but they were now adjusting to the new politics. The advent of mass politics, as represented by the PPP of 1953 and by the PPP and PNC subsequently, obscured their power and influence. In the 1961 election battles the PNC had had to come to grips with its enormous power and influence. Dr. Jagan was never exposed to this and even when he was, he did not take the UF seriously; then it was too late for him to really maneuver the government into a position to be able to deal with them. In concluding, we see the root of the riots similarly to the way the Commission did:

> The leaders of the People's National Congress were actuated through the failure of their ambitions and a realization that there was no future for them as Dr. Jagan's allies and supporters. . . . The Civil Service Association were moved to action by the procrastination of the government and the unsatisfactory response they had received to their demand for high salaries and better conditions of service. The trade unionists though professing to be completely free from political taint, made common cause with the Civil Service Association and with the politicians, and a gathering together of all these forces was made possible by the fact that Dr. Jagan was not endowed with the breadth of vision which could have enabled him to foresee that his purpose was progressing towards a lamentable end. Nor did he possess the nimbleness of intellect, or the dexterity of political maneuvering which allows a politician to change his plan of action without incurring the odium of his supporters or inviting the derision of his opponents.[53]

The Making of a New Elite: The Civil Service

Reference has already been made to the active role that many Guyanese Civil Servants played in the political movement of 1953. The interest of these civil servants in assisting the early PPP in the decolonization process was fired by the nationalism sweeping the country at that time. However, as time went by their position grew strong and they realized their potential for achieving greater benefit and power, they changed their view. For some time the members of the lower echelons of the service, which tended to be mainly African, had complained of discrimination and a lack of promotional opportunities despite the fact that they were just as qualified, and in some cases more qualified, than those who were promoted. Their contention was that Africans, not favored as a group by the administration, could only rise in most cases to junior administrative levels, whereas the mulattoes, Chinese, and Portuguese could rise to the senior levels because they were more acceptable, or to be more precise, because they were "fairer in complexion."

A change of the system would have benefited most of the African and

Indian members of the civil service. This mistrust for most of the senior and top civil servants manifested itself politically in the form of attacks by senior People's Progressive Party leaders on civil servants during the campaign and while in office. It also prompted PPP ministers to ignore "heads of departments" and to take "junior officials" into their confidence when formulating "Departmental Policy."[54] The matter seemed important enough to warrant special treatment by the Commission, that subsequently investigated the suspension of the constitution.[55]

Realizing that a problem existed within the service, the British Government, after the suspension of the constitution, embarked on a program of recruiting and training the locals in an attempt to professionalize the service, and to give it a more Guyanese character. The training that most of the civil servants received was minimal, yet adequate for their new jobs as instruments in the development process, but it was also limiting in another way. Once those who had gone on the six-month or one-year courses were designated "trained" and advanced in the civil service, they then guarded their new positions jealously, sometimes becoming more ineffective than those who had vacated the post. These people were only trained for some particular occupation or practice. Since they had not been trained to think, many were unsuitable when promoted to the more senior level; this tended to make them insecure, and as a result many of the civil servants, who in 1953 were very progressive in their political outlook, were by 1960 quite lukewarm to change.

All this time the representative association of the civil servants, the Civil Service Association (CSA), was deliberately trying to strengthen its organization and in its political associations,[56] so that civil servants, in addition to becoming the bureaucratic backbone of the country, also possessed an organization that could represent them adequately at both an industrial and political level. This put the civil service in a very pivotal and enviable position between 1962 and 1964 to bargain with the government and even with their associates in other unions.

New Tactics: Oppose and Depose

The February 1962 riots had shown how vulnerable the government was. The embarrassment brought about by the opposition, rather than promoting a responsible attitude between the government and itself, only succeeded in promoting further irresponsibility on all sides. As the government went on with business as usual, an uneasy calm prevailed over the city in the months following the riots. This attitude caused PPP General Secretary Mrs. Jagan to write two months later: "The crisis has, however, not stifled the demands for independence for British Guiana. The Conference for discussions on a date for independence goes on as previously planned, in May."[57] What the PPP did not realize then was that the riots had effectively erased their long held claim that the country was solidly behind them. For the first time, the PPP's detractors could legitimately accuse them of not having the full support of the people. The Jagan government from that time on was "in office but had lost effective power." This untenable position of the government gave greater force and legitimacy to the heretofore muffled PNC's cry for "Proportional Representation." "P.R. or Nothing" became the slogan of the PNC and UF. The PNC had suggested sometime earlier that the electoral system be changed from simple majority constituencies to one of Proportional Representation, since the PPP had won the 1961 election, gaining a clear majority of seats while getting less than fifty per cent of the votes cast. With the UF also supporting this change it gave the PNC demand greater credibility.

The first signs of apprehension from London occurred just prior to the convening of the planned Constitutional Conference. Rather than specify the date for the independence conference, the Colonial Secretary announced on May 11 the appointment of a Commonwealth Commission to investigate and report on the riots of February 1962. Upon completion of the Report, a new conference was set for October 1962. The act of postponing the independence conference and of subjecting the country to a long investigation contributed even further to the weakening of the government. The opposition grabbed the initiative for the remaining years of the PPP government. The opposition took the investigation as an opportunity to show their strength versus that of the governing party. They also used the Commission's umbrella to question the decisions made by the PPP government and questioned PPP leaders intimately about their political philosophy. The act of postponing the originally scheduled conference further convinced the opposition that London was beginning to take them more seriously even if the PPP government at home was not.

Constitutional Conference II

List of those attending the conference

Mr. Duncan Sandys, M.P., Secretary of State for the Colonies (Chairman)
Mr. Nigel Fisher, M.P., Parliamentary Under-Secretary of State
Mr. Hilton Poynton, Permanent Under-Secretary of State

Mr. A. R. Thomas ⎫
Mr. R. W. Pipers ⎬ Colonial Office
Mr. N. B. J. Huijsman ⎭

Mr. Ralph Hone ⎫
Mr. J. A. Peck ⎪
Mr. Ralph Grey, Governor of ⎬ Legal Advisers
  British Guiana ⎪
Mr. M. Shahabuddeen ⎭

Dr. C. B. Jagan, Premier ⎫
Mr. B. H. Benn, Minister of Natural Resources ⎪
Dr. F. H. W. Ramsahoye, Attorney General ⎪
Mr. Ashton Chase ⎬ People's Progressive Party
Mr. Moses Bhagwan ⎪
Mr. J. B. G. Kelshall ⎭

Mr. L. F. S. Burnham ⎫
Mr. N. J. Bissember ⎪
Mr. W. O. R. Kendall ⎪
Mr. J. Carter ⎬ People's National Congress
Mr. E. F. Correia ⎪
Mr. C. A. Merriman ⎪
Mr. H. M. E. Cholmondeley ⎭

Mr. P. S. D'Aguiar ⎫
Mr. R. E. Cheecks ⎪
Mr. S. Campbell ⎪
Mr. L. A. Luckhoo ⎬ United Force
Miss M. A. Jardim ⎪
Mr. J. E. DeFreitas ⎪
Mr. R. M. Delph[58] ⎭

It was the sincere impression of the leaders of the PPP that they were traveling to London for a conference to discuss the last details before independence was granted. True, they had begun to have second thoughts when the conference was postponed, but the PPP still felt its position was good. The opposition parties, on the other hand, were becoming more aware of their power. The signals that they had received through the appointment of the Commission of Inquiry gave them even more confidence. This caused the opposition parties to demand, "No P.R., No Independence" and further, "Elections before Independence."

But if it was the PPP's impression that independence was the next step, they must have detected a shift in the British Government's position with the opening remarks of the Colonial Secretary. He said, "At the last Conference, held here in 1960, it was agreed that as the next step in constitutional advance British Guiana should be granted full internal self-government; and that after an interval a further Conference should be convened to discuss the final preparation for independence."[59]

At the 1960 Conference the PNC had raised the possibility of having PR as the election system, but the British Government and other parties at the conference would not even entertain the thought. The British were preparing their colonies for independence along the Westminster model, and PR was not part of the system it used. However, with both the UF and the PNC pushing for PR with the support of the AFL-CIO, and with a keener American State Department interest in the final outcome, the PR arguments were given better reception. This happened much to the chagrin of Dr. Jagan:

> We argued that the issue of the electoral system had already been settled in 1960. The opposition, however, based its case on the point that we had not been elected by a majority of the electorate. I said that this was spurious, that as in other countries like the United Kingdom it was immaterial whether we had concentrated on winning a majority of seats, not votes. Indeed that was why we had contested only 29 of the 35 seats. Moreover, the constituencies had been delimited not by my government, but by a retired High Court Judge appointed by the British Government. No objection had been raised by the opposition parties with regard to the delimitation of the boundaries by the Commissioner. Indeed, no issue had been made by the opposition on the system of voting either at the end of the Constitutional Conference in 1960 or at the time of the elections in 1961. It was only after the opposition had failed to win a majority of seats that they had resurrected their early 1960 demand for the Israeli list system of PR. We were not prepared to accept; theirs was not a demand based on principle but merely a maneuver to remove us from office (WT, 267).

The PPP argued further that Proportional Representation as a system was unsatisfactory, even in those countries where it was then being used. They suggested that it encouraged a multiplicity of parties which, in turn, lead to weak and unstable governments. They conceded to the opposition's stand—elections before independence, but asked for a lowering of the voting age to 18. They also suggested that it would be wrong for the PPP to go to the polls so early after such a controversial budget, and with so much adverse press publicity still fresh in the minds of the electorate, but this was not accepted by the opposition. In an effort to have the conference come to a fruitful end, Dr. Jagan made a number of proposals for consultations and constitutional changes. These too were found not acceptable. He then proposed a coalition with the PNC, offering them "four out of ten Ministries in the Council of Ministers and the post of Head of State with powers of veto on vital questions pertaining to the importation of military equipment, the establishment of foreign bases and the declaration of war" (WT, 269). This was also rejected. At this point, the Colonial Secretary asked that he be allowed to arbitrate, but this was rejected by all sides and caused the constitutional conference to end in deadlock. Dr. Jagan himself saw the breakdown of the talks in this way:

> The talks thus broke down, principally owing to common interests of the British government and our Opposition not to transfer residual powers to my government. The intransigence of the Opposition of the insistence of the British government on the principle of unanimity were two sides of the same coin. (WT, 269)

The official report saw the reasons for the failure of the conference in a somewhat different light: "A number of constitutional points were settled. But it was found that no substantial progress could be made until decisions were reached on three major questions:

1. Should elections be fought on the basis of single member constituencies as at present or on the basis of proportional representation?
2. Should the right to vote be accorded at the age of 21 as at present or at the age of 18?
3. Should fresh elections be held before Independence?

The People's Progressive Party advocated single-member constituencies, voting at 18, and no elections before Independence. The People's National Congress and the United Force asked for proportional representation, voting at 21, and fresh elections."[60]

Local Analysis of Political Change

The inconclusive break-up of the constitutional conference was of consequence to all of the parties. To the PPP it was a serious blow. It damaged the party's credibility. It was clear that the PPP would have to have much broader support in order to win independence for the country and also modify its ideological stand so as to gain acceptability; but while it strove for this, it also knew that the opposition was in a strong position to make significant demands on it.

On the other hand, the break up of the talks was a triumph for those who had opposed the government and precipitated the unrest. They were able to read the change of mood in London, Washington, and Guyana. Time, they knew, was what they needed. The 1962 riots had shown them that unrest could not only buy time but also political leverage. They knew too that Dr. Jagan and his government would now have to pay more attention to their sentiments, or run the risk of more internal dissent.

But as these changes were taking place, many members of the middle class who saw no end to the civil strife began to emigrate to Britain, Canada, and Caribbean territories. The saying among many people was "you either stan and bun or cut and run." Translated, this means that you either stay and fight or run as soon as possible.

The months that followed Black Friday saw a sharpening of racial divisions and a few minor incidents of racial conflict. One such incident took place on Friday, April 5, 1963. The British Guiana Rice Workers Union, a TUC affiliate, opposed the Rice Marketing Board Workers Union, a People's Progressive Party affiliate, over the loading of a Russian ship with rice bound for Cuba. The Rice Workers Union, which had at the time been negotiating wage increases, called a strike when talks reached an impasse, but before the Russian ship had even arrived to take the rice, there was a rumor that the ship was bringing a shipment of arms consigned to the People's Progressive Party. These arms, it was said, were taken off by the PPP when their agents met the ship outside Guyana's territorial waters in small boats.

On the afternoon of the strike, Mrs. Jagan's car arrived at the Rice Marketing Board with gifts for the captain to take to People's Progressive Party students who were being trained in Cuba. The strikers demanded that the police search the car as it left the wharf. Fights

broke out between members of the rival unions; her car was damaged
and the car of the head of the Rice Marketing Board Workers Union
was set on fire. Trouble soon spilled over into the streets and into the
city center. People hurled bottles and bricks at the police who re-
taliated with tear gas and gunfire. Crowds broke into stores and looted
them. The day ended with one person killed and 20 others injured.
More than 100 people were arrested. Damage was estimated at
$100,000.[61] This incident shows the extent to which the people were
prepared to go in order to resist or question every PPP gesture. It also
shows the degree to which violence had then become part of the
political process. In the climate of a communist scare over Cuba within
the U.S. at that time, such behavior in Guyana was interpreted in
Washington as the people's attempt to resist communism.

Violence with Purpose

The PPP had over a period of time been given scholarships by the
governments of a few socialist countries, and these scholarships were
channelled through and administered by the PPP's youth arm, the
Progressive Youth Organization (PYO). In addition, the PYO was,
through affiliation with other socialist organizations, awarded fellowships to travel to international political youth conferences. The control
of these scholarships and fellowships gave the organization a certain
amount of power; as a result of its power and militancy, it began to
exercise an influence that during 1961–1964 could not be ignored. The
organization, through its ability to allocate scholarships and fellowships, attracted groups who wanted to further their education, and
who, in many cases, wanted to identify with its ideology. From time to
time PYO detractors would spread rumors, saying that these young
men were not sent on scholarships to study the subjects they claimed,
but they were being trained as communists and guerrillas. This caused
many people then to argue that the PPP were the real instigators of
violence and were people to fear. Thus, violence against them had to
be initiated as a self-protective measure. This perception by the people
fitted in quite nicely with the overall strategy of those who opposed the
government politically. The overall strategy of the PNC and UF of
opposing the government was shown once again when suddenly, on
March 25, 1963, the PPP government introduced a Labour Relations
Bill into the legislature.

Labour Relations Bill: Further Conflict

The publication of the Labour Relations Bill came as a surprise to everyone, as neither the unions nor the political opposition were consulted. Dr. Jagan had realized, from the time he entered politics, the importance of having the support of the unions. This he knew from his experience in the MPCA, when he attempted to gain recognition for the GIWU in 1948 and also through legislation in 1953. The Labour Relations Bill of 1963 was aimed at gaining recognition for the PPP-affiliated GIWU. One might be tempted to ask why the persistence over union recognition when the party was in control of the government itself? One answer might be that the PPP was not in control of the government; at least not fully. This was an attempt to secure a strong base with a strong organization which was, on the whole, opposed to it. In addition, the PPP government imagined itself to be under attack from everyone and in reality the government by its policies and actions had alienated even those who would have worked along with them. Dr. Jagan showed by the way he ran his government that the art of rebellion could be marshalled more easily than the technique of government, even when it is acknowledged that the task before him was at all times a gigantic one. In meeting this test, Dr. Jagan and the PPP failed to use the support and loyalty placed in them by a large cross-section of the people. Consequently, confidence dwindled at every crisis.

Again, few could doubt that the Labour Relations Bill was improper or ill inspired, but that its timing was crucial. The unions, which had by then, with the help of the AFL-CIO and AIFLD, come to regard themselves as "freedom fighters," saw the bill as an attempt by the government to muzzle their influence and militance. This determined them to put up a fight. The government saw the unions as that group which the opposition parties could influence to oppose and obstruct the government. Probably because the unions were known to be well organized but not financially strong, the government figured that opposition to the bill would be all rhetoric. But the government did not anticipate the help that the international friends of the unions would be prepared to give.

Richard Ishmael, then President of the MPCA (the recognized union in the sugar industry) and head of the TUC, immediately declared the bill "dangerous." The intent of the bill was to give the Minister of

Labour unlimited power with respect to dealing with inter-union disputes. It also provided for the recognition of unions that were truly representative of workers in place of those which were more "company unions." A section of the bill entitled "Objects and Reasons" reads as follows:

> This Bill seeks to ensure the compulsory recognition by employers as bargaining agents on behalf of workers of those unions which, after due inquiry, appear to the Minister of Labour, to be truly representative of the workers in a particular industry, trade or undertaking.

Further, it stated:

> The Bill seeks to enable the Minister, after due investigation, to direct that certificates be issued to certain Trade Unions, and to provide that, from the date of such certificates, the employers concerned shall be bound to deal exclusively with such trade unions in respect of all questions arising between any worker and his employer, in connection with the terms and conditions of his employment. Provision is made whereby an employer who fails to recognize and deal with any such Trade Union, shall be liable to a penalty not exceeding five hundred dollars for each day during which he continues to fail to recognize such Trade Union.[62]

On April 18, the Trade Union Council Delegates' Congress decided to call a strike protesting the proposed Labour Relations Bill. The TUC declared that the strike was being called "in defense of Trade Union Rights and not for political revolutionary purposes." At a meeting held on the Parade Ground the following day, six unions struck: the Man Power Citizens Association, Transport Workers Union, National Union of Public Service Employees, General Workers Union, Rice Workers Union, and Clerical and Commercial Workers Union.[63] By April 21, fourteen other unions, including the Civil Service Association, joined the TUC action.[64] The whole country became paralyzed with a cut off of most commercial activity and government services.

Meanwhile, in Parliament, the debate over the bill continued. On April 22, all of the opposition members walked out of the Legislature in protest against the use of "scab personnel" to replace the regular *Hansard* reporters who were on strike.[65] In the absence of the opposition, the bill was passed. However, it did not become law because it did not go to the Senate before the house was prorogued, and as a consequence, the bill lapsed.

The Post Office Workers Union joined the strike on April 24. Two days later, civil servants voted overwhelmingly to remain on strike. Because of the tension in the city, the police refused permission for the TUC to hold their traditional May Day rally on May 1, but the ban was defied and the rally was held without incident.[66]

Ironically, the strike had the support of many business enterprises, which in many cases paid some workers and encouraged others to stay out from work. In other cases, the premises of some establishments were locked and just never opened. "The Shipping Association also supported the strike and some companies in the Association refused to unload ships already in harbour and to bring in other ships which were bound for British Guiana. They even refused to allow goods unloaded in Curacao, Barbados, Trinidad and Surinam to be transported by Government boats and small private craft, their excuse being that their ships would be 'blacklisted' in the world's ports by the TUC through ORIT and ICFTU" (WT, 275).

The attitude of the Shipping Association caused many shortages, which in turn encouraged hoarding. Many people began turning more to local sources for supplies, and soon a wide number of local substitutes replaced regular imports. As a result, foods classified previously as poor people's food regained a certain prominence in the local diet.

Before the shipping lines closed, the airlines closed. With a general strike going on, the country was very quiet. Nevertheless, many knew the effects of a protracted strike, especially when essentials like oil ran out. Of this crucial situation, Dr. Jagan wrote:

> Realizing that the fuel oil situation would soon become critical, I requested the Governor to seek the help of the British Government to get oil supplies from other sources such as Venezuela and the Netherlands Antilles or through the British Navy. I was told by him not long afterwards that this would not be practical. It was at this stage that I appealed to the Cuban Government for help.
>
> The Cuban Government readily agreed. But its problem was to get an available tanker. Our problem was to get storage tanks; the U.S. Government refused to allow my government to utilize unused fuel tanks at its de-activated Atkinson Field Air Base although it had been under lease to the British Guiana Government. The U.S. oil companies also refused to allow us the use of their storage tanks at Ramsburg. At one stage, my Council of Ministers considered requisition of the tanks under the emergency. But the Governor would not agree. We thought of Nationalization, but many blocks, legal and otherwise, would have been put in our way. The Companies could have applied to the Supreme Courts for "prompt and adequate compensation" under the "protection

of property" clause which had been unilaterally written into our constitution by the British Government in 1961.

Finally we were able to store fuel in the tanks of the Electricity Corporation in Georgetown and in the Shell storage tanks at New Amsterdam. The Cuban fuel and gasoline really saved my government. When the tanker arrived there was only one day's supply left in the storage tanks of the Electricity Corporation, and the emergency supplies of the police were running low. Later in July, the Soviet Ship, Mitshwnsh brought in wheat flour and broke the food blockade (WT, 277–278).

Though the PPP relieved the oil shortage, the oil's source was another fact to be used in the opposition's drive to convince people that the PPP was communist.

Though "Passive Resistance"[67] became the cry of the protesters, there were continuous incidences of violence throughout the duration of the strike.

On May 4, the police raided the headquarters of the People's Progressive Party, the People's National Congress, and the United Force. At Congress Place, headquarters of the People's National Congress, the police found and seized a quantity of ammunition and other material, and also Plan X-13, a detailed account of a PNC terrorist gang. At Freedom House, the headquarters of the People's Progressive Party, they found cutlasses, knives, a stolen bicycle, and three wanted men. They also took away a safe for which a key could not be found; later it was found to contain one unlicensed automatic Lugar pistol and ammunition. Nothing was found at Unity House, headquarters of the United Force. The finding of Plan X-13 at Congress Place suggests that the PNC was more involved in the actual violence than was ever known before. The plan was a detailed document of PNC line of command in planning and executing violence.[68] This searching of the three political party head offices suggests that there was some concern and evidence to the police that they were all engaged in some sort of organized violence.

A few days later, on May 15, the police swooped down on the residence of a People's Progressive Party activist, Eric Gilbert; they found a submachine gun, a hand grenade, and ammunition in a carton marked "rejected rice." The weapons found confirmed the widespread belief that the People's Progressive Party was receiving arms from Cuba and was secretly unloading them at the Rice Marketing Board. On May 18, the police had to use tear-gas against strikers who carried out a passive resistance campaign, blocking operations by scabs of the Government's Ferry Service.

The strike began at first as a "week of Sundays," with very few people on the streets and almost no activity throughout the country. As the government attempted to get its business to return to normal, peace developed into violence when the police clashed with strikers who were practicing passive resistance against government scabs. Passive resistance, begun by the unions, was eventually taken over by the PNC. Because of the coincidence of its initials with those of Proportional Representation, the PNC claimed it as their own and, to a large extent, directed it. The PNC's General Secretary, Mr. H. Green, was very prominent in these operations.

Some civil servants and government workers decided by the end of May that the General Strike had gone on for a reasonable period of time and felt they had made their point. As a result, a few people returned to work after the government had appealed for them to do so and had assured them that their safety was guaranteed. To augment the skeleton staffs prepared to operate certain essential services, the Government, on May 9, asked the governor to sign a ten-day emergency proclamation giving the government the power to deal with the situation. The next day the government issued a release asking that skilled people register for temporary jobs since certain workers persisted in remaining at home while essential services needed to be carried on. This quickly became a racial issue as most of those who registered for jobs were Indian and tended to support the PPP and the strike breakers were taking jobs vacated by opposition sympathizers and mostly Africans. This only exacerbated the racial tension which was already high throughout the country.

Opposition Parliamentary Maneuver

In the meantime, the ten-day emergency proclamation was scheduled to come to an end, on May 19. The government introduced a motion in the legislature seeking an extension. After three days of debate, during which time the Government used up much valuable time speaking in favor of the emergency order, it realized that time was crucial. The opposition decided that all of its members wanted to speak. An attempt to cut off debate met with no success since there had been too many PPP speakers.

It was known by the opposition that if the emergency order was not extended by midnight, the People's Progressive Party Government would have to once again call on the Governor to sign a new proclamation. The PNC, therefore, used one of the most effective tactical maneuvers in the history of that body. By 11:45 p.m., it was apparent that the Government would have the emergency order extended by a vote in the legislature, but at that point Mr. W. O. R. Kendall (PNC) jumped to his feet and proposed an amendment to the motion that was seconded by Mr. Burnham. The leader of the House, Mr. Brindley Benn, asked the speaker, Mr. Rahman B. Gajraj, to rule the proposed amendment out of order, but the speaker allowed the amendment. By then it was a few minutes to midnight, and Mr. Burnham began speaking on the amendment. He was still speaking when the clock struck, and the adjournment had to be taken. The emergency order had lapsed. On May 22, the Governor signed new emergency regulations at the government's request.

This incident shows the careless way with which the PPP handled very important affairs, and the cunning the opposition used at all times to embarrass the government. In a climate of fierce opposition to the government, this ineptitude only caused the PPP to lose yet more respect; and it showed the opposition as being even more powerful than they really were. Thus the PPP even in the legislature, where it had an unquestionable majority, could not see its own legislation through. With a general strike in progress and opposition forces in the streets and at rallies continuously, the incident damaged the prestige of the PPP further. Outwitting the PPP in Parliament bolstered the opposition's prestige among elite groups even if it did not win votes. The opposition parties were bent on demonstrating that they were an effective alternative government and that it was they, not the PPP, who had real power. Denying the government's extension of the emergency had the humiliating effect of sending Premier Jagan once again to Her Majesty's representative to ask for another order to be signed.

On May 28, the Speaker read a statement to the Assembly deploring the conduct of certain members of the house on the night that the emergency order was debated. PPP members, annoyed that the Speaker had allowed the opposition motion, had jeered and hurled abuses at the Speaker as he left the chamber. The Speaker, after declaring that "grave disorder exists in the House," adjourned the Assembly to an unspecified date.[69]

Forbes Burham, leader of the People's National Congress, was also Mayor of Georgetown during this time. In his capacity as Mayor, he had refused to have the strike breakers operate the council's equipment while its regular workers were out on strike. Thus, on May 28, the government began engaging private contractors to collect the garbage around the city. The government had to use the emergency powers given them to forcibly open the municipal markets so that huskers could salvage their goods and begin trading.

The Road to Conflict

A few days earlier, Mr. Claude Christian, the Minister of Home Affairs, fell ill while attending a meeting at the PPP head office and died later. At his funeral on May 30, antigovernment crowds jeered at People's Progressive Party Ministers as they arrived at the church; when Dr. Jagan arrived at the Cathedral in an open-neck shirt (a Gueyebera, later made the official dress of the nation) the crowds jeered at him even more. Upon hearing the jeers, Mrs. Jagan responded by giving the crowd the PPP salute, which aggravated the huge crowd even more. As the last rites were being performed in the cemetery, the crowd began to throw bottles and stones at the PPP officials gathered at the graveside. The police used tear gas to disperse them. As the crowd dispersed a rumor circulated that a child had been trampled by a mounted police during the incident, whereupon the crowd turned into the city and began rioting and beating Indians. Tear gas was used once again to quell the riots. That evening twenty-five people were admitted to the Georgetown Hospital and some twenty arrests were made.

In response to the violence against Indians living in the urban areas on May 20, violence erupted on the East Coast of Demerara against Africans where the Indian population was predominant. Several Africans in that area were beaten and one Desmond Doris was hacked to death at Cummings Lodge.[70] On June 1, Georgetown had again been declared a proclaimed area and a ban was imposed on all public meetings and gatherings.

As the strike dragged on with no end in sight, some people began drifting back to work. Both government and business began operating on a limited scale. On June 10, the TUC strike effort moved into a new phase of passive resistance. This was to counter the government's efforts to get certain essential services running and certain government offices reopened. The campaign took the form of sit-ins at the places of work. The exercise was carried out around the Public Buildings and other ministries, at Sandbach Parker, and the Royal Bank of Canada. Dr. Jagan's personal remembrance of that day was: "On the morning of that day (June 10) when I entered the Public Buildings, seat of government, there were several people waiting at the entrance. They followed upstairs. Soon after, I saw them squatting on the floor outside my office. They were quickly joined by a large number of others who sat on the desks and chairs of officers of the Ministry and on the floor of the various rooms. The same invasion and obstruction occurred at the Ministry of Finance and other offices in the Public Buildings.

"I left the Public Buildings at about 9:15 a.m. to proceed to Le Resouvenir, East Coast Demerara, to deliver a lecture at Accabre College. I returned at about 11:30 and remained at home, as I was advised not to return to my office because the crowds in the office and in and around the Public Buildings had become larger and the police were using tear gas to disperse them" (WT, 285–286). It was clear that the strike had gotten out of hand. The unionists were upset that their efforts did not completely cripple the government, and the government, even though it had become ineffective, was intent on not resigning. A stalemate had been reached, but none was willing to give in. Dr. Jagan's recollections illustrate how difficult the passive resistance campaign made his work situation. For the other civil servants, it was somewhat worse since the use of tear gas to disperse the demonstrators outside the building invariably affected those inside the buildings. Work was made uncomfortable. The evening of June 10 ended with the police discovering and foiling an attempt to blow up the Rice Marketing Board. The establishment was viewed as being totally under the control of the PPP and a source of PPP finance.

On June 12, another sit-in occurred outside the Public Building where the Council of Ministers were meeting. After the Ministerial meeting, Senator C. J. Nunes, Minister of Education, was mobbed and beaten while attempting to walk through the crowd on his way to his office a short distance away. Dr. Jagan was also mobbed as he attempted to leave in his limousine. His security guards, fearing for his safety, fired shots to clear the protestors. Four people were injured as a result of the incident and once again the crowd turned into the city and rioted. Thirty-five people were reported injured and thirty were arrested.[71]

Judicial Rejection Bill Lapses

During this time, the Legislature did not convene, as the speaker had insisted that Dr. Jagan and his colleagues apologize for their unparliamentary behavior on the evening of May 19; and they were all suspended until they did so. Rather than apologize, Dr. Jagan and his colleagues brought a court injunction against the speaker, but lost. The PPP was then faced with a predicament. If they called a meeting of the house to see the Labour Relations bill through, or to have any other type of legislation passed, the opposition could easily ask for a suspension of the standing orders and bring a motion of no confidence in the government. With some PPP members on suspension, such a motion would be sure to pass. The government would then have no alternative but to resign. Instead of running such a risk, Dr. Jagan prorogued the house, thereby avoiding an apology but also causing the highly controversial and hard fought-for Labour Relations bill to lapse. Again because of its own lack of foresight the PPP had to retreat.

The failure of the PPP to see the bill through because of its own impetuousness could only be termed a victory for the opposition. No doubt the tense and unstable domestic situation had had an effect on the PPP legislators, and their abuse of the Speaker was simply a sign of disgust. It was exactly the sort of situation the opposition was intent on generating, however, and the PPP parliamentarians fell for it.

The general strike continued despite the fact that the Labour Relations bill had lapsed. The problem was to negotiate a back-to-work settlement and it was the Jagan Government, not the Labour Relations bill, that was now the issue. The bill had only been the pretext for the strike; the real issue was still the government. The back-to-work negotiations dragged on and the strike dragged on.

Once again the PPP Government had persuaded the Cuban Government to send Guyana more essentials such as flour, fuel, and oil in exchange for the rice that Guyana sold to them. The presence of Russian and Cuban ships in Port Georgetown only aggravated the opposition to the government. On June 13, the Cuban ship "Maria Therese" arrived and unloaded a shipment of Russian flour. On June 20, the U.S. Government and oil companies refused the Government the use of its installations to store refined Cuban oil. On June 21, the tanker left without being allowed to discharge its cargo.

PR and the Parties

That evening the People's National Congress held a meeting in Ruimveldt, just outside the proclaimed area. At the meeting, Burnham declared his intention to take full part in the demonstrations against the government and announced that thenceforth the People's National Congress would take over and stage bigger Passive Resistance campaigns than the ones promoted by the TUC. The following day, the police had to use tear gas to disperse People's National Congress demonstrators at several ministerial offices.

On July 6, the Government reached a back-to-work agreement with the business community, but talks with the unions proved more difficult. Bargaining between the government and the union was so difficult that the TUC sent for the help of Mr. Robert Willis of the British TUC. He was sent to Guyana from London on June 29. He worked out an agreement, but the TUC still failed to reach a compromise with Premier Jagan over the re-introduction of the Labour Relations Bill.

Meanwhile, on July 1, violence had broken out between Indians and Africans on the East Coast. Bevan Williams, a young African of sixteen, died from gunshot and cutlass wounds. Nine other people were seriously injured and rushed to the hospital. The disturbances continued for the next two days. The People's National Congress took Bevan Williams' funeral as an opportunity to demonstrate its solidarity with the people on the East Coast and its own political strength. Some five thousand supporters followed Forbes Burnham and members of the People's National Congress Executive in the funeral procession from Georgetown to Plaisance, a village on the outskirts of the city. That day, disorder broke out for the first time in a new area—the West Coast of Demerara. Here more than 150 people were injured and over 100 arrested.

On July 5, in separate talks held between the TUC and Dr. Jagan, Mr. Robert Willis finally forged an agreement acceptable to both parties. The strike ended on the following day. The agreement read:

Agreement Between the Government of British Guiana and the British Guiana Trade Unions Council After the 1963 Strike

1. *The Red Line:*
   The suggested Red Line shall not be introduced. The strike period shall not be regarded as a break in service.

2. *Victimisation:*
   The parties to this agreement are agreed that there shall be no victimisation on either side.

3. *The Labour Bill:* Labour Relations Bill 1963 having lapsed will not be re-introduced in its original form or its amended form in which it was passed in the Legislative Assembly.

4. (a) In any labour matter that may arise in future, Government will consult with the Trade Unions concerned and/or with the British Guiana Trades Union Council.

   (b) In particular, all Bills affecting labour matters shall, before presentation to the Legislature, be submitted to the Trades Unions concerned and/or to the Trades Union Council for consideration and recommendation.

   (c) To facilitate the implementation of (a) and (b) a Joint Standing Committee of Government and the Trades Union Council shall be established. The functions and composition of this Committee shall be agreed between Government and the Trades Union Council. Ad hoc Tripartite Committees may be appointed from time to time. The functions and composition of such Committees shall be agreed between Government and the Trades Union Council.

   (d) It is further agreed that a specially appointed Ad Hoc Tripartite Committee shall examine the existing labour laws in order to make recommendations to the Government for the consolidation and/or amendment of these laws, and the enactment of any new legislation which may be considered necessary. Until this Committee has reported—which shall be done within a reasonable period, say four months—the Government will not introduce any new bill dealing with labour legislation, except with the agreement of the Tripartite Committee.

5. Immediate payment of resumption shall be made of wages and salaries earned by Government employees up to the time the strike started. The Government will make available to its employees who were on strike, loans of two weeks' wages or half-month's salary—repayments to be made over a period of six months, but not including December, in equal weekly or monthly installments commencing two months after resumption of work. On resumption the staff Associations shall have the right to pursue through normal industrial relations channels, including Whitley Council

Machinery, the question of no loss of income or the conversion of the loan to a ex gratia payment, also the period of repayment of loan.

6. *Emergency Measures:*
   In order to avoid hardships, these shall be gradually withdrawn as the situation warrants.

7. All scabs to be immediately withdrawn.

8. The proposal for Government Employees to opt out of the service and the attendant conditions thereon shall be pursued through the normal industrial relations channels.

9. These conditions shall be applied to resumption of work by all employees of the Government, including part paid and contract officers.

10. Special Committees will be appointed (preferably under the chairmanship of the Secretary to the Treasury) to consider other matters which may arise out of the resumption of work. (A list of these matters will be forwarded.)

(Sgd.) Cheddi Jagan, Dr. the Hon. C. B. Jagan Premier of British Guiana	(Sgd.) Richard A. Ishmael, President, Trades Union Council
(Sgd.) Ranji Chandisingh, Hon. Ranji Chandisingh Minister of Labour, Health & Housing	(Sgd.) J. H. Pollydore, General Secretary B. G. Trades Union Council
(Sgd.) F. Ramsahoye, Dr. the Hon. Fenton Ramsahoye Attorney General	(Sgd.) Robert Willis, General Council British Trades Union Congress

Dated this 6th day of July 1963.[72]

The strike was the longest general strike ever recorded in Guyana, having lasted eighty days, and accomplishing nothing for any of the parties. The PPP still did not have a bill, after incurring opposition, riots and disorders. They, because of their loss of nerve, caused the bill to lapse when they did not apologize to the speaker. On the other hand, the opposition had embarrassed the government in and outside the legislature. They showed that they were more resourceful and cunning than the PPP, but they also caused severe economic dislocation within the country. Some had hoped to force the government to resign, but this never happened. At the end, all parties were exhausted and the situation had reached a stalemate. "In a typical South American state . . . such a stalemate would have been broken by a military coup, since historically it has been the Army's role in such countries to take over when in its opinion the demagoguery and instability of civilian regimes threaten chaos."[73]

Even though the General Strike had ended, violence continued in a sporadic fashion throughout the countryside as people attacked each other for their political beliefs or because of their ethnic origins.

These developments were viewed with such concern that the Colonial Secretary, Mr. Duncan Sandys, paid a visit to Guyana on July 10, 1963, to make a personal assessment of the situation. It was the first time that a British Colonial Secretary had gone out to a colony to make a personal assessment of a "crisis." During his visit, Mr. Sandys encouraged the parties to form a national government. The PPP opposed this idea since they had always maintained that a coalition was possible and only desired between the PPP and PNC, but saw the ideology of the UF as being too far to the right for compromise. The first meeting to try to forge a national coalition was held with Colonial Secretary Sandys present. Dr. Jagan said that his government was willing to work with the People's National Congress, but he insisted that he was not interested in forming a holding government only. He was willing to begin discussions between the PPP and PNC on a program for the purpose of forming a coalition of a more lasting nature. He was also interested in having the PNC support a firm date for independence and a bill for a Guyana Army, which it was contemplating. Burnham thought a coalition could only be a short-term arrangement and had also demanded that a referendum on proportional Representation be held. An agenda was drawn up and it was agreed that the representatives of the two parties would meet on July 18 to begin formal talks. When these talks convened, the People's National Congress refused to discuss a coalition while Guyana remained in a state of emergency. The talks were suspended and never reconvened.[74]

The breakup of the coalition talks is symptomatic of the inability of either party to compromise, and the desire by each for total power. The party which happens to be in a weaker position always tries for compromise while the stronger party bargains, trying to humiliate and reduce its opponent. The PNC's refusal to attend any talks until the Emergency Order was lifted suggests that the People's National Congress was not interested in a coalition, but in using the event as another political platform, while trying to buy time in the hope of itself becoming the government.

In the meantime, GIMPEX, a company owned by the People's Progressive Party, became another center of controversy. On July 23, the *Graphic* newspaper gave prominence to a report that the government had entered into negotiations to borrow money from GIMPEX, the import/export trading arm of the People's Progressive Party. The report was based on the announcement in an extraordinary issue of the *Official Gazette*, which announced that legal provisions had been made for the Government to negotiate loans for purposes of emergency. On July 25, Dr. C. R. Jacob, Minister of Finance, announced that the Government had found it necessary to borrow $1.7 million from GIMPEX "to help in a difficult but brief period." The loan, it was stressed, was to be repaid at an interest rate of 5½ percent over a period of six months.

For the PPP Government it was a practical move; politically, it was disastrous.

It confirmed some suspicions about the People's Progressive Party that were abroad at that time. Throughout the strike the Trade Unions had accused the PPP government of using the strike to enrich itself. All Cuban goods were channelled through GIMPEX so that the PPP indirectly collected the commission.

The United Force used the loan as evidence that Dr. Jagan and the PPP, being Communist, would like to take complete control of the commercial sector of the economy. Furthermore, D'Aguiar accused the People's Progressive Party of receiving large sums of money from Communist sources through its GIMPEX trading arm. It confirmed that the PPP had large sums of money to mount a strong election campaign.

During the General strike, racial violence on an unprecedented scale began and increased over the months throughout the country, at times with ferocity in the rural areas. The increase in violence took on a more and more racial character as it continued. At its inception different groups were attacked because of their political affiliation, later because of one's ethnic origin one was presumed to support a particular party. Violence had become racial rather than political. Nevertheless, the Government revoked the Emergency Order on September 4, 1963, just prior to the reconvening of the Constitutional Conference in London.

Constitutional Conference III

Prior to the conference, the PNC was insisting at its political rallies that the scheduled conference be held in Guyana. Burnham's contention was that since the conference had to do with Guyana and the Guyanese people, it should be held in Guyana. No one concerned, however, including many among the PNC itself, took the demand seriously. The three parties arrived in London and the conference began on October 22, 1963. The Party's representatives were:

Mr. Duncan Sandys, M.P., Secretary of State for the Colonies (Chairman)
Mr. Nigel Fisher, M.P., Parliamentary Under-Secretary of State
Sir Hilton Poynton, Permanent Under-Secretary of State
Sir Ralph Grey, Governor of British Guiana

Dr. C. B. Jagan, Premier
Mr. B. H. Benn, Minister of Natural Resources
Dr. F. H. W. Ramsahoye, Attorney General   PPP
Mr. Ashton Chase
Professor J. A. C. Griffth (advisor)

Mr. L. F. S. Burnham
Mr. N. J. Bissember
Mrs. W. Gaskin   PNC
Mr. C. M. Llewellyn John
Mr. H. M. E. Cholmondeley (advisor)

Mr. P. S. D'Aguiar
Mr. R. E. Cheeks
Mr. S. Campbell   UF
Miss M. S. Jardim
Mr. L. A. Luckhoo (advisor)[75]

At the opening of the Conference, the Colonial Secretary asked whether the parties had reached an agreement on the outstanding issues. After a negative reply, he suspended the plenary sessions and began a round of personal discussions with the different delegations while the delegations themselves had meetings with each other, none of which broke the deadlock. The attempts to narrow the differences having failed, and all hopes of a positive result unlikely, Dr. Jagan suggested that the British Government, in the person of the Colonial Secretary, arbitrate in the matter. In making his request, Dr. Jagan praised "the high sense of fair play and justice" of the British in which he had come to believe. Mr. D'Aguiar readily agreed with Dr. Jagan in his request, but Mr. Burnham objected. He said that the problem was a domestic one, and should be settled by the Guyanese leaders themselves. After a warning by Mr. Sandys about the possible delay of independence that might result from his action of not agreeing to

arbitration, Burnham agreed.[76] The Colonial Secretary then prepared
a letter for the leaders to sign. It read:

> At your request we have made further efforts to resolve the differ-
> ences between us on the constitutional issues which require to be settled
> before British Guiana secures independence, in particular, the electoral
> system, the voting age, and the question whether fresh elections should
> be held before independence.
>
> We regret to have to report to you that we have not succeeded in
> reaching agreement; and we have reluctantly come to the conclusion
> that there is no prospect of an agreed solution. Another adjournment of
> the Conference for further discussions between ourselves would there-
> fore serve no useful purpose and would result only in further delaying
> British Guiana's independence and in continued uncertainty in the
> country.
>
> In these circumstances we are agreed to ask the British Government
> to settle on their authority all outstanding constitutional issues, and we
> undertake to accept their decisions.
>
> (Signed)　　　　　　　　Cheddi Jagan
> 　　　　　　　　　　　　L. F. S. Burnham
> 　　　　　　　　　　　　P. S. D'Aguiar[77]

The Secretary of State announced his decision at the final plenary
session on October 31, 1963. In announcing his decision the Secretary
said:

> I have listened carefully to the arguments advanced in favor of single
> member constituencies ("First past the post"), and those advanced in
> favor of various types of proportional representation. I must, however,
> say that I got the impression that the advocates of the different solutions,
> while propounding impeccable principles, were more concerned with
> their own electoral prospects than with the furtherance of racial har-
> mony in British Guiana.
>
> After taking into account all that has been said, I have tried to examine
> this problem with complete objectivity and with one aim only, namely to
> assess what electoral system would be most likely to give your country
> peace and good government. . . .
>
> In the light of these various considerations, I concluded that it must
> be our deliberate aim to stimulate a radical change in the present pattern
> of racial alignments. It was therefore my duty to choose the electoral
> system which would be most likely to encourage inter-party coalitions
> and multi-racial groupings and which would make it easy for new parties
> to form. Having thus denied the objective, the answer was clear. British
> Guiana must change over to a system of proportional representation. . . .

However, once these new parties, some of which may still have racial connections, have been brought into being, it is to be hoped that some may amalgamate into larger multi-racial groupings and contest subsequent elections together. To encourage this process of fusion, it may well be desirable, after the first election, to introduce a minimum qualifying percentage. The land at which this would be fixed need not be determined now.

No case has been made to show that a lowering of the voting age would help to solve the problems which face British Guiana. I do not therefore propose to make any changes. . . .

Another question I was asked to decide was whether there should be fresh elections before independence. If it were proposed to retain the existing electoral system, there would be no justification for holding further elections. However, since the system is to be changed, it is clearly right that fresh elections under the new system should be held before independence. Preparations for them should be put in hand as soon as practicable.[78]

Analysis of Sandys' Decision

The Secretary of State for the Colonies, Mr. Sandys, gave the opposition everything they asked for. Premier Jagan had gambled and lost. Dr. Jagan knew from 1962 onwards that he was losing ground with every crisis. The 1962 budget riot was an indelible blemish on his record. That crisis, followed by subsequent crises, showed that while the PPP could win successive elections they had not mastered the art of government. In addition, events in Cuba, the missile crisis, the expropriation of American business, and general fear of what was perceived as a Communist threat in the Caribbean caused a hardening of American attitudes, which in turn seems to have had great influence on the final British decision. Dr. Jagan's decision to ask the British Government to arbitrate was a direct result of the position in which he found himself domestically; he was surrounded by two opposition parties whose constituency, though smaller than the PPP's, were able to paralyze the government because of their location in the urban centers and in the government service.

Dr. Jagan's style of running his government did not give him the leverage of appeal to any of the opposition supporters nor did he try very hard to do so. While in 1957, Dr. Jagan had had that sort of credibility, by 1961, because of his persistent fear of the old establishment and his own inability to deal with the conservative elements within his own party, he was never able to broaden his party's political base. Thus when the 1962 budget was presented, there was very little sympathy for the PPP government except from its own people. The enormous sacrifice the people were asked to make demanded that the government show a greater sympathy with the groups who felt they were making more of a sacrifice. The government did not show from its rhetoric that it had any such intentions.

Before 1961, Dr. Jagan and the PPP were accustomed to the Parliamentary opposition of the PNC. After 1961 this situation changed with the election of the UF. Dr. Jagan, who had indirectly cooperated with the UF by not putting up any candidates in Georgetown, thus lessening the PNC's opportunities, gave the UF the parliamentary legitimacy it needed. It was the UF that, in turn, precipitated the militancy of the PNC and alienated all of the opposition forces from the government. In a way, Dr. Jagan's 1961 decision had come to haunt him.

To a large extent, the same argument holds true for the events that led to the 1963 general strike over the Labour Relations Bill. Here, Premier Jagan once again grossly underestimated his opposition. Even though his implied source of attack was the rather weak MPCA union, he did not seem to realize how much the international and especially the domestic situation had affected his position in government. Instead, he seemed to cling to his electoral majority like a security blanket, but even this majority he could not use effectively. He could not take the risk of silencing the opposition demands for PR by holding a referendum. On the other hand the PNC had come to realize by then that only a change in the electoral system could bring them victory at the polls. The figures speak for themselves.

TABLE 5

		Votes (%)	Seats (%)
1953	PPP	51.00	75.00
1957	PPP (Jaganite)	47.50	64.28
	PPP (Burnhamite)	25.48	21.43
1961	PPP	42.63	57.14
	PNC	40.99	31.43

Dr. Jagan knew that the opposition would win a referendum. Rather than try for a compromise at home, which would have taken time, he opted to put his faith in "British Justice." Dr. Jagan's main mistakes seem to have been his bad timing and a failure to share power, or at least to appear to do so. The PNC, on the other hand, had very little chance of ever forming a government. It increased its power and influence only by allowing the PPP to make mistake after mistake on its own. As the opposition strength increased, their demands increased. With a favorable international climate, the opposition could assert itself both at home and abroad. They probably knew this despite the protestations of Burnham about signing Sandys' letter.

Premier Jagan was his own worst enemy. He lacked political vision and most of all administrative ability. His dissatisfaction and distrust of the police, primarily because they were reluctant to use more drastic measures to deal with demonstrators, suggests a certain lack of foresight. Even if the police had succeeded in dispersing the demonstrators by the most violent means, the result would have most likely been the stimulation of civil war. Should such a situation have occurred the result would have been the same, the re-entry of the British government and the imposition of a solution.

Dr. Jagan saw this reluctance to use force by the police in totally racial terms, and as a result after 1963 saw his salvation in having the racial imbalances in the services corrected. His answer was the creation of the Special Service Unit (SSU) after the 1963 riots. No one can argue with the need for a country, aspiring to independence, to have an army of its own. However, suspicions must be aroused when it is created after inferences are made about the police and other forces. It was his failure to inspire confidence and loyalty in the people with whom he had to work that caused the PPP to raise the argument of imbalances in the Government services. The PPP, after suffering the embarrassment of the government service going on strike twice in two years, began to feel that if a majority of government workers had been supporters of the PPP, they would not have set out to deliberately embarrass the government; hence, their charge of racial imbalances in the government service had political overtones. In a way, their charge played into the hands of the opposition. They were then seen as the only hope for those who thought they had to protest their own careers.

PR or CR

On November 9, 1963, Dr. Jagan returned to Guyana, a very bitter man. In a number of speeches to his supporters, he urged them to protest the Sandys decision. He urged them to join in the battle to fight imperialism as Castro had done: "No PR, or DEATH"; "PR and CR"; "WE PREFER DEATH TO PR." (CR was a local term for giving someone a beating.) These slogans were added to the walls and surfaces already painted with the opposition signs, up and down the coast.

Early in 1964, the People's Progressive Party stepped up the Guyana Agricultural Workers Union's bid for recognition as the bargaining agent for sugar workers. The demand took a violent form. Members of the recognized MPCA were attacked and beaten. For weeks a reign of terror raged on the sugar estates throughout the country. In the city and in the rural areas, interracial violence continued on a small scale, and in some instances, those involved met death with such horrendous butchery that it defies description.

It could be said with some certainty that the violence in the city in 1962–63 had influenced the final outcome of the constitutional talks. This was violence and coercion by the opposition. In 1964 the PPP seemed to feel that violence could somehow reverse the decisions that had been made. The demonstrations launched by the PPP in November and December of 1963 to protest the Colonial Secretary's (Sandys') decision culminated with a giant march into the city of Georgetown on February 9, 1964. As Dr. Jagan himself explains:

> We wanted to afford our supporters the opportunity to demonstrate their confidence in the leaders of the party in the face of the British government's betrayal at the London talks. (WT, 350)

The marches began at both ends of the coastal strip where most of the Guyanese people lived. One began at Crabwood Creek and covered a total distance of 115 miles. The other began at Charity and covered about 50 miles. Both marches held meetings at PPP strongholds along the way and culminated at the rifle ranges in Georgetown. The PPP demonstrations did not have the use of a more convenient meeting place in Georgetown because the Mayor (Forbes Burnham) and City Council had refused the PPP permission to hold their demonstrations and rally at the Parade Ground as they had requested (WT, 350–351).

Prior to that Dr. Jagan had called on the PNC to reject the Sandys decision, and suggested that the PNC and PPP should "carry out a united attack against the United Force." The People's National Congress rejected the offer while reminding the PPP that in 1961 it had asked its supporters to vote United Force. "Now (Burnham said) the People's Progressive Party wanted the People's National Congress to undo this for it."[79] Dr. Jagan's suggestion to the PNC shows the political position in which he found himself, a situation from which he seemed powerless to disengage the PPP from 1962 on. The rejection by the PNC of Dr. Jagan's request, and its failure to stimulate some discussion toward finding a compromise around which some sort of national unity could be built, could only be seen as lack of foresight due to their own ambitions. 1964 was the PPP's lowest point and the PNC's highest. It was a time when both parties could and should have been in a position to negotiate a national consensus. The failure to reach some compromise calls into question the principles the two major party leaders proclaimed that they possessed. Each major party thought it could win and govern on its own without the cooperation and assistance of the other. Power rather than principles seemed to be their major consideration.

On February 11, the General Secretary of the People's Progressive Party, Mrs. Jagan, sent a letter to the People's National Congress, asking that the two parties meet to discuss restrictions of their political activity because of violence. The People's National Congress showed no interest in discussing the subject. In the meantime, the inter-union dispute continued with ferocity on the sugar estates. There were daily reports of intimidation, murder, arson, and beatings. In the city of Georgetown, violence also increased. Bombs were thrown into the homes of people with known party affiliation, and prominent citizens were shot or shot at. On March 31, the editor of the *Evening Post* and the *Sunday Argosy* was shot. The following day another prominent journalist, the Commissioner of Police, and a senior Civil Servant received threatening letters.[80] The president of the TUC narrowly escaped death when someone shot at him while he was in his car.

Despite the increased turmoil throughout the country, Dr. Jagan and the PPP were still working tirelessly to try to reverse the decision made by the Colonial Secretary Sandys.

Dr. Jagan asked President Nkrumah of Ghana to send a goodwill mission to try to mediate between the PNC and the PPP:

> I had asked Dr. Nkrumah to aid the mission with the object of achieving a coalition between the PPP and the PNC and the adoption of a mixed electoral system similar to that in force in Surinam. I had done so be-

cause of my respect for the President and the confidence which the
Guianese people had in the progressive and dynamic role Ghana was
playing in Afro-Asia. I felt that since these countries were pursuing a
non-aligned course and moving in the direction of socialism, they could
play a great part in bringing about a better understanding between the
PPP and the PNC. Besides I was anxious to get African countries to
become more knowledgeable about our affairs since the PNC and the
African Society for Cultural Relations with Independent Africa
(ASCRIA) had launched a propaganda campaign at home and abroad to
the effect that my party was racially motivated and was discriminating
against Negroes. (WT, 351–352)[81]

The Ghana Mission arrived in Guyana on February 9, 1964, and was
given a mixed reception by the press and an official welcome from the
PNC. There was some opposition and demonstration from the United
Force against the mission. At the conciliatory meetings, the two parties
did not reach agreement and the mission left Guyana ten days later
with the two parties nowhere nearer agreement than before. The inter-
union dispute in the sugar industry continued with an increased
momentum during this time. On February 17, a work stoppage was
ordered by the GAWU on all of the sugar estates. The estate authorities decided, since the African workers who tended to be factory
workers were not going to strike, to recruit scabs to fill the jobs vacated
by the Indian strikers. In many cases the scabs were Africans. This
policy eventually led to open violence between the two groups. Violence against scabs living in villages along the coast broke out.

On March 4, a bomb was thrown into a bus conveying scab workers
to Plantation Albion at Tain. Two men died as a result of their injuries.
On March 6, a tractor driven by a scab ran over a group of female
demonstrators who had squatted on a bridge leading to a factory. One
woman, Kowsilla, was killed and two others were seriously injured.
The incident sent the picketers into a rage; eventually tear gas was
used to disperse the demonstrators.

On the estates the situation became worse—the violence no longer
took the form of an inter-union dispute, but developed into open racial
strife. Within a few days it almost reached the point of civil war. On
March 23, a bomb was thrown into a school bus at Lusignan on the
East Coast. One 13-year-old boy, Godfrey Terxiera, died as a result
and 11 other children were injured. In New Amsterdam a bomb exploded in the home of Joseph London on March 27; both he and wife
were seriously injured. On the West Coast, a gasoline station owned

by Razack Mandal was blown up on March 31; at Canje a young man was killed on April 15 when a grenade exploded in his hand. On April 20, riots broke out at Lenora where stores were looted, several people were severely beaten, and one man died.

On May 7, the Sugar Producers reported that in the fifty-seven days since the dispute had begun, sugar cane worth $2.5 million had been destroyed by arsonists. The whole of the West Coast of Demerara was gripped by civil strife. On April 20, five people were shot and over twenty hospitalized. On April 24, all of the Africans living in the village of Tuschen were chased out. The newly formed African Society for Cultural Relations with Independent Africa (ASCRIA) issued a release asking that armed assistance be sent to the West Coast to save the lives of Africans who were being butchered. On April 28, the senior coordinating alder of ASCRIA began a round-the-clock vigil in front of the Governor's office in protest against what he described as "armed terror by the government party against Africans in West Demerara."[82]

Eventually violence enveloped the whole country. No place was safe; neither the cities, towns, nor rural areas. Communities in which people of a different ethnic origin had lived side by side for generations were split. Minorities found themselves having to leave their homes and flee to villages where their racial group was in a majority. Houses were pulled off their blocks, sometimes with their occupants inside; others were put to the torch. Lamp posts were cut down to disrupt communications. Murder and arson became an everyday occurrence.

Fire was set to several houses belonging to minority groups in Cashba, Uictvlugt, Tuschen, and Meeta-meer-Zorg on May 13. Violence on the West Coast continued at an unprecedented level, with sporadic violence on the East Coast.

On May 22, the Governor took the situation into his own hands and declared a state of emergency. Nevertheless, Mr. and Mrs. Sealy, two Africans from the village of Buxton, were hacked to death on May 23 as they tended their farms in the backlands. The news caused an outbreak of violence in several parts of the country.

In Georgetown people were beaten, some severely, and robbed that very night. Afro-Guyanese farmers were ambushed, shot, and killed in the Mahaicomy River. Several other killings took place in the same area. That weekend, large-scale violence erupted at McKenzie (now renamed Linden), where Africans are in a majority. When the situation was brought under control, two people had died and many others were hospitalized. Over 200 houses and businesses were completely burned. The total Indian population of that area had to flee to the coast. Thereafter, the police and British Army launched a massive search for arms and ammunition across the country.

On June 12, Senior Civil Servant Arthur Abraham and seven of his nine children were burned to death in their home in Georgetown. Mr. Abraham's daughter was an active United Force executive member. Their deaths sent the recorded figure to 43 in 121 days of upheavals. The next day, June 13, the Governor stepped in and ordered the detention of 33 persons belonging to the People's Progressive Party and the People's National Congress.

The governor, with the assistance of British Troops and local forces, began to take more personal control of perserving domestic order; nevertheless, sporadic violence continued. Amid the hellish turmoil, registration for the elections proceeded as scheduled and the election date was fixed for December 7, 1964.

New Parties: Hopes for Support

As had been predicted by Colonial Secretary Sandys, a number of new political parties sprung up as elections were announced. The Guyana United Muslim Party (GUMP) formed to appeal to the Muslim section of the Indian population. The party was led by Mr. Hoosein Ghanie. The Justice Party (JP) was led by former PPP minister Mr. Balram Singh Rai. (Mr. Rai had left the PPP after losing a struggle for the Chairmanship of the party.) Mr. Jai Narine Singh, who had formerly been associated with the PPP, the PNC, and was head of the then defunct Guyana Independence Party, was also closely associated with the JP. The Peace and Equality Party (PEP) was headed by Mr. Kelvin de Freitas, and the old National Labour Front (NLF) was led by Mr. Cecil Grey. Of the new parties, the ones thought to be in any serious contention for votes and that mounted serious campaigns were the Guyana United Muslim Party and the Justice Party. It was the intention of the leaders of these parties to try to appeal to the supporters of the People's Progressive Party. The PPP, the PNC, and the UF each had modern, elaborate and well financed campaigns, the best that the country had seen until then.

Apart from its manifesto, the PPP had to stand on its record in government. The PPP platform speakers defended against opposition accusations of the administration's ineptitude and racist tendencies. They accused the main opposition parties of being "reactionary" and of not giving the duly elected government the cooperation it deserved in trying to bring about social reform. It accused the opposition of being caught in a position of advocating the cause of those who were intent on preserving their positions of privilege. These accusations were aimed especially at the PNC, which the PPP always said was closer to itself and was working for the same ideals even though employing different tactics. The PPP further accused the PNC of being racist in trying to appeal particularly to the African population and of espousing the cause and grievances of the civil servants who were mainly African. The civil servants, the PPP claimed, tended to be a privileged group relative to the rest of the society, and their fight was one that would benefit and improve their position only. In addition, the PPP felt that the general ideology of many of the top civil servants was not one for the promotion of rapid change. The PPP then was interested in finding and promoting those who could help them execute their policies.

PNC platform speakers, on the other hand, accused the PPP of lacking administrative ability and of governing on behalf of one group of people only—PPP supporters. It also accused the PPP of wasting money on the Del Conte road project.

Over $1 million was allocated and spent by the company before the project was brought to an end because of mismanagement. At the end of the scandal the government did not even salvage the machinery used by the company. The PNC held this up as a classic case of government carelessness. It offered its slate of candidates as a group of educated, knowledgeable, and able administrators.

The PNC dwelt constantly on the topic of peace and stability and blamed the PPP government for not being able to control the forces of violence. It contended that the violence was a direct result of the mismanagement and fear that the PPP government had produced by its policies and method of governing. The PNC speakers said that their party needed a chance to show the Guyanese people the level of performance they were capable of as an alternative to the PPP. They implored the electorate to give them a chance since Jagan had already had a chance to show what he could do. The PNC leader, Forbes Burnham, was stronger in his speeches. He said that independence was inevitable no matter who won the election. He exhorted the Guyanese people to make up their minds once and for all—Burnham or

Jagan, while he dismissed all thoughts of a coalition with the United Force, a popular suggestion at the time. He said that his party would take no part in a PNC-UF, or any coalition. The PNC stated their plan for social and economic development of the country in a manifesto entitled "New Road."

New Parties in the Elections

The Peace and Equality party never seemed to launch a campaign. What little it did caused no serious differences, as the results indicated, since the party ended with 224 votes. The National Labour Front likewise did not seem to have a chance nor did its leaders even pretend that it was in a national campaign. The party collected a meager 177 votes. The Guyana United Muslim Party and the Justice Party were the two new parties most commentators expected to make a good showing. It was expected that the GUMP would concentrate, as indeed it did, on the Muslim section of the Indian population that traditionally supported the PPP. The Party's appeal was mainly religious, as one of its pamphlets shows: "A Vote for GUMP is a vote for Allah." Contrary to what was expected, the party made a very poor showing at the election, polling only 1,194 votes.

The Justice Party (JP) was the newcomer to watch. The party had as its leadership two politicians who had been on the national scene for some time, and Balram Singh Rai was known to have had substantial support while in the PPP. Jai Narine Singh had been in the PPP of 1953, was a minister and a legislator for the PPP (Burnhamites), and also a past president of the old East Indian Association. It was thought that of all the new parties, the JP had the best chance of wresting a substantial number of votes from the PPP, especially since they concentrated their appeal to the same constituency—the Indian vote. The JP mounted what appeared to be a well financed and organized campaign. Its platform speakers stressed that the PPP was not only Communist, but anti-religious. Despite this, the party's efforts only yielded 1,334 votes. None of the four new parties managed to qualify for even one seat in the Legislature.

From the time the date of the election was announced, there was a marked decrease in the violence throughout the country. The election was conducted under the system of proportional representation, with each party submitting a list of its candidates in order of preference. Under this system, votes are cast for the party and not for particular individuals. A party, however, because of its traditional support could predict a certain number of safe seats. This meant that those at the top of the list were automatically likely to become legislators in the case of the main political parties. The idea of the system was to get the party working together as a whole unit. But this made the leaders of these parties more vulnerable to the accusation of favoring some people. Those at the bottom of the list in some cases thought that they had less reason for enthusiastic work than those who were at the top.

Registration and Voting

At registration, 247,604 electors were on the voting list out of a voting population of 605,000. A total of seven political parties contested the elections. The parties each put up candidates that reflected the level of its expectations.

Guyana United Muslim Party (GUMP)	14 candidates
Justice Party (JP)	36 candidates
National Labour Front	6 candidates
Peace and Equality Party (PEP)	2 candidates
People's National Congress (PNC)	53 candidates
People's Progressive Party (PPP)	35 candidates
United Force (UF)	53 candidates
Total	119 candidates

On election day, December 7, 1964, voting was very heavy. The parties had reminded the people that every vote counted. At the election 238,530 persons, 96.9 percent of the electorate, cast their votes. The parties received respectively:

TABLE 6

People's Progressive Party (PPP)	190,332	24 seats
People's National Congress (PNC)	96,651	22 seats
United Force (UF)	29,612	7 seats
Justice Party (JP)	1,334	
Guyana United Muslim Party (GUMP)	1,119	
Peace and Equality Party (PEP)	224	
National Labour Front (NLF)	177	
Total		53 seats[53]

The voting showed no change in the ethnic alignments of the political parties. In many cases it was more pronounced. It affirmed the dominance of the PNC and the PPP as the only parties with any mass following. Little can be added to what has already been said about the election. But the comment of one member of the Commonwealth Team of Observers is fitting: "In British Guiana the atmosphere is charged with fear. The election therefore was not for the support of any programme. It was a racial census as the analysis of voting would clearly show. It was a race in search of security and this also accounted for the heavy polling."[84]

The large turnout at the polls was an indication of the importance almost every Guyanese attached to the final outcome. In terms of percentages, there were some notable shifts when compared with the 1961 result; the new systems, however, produced a different result:

	1961 %	1964 %	% Change
PPP	42.63	45.84	3.21 increase
PNC	40.99	40.52	.47 decrease
UF	16.38	12.41	3.97 decrease

While there were slight shifts in the percentages of votes gained or lost, the percentages made a great difference in the number of seats which each party was awarded.

TABLE 7

		Seats 1961	Seats 1964
PPP		20	24
PNC		11	22
UF		4	7
	Total	35	53

The results show quite clearly that under the system of proportional representation, even though the PPP had an *increase* in popular support, the opposition parties (PNC and UF) made a substantial gain in the number of seats they got in the legislature in relation to those of the PPP. Hence the reason why the PPP, within a week of the election results, were holding rallies up and down the country shouting "cheated not defeated."

As head of the party that had polled the most votes and had won the most seats,[85] but not sufficient to command a majority in Parliament, Dr. Jagan was asked to form a new government. When Jagan was not able to do so, the governor called in Forbes Burnham to take up the task on December 13. The formation of a PNC-UF coalition government did not come as a surprise to most of the PNC and UF supporters who had opposed the PPP government from 1962. It is true that Burnham had said during the election campaign that he would not form a coalition government under any circumstances, but this was interpreted by the voters as a ploy to try to win his party as much electoral support as possible to increase his party's say within a coalition.

PPP Leaves Office

Because the PPP felt that it was "cheated not defeated," Dr. Jagan refused to resign. The constitution had to be amended to enable the Governor to revoke his appointment. The departing of the PPP from government marked the end of seven years of continuous political rule. During the period 1961–1964, the government, though given much more autonomy than before, constrained itself because of its ideological stand, its style, and use of power. This constraint, in turn, gave the government an illusion of being much weaker than it really was.

The years 1957–1964 were to be the years of political maturation. Instead, they turned out to be years of confrontation and struggle for power between rival parties. The division of the two major parties along ethnic lines only produced more interracial conflict. Even though the PNC-UF formed a viable government, they still had to contend with the fact that the largest ethnic majority in the country was not adequately represented within their own political structure.

The PNC-UF Coalition

The formation of a coalition government between the People's National Congress and the United Force in December 1964 allayed the fears of many Guyanese who were deeply disturbed about the violence during the preceding years; much more, it was welcomed by all of those who were working for the defeat of the PPP. Externally, it was also welcomed because the UF was seen as a stabilizing influence to the Socialist tendencies of the PNC. The alliance created between the PNC and the UF prior to the election was only formed, however, in an attempt to oust the PPP from office: the PNC and UF had little in common. The PNC espoused a brand of socialism, and the UF advocated a strong capitalist ideology. As a matter of fact, most observers knew that a more likely combination would have been a PPP-PNC coalition, since both of these parties claimed to be socialist. But by 1964, at the end of the election, so much ill-feeling existed between the PPP and PNC supporters that a coalition between the two was impossible.

Premier Burnham presented a fifteen person cabinet of twelve PNC and three UF ministers to administer the country's affairs. Though a coalition in principle from the beginning, it was dominated by the PNC. But for S. S. Ramphal, who was brought back from Jamaica to assume the post of Attorney General as a technocrat, each member of the Cabinet had a political base of his or her own. These factors reassured skeptics that Premier Burnham was really serious when he said that his government would be a "consultative democracy."

The strategy of the PNC from the time it took office was geared toward the early achievement of independence and securing the government for itself. To do this, it tried to restore confidence at home and abroad very quickly, and begin a dialogue with opposition activists and supporters through its position in government. The party's whole thrust was one of conciliation. Even though the violence had abated substantially when the new government took over, Burnham kept the emergency in force so as to deal with any dissidence that might surface. The impression conveyed was that the government was going to be tough yet sympathetic.

First, the tactic of confidence. Apart from the fact that the coalition itself generated confidence because of its composition, the government gained greater confidence among opinion leaders by the appointments it made. By launching a high program of renovation and rebuilding, it was able to put a number of unemployed people, many of whom were its supporters, to work. PNC ministers visited areas of strong opposition support to hear their grievances and anxieties. The government also appointed a committee to advise on "what steps and action may be taken to rehabilitate and bring assistance to those persons, those Guyanese, who have in any way suffered as a result of the disturbances which plagued our country from 1962–1964."[86] To further allay the fears of opposition supporters, the government invited the International Commission of Jurists to investigate allegations of imbalances in the government sector.[87]

The Government was able to undertake many of its programs within months of assuming office because of the large sums of aid that the USA, Canada, and Britain rushed to extend to it as its needs became known.[88] The lucrative Cuban rice market was given up by the government, but the subsidy paid to the farmer remained unchanged.

Nevertheless, the East Indian population remained somewhat uneasy toward the coalition. They saw it as African dominated and were justifiably suspicious in view of the fierce opposition of two races from 1962 to 1964.

Secondly, politics. PNC ministers, as the UF was to complain later, spent as much time on the road as they spent in their offices. These ministers were constantly campaigning in areas where their own support was strong, but also in areas where the opposition PPP was strong. They tried to reassure PPP supporters that they were safer under the PNC-UF coalition. They reminded them that their cooperation was necessary because the PNC was in charge of the allocation of funds for the improvements to their drainage and irrigation for their rice lands and for other village improvements. This ploy gave the PNC ministers and activists an opening to begin a dialogue with staunch PPP supporters in the rural areas.

Against the United Force, the PNC tactic was simple; it took credit for every achievement made while at the same time it complained of not being able to do more because it was saddled with an incompatible coalition partner. As time went on, the operative expression of the PNC ministers changed from "PNC-UF Government" to "PNC-led Government."[89]

In November 1965 the parties went to London again for constitutional talks. On this occasion everyone was reasonably certain that independence would be granted to the country. Dr. Jagan and the PPP, who had at first refused to take up their seats in Parliament because of their objection to PR, eventually did so in April 1965, but refused to attend the talks. They objected because the government, still operating under the existing emergency, had detained sixteen PPP leaders and activists for the preservation of law and order. The Secretary of State himself appealed to Dr. Jagan and the PPP to attend the conference, but Dr. Jagan rejected his appeal. The Conference proceeded with only the PNC and UF in attendance.

The Conference ended with the PNC, the UF, and British Government agreeing that "British Guiana should become independent under the name Guyana on 26 May 1966."

NOTES

1. Simms, *Trouble in Guyana*, pp. 153–154.
2. V. S. Naipaul, *The Middle Passage* (London: Andre Deutsch, 1962), p. 132.
3. Simms, *Trouble in Guyana*, p. 153.
4. Arthur M. Schlesinger, Jr., *A Thousand Days—John F. Kennedy in the White House* (Boston: Houghton Mifflin, 1965) pp. 774–777.
5. Ibid., p. 773.
6. Ibid., pp. 777–779.
7. Simms, *Trouble in Guyana*, p. 155.
8. Fourth Committee 1251 meeting, December 15, 1961 (A/C.4/S514), p. 603.
9. Ibid., p. 603.
10. Ibid., p. 604.
11. Fourth Committee 1252nd Meeting. Monday 18 December 1961 (A/C.4SR1252), p. 612.
12. Ibid., p. 611.
13. Ibid.
14. Fourth Committee 1254th Meeting, Tuesday, 19 December 1961 (A/C.4/SR/1254), p. 619.
15. Report of a Commission of Inquiry into Disturbances in Business Guiana in February 1962, Col. 354, p. 13.
16. Ibid., pp. 14–15.
17. *Graphic*, January 31, 1962; *Chronicle*, February 1, 1962; *Chronicle*, February 4, 1962.
18. Report of a Commission of Inquiry into Disturbances in British Guiana in February 1962, Col. 354, p. 13.
19. *Graphic*, Thursday, February 8, 1962. Since the appointment of Jack Kelshall as Dr. Jagan's Private Secretary the UF had waged a verbal and press battle against his presence in the country. They interpreted his presence in the country as indicative of Jagan's intent on turning Guyana into a communist state.
20. *Hansard*, February 9, 1962.
21. Ibid.
22. Ibid.
23. Simms, *Trouble in Guyana*, p. 158. See also Jagan, *The West on Trial*, pp. 258–259; Dr. Jagan claims that the group was led by Dr. Ptolemy Reid, then an executive member of the PNC. He later became Deputy leader and Deputy Prime Minister. The Report of a Commission of Inquiry into Disturbances in British Guiana in February 1962 names him as the person who obstructed the vision of Dr. Jagan's driver thus impeding his exit.
24. Report of a Commission of Inquiry into Disturbances in British Guiana in February 1962, Col. 354, p. 26.
25. Interview with General Secretary of the TUC.
26. Report of a Commission of Inquiry into Disturbances in British Guiana, in February 1962, Col. 354, p. 35.
27. Ibid., p. 35.
28. Ibid., p. 30.
29. Ibid., p. 35.
30. Ibid., p. 36.
31. Ibid., p. 54.
32. Ibid., p. 41.
33. Ibid., p. 41.

34. Ibid., p. 30.
35. Ibid.
36. Ibid., p. 36.
37. Ibid., p. 37.
38. Interview with PNC executive member.
39. Report of a Commission of Inquiry into Disturbances in British Guiana in February 1962, Col. 354, p. 29.
40. "Esoteric Communications—ostensively ideological or theological communications but actual policy directions by ruling elites to sub-elites." For a full treatment of the subject see William E. Griffith, *Communist Esoteric Communications Explication de Texte*, Centre for International Studies, MIT, Cambridge, Mass. 1967.
41. Mrs. Jagan's analysis of these events suggests that this was considered, but then dismissed. "A counter-demonstration of its strength by bringing its supporters into the city could only have produced civil war." Janet Jagan, *Monthly Review*, April, 1962, p. 566.
42. Report of a Commission of Inquiry into Disturbances in British Guiana in February 1962, Col. 354, pp. 37–39.
43. Ibid.
44. Ibid.
45. Ibid.
46. Ibid.
47. Ibid., pp. 44–45.
48. Ibid.
49. For a different analysis of the events and actors, see Janet Jagan, "What Happened in British Guiana," *Monthly Review*, April, 1962, pp. 559–567.
50. Ibid., pp. 562–563.
51. Report of a Commission of Inquiry into Disturbances in British Guiana in February 1962, Col. 354, p. 50.
52. Simms, *Trouble in Guyana*, p. 157.
53. Report of a Commission of Inquiry into Disturbances in British Guiana in February 1962, Col. 354, p. 52.
54. Report of the British Guiana Constitutional Commission 1954, Cmd 9274/253.
55. Ibid., pp. 52–53.
56. For an excellent analysis and history of the organization see Harold Lutchman's *Interest Representation in the Public Service*, (P.S.C. Publication, 1973).
57. Janet Jagan, "What Happened in British Guiana," *Monthly Review*, April 1962, p. 567.
58. British Guiana Independence Conference 1962 HMSO London Cmd. 1870 Annex A, p. 5.
59. Ibid., p. 6.
60. Ibid., p. 3.
61. *Chronicle*, April 6, 1963.
62. As quoted in the *Freedom Strikers*, an account of the 1963 general strike by the TUC, p. vii.
63. Interview with trade union leader.
64. *Graphic*, April 21, 1963.
65. Minutes of the Legislative Assembly, April 22, 1963.
66. *Graphic*, May 2, 1963.
67. Passive Resistance PR was a very apt slogan for the two opposition parties who were advocating Proportional Representation PR as the new form for elections.
68. For details of the PNC's Plan X-13, see Jagan, *The West on Trial*, pp. 282–283.

69. Minutes of the Legislative Assembly, May 28, 1963.
70. *Chronicle*, June 2, 1963.
71. Ibid.
72. Harold Lutchman, *Interest Representation in the Public Service*, P.S.A. 1975, pp. 278–279.
73. Newman, *British Guiana*, p. 95.
74. The report of the 1963 Constitutional Conference gives as the reason for the breakdown of talks "disagreement over the allocation of Cabinet Seats." See Cmd. 2203, 1963, p. 3.
75. British Guiana Conference, 1963, Cmd. 2203, Annex B.
76. British Guiana, Independence Conference 1963, B.G. (H) (63) rth Meeting, Copy No. 37.
77. British Guiana Conference 1963, Cmd. 2203, 1963, p. 4.
77. British Guiana Conference 1963, Cmd 2203, 1963, p. 4.
78. Ibid., Annex A, pp. 6–8.
79. Ibid.
80. *Chronicle*, February 18, April 1, April 10, 1964.
81. Dr. Jagan in his memoir insists that a tacit agreement was reached but Mr. Burnham reneged after the mission had left.
82. *Chronicle*, April 29, 1964.
83. British Guiana, Report by the Commonwealth Team of Observers on the Election in December 1964, Col. No. 359, p. 4.
84. Ibid., Appendix VII, memorandum by Ali Mirza, p. 14.
85. Dr. Jagan states that he had "offered the PNC leadership a coalition based on parity in the Council of Ministers and a negotiated settlement on the premiership," (WT, 377).
86. Forbes Burnham, "Report to the Nation," Guyana Information Services, 1965, p. 18.
87. Ibid.
88. Ibid.
89. Report of the British Guiana Independence Conference 1965 and Cmd. 2849, p. 6.

PART 2

Independence
and
Development

CHAPTER 8

Agreement and Dissension after Independence

THE Commonwealth students in London during the 1960s referred to the granting of independence by the British Government to their colonies as "the briefcase revolution." It was a revolution where administrative control was signed over to the native government after a certain period of tutelage and negotiation. But the lowering of the Union Jack and the hoisting of the flag of the newborn nation was only an outward manifestation of the intense struggle which was about to begin. It was the inevitable result of the extreme artificiality of colonial society and government.

Before independence, the politicians had made the usual grandiose promises to the people. And, of course, the various individual groups had their own ideas of what the promised economic and political freedom would mean. The politicians had skillfully aroused the latent passion, pride and ingenuity of their people which had been held in check by administrative rules and laws instituted by the colonial power. Their job after independence was to satisfy the expectations of their people, while holding on to their own political base. At the same time they had to provide the stability to attract investments and the necessary skilled personnel. The challenge of reconciling these contradictory policies required more skill than had been required to oppose an already foundering colonial government. To do so with a nation bristling with expectation after years of political activism and struggle is a staggering objective for any administration.

The Economic Outlook: 1966

Domestically the economy of Guyana had been revived and was beginning to grow. In his budget speech on April 5, 1966, the Minister of Finance, Peter S. D'Aguiar, was able to report, "In 1965 we made a good start. We repaired the damage to the economy caused by the events of the past three years. We restored confidence in good government.

"As I predicted in my Budget Speech last year, the economy has passed out of the doldrums of 1962, 1963 and 1964, and has recovered its momentum. Production in 1965—about $325M in terms of the gross domestic product at factor cost—was 8% higher than in 1964 and would have been higher still but for the present unfavorable market conditions for our principal agricultural exports, sugar and rice. However, bauxite and alumina exports were 13% higher in value than the previous year, pushing domestic exports up to about $165M—$5M more than the previous year's." In outlining the government's aims for that year Mr. D'Aguiar went on to state: "The 1966 Capital Estimates continue to aim at the objective of stimulating employment and income. Total expenditure this year at $45.9M is the highest ever projected for any single year. There is a heavy accent on construction—mainly roads, on which $7M is to be spent. Some $3.6M is to be spent on sea defenses and drainage and irrigation works; $6.9M on public buildings, housing and site development; $5.2M on railway, steamer and air transport (including Atkinson Field Airport); $2.4M on schools; $2.7M on geological, hydrological and topographic surveys; $3M on the armed forces and police; $2.3M on industry and credit." The Finance Minister went on to outline how he proposed to finance the massive public works improvement, and development he had outlined. "The funds in sight for financing this programme of expenditure total $42.2M; CD and W grants—$6.1M; USAID grants—$5.5M; United Nations grants—$1.0M; and grants from Canada, West Germany and other sources—$2.9M; together with $2.0M from Exchequer Loans; $2.3M from USAID loans; $1.2M from contractor-finance; and $21M from other borrowing—mainly local. The profits of the national bingo and lottery will add $1.2M. All but $10M of this is reasonably assured."[1]

Both in 1965 and 1966 budgets placed a heavy emphasis on rebuilding and improving the country's infrastructure, which had been neglected or destroyed during the years of PPP government. The sources of the aid for this rebuilding give a clear indication of the confidence the Western governments had in the PNC-UF coalition and suggest how anxious they were to see it succeed. The success of the PNC-UF coalition in obtaining aid and in improving the economy did not prevent them from competing individually for electoral support and maneuvering for political advantage. The need for skilled and unskilled workers to man these projects saw the PNC emerge as the main dispenser of patronage. Congress Place, the PNC head office on Camp Street, functioned almost exclusively as an employment office. Party activists were given first preference on most unskilled, low-level jobs. Sympathizers and others were coerced or voluntarily joined the party in large numbers so as to obtain employment. The ability to deliver jobs, coupled with the large amounts of international aid it was then receiving, made the PNC very credible in the eyes of an electorate tired of political conflict. Coupled with the fact that a $300M seven-year development program (1966–1972) had been laid before the house a few weeks before the budget was, people seemed sure that the PNC-UF was going to be in office for sometime and that these sources would continue to finance the country's development. By running the government in a way in which seemed fair and competent, the coalition undermined the confidence of some of the PPP's political supporters.

Old Problems, New Realities

Colonial economies as they exist prior to independence are usually dependent, existing primarily for the production of raw materials for the "mother country." Such an economy is a partnership between the government of the colony, headed by the governor, and the business enterprises, mainly from the mother country. Much of the policy which guides a colony is written and enforced against this backdrop. Not much encouragement is given to the development of indigenous business unless it is service oriented and does not compete with trade from the mother country. The result of this colonial policy for Guyana was that its large sugar estates produced raw sugar which was sent to London, refined, and re-exported back to Guyana. Bauxite, the country's main mineral resource, was sent to Canada and the U.S. to be processed into aluminum. The government, headed by the governor, was authoritarian and represented not the people of Guyana but the business interests and a relatively small local group.

Because the local non-white civil servant or business executive was seldom allowed to rise above a certain grade in his profession, no true meritocracy was ever established. This is why the radical political parties such as the PPP in 1953 were supported by such a large cross section of people—the workers, the lower level civil servants and the semi-professional groups. Independence meant access to jobs, affluence and power.

In order to fulfill expectations without altering too much the party's plan, the post-colonial must appeal to everyone, which imposes strains on its manpower. A larger bureaucracy is necessary. The government must also reorganize and reorientate the civil service, already too small for its new responsibilities, to its new larger role. The vacuum created by the departure of the expatriate senior civil servants creates a hasty and sometimes antagonistic jockeying to fill the vacated positions. This vacuum, which permeates every branch of government, the police, the army and the civil service, can be a source of much power to the politician if he can establish himself as the sole arbiter for the internal maneuverings.[2] In most cases, the minister or party to which he belongs will appoint someone whom they feel is loyal and sympathetic to their policy. The ability to appoint the top administrators becomes a crucial link in the party's strategy to remain in office for any length of time. At the same time, the government also succeeds in significantly reducing the power of a potentially strong interest group—probably the one group with enough technical and political know how to question government policy and propose alternatives. An important section of the middle class is thus bought off quite early by the politicians. It is against this backdrop that Guyana became independent on May 26, 1966.

Not long after independence Prime Minister Forbes Burnham traveled to Canada, to the Commonwealth Caribbean heads of Government Conference in Ottawa. In the years prior to independence Canada, as a more affluent commonwealth nation, had given increasing amounts of aid to Guyana and the Caribbean nations. This conference was called to discuss aid to all of the Caribbean nations rather than have each country compete with each other for aid and for the financing of similar projects. After the conference Prime Minister Burnham went on a tour of Canada. Among the places he visited were the plants of the Aluminum Company of Canada (Alcan) and the Canadian Multi National Corporation, which was the main extractor of bauxite in Guyana. Burnham was impressed with the number of jobs and wealth that this industry, whose main raw material supplier was Guyana, could generate. In talking with the Company's management he extracted an agreement from them to expand their operations in Guyana when the large amounts of electrical power necessary became available. Burnham knew that hydroelectricity was particularly suited for Guyana, with its many rivers, and that plans were already being made by his government for a hydroelectric project. Thus was the economic model for Guyana crystalized in Burnham's mind. Bauxite would serve as a lead to creating an industrial base, a co-operative sector and a strong agricultural sector.

Grants to the government from Western Governments and international organizations in 1965 and 1966 were double those of 1964. In addition the government was quite successful in attracting back to the country many of those Guyanese who had gone abroad to study and work. Even a few of those people who had emigrated earlier to Britain and North America returned. The return of these people, the steadily increasing economic activity, and the high credibility of the government all fueled the hope most people had for a prosperous future.

Meet the People Politics

Before independence the official religious emphasis in the country had been entirely Christian. No official recognition had ever been given to the religions of the Hindu and Muslim sections of the country, even though they comprised nearly 50% of the population. The coalition government consented to the introduction of a private bill making four Hindu and Muslim religious festivals national holidays. By so doing, the government reinforced its seriousness in building and recognizing the varied cultural heritage of the different cultural groups. This gesture helped allay some of the fears many Indians had when the government came to office, that their interests would be neglected.

Through all of this excitement the PNC never stopped campaigning. The UF leader and ministers objected to the constant absence of PNC ministers from their desks. The difference in ideology and emphasis between the UF and the PNC was most apparent at the cabinet meetings, when major decisions had to be made. The PNC members of the Cabinet complained that the UF was seeking to influence the cabinet out of proportion to the representation it had achieved at the election.

Peter D'Aguiar was forceful in articulating his views and threatened constantly, as the leader who held the "balance of power," to resign and bring the government down after him.

On February 5, 1965, Mr. Burnham appointed F. O. Pilgrim as his public relations officer. Soon after taking up his appointment Pilgrim suggested that the Prime Minister undertake a number of "meet the people" tours throughout the country to both strengthen his image and improve his party's support. The first tour was planned for the PNC stronghold of Linden and took place on March 9, 1965. The response to the experiment was so successful that such tours became a permanent feature on the Prime Minister's schedule. Successful visits were made soon after to the PPP strongholds on the West Coast, Annandale, and to the squatters' areas outside Georgetown where the PNC enjoyed virtually no support. These forays into what used to be impregnable PPP strongholds seem to have convinced the PNC that its chances of winning over some PPP support were enhanced by its being in office. As a result, the PNC-UF coalition made a special effort to be even-handed in making senior government appointments. On his tours the Prime Minister was accompanied by members of his staff who made notes of the complaints made and passed these on to the appropriate ministry for action. Because these complaints were made to the ministry by way of the Office of the Prime Minister, they were usually resolved quickly. The prestige of having the Prime Minister visit a town or village and the chance of having their problems resolved made every village clamour for a visit.

The PPP, the Government and the Rice Industry

Shortly after forming the new government in 1964, the PNC-UF coalition arbitrarily gave up the lucrative Cuban rice export market. Even though the Cubans paid a higher price for the rice it received from Guyana than could be obtained on the international market, trade between the two countries was contrary to the policy of the U.S. and the West. It was also contrary to the U.S.-inspired O.A.S. trade embargo against Cuba. Because the PPP had used the Cuban rice arrangement both as a party arrangement as well as a government arrangement, the policy, though a good one at the time, came to be seen in purely political terms within the country. By appointing GIMPEX, the PPP's business arm, as agent for the procurement and shipment of the rice, the PPP made what should have been a business deal a political one. The Cubans, on the other hand, by sending the PPP gifts (like a printing press) which contributed to the strengthening of the PPP, detracted from the purely "businesslike" nature of the deal and angered the opposition parties. So, upon coming into office the PNC-UF coalition had not only external pressures, but their own political reasons as well for giving up the Cuban rice market.

However, even though rice cultivation had been put on a firm economic footing by the Jagan government from 1957–1964, the industry was plagued with problems. Several countries, including the United States, had entered the market and developed a better strain of rice, therefore enabling them to plant less acreage, get a better yield, and so acquire the most lucrative markets. In Guyana the industry suffered from inappropriate mechanization. Because the variety of paddy cultivated was unsuited for mechanical harvesting, yield per acre fell and total output only increased marginally in response to a sizeable expansion of the total acreage under cultivation.

The government responded by reorganizing the Rice Marketing Board, which had the exclusive authority for buying and selling rice in the country. They expelled all known PPP members from it and replaced them with professionals more sympathetic to the coalition government. The new board then reduced the price paid to farmers for certain grades of rice. The grades affected were the lower ones. It was hoped that this would cause farmers to produce a better quality of rice and increase productivity. By reorganizing the rice industry the government inadvertently accomplished two objectives. First was making the industry more efficient, as the Finance Minister stated: "We must improve the efficiency of the rice industry both in its husbandry and its marketing. There is no lack of markets for rice, but we are not producing at a price or of a quality, and not marketing in forms that enable us to sell profitably in the highly competitive and sophisticated world market. The industry by its defects in this respect and by living beyond its means has built up a huge debt of some $20M.

"The higher level of exports projected ($20M more), the higher level of Government expenditure I shall now propose (at least $15M more is feasible), and I hope a higher level of private investment expenditures, should raise production and expenditure this year at least 10% over last year's."[3]

Second, by making the industry more commercial the government

was indirectly putting the burden of improving the industry on the
farmers themselves. In political terms this meant that the rice farmers,
the backbone of PPP support, had to become more independent of the
government if they were to survive, and needed to spend their own
money to do so. Taken a bit further, that meant diminished contributions to the PPP. "Despite a flattering supposition to the contrary,
people come readily to terms with power. . . . But as the ghosts of
numerous tyrants, from Julius Caesar to Benito Mussolini, will testify,
people are very hard on those who, having had power, lose it or are
destroyed. Then anger at past arrogance is joined with contempt for
weakness. The victim or his corpse is made to suffer all available indig-
nities,"[4] and this was the case with the PPP by 1967.

Self-Analysis and Mid-Term Campaign

On January 17, 1967, the Evening Post carried the headline: "PNC
Put Election Campaign into Gear." The report stated that the Prime
Minister had made a number of administrative changes in preparation
for elections. The article also noted that the Prime Minister had told
the general council of his party that the PNC campaign for the next
election had in fact begun. Though it did not evoke any comment from
the other parties, it disturbed the PNC that the news was leaked to the
press as they were trying to proceed with their election strategy with
the utmost secrecy. The PNC, however, had a big advantage in terms
of appealing to the people over the other political parties. They dominated the coalition government and were fully in charge of allocating
all lower level, mainly unskilled, government jobs.

The PNC paper, the New Nation, on February 12, 1967, showed
pictures of the party's chairman, Mrs. Gaskin, and many other senior
party officials addressing meetings in areas where the PNC enjoyed
strong support. The caption said quite clearly that the meetings were
the beginning of the PNC's election campaign. Everyone knew that
elections were almost two years away so little attention seemed to be
paid to these activities. This mid-term campaign by the PNC lasted
nearly six weeks and produced severe strains in the cabinet. The PNC,
on the other hand, always disgruntled at having to share power with
the UF, made up their minds at the inception of the coalition to win
the next election outright. Their problem, however, was that people's
interest had changed from politics to economics and the PNC found

great difficulty trying to rekindle the former level of political interest of its supporters.

The papers presented at the annual delegates congress of the PNC in April 1967 at Anna Regina provided an interesting analysis of the way the party saw itself and its strategy for the elections that were eventually to take place in December 1968. The party's General Secretary, Mr. Hamilton Green, set the tone for the conference when he said "we have with some examination and correction a party capable of being the government as a single entity." As leader of the party, Mr. Burnham's speech to the congress was a brilliant one. It was confident, persuasive, encouraging and flattering. He began by saying:

"Last year, Congress was held on the eve of Independence, just after a year of office. The enthusiasm from the latter had hardly worn off and anticipation of the former created a great deal of hopeful emotion.

"Now, however, we are nearly a year from Independence and more than half way through one term of office in Government. The exercise, therefore, this year should be to make a realistic assessment of our achievements and failures, concrete plans for tackling the national problems which still remain and strengthening the Party for the tasks, electoral and otherwise which must be accomplished."

After outlining the government's policy and intentions in several key areas of the economy and its success thus far, he turned his attention to the business at hand. He went on:

So far, I have been outlining some of the proposals and goals of the Party in office and pointing to the role of the groups, the activists and the rank and file. This role, however, cannot be effectively played unless we get our party machine back to the point where it was in December, 1964, and the members become more actively involved.

After the Herculean effort of 1964 and the end of one period of our country's history, many party members felt that the millennium had come—that there would be full employment and all the problems would silently fade away. This attitude gained even more currency after the achievement of Independence in spite of the frequent warnings of the party leadership.

For instance, the point was not convincingly brought home to the membership that there were not enough jobs for all who were unemployed and that the emphasis would have to be on self-employment especially on the land. At the same time, a sufficiently vigorous campaign was not waged to reorient the many young men and women who felt that farming was and is an undignified and unrewarding occupation. Day after day enough was not done to develop initiative and self-reliance amongst comrades. And even where these qualities were present the institutions and agencies did not exist to give the proper assistance and encouragement. We have in many instances been stumbling in the dark.

There can be no doubt that though there has not been real disenchantment amongst our members, there has been a great deal of frustration and belly aching. This indicates a weakness in the leadership at various levels—national and group.

Conscious of this, I have reorganized the Cabinet so that with a full time Deputy I may be able to devote more time to the Party and its organization. I have found that though hundreds of groups still continue to exist and meet from time to time, most of them lack specific purpose and projects and are not *au fait* with Government's policy, tactics and strategy. They are loyal but grouping.

These groups require more purposeful contact with the centre and a greater attempt must be made to recruit into them party members and supporters in the area who can add more zest and life. The party group must become the place where things are happening and where people come to be informed, educated and led.

The first task is that of the national leadership. Unfortunately, the greater part of this segment of the Party is in the Parliament and Cabinet with all the pressure on time and energy that that means. But the middle leadership in the context will not be inspired unless there is a lead from the centre. And those at the centre, including myself, have got to show more realistic humility.

Our top leadership consists predominantly of those who in the rough and tumble of the last period stuck to their guns and the Party loyally— people who far from being ashamed were proud of their PNC connection.

But this is a new period where more than courage and devotion are necessary. There must be a re-examination of our ideological position and an interpretation and application of our philosophy to the facts and situation. For instance, what does socialism in our circumstances mean? What tactics must be distinguished from strategy? All this is necessary but can only be done if we meet periodically. Too many of our top leadership are too tired or self-opinionated to do it and important briefings, seminars and discussions are missed on the flimsiest of excuses.

This is the era of organization, mobilization and indoctrination. The blind will lead the blind into the bottomless pit. If we do not have our goals and strategy clear, how can we communicate them? Organizing for opposition differs in important aspects from organization and a people for the march forward. Flowery speeches and bold and dramatic but empty postures wear thin. Fine promises divorced from the realities and performance boomerang. Unhonoured undertakings breed contempt and disillusionment. Such undertakings may be seriously and honestly meant but unrealistic if the facts are known. Tell the people the truth, take them into your confidence, they will understand. But you cannot tell the people the truth unless you know it. Positions and situations have to be thought out and new initiatives shown. Dedication and time-consuming preparation is necessary. If you cannot rise to these, like the unbeaten world champion, retire. Words no longer satisfy people.

On the fringe of the Party are some young men and women of imagination, earnestness and ability. The older brigade fear them often at the subconscious level and imagine that they are out to storm certain untrenched positions won after years of sweat, toil and blood.

Many of these young men and women on the other hand for fear of earning enmity, fail to throw themselves into the movement whole-heartedly. Others rationalize their own laziness and selfishness and adopt a supercilious and superficial attitude—criticizing but not doing. The old must adapt, the new must work. Our future and destiny and those of our nation are at stake. One group of people cannot carry out all the tasks. . . .

He then went on to spell out his proposal for dealing with his malaise:

As part of the operation of getting close to the people and knowing their problems and learning their ideas, it has been decided that once every quarter, all the legislators, including Ministers, except one (Comrade Reid or myself) will spend one week in an area of the country. During this week, the legislator will hold meetings, visit and learn of the areas' problems and explain the Party's and Government's policy frankly. I, myself, will endeavour to spend one week in at most three out of town in various parts of the country.

The speech shows Forbes Burnham at his best, as a politician and leader, in analyzing the PNC's position while at the same time preparing his supporters for the campaign ahead. It also shows the PNC determination to win the forthcoming elections single handedly. Mr. Burnham then went on to make what appeared to be an insignificant suggestion at that time. He said:

The PNC has many members and supporters in countries like U.K., U.S. and Canada who are keenly interested in the fortunes of the Party and the nation. There are several organized groups in these countries and these, from time to time, send assistance to the Party. The U.K. groups are formed into a Branch which publishes a periodical—*GUYANA.*

We have got to keep in very close touch with these groups and supporters, and all members and groups of Guyana who know of any relatives or friends abroad are asked to forward the addresses and occupation, if known, to the General Secretary of the Party. PNC members and supporters abroad not only can assist the Party with funds and gifts, not only can they help to project a favourable image of the Party and nation abroad, but are also of inestimable importance since they retain their citizenship and right to be registered and to vote.

In summing up, Mr. Burnham turned his attention to his party's strongest opposition to the PPP. He analyzed their position in this way:

Our main political opponent remains the PPP. Its leadership is now sharply divided over tactics, foreign commitments and the sharing of finances. Some are disgruntled, others are disillusioned and still others are convinced that the Party has no electoral future. Now is the time for us to strike. There are many followers at all levels who can be weaned away. This calls for tact and understanding not only of the situation but also of the tactics which may be pursued by our party leadership.

The PPP is caught on the horns of a dilemma. It continues in some places to mouth leftist and communist slogans and in others, pursues a racist line alleging racial discrimination at every turn and opportunity. It is feeding on itself.

It must not, however, be imagined that this monster is dead. It still has strength left. It still has the ability to confuse by striking postures and appearing to champion the cause of the working class which is betrayed when in office. Some people have short memories and may be inclined to listen, forgetting the crimes, the incompetence and the ruthless discimination which marked the PPP's term of office.

We must remain united exposing these political hypocrites at every turn, their past incompetence, their racism, their dishonesty and basic disloyalty, as shown over the Ankoko affair. They will plan and will attempt to infiltrate the Trades Union Movement and the PNC. Though the former is not officially affiliated to the latter, there is no doubt that our members form a majority of the membership and the leadership of the Movement. We must be forever on guard, examine many of their newly arrived "progressives" and "workingclass champions." We must examine ourselves and the leadership we have put in office in the Trade Union and bring our influence to bear, to ensure that all is well. You know and I know that all is not well and that our enemies are planning to take over the Trade Union Movement to wreck the economy of the nation.[5]

As is to be expected, the PNC leader overstated the PPP's situation. True the party had suffered a serious setback when it lost the 1964 election, and many of its supporters had become very disillusioned, but the PPP still retained a strong political base. The PNC had had some spectacular success at recruiting parliamentary PPP members but their success with the ordinary PPP supporter was not tested and was marginal at best. In 1966 the PNC had persuaded two PPP parliamentarians, George Bowman and Mohammed Saffee, to leave the PPP and join the PNC. The defection of these two prominent members of the PPP to the PNC was the first such defection in the modern parliamentary life of the country and was a severe embarrassment to the PPP. The third defection later in the year was more spectacular. Zehuradeen, the next man on the PPP list to become a parliamentarian should anyone resign or die, entered the house late in 1967. Rather than sit with the PPP in opposition, he requested that he be allowed to sit alone with no party affiliation in the opposition. In his first speech in parliament, he denounced the PPP and praised the PNC-UF coalition for the splendid job it was doing. Wide coverage was given to his speech by the press, and again the PPP was not only embarrassed but humiliated. Shortly after, Zehuradeen announced that he had decided to join the PNC. The defections of the first two parliamentarians were a total surprise to the PPP and to political observers. However, Burnham's stage managing of the Zehuradeen defection should have been anticipated by the PPP as he had already enticed two of their parliamentarians to leave and join the PNC. It should have become clear by then that the PNC leader was seeking to increase his party's parliamentary strength while dealing its main opposition some hard psychological blows. For Prime Minister Burnham and the PNC, the defections were another illustration of their brilliant use of parliamentary strategy. Among the rank and file PNC membership, however, some began to grumble that the party, in an effort to broaden its base, was rewarding the newcomers much more than their "stalwarts."

Coalition Differences

The United Force faction in the coalition had always had differences with the PNC on issues of policy. The increased activism of the PNC caused the coalition partners to clash on political grounds. As PNC ministers took off on their week long "fan-out" campaign, UF leader Peter D'Aguiar accused the PNC in the press of spending more time politicking than working. Forbes Burnham defended the action of his ministers by saying that the tours were the PNC's way of keeping in touch with the people. But there was a much more serious quarrel brewing within the PNC-UF coalition. Burnham had begun and was determined to accelerate the repatriation of Guyanese, qualified and living abroad, to fill some of the many positions in the government occupied by expatriates—mostly Englishmen. This philosophy often clashed with that of Minister of Finance, D'Aguiar, who preferred to find people with the best skills and experience no matter what their nationality. It was on this question that Burnham and D'Aguiar quarreled late in 1967, which ended with D'Aguiar's resigning as a minister in the government. Because he did take his party with him, D'Aguiar's resignation did not have the catastrophic effect it could have had. Such a move would have caused the government to fall and forced a general election on the country. The UF, however, was not prepared for elections. Since the 1964 election the UF and its membership became remarkably complacent, but for their participation in the coalition. D'Aguiar's attacks on the government were echoed by the PPP, who hoped that a PNC-UF quarrel would lead to a break up of the coalition, and make possible the PPP's returning to office. This did not happen. Rather, Peter D'Aguiar took a seat on the back benches of the government.

A few weeks after Mr. D'Aguiar's resignation, a UF member of the coalition, Mr. Mohamed Kassim, announced that he had joined the PNC. His defection had caused serious strains between the PNC and UF coalition. Mr. D'Aguiar had urged Mr. Kassim to resign as a UF member of parliament much earlier when it was discovered that the Ministry of Works and Hydraulics which he headed had made several unauthorized payments of large sums of money for work done on road building projects. Mr. Kassim refused to resign and was supported by the Prime Minister. Even as head of the UF, Mr. D'Aguiar could not force Mr. Kassim to resign, especially since Kassim had the Prime Minister's support. D'Aguiar nevertheless insisted that the Prime Minister relieve Kassim of his post, to be replaced by a loyal member of the UF. This the Prime Minister was forced to do as the UF had joined the coalition with the understanding that they would control a specified number of ministries. With Kassim gone, the US voting strength in Parliament was reduced by two to five, another UF member, Mr. Prashad, having left the country on a long extended holiday. Even though the constitution allowed elections to be held anytime before March 1969, it was clear to political observers that the PNC was feverishly preparing for a surprise election very soon.

On October 23, 1968, the parliament passed a Representation of the People Act (Adaptation and Modification of Laws). The act sought extensive amendments to the Elections Regulations of 1964, the effect of which had been to greatly reduce the powers of the election commis-

sion. Apart from legislating the registration of Guyanese living overseas, the bill included a provision for an expansion of the use of the
proxy vote. It was proposed that the number of proxy votes any one
person is entitled to cast be increased from three to five. The PPP
objected vehemently to these proposals, citing the opportunity for
wholesale abuse of such a liberal system. The provision for this change
to introduce overseas voting was written into the Independence Constitution and was agreed to by both the PNC and UF. But the UF at
that time was a friendly coalition partner and probably expected to
benefit handsomely from an overseas vote. However with a cooling of
the PNC-UF friendship, they did not think they were as likely to
benefit as much from such a measure. Since the PPP had boycotted the
independence conference in protest over the British attitude toward it,
the party lost its opportunity to object to this provision at that time.
Despite the PPP and the UF's strong objections to the amendment,
the PNC determined to push it through parliament.

Earlier, on November 18, 1967, the National Registration Act had
been passed. It was described in its heading as "An act to provide for
the establishment of a National Register, for the use of identification
cards and for purposes connected therewith." The PPP and UF had
supported this measure. When the National Registration office was set
up the Minister of Home Affairs, Mr. C. M. L. John, had said that it
was set up to assemble "a complete and permanent record of all persons in the country"[6] for statistical purposes. Subsequently, it leaked
out that the office was also undertaking the registration of Guyanese
living abroad. The PPP and UF objected when the Minister revealed
that the center would provide from its records a register of electors for
use at the elections. In the meantime, Burnham leaked to the press the
fact that Dr. Jagan and Mr. D'Aguiar had been having a series of secret
meetings. These meetings were undoubtedly to discuss the possibility
of both parties mounting joint opposition to the bill. The news shocked
supporters of both parties in the coalition. The specter of uncertainty
was again raised as people saw new political alignments developing
once more. Both the PPP and UF had realized that the piece of legislation before the house was a devious attempt by the PNC to enhance its
support at the polls. Everyone knew that the majority of those who had
emigrated, during the PPP tenure of government, were heavily PNC
with a UF minority. The successful passage of the bill would condemn
both the PPP and the UF to opposition status for some time to come.

The UF, still a partner in the coalition government, decided to call the PNC's bluff. When the debate began in parliament, the UF vacated their seats on the government side of the house and sat on the opposition side of the chamber. While this was in part a symbolic gesture it marked the beginning of the end of the coalition between the PNC and the UF. In the house at this time the PNC commanded 26 votes, the PPP 21 votes, and the UF 5 votes, with one UF vote on prolonged holiday as stated before. When the vote was taken, one UF member, the ex-unionist Rupert Tello, voted with the PNC. The coalition had effectively splintered. The PNC, which had begun as a minority party, now had a majority in the parliament, the cause for great rejoicing in the PNC benches. The legislature looked as follows:

TABLE 8

1964	Seats	1968	Seats
PPP	24	PPP	21
PNC	22	PNC	27
UF	7	UF	4
		Absent	(1)

One must admire the shrewd political mind and brilliant parliamentary strategy of Forbes Burnham. He played both the UF and the PPP a patient and calculating political game, so as to ensure the PNC's future and to maximize the PNC's continuing success at the polls. But although Burnham may have gained political power he in the process destroyed the legitimacy which the coalition commanded and which the PNC by itself never could fully muster. The PNC may have had the political support, but the UF had great influence among the business community and other professional groups. For some professionals and businessmen who had remained in the country all along, the break up of the coalition was a signal that politics would be the major preoccupation of the government for some time to come. For them, their last option had to be exercised: emigration.

Later, when questioned by this writer, Forbes Burnham said that the strategy he used of weaning parliamentary members away from their parties was the same one he had intended to use in 1953 after losing the struggle within the PPP to become its leader, had the British Government not suspended the constitution. Whether in 1953 Forbes Burnham would have been able to pull off such an act is a subject for debate. However, his success in 1968 in attracting PPP and UF parliamentarians to the PNC camp, while brilliant, seems to ignore the sentiments of the Guyanese voting public. By not giving any one party a clear majority the electorate seemed to be expressing a preference for some type of multi-racial and multi-party balance, as neither of the major parties by themselves had this composition, a fact which the PNC did not seem to take seriously. In 1953 the PPP attracted a broad following of Indians and Afro-Guyanese, with a sprinkling from other ethnic groups. Some of the sentiment and euphoria of that 1953 victory was present in the PNC-UF victory of 1964. Though the two are different in many ways, the outright rejection by the electorate of all parties with a blatantly racial posture suggests that the electorate favors a party with a broad base of appeal or some type of coalition politics. In 1968 the inability of both Dr. Jagan and the PPP and Forbes Burnham and

TABLE 9
Parliamentary Candidates of PPP (1953)

INDIAN (12)	AFRICAN (7)	MIXED (2)
1. C. B. Jagan	1. L. F. S. Burnham	1. Martin Carter
2. Dr. Sirpaul Jagan	2. Sidney King	2. F. Van Sertima
3. Dr. J. P. Latchmansingh	3. Jessie Burnham	**WHITE (1)**
4. Mohammed Khan	4. Ashton Chase	
5. Dr. R. Hanoman	5. George King	Janet Jagan
6. Mr. S. Latchmansingh	6. Jane Phillips Gay	**CHINESE (1)**
7. Amos Rangella	7. Fred Bowman	
8. Ramkarran		Clinton Wong
9. Ajoblha Singh		
10. Jenarine Singh		
11. Pandit Misir		
12. Chandra S. Persaud		

Source: From *Political Parties in a Bifurcated State: The Case of Guyana*, R. Premdas University of Illinois unpublished Ph.D. thesis 1970, p. 32.

the PNC to provide this diversified appeal is due to their own inability as leaders to withstand the majority sentiment and pressures within their respective parties. In both cases the absence of strong and competent men of opposite views in their cabinet is still a severe weakness.

In November of 1968 the PNC introduced yet another amendment to the election regulation. This proposal sought to have the candidates of each political party listed in alphabetical order rather than in order of preference, as was done in 1964. There was no reason given for this change except that it suited Prime Minister Burnham's purpose. Again both opposition parties objected to this measure, but the PNC could afford to ignore their appeal.

Analysis of the Legal Changes in Election Law

The introduction of the registration of Guyanese residents abroad as legal voters in national elections came as a surprise to the opposition. The UF had agreed to the measure at the constitution conference in 1965, when it and the PNC were on more friendly terms. Their objection to the legislation in 1968 was either a realization after the fact that their role in the coalition had diminished, or an indication that the PNC was able to slip it by them at the constitutional conference.

If the first piece of legislation gave the PNC the built in electoral advantage it sought, a second piece of legislation gave Forbes Burnham all of the personal power he craved. By submitting the list of candidates by preference as was done in 1964, every party leader was forced to give a rough order of seniority for those whom the party wanted to be elected to parliament. This meant the leader's name would be first and the others would follow, 53 in all. Based on the percentage of votes a party expected, there was a rough knowledge of who would be elected and who would definitely be excluded. However, by submitting a list alphabetically, with one name designated as leader, the leader is assured of his complete dominance of his party and everyone else is automatically leveled. The only justification the PNC could offer for the change was that it made everyone work equally as diligently for the party to earn selection by the leader. But it also gave the leader the flexibility to pick and choose, leaving the process open to whim.

The increase in the number of proxy votes a single person could cast for someone either disabled or temporarily out of the country was also designed to help the PNC. Its membership tended to vote less often and to travel; this device enabled the party to get every last vote. The opposition UF and PPP did not object to these measures on the basis of their legality. Instead they argued that these new pieces of legislation were open to abuse. One would have expected some concession by the PNC in light of the objection from both opposition parties and in order to retain some competition in the system. But their thirst for power was so great that they saw no need to compromise. In that sense both the PNC and the PPP, when in office, have displayed an uncompromising streak and a willingness to control every aspect of its environment through legislation or otherwise. They seem to feel that absolute control is necessary for development; experience, however, has been to the contrary. The greatest bursts of spontaneity occurred in Guyana at precisely those times when people had gained a measure of freedom from administrative (1953) or political (1964) control. And in 1964 the government, being aware of this, channeled it to good use. The huge success of the self-help groups is an example of this. Winning elections demonstrates an organizational ability and political acumen, governing requires adroitness and foresight. The spirit of consultative democracy adumbrated by the Prime Minister in 1964 was being replaced.

Self-Help and the Economy

It was clear from the beginning of the campaign that rejuvenation of the economy was going to be the main PNC argument why they should be reelected. It was that part of their record of which they were most proud and which they touted most. Even though the PNC-UF coalition had succeeded in stimulating greater economic activity, much of it was rehabilitation and reconstruction. Only two new significant economic projects were undertaken and completed: 1) The Timehri Linden Highway and 2) The new Airport and Terminal. This is not to belittle the reconstruction done, and the amazing speed with which it was accomplished, due to the enthusiasm of the government and the people. For the Guyanese people, who had seen nothing but civil strife and political wrangling, the difference in economic activity between the PPP and the PNC-UF coalition was remarkable. In three years the PNC-UF government could boast that it had rehabilitated every section of the infrastructure of the country which the PPP government had allowed to deteriorate. In doing so the government relied on domestic borrowings and a large infusion of foreign aid. From January 1, 1965, to December 31, 1967, it raised $49.1 million[7] in bonds and treasury savings certificates. The rest came in the form of generous grants and loans from Western governments and United Nations agencies (see the accompanying tables). The generous infusion of capital from Western nations was in part to bolster a government more to its liking than the PPP.

But the ordinary people of the country also responded to change of government in a positive way. Self-help, a method of community involvement in erecting projects, had been tried once before in the country by the interim government of 1953–57 with little success. However, with limited capital to spend, the coalition government rekindled the idea. No one then anticipated the success this policy would have. From every area of the country, communities flooded the department with proposals and plans for the improvement of their communities. The accomplishments were most spectacular in the area of school building, though the projects in other areas were just as successful. One writer described the school building program thus:

"With our very young population, the provision of schools is a major problem. It is still a problem, but much less so at present as village communities through self-help methods have been building about one new school each month, many of them in the range of 800 to 1,000 school places. Already 10,000 new school places have been added and another 6,000 will be provided by mid-year when 13 schools, now in the course of construction, will be completed."[8]

As independence approached in 1966 the government had asked each community to submit a proposal for a project to commemorate independence, so that along with their other festivities the communities would have an "independence self-help project" to work on. It was a wise idea, taking advantage of the public euphoria and the government's popularity to enhance the economy of each community. More than 150 communities submitted proposals and had projects approved. These projects ranged from digging drainage and irrigation canals and wells, to building bridges and constructing a science laboratory and a cottage hospital. The response was so great that strict proce-

TABLE 10
Investment In The Public And Private Sector

	Public	Private	Total
1960	$16.6	$63.0	$79.6
1961	23.3	54.1	77.4
1962	20.1	39.8	59.9
1963	12.4	32.4	44.8
1964	9.9	49.4	59.3
1965	16.4	53.8	70.0
1966	26.3	60.0	86.3
1967	27.2	77.8	105.0
1968	37.6	58.4	96.0
1969	40.4	59.3	99.7

Source: Economic Survey of Guyana (1965 and 1969) by the Statistical Bureau Ministry of Economic Development.

TABLE 11
Net Investment, Loans and Grants Received Over A
10 Year Period

	Loans Millions	Grants Millions
1960	$ 7,412	$ 4,944
1961	7,267	7,142
1962	10,521	6,809
1963	5,437	4,933
1964	2,496	6,337
1965	1,870	11,684
1966	3,707	10,655
1967	9,900	8,045
1968	12,592	5,795
1969	17,133	4,080

Source: Taken from Economic Survey of Guyana 1965 and 1969 by Statistical Bureau Ministry of Economic Development.

dures had to be set up to ensure that economically necessary projects were funded first. The government assisted with these projects by providing the raw materials and a technical supervisor. The people gave their labor voluntarily. As the success of the program became known, the World Food program and USAID began assisting by donating food packages for self-help workers. By the end of 1968 the government could boast that self-help program had contributed over $12 million to the nation's product.[9] These accomplishments do not suggest that the Guyanese people were in any way lethargic as Mr. Burnham had suggested in his 1967 address to his party's congress. If they were lethargic, it was only toward politics. What the PNC leader was really complaining about was the failure of the political parties themselves to keep their supporters politically charged for their own purposes.

For even in this area the government sought to gain some political capital. Within the Community Development Department (then part of the Prime Minister's portfolio), the government created a category called the Community Development Worker. The person appointed was usually a community leader who worked along with the Community Development Officer, the civil servant responsible for implementing the particular project. He acted as the on site manager of the project. Needless to say the government appointed mostly PNC activists and former voluntary workers to these jobs, thus rewarding these former voluntary workers and thereby strengthening the party organizational structure at the lower level.

Caribbean Relations

The PNC had declared long before it came into office that it intended to pursue a non-aligned course in international relations. This posture seemed to suit their coalition partner, the UF.

Caribbean relations were the main foreign policy interest of the PNC-UF coalition. The country's foreign policy was totally in the hands of the PNC. For the first eighteen months Mr. Deoroop Mahraj was given the responsibility for External Affairs. Thereafter the post was taken over by Shridath S. Ramphal, who added the responsibility to that of Attorney General.

For administrative and economic reasons, the British Government had the same policy for all of its Caribbean colonies. The Caribbean people themselves, because of migration and a similarity of experience, developed a bond among themselves. The sharing of a common cricket team and the participation in other activities made the people of the different islands friends and rivals. Guyana, because it was the only English speaking country in South America and because it was a British colony, shared in these activities with the islands. As it became obvious that the islands would soon become independent, the British Government and Caribbean politicians formed what all thought was a more viable "Federation of the West Indies," made up of the different English speaking Caribbean islands in 1960. The Guyana government headed at that time by Premier Cheddi Jagan opted not to join the Federation. In 1962 the Federation collapsed, "perhaps, partly because of the strenuous efforts of a generation of committed West Indian politicians to secure and strengthen it as the focus of West Indian political aspiration."[10]

Because Guyana did not participate in the initial attempt at Federation, Forbes Burnham, when he was elected in 1964, with a declared commitment to West Indian unity was able to bring new life to the idea. After having convinced Mr. Barrow, the Premier of Barbados, of the need for another attempt at Caribbean unity, the two Premiers and Chief Minister Ver Bird of Antigua signed in December 1965, at Dickenson Bay Antigua, an agreement bringing the Caribbean Free Trade

Area, CARIFTA, into being. Two years later in 1967 the other islands which had participated in the defunct Federation all agreed to join CARIFTA, with the purpose of pursuing a program of economic integration leading to the establishment of a Caribbean Economic Community. Forbes Burnham gained much popularity and prestige both in the Caribbean islands and in Guyana for initiating and leading the new movement for Caribbean Unity.

Besides the Caribbean islands, the coalition government was required to deal with the dispute with Venezuela and Surinam over Guyana's border.[11]

Border Disputes

When Venezuela became independent in 1830 the new republic sought to have its borders clearly delineated. It raised the issue of the eastern borders with Great Britain, whose colony, British Guiana (as Guyana then was) bounded Venezuela on the east. In 1840 Britain attempted to delimit the boundary but Venezuela did not accept the recommendation. The dispute dragged on until 1894 when on Venezuela's insistence, U.S. President Grover Cleveland forced Britain to submit to arbitration. The final Treaty of Washington was signed on February 2, 1897, and ratified and exchanged in Washington on June 14, 1897. For over half a century no objections were raised by either nation. In 1962, Venezuela unilaterally announced that it regarded the award given in 1899 as being null and void. Its sudden action was prompted by the posthumous publication of the memoirs of a junior member of the staff of its Venezuelan negotiating team. His account of the original treaty as a deal being made to favor the British was based on little real evidence. After a British invitation to the Venezuelans to examine the original documents, the Venezuelan government still remained unconvinced. Because Guyana was at that time close to obtaining independence, they were anxious to have the dispute settled.

The Geneva agreement (between Guyana and Venezuela) was signed in February 1966. The agreement set up a Mixed Commission "with the task of seeking satisfactory solutions for the practical settlement of the controversy between Venezuela and the United Kingdom which has arisen as a result of the Venezuelan contention that the Arbitral Award of 1899 about the Frontier between British Guiana and

Venezuela is null and void."[12] The other provision specified in the agreement was that "no new claim, or enlargement of an existing claim, to territorial sovereignty in these territories shall be asserted while that Agreement is in force, nor shall any claim whatsoever be asserted otherwise than in the Mixed Commission while that Commission is in being."[13] The intent of the second provision was to prevent the claims from growing and to avoid an escalation of the problem in the international arena.

Despite the formation of the Mixed Commission, Venezuela continued to provoke economic, political, and security attacks upon Guyana. On October 12, 1966, the Venezuelan army occupied the Eastern half of Ankoko island. The island was a part of Guyana adjacent to Venezuela and part of its claim. Sometime thereafter operatives at the Venezuelan embassy in Guyana tried to inveigle a meeting of American Indian chiefs to support a resolution in favor of Venezuela's claim. The most damaging Venezuelan ploy was the payment by the Venezuelan foreign Ministry for advertisements in the British press urging investors not to commit funds for any development projects in the disputed area. But the Mixed Commission continued to meet. Its work culminated in the Protocol of Port of Spain signed on June 18, 1970. The intention of the protocol was to freeze the dispute for 12 years while both Guyana and Venezuela worked at improving their relations. During this time neither of the parties was expected to do or say anything that could be construed as a violation of the Geneva Agreement. Despite this, every Venezuelan President since than has made some major statement about the dispute. Venezuela gave notice that it was not going to renew the Protocol of Port of Spain, long before the final six months stipulated in the Protocol. These renewed claims by Venezuela again caused Guyana to invest valuable time and resources to non-development areas.

The dispute with Surinam, like the one with Venezuela, also began in colonial times. The country of Berbice, now part of Guyana, was originally settled in 1627 by the family of Abraham Van Perre, a Dutch citizen. Surinam (formerly Dutch Guiana) was settled by Lord Willoughby and Lawrence Hyde under a grant from Charles II, King of England. In the beginning then Surinam was British and Guyana, including the country of Berbice, was Dutch. However, as European rivalries in the New World continued in the seventeenth and eighteenth century, the colonies changed hands several times between the time they were settled and 1803, when they were beginning to be seen as more permanent parts of European empires. The Peace of Paris of 1815 returned Surinam to the Dutch, who had held it until shortly before then, and the three colonies of Demerara, Essequibo, and Berbice, now Guyana, to the British. But once again a formal treaty was signed for countries where the boundaries were not clearly defined. Up to this time the Corentyne River was taken to be the boundary between the two countries. However, the upper reaches of the river remained largely uncharted. In 1841 the British commissioner Sir R. H. Schomburgk explored the Corentyne River and discovered that in its upper reaches it had two branches, the Kutari and the Curuni, which united and flowed into the Corentyne. Following his discovery, maps produced in both Britain and Holland showed the boundary as being the Corentyne and the Kutari, as its source, forming the boundary.

In 1871 Barrington Brown, a geologist, discovered while carrying out a survey, a river on the Guyana side of the border which he called New River. He felt that the river was larger than the Kutari and that it was the source of the Corentyne. Despite his finding, both his and subsequent copies of maps stuck to the original boundaries.

At the time when the Guyana/Venezuela border dispute was submitted to arbitration in 1899, W. L. Loth, a land surveyor in Surinam, produced a map which for the first time showed New River as the continuation of the Corentyne River. The Dutch government used this and Barrington Brown's remarks to protest to the British Government. To this the British Foreign Secretary Lord Salisbury replied that it was not too late to reopen this particular issue as the Kutari had long been accepted on both sides as the boundary.

In 1910 the upper reaches of the Corentyne River were again explored and surveyed, this time by Lieutenant C. C. Kayser of the Dutch Navy. He discovered another large branch of the Corentyne River which entered it on its eastern side about twenty miles below the New River. This river he named the Lucie River. His discovery prompted much academic discussion about the rivers and the two countries in Holland. However, the Dutch government refused to be drawn into the debate. The Dutch government could find no justification for making a renewed claim even after they had taken measurements of comparative flows of the rivers in 1920.

In 1929 news that the disputed area contained possible oil reserves brought the conflict to life once again. On August 7, 1929, the Netherlands Minister sent a letter to the British Foreign Secretary asking for the conclusion of a treaty between Britain and the Netherlands. This opportunity was taken because Brazil at that time was seeking to have its boundary with Guyana demarcated. The Netherlands government was invited to participate since decisions involving its territory were going to be affected also. Following intensive negotiations, the three countries agreed in 1936 to settle the problem based on a Dutch plan put forward three years earlier. This agreement was then signed by the three representatives. The treaty was all but signed when World War II broke out. Even though agreement had been reached, the actual signing of the treaty never took place. This remains the basis of the dispute between Guyana, the former British colony, and Surinam, the former Dutch colony. After a number of border violations and name calling, the dispute was finally settled in 1970.

New Actors

During the 1964–1968 tenure of the PNC-UF coalition, two organizations gained some prominence within the country. These were Ascria and MAO.

Ascria: The Association for Social and Cultural Relations with Independent Africa was formed by Eusi Kwayana, formerly Sidney King, in 1964. The organization was formed in response to long interunion dispute in 1964 during which time Africans living along the East and West Coast were beaten, terrorized, chased from their homes in the rural areas, and sometimes killed. With independence approaching, ethnic pride grew in importance. The Indians had arrived in Guyana much later and under different circumstances from the other groups and had preserved many of their customs. Some leaders sought to cultivate and use this as an instrument for political gain and to abuse other ethnic groups. In the past the Africans had done everything possible to shed their identification with things African. Only in the rural areas were a few customs handed down by slaves preserved. This cultural gap among the Africans was what Ascria wanted to fill.

Shortly after the coalition government came into office, Eusi Kwayana undertook a long, semi-official trip to a number of African countries to establish cultural and political contacts with them. His appointment as head of the Guyana Marketing Corporation shortly after was a signal that the man who was once kicked out as General Secretary of the PNC was again in favor with the party. Despite his change of political opinion, he has always held a mystique in Guyana for his passionate belief in his cause, his simplicity of lifestyle, and his scrupulous honesty.

Despite no clear identification with the PNC, the jobs Kwayana held caused most people to see him and his organization in a certain light. He was appointed chairman of a committee to investigate changing of the Guyana Co-op Credit Society into a Co-op Bank, chairman of a Cooperative Insurance Committee and head of the Guyana Marketing Corporation. As head of the Guyana Marketing Corporation, Mr. Kwayana was in charge of the pricing, purchasing and marketing of all products except rice. The corporation employed large numbers of people and was a major source of employment for PNC activists. As a result, he had a working relationship with the PNC head office—Congress Place—which acted as an unofficial conduit for those seeking employment. Not long after he emerged as a close advisor to the Prime Minister on domestic political and economic policy.

It was a coincidence that Ascria's formation took place at the same time as the rise of the civil rights movement in the USA. The movement in the U.S. provided Ascria with the literature, slogans and style which it could draw upon to reinforce its seriousness as a cultural leader and have people pay attention to its social and economic proposals. The organization's aims were to promote the revival of African culture in Guyana; to stimulate pride among Africans in their heritage through the importation of books and the documentation of local customs; and to promote the association and activities and contact with Black Africa. Its main economic objective was the return to the land by Afro-Guyanese.[14] By 1968 Ascria had become a strong cultural organization with an active membership. This happened at the same time that the PNC, with whom its membership overlapped, was suffering from severe sluggishness. These new members seemed to use Ascria as a means of reinforcing their claim to obtaining appointments within the government. As the PNC-UF coalition government had moved towards the center by trying to balance the appointments they made, showing no strong bias to one or another ethnic group, these people sought the influence of Ascria to help in getting an appointment.

The appointment of Eusi Kwayana to high office by the PNC-UF coalition and his rise as an adviser to the Prime Minister was very similar to the experience of the PPP while in office. In both cases the parties sought to have the ethnic cultural organizations of a majority of its members closely allied to them. And of course these groups have sought to have the parties favor the ethnic group whom they represented. In the PPP's case, after it became closely allied with the Hindu Maha Saba and the Muslim Islamic Anjuman, Dr. Jagan was under constant pressure to favor Indians in his appointments. The same was true of Ascria and the PNC. In a country where government is the main employer, such group influence eventually puts the politician at a disadvantage by impairing his flexibility and curtailing his ability to maneuver politically.

Ratoon: Because Forbes Burnham was instrumental in rekindling the fire of West Indian unity, his popularity went up dramatically among West Indian academics. No group had lamented more the downfall of the Federation. In the interim, these scholars had provided the economic framework on which political organizations ought to be based. The academics at the University of Guyana, however, remained skeptical about Burnham. As the PNC-UF coalition sought to get public opinion on its side using every means possible, a number of scholars and their friends formed the Ratoon group. This group, through their own paper of the same name, interpreted the information provided by the government and provided that which was not given officially. They also put out their own position papers on government programs. Ratoon had great appeal to the informed electorate who were tired of reading reprinted government releases in the press and seeing status quo analysis in the national newspapers. The paper provided such stimulation that top PNC members and government officers all clamored to read it. The group was very critical of the government's attachment to the U.S. and to the free enterprise system. They called for the nationalization of most of the foreign mining companies and withdrawal of the Peace Corps. They advocated a strong Guyanization policy and greater regional integration.

The popularity of the Ratoon group among the attentive public in the main urban areas disturbed the PNC. But it was the PNC's own refusal to be open with information and its attempts to limit discussion which contributed to Ratoon's popularity.

This was the environment in the country when the PNC called a national election for December 15, 1968. As had already been pointed out, only the PNC seemed prepared for the election. The PPP had suffered a great loss of prestige because of its parliamentary defeats and there was conflict among its top leadership over strategy after having lost the 1964 election. With no spoils to share, activists were not as enthusiastic and its rank and file members did not have as much to contribute to the party.

The U.F. found itself outmaneuvered and was then part of the opposition. Its members were either migrating to Canada or were resigned to not having a strong voice in government. Their failure to command much of the spoils of office for their members left the party severely weakened and in disarray.

Election 1968

In many respects the election of December 16, 1968, was a test of the preparedness of the parties organizationally and financially, and the PNC shone bright. By contrast the other parties lacked brilliance. The PNC ran their campaign as though it was their last. They exploited their incumbency to the fullest. Business, both foreign and domestic, which had done very well in the preceding four years, were called upon and contributed generously in cash and in kind. Not only were there a number of self-help and other projects to be opened at this time, but the Prime Minister made monetary grants to nearly every village he visited.

The opposition PPP campaign was a good one, as all PPP campaigns have been over the years, but it lacked the passion of its former campaigns. In April of 1968, the government had established the National Registration Centre for obtaining what the Minister of Home Affairs, Mr. C. M. L. John, called "a complete and permanent record of all persons in the country." Gradually, the opposition parties and the public learned that the office was also registering Guyanese residing overseas. The PPP reacted strongly against this. Their attempts to have some of their activists and sympathizers included among those who did the registration in Guyana and abroad were blocked by the PNC. Every aspect of the preparations for elections was handled solely by PNC activists. When the PPP accused the PNC of monopolizing the registration, the PNC denied it. Because of this change and other administrative changes in the election procedure, the PPP and UF filed separate injunctions against the Election Commission. The promised identification cards required by the PNC for all voters were not ready for the election and were never issued because of incompetence. There was so much contention over the local electoral list after it was released to the parties that the *Evening Post* of December 9, 1968, concluded: "The whole future of this country is at stake right now. The four years of what has been achieved since 1964 is all hanging in the balance, just because incompetence and inefficiency have dominated the preparation of the election machinery under the very noses of those whose job it was to make sure that all was going well."[15] By trying to undertake the organization of the whole election themselves and so gain the maximum political advantage of incumbency, the PNC undermined the honesty and confidence of the whole election process.

Overseas registration was another fiasco. Registration was conducted in 55 countries rather than in just the large centers of Guyanese settlement: the UK, the USA and Canada, and the Caribbean area. At every stage of the election proceedings, both the PPP and UF protested but the PNC stood firm and did not allow the opposition to participate in registration. Only in the UK, where both parties protested, were four UF supporters included as registration officers.[16] The discrepancies found in the UK list by the PPP and the UF were many. The story was taken up by the British press, giving some publicity to the opposition's point of view.

In its campaign the PNC labeled itself as the party of "Peace Not Conflict." Burnham told voters that he did not have the stamina to deal with another coalition government. He and speakers from his party rattled off a long list of the accomplishments and the projects which had been completed by the PNC-led coalition. In the area of foreign affairs PNC speakers touted the government's accomplishments in the formation of CARIFTA and in the progress in the talks on the two border disputes. They also reminded people that should the PPP win, the country would return to the violence, killings, and looting of 1962–64.

Because of the PNC's success in government, the PPP and UF protests were not given the attention it ought to have been by the press and by voters. The PPP accused the PNC of preparing to rig the elections, of destroying the rice industry, and of being under the thumb of the American government. The UF ran a rather lackluster campaign. They accused the PNC of misusing its authority and of wanting to run the government alone. In the midst of opposition protests and delays, the elections were held on December 16, 1968. The results were as follows:

PNC	51.81%	30 seats
PPP	36.49%	19 seats
UF	7.4%	4 seats

Winning the election and being able to form a government was the PNC's greatest triumph. They had full control of the Parliament and the authority to make all of the changes they claimed they needed to make.

The Election Analyzed

Most people would agree that the preparations and the execution of the election was handled badly by the PNC. However, the PNC got away with it, not because the opposition parties did not protest but because the electors themselves had been generally pleased with the job the PNC-UF coalition had done, contrasted with the previous years of PPP rule. They were, therefore, prepared to overlook the PNC manipulation of the election process to ensure victory at the polls.[17]

The results showed that the PNC had stretched the rules significantly to favor themselves. In doing so they may have damaged an important aspect of the election process, the integrity of the system and party competition. It also meant that election results could no longer be analyzed by the conventional methods. Future analysis had to be based on conjecture and on much less precise information. A comparison of some of the election statistics shows where the PNC gained much of its advantage. When we look at the proxies cast, the advantage gained by the PNC is clear.

TABLE 12
Proxies as a Percentage of Votes Cast, 1961–1968

	Votes Cast	*Proxies*	*Proxies % of Votes*
1961	220,125	300	0.5
1964	240,120	7,000	2.5
1968	314,216	19,297	7.0

Source: From *Race Vs. Politics in Guyana*, J. E. Green, ISER, UWI, 1974, P. 28–30.

While most politicians do what they can get away with, a line must be drawn between the desire for power and the maintenance of a certain degree of fairness and objectivity. The clever politician is the person who is sensitive to this imaginary line and who can conduct his affairs in such a way as to allow some infringement of the rules while maintaining public confidence in his own and in the opposition's camp. While the election results of the vote within the country had a degree of plausibility about it, depending upon which year is used as a base in judging the percentage growth in population, the inclusion of the overseas vote over the objection of both opposition parties gave the PNC what some commentators considered too much of a lopsided vote.[18]

TABLE 13
Comparative Summary of Ballots Cast in Five General Elections[18]
1953–1968

Year	No. of Electors on Register	No. of Votes Cast	Percentage
1953	208,939	156,226	74.8
1957	212,518	118,564	55.8
1961	246,120	220,125	89.4
1964	247,604	240,120	96.9
1968	297,404 Local vote only	—	93.5
1968	369,088 Including foreign votes	314,216	85.1

Source: Report [293]

Getting power is one thing. Using power effectively to move a society forward politically and economically requires political ingenuity, flexibility, and luck.

NOTES

1. Budget Speech 1966—The Hon. Peter S. D'Aguiar, Minister of Finance. British Guiana House of Assembly, April 5, 1966. The Government Printery, Georgetown, British Guiana.
2. For a very detailed article on this subject see M. K. Bacchus The Ministerial System at Work: A Case Study of Guyana. Social & Economic Studies, University of the West Indies Vol 16, 1967 p. 34–56.
3. Budget Speech 1966—The Hon. Peter S. D'Aguiar, April 5, 1966.
4. John Kenneth Galbraith, The Great Crash, p. 136.
5. Leader's Address to Congress, 1967. By Forbes Burnham, p. 16 Unpublished.

6. A History of Guyana by Dwarka Nath, Published by the Auther, London 1975, p. 146.
7. Pease, Self-Reliance from past chaos—Address by L. F. S. Burnham to 11 Congress of the PNC—April 14, 1968, p. 7. Published by PNC.
8. New Commonwealth Trade and Commerce—Guyana, L. Searwar New Commonwealth London, November 2, 1967.
9. Address to Congress by L. F. S. Burnham, 1968. See also United Nations in Guyana—UNDP—Guyana—Guyana Lithographic.
10. The Prospect for Community in the Caribbean—Hon. Shridath S. Ramphal Ministry of Foreign Affairs—Georgetown 1973.
11. In this section I have drawn heavily on *Guyana/Venezuela Relations* Ministry of External Affairs—Georgetown, September 1968.
12. Guyana/Venezuela Relations—Ministry of External Affairs, Georgetown, September 1968.
13. Ibid.
14. See also J. E. Green Race vs. Politics in Guyana. Institute for Social and Economic Research UW9 1974. p. 45–46.
15. Quoted in Dwarka Nath, A History of Guyana, Vol. III, Published by the Author, 30 Croother Rd., London, 1975, p. 153.
16. Ibid.
17. For a complete study of the 1968 election see J. E. Green, Race Vs. Politics in Guyana, ISER, University of the West Indies, 1974.
18. Ibid., p. 19.

CHAPTER 9

The New Road

PRIME Minister Burnham set about establishing his new government in December 1968. The cabinet appointments gave a hint of Burnham's new strategy. Under the old system of constituency voting, individual parliamentarians built their own political base even though they were under the aegis of a party. Despite the change in 1964, many of the older representatives continued to command support from the areas they had previously represented. This meant that within their party they carried a certain amount of clout, which the Prime Minister, as leader of the party, would have to acknowledge in making appointments and in formulating policy. The leader had to satisfy different factions in forming his cabinet and in making other appointments.

Burnham's new system of Proportional Representation eliminated the power base concept, but the system of listing candidates in alphabetical order gave the party leader the flexibility of excluding at the last minute anyone he desired to drop from among his parliamentary party. The PNC parliamentary list announced in January 1969 contained just such a surprise. A number of ministers lost their portfolios and were not even returned to the house as back-benchers. The more prominent Mr. W. O. R. Kendall and Mrs. W. Gaskin were given ambassadorial appointments while some were given less important jobs and yet others disappeared from politics. The changes in the PNC benches were made at two levels. First, the average age of the new group was substantially lower than the group before; and second, they were, as a group, less well educated. In the opposition benches the PPP also introduced many new faces into the house. As a matter of fact the PPP's new group had greater balance of ethnic representation than before. The other opposition party, the United Force, returned the same slate to parliament.

Among the PNC benches, while there was a wider general distribution in social background, the number of technocrats appointed went from one to five. In 1964 S. S. Ramphal was appointed Attorney General because of his knowledge of the law. As a technocrat he served as a minister within the cabinet and had a seat in parliament, but he had no vote. The position was that of a specialist, which the governing party felt it could not fill from among its parliamentary ranks and filled from outside. During the four years in which he served, Mr. Ramphal proved himself to be brilliant at the law and an able administrator and skillful parliamentarian. His position in the government was greatly enhanced when he took on the added responsibility of foreign affairs, for he was as brilliant at that as he was at law. But it was not for this reason that the number of technocrats was increased, since none of the appointees, even though qualified, could have been called experts.

Their appointment was an attempt by Burnham to create a new structure within the party and government. The party gave broad representation at the parliamentary level to its supporters from which a number of ministers were chosen, but a inner cabinet of technocrats was created to help make and formulate policy. Most of those selected, while respected in their individual fields, were a mixed group of professional and independent men. Some observers speculated that it was the Prime Minister's device to get good men to work with him while not having to worry about the possibility of their ever becoming strong enough to challenge his position.

The appointment of Hamilton Green, the General Secretary of the PNC, as a technocrat lends some validity to this view. Mr. Green's appointment as a minister was very interesting for two reasons. First it was a recognition that a party bureaucrat could within his party become a highly trained and disciplined administrator. Secondly his appointment spelled the demise of the PNC as a party with any vitality. Upon his appointment as a minister Mr. Green did not relinquish his post as party secretary, rather he sought to do both jobs. By not appointing able assistants and not delegating any authority in his capacity as general secretary the party structure suffered despite his attempts to have departments of the government assume some of these functions.

Within a few days of the government's election victory it had to face its first crisis. On January 2, a number of wealthy white families (including the Hasts and Melvilles) tried to lead a rebellion in the sparsely populated cattle ranching area of the Rupununi. The families hoped to declare the secession of the border area with the help of the Venezuelan Government. Though the area lay adjacent to the Guyana border with Brazil it was part of the territory claimed by Venezuela.

On the day of the rebellion a heavily armed group opened fire on the government compound at Lethem. When the fighting was over seven policemen were killed and a number of government officers were wounded and the others taken hostage. The rebels then blocked the airstrips in the area to prevent entry or exit. The government in Georgetown (300 miles away) dispatched troops to the area, who were able to land and eventually restore order. The leaders of the rebellion fled to Venezuela while the Indians whom they had enticed to assist them fled to Brazil. A few days later, on January 4 in Caracas, Mrs. Hart, claiming to represent a secessionist "provisional government of the State of Essequibo" asked the Venezuelan government for support. The Venezuelan government termed the rebellion a domestic matter for the Guyana government and denied any participation by Venezuela. A few days later on January 7, Mrs. Hart again pleaded for Venezuela's military support "in order to recover territory which belongs to it historically."[1] She went on to state that "we intended to create an independent state of Guyana Essequibo, associated with Venezuela, as a first step towards eventual territorial and administrative integration." Rather than responding as the rebels asked, the government of Venezuela granted them political asylum.

On January 8, the government of Guyana handed the Venezuela mission in Guyana a note alleging that Venezuela had supplied arms and given aid including supervised training to the rebels in Venezuela. It was also stated that in addition to the 20 suspects detained, some 300 rebels had been arrested in Brazil by the Brazilian security forces and that their extradition to Guyana was being negotiated. This event put both opposition leaders in an awkward position. Dr. Jagan, the leader of the PPP, was still bitter over the loss of the election and was still on his campaign to expose a regime which had come to power by fraud. Both he and Peter D'Aguiar had travelled to Europe, the Caribbean, and North America for this reason and had managed to embarrass Prime Minister Burnham and the PNC. But by responding immediately with military force and by denouncing Venezula's territorial claims, the PNC government quickly gained national sympathy for their plight. As a result Dr. Jagan had to support the government's position and condemn the Venezuelan attempt to subvert the country's independence and territorial integrity. His support for the government's position in the interest of national unity coming so soon after the election gave the impression to the public at large of PPP acceptance of the election result probably earlier than they had intended. The UF's plight was different. The party had enjoyed near total support in the area. The Harts and Melville's were whites and known UF supporters. Peter D'Aguiar and the UF disassociated themselves from the uprising but provided legal assistance to those charged with having participated or associated with the event.

In addressing itself to the country's problems, the PNC had to first deal with some internal conflicts in the Civil Service. Among the first number of students who had gone off to university many had studied the classics and liberal arts, subjects which were valued, but not as the proper education for top administrators, who were required to provide practical direction for national development. As a result, the politicians began to search for more qualified specialists. This change of emphasis meant that many of the people trained prior to independence found their careers advancing more slowly than before. As these changes were being made there seemed to be no clear direction, no clear plan being followed. The Development plan had long been discarded and the infrastructural work embarked on in 1964 had been more or less completed. Much more important was that overseas aid and grants had begun to dwindle. In the *Official Gazette* the names of ministers and top government officers acquiring houses began to appear more often. It was apparent that these officials had begun to make themselves more comfortable. And with the creation of new government ministeries and new government corporations there was a plethora of officials, all being chauffered here and there. It marked a change in the government's style of management.

Co-Operative Republic

On March 20, 1979, the government gave notice in Parliament that it intended to introduce a motion to have the country change its constitutional status to become a Republic. Though this provision was written into the report of the conference, no one quite expected the PNC government to exercise this option so soon. The report stated:

"There will be provision for the Parliament of the new State, if it so wishes, after 1st January, 1969, to bring into operation scheduled amendments establishing a Republic on the Parliamentary system."

In moving the motion in Parliament on August 28, 1969, the Prime Minister gave his reason for the constitutional change.

"Mr. Speaker, if this Motion is passed and the day proposed in the Motion sees the fulfilment of our intention, there will cease to be a Governor-General in Guyana and in his place as titular Head of State, there will be substituted a President. The President, who will have to be a Guyanese citizen, not disqualified from being a Member of this Assembly, and of the age of 40 or over, will be elected by the Parliament by secret ballot.

"Looking at it as a matter of mere words and lifeless form, one would come to the conclusion that all that would have been done was to substitute a President for a Governor-General, except of course that whereas the Governor-General is appointed by Her Majesty the Queen on the advice of the Prime Minister, the President will be elected by the National Assembly by secret ballot.

"The powers of the President as proposed in Schedule II of the Constitution will be no greater and no less, as I understand it, than the power of the Governor-General. But when one departs from the mere form, I would submit, sir, that there will be a difference between Guyana, a Monarchy, and Guyana a Republic. In the first place, though we accept the fact that Her Gracious Majesty Queen Elizabeth II is Queen of Guyana merely titularly and exercises no executive powers within her Dominion of Guyana, though we accept the fact that Her Majesty's representative the Governor-General performs his duties in the name of Her Majesty the Queen but again on the advice, which has to be taken, of the elected Ministers of the Government, one must confess that looking at the history of Guyana, looking at our own former connection to a relationship with the United Kingdom, a natural fulfilment of our history should be the cutting of even formal ties with the Queen or the Royal House of Great Britain. Now that we have matured, the element of bitterness has lessened, if not disappeared, but I would submit, that in the context of Guyana there is an indescribable incongruity between having the Queen of Great Britain, the Queen of Guyana.

"Moving to the status of a Republic represents, to my mind, a further step in the direction of self-reliance and self-confidence. It is to be noted that there have been other Constitutions promulgated within the Caribbean and outside of the Caribbean before and subsequent to the Guyana Constitution. It is to be further noted that in most of those Constitutions the monarchy has been retained. And in moving this Motion, I desire to make a special point. We, in Guyana, have decided that the monarchy should go. But we do not criticize anyone more knowledgeable of his own circumstances and environment outside of Guyana who wants to retain for his particular country, the monarchical system, because every politician, every Leader of a country, must be deemed to be more conversant with his own circumstances and attendant facts than outsiders."[2] The Prime Minister then went on to announce that the country would become a co-operative republic on February 23, 1970. The date chosen was the date of the Berbice Slave rebellion of 1763. Burnham chose this date because he saw it as the first attempt by Guyanese to gain their independence. In 1970, Coffey the leader of that rebellion, had officially been made a national hero.

The word *co-operative* was added to *republic* to indicate the government's economic preference. The Prime Minister put it this way:

"With the establishment of the Republic it is proposed that a serious and earnest effort be made to establish firmly and irrevocably the co-operative as the means of *making the small man a real man and changing, in a revolutionary fashion, the social and economic relationships to which we have been heir* as part of our monarchical legacy.

"On economic grounds, our continued membership of the Commonwealth is justified. There are some who would explain their membership in terms of philosophy, concept, Westminster model, but this sometimes seems empty when one looks at the different and differing constitutional and parliamentary systems to be found in the Commonwealth. Most of those who speak on this subject will admit that, economically, it is advantageous to be a member of the Commonwealth. It may be that some day membership of the Commonwealth would have some new dimension attached to it, maybe, but as I see it—and speaking for myself and, I believe, the majority of my colleagues—the economic justification is predominant. And I may remark that there is no difficulty in our remaining a member of the Commonwealth.

"It has been suggested in some quarters that the republican system as envisaged in Guyana removes the protection of Her Majesty the Queen, of her loyal subjects in her dominion of Guyana. That is a good reason for ending the monarchy in Guyana because, psychologically, there are so many unemancipated minds who still believe that protection can come from without an independent country. It is in their interest and the interest of the progress of the country that the monarchy be removed so that there can be no illusions and it can be recognized that power and protection are to be found here in Guyana."[3]

If Forbes Burnham was confident in the new direction his government was about to take, not everyone else was. The United Force was not convinced of the necessity for a change. They argued that the change to the Republican system would remove the protection of Her Majesty the Queen of her loyal subjects in her dominion of Guyana. But it was precisely this psychological dependence that the PNC said it wanted to eliminate.

The PPP agreed with the motion in principle but had some reservations. They agreed with the usefulness of replacing the Governor General with a President. However they did not altogether agree with the legal changes which had to be made to support it. Under the monarchical system with a Governor General resident in Guyana, the final Court of Appeal had been Her Majesty in Council of the Judicial Committee of the Privy Council. The loss of this final right of appeal the PPP felt would be unfortunate. As a compromise, PPP backbencher Mr. D. Jagan, brother of the PPP leader, suggested that the government try to have established a West Indian Court of Appeal. This he felt would be subject to less political pressure while maintaining a local and regional flavor. Although the government thought the idea had some merit, they did not take it seriously. In rebutting the opposition's concerns the Prime Minister said:

"Traditionally, our final Court of Appeals has been Her Majesty in Council or the Judicial Committee of the Privy Council.

"Lest there be any illusions, lest there be any suggestions that the cards were not put on the table, and today is the day for putting the cards on the table, let me first observe that there is an inherent inconsistency behind Guyana becoming a Republic and Guyana still having Her Majesty's Privy Council, the Judicial Committee or what have you, as the final Court of Appeal.

"To continue to have the Judicial Committee of the Privy Council as the final Court of Appeal is to admit our inferiority which our erstwhile masters have attempted to instil in us, it is to admit that we are incapable of finding within the boundaries of our country such legal talent and such sense of justice as would lead us to leave the final arbitrament of matters legal to our fellow Guyanese.

"Far be it from me, Mr. Speaker, to suggest that the Judicial Committee of the Privy Council does not consist of eminent lawyers. Far be it from me to attempt to suggest that it might not be the font of justice, but far be it from me, a nationalist, to tolerate this inconsistency, this incongruity so far as I have any power to bring it to an end. Those who have ears to hear, let them hear."[4]

The Small Man Will Become a Real Man

The Prime Minister described the co-operative as the instrument through which "the small man will become a real man." What he meant was that the people were going to have a say in the economy commensurate with their political strength. An indication of what many people thought of the idea can be seen from the number of sayings ridiculing the idea which sprang up soon after. "The only real man is the smart man," some people retorted. "The small man is a smart man." Not many people regarded this apparent tilt to the left by the PNC government seriously. Some saw it as an attempt to force the wealthy to divest themselves of their property after the government ministers had themselves purchased a number of properties earlier. They saw a clever attempt by the government officials to supplant them. However others interpreted it as a move to the left. Whether this move was the result of the constant attack of the Ratoon group, which constantly accused the government of being pro-American and pro-business, or because of a reduction in aid or a genuine commitment on the part of the PNC is uncertain. However two points must not be discounted. By 1970 Burnham, fresh from winning his second election, and with a good reputation in the Caribbean, was anxious to establish himself as a radical at home and was more anxious to enlarge his reputation beyond the region. It is quite possible that as he saw himself gaining the support of the radical professors at the University of the West Indies (UWI), he became determined to keep in the forefront of political and economic change.

The establishment of the Guyana National Co-Operative Bank in February 1970 was the pride of the government. It was designed to be the institution which assisted the government in its economic formation by providing funds for industrial development. Though the bank itself did well, it soon became obvious that it was only being used by small depositors. The government then mounted a campaign to "minimize the banks" by forcing local business, top government officials and state businesses to use the Co-op bank. They hoped to reduce the business done by foreign banks to a minimum. But the very government officials feared that once their money was in a government-sponsored bank, the government would have access to their records.

While answering questions at a news conference on February 13, 1970, Prime Minister Burnham, in response to a question, stated that the government had decided to pursue a policy whereby the state would have a minimum participation of 50 percent in all agreements for the exploitation, development and ownership of the country's resources. When asked if this policy would extend to the country's major industries—bauxite and sugar—the Prime Minister stated that the cabinet had already decided that the government should have dialogues with the bauxite and sugar companies with a view to its obtaining a participation of over 50 percent in them. The idea of nationalization was not new to the people of Guyana. As far back as the mid-1960s Dr. Jagan had argued that these companies ought to be taken over by the government. Since then the economists at the University of the West Indies had done substantial research on the nature and financing of those industries and the need for Caribbean governments to get a larger share of the revenue generated, either reinvested or through taxes. The Ratoon group in Guyana had published a number of articles on the bauxite industry and an exhaustive study of the sugar industry. The PNC had not previously expressed any strong commitment to the policy of nationalization of private industry. However, a declining foreign aid, a birthrate rising at 2.8 percent per year, and a high unemployment rate may have made this more inevitable. Besides Mr. Burnham may also have desired the support plaudits of U.W.I. academics and other radical groups in the region which had advocated this strategy for some time. As has been pointed out earlier Forbes Burnham in his youth was academically inclined and a student leader. His desire for the approval of the academic community never waned.

Local Government Elections 1970

The local government elections of June 1970 were the first to be held in the country since 1956. While political parties had campaigned for national elections from 1950, no local government elections had ever been held in all these years. The Marshall report of 1955 made a number of recommendations for improving local government representation. The Jagan government, when it was in office, had refused to hold local elections because it knew the PNC would win a majority of them. Instead it appointed replacements when necessary and shelved the idea of elections. The PNC had protested, but the government was able to hold them off.

PNC preparations for these elections were just as sloppy and disorganized as they were for the general elections, but it was of no consequence. Protests by the opposition parties made no difference, as the PNC was maneuvering the system in such a way to win most of the districts outright. In the end the PNC, as was expected, won a majority of the municipal districts and the PPP won the others. The UF won none.

Though the outcome was no surprise, the disparity between the results was for many cause for concern. Again the PNC wins reflected a percentage of votes higher than anticipated in many areas while the other parties had a lower than expected result. The PNC then had increased its power by controlling not only the central government but the municipalities also.

Although both of the main parties conducted energetic campaigns, the attendance at their rallys was noticeably small. And those who did come were young and not charmed by the speeches of either Dr. Jagan or Mr. Burnham. To the young, the jokes were not funny, nor the rhetoric poignant. After more than twenty years in politics, both Jagan and Burnham sounded tired and well past their prime.

Hinterland Mahdia Road

In August 1970 the government's policy to develop the interior got a great deal of publicity when it brought a number of University of the West Indies (UWI) students from all over the Caribbean to work on the road to Mahdia in the Hinterland. The students were flown to Guyana and maintained at government's expense. Few besides the Prime Minister and his cabinet agreed that the project was necessary in view of its cost. The students did work on the road and completed a substantial portion of it, but most regarded it as a summer holiday. The government insisted that the road was the first in a network it intended to build at a low cost to open the interior to development. From the outset it was known that such a project would take lots of money just to begin and much more to maintain, given the terrain of the area. However the government proceeded even though a continous flow of funds for the project was not assured. On subsequent summers Guyanese students studying abroad on government scholarships were brought home, again at government expense to work on sections of the road. In 1983, the network of roads the government promised it would build still had not been completed.

In December 1970 the government announced that it had established resident diplomatic relations with the USSR. In view of the country's recent history the announcement was an important one. Indeed the reactions by columnists in the press were cautious and in some cases defensive and sympathetic.

Carl Blackman, Editor of the Sunday Graphic, wrote "After all, the reason for Marxist Cheddi Jagan's downfall was the fear at home and abroad that if he stayed in power, he would have opened closer diplomatic relations with Communist countries, especially Russia. Then Russian technicians would have flooded the country, the argument went, and soon Guyana would have been turned into a great Red springboard for an offensive in South America. Burnham owes his rise to power to these fears, and on the face of it he seems to be the last man likely to let the Russians in, especially since the Russians are more friends of Jagan's than his."[5]

A few weeks later Guyana's ambassador to London, John Carter, presented his credentials in Moscow and the Russian Ambassador to Brazil presented his credentials in Georgetown. It had been suggested by some people that the establishment of diplomatic relations was done to create the appearance of a nonaligned position.

Wider Horizons

Attending the Lusaka Conference widened Forbes Burnham's political influence. Having rubbed shoulders with his Caribbean colleagues and succeeded in emerging a leader, he now sought to test himself in a larger area. The country's reputation was already very good and was still improving. The speeches of Minister of State S. S. Ramphal at the United Nations were all extremely well received. And the work of other Guyanese diplomats in the committees of many organizations were accorded high credit from their counterparts. Burnham's arrival in Lusaka was the climax to the groundwork laid by a competent staff. Speaking after several established leaders of the nonaligned movement had done so, Prime Minister Burnham ended by pledging to give $50,000 per year to support the freedom fighters in Southern Africa. The announcement was a masterful stroke of diplomacy and immediately gave him a leadership status within the Afro-Asian block. The African countries in particular were pleasantly surprised at Guyana's generosity, while also being slightly embarrassed that they themselves had no such program for a policy to which they were dedicated. In Guyana however the news of Burnham's pledge got a mixed reception. While most people felt sympathetic with those still struggling for independence, they did not think that Guyana with its own problems ought to be financing the operation.

On his way home from the conference, Forbes Burnham made official visits to several African countries and to Czechoslovakia. With his reputation from the conference riding high, he was treated royally at every stop. In his briefings and tours he was particularly interested in the economic direction of these countries, especially those which had just acquired a majority of the shares of the large industries operating within their borders. The final official stop in his tour was Czechoslovakia. Here the Prime Minister was particularly interested in their alumina and aluminum plants and the contribution they made to the economy of that country. The trip itself crowned Burnham's career. He had conferred with and measured himself against some of the most well-known leaders in the nonaligned movement and found himself equal to them. Back home he was ready to make some difficult decisions.

Bauxite and Nationalization

In November 1970 the Government of Guyana invited the Demerara Bauxite Company, Demba, a wholly owned subsidiary of the giant Canadian Multinational Aluminium Company of Canada, Alcan, to negotiate items of a new relationship with Guyana.[6]

Demba had been extracting Bauxite from Guyana since 1917, and according to Demba's President was the oldest and largest undertaking owned by Alcan. In 1969 the company mined over four million tons of Bauxite in Guyana. Two types were mined in Guyana, metal grade ore and calcined. Of the metal grade ore mined, some of it was shipped as

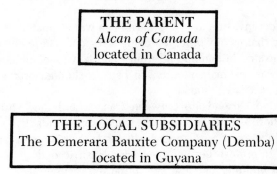

pure ore to other countries and some was shipped as alumina (the intermediate process between bauxite and aluminum). The calcined bauxite, the bulk of what was produced, was all shipped out of the country, to be used in the abrasive and refractory industries in the more industrialized countries of the world.

Background Canada Caribbean Relations

Because the Caribbean nations are all Commonwealth countries, Canada enjoyed extremely good relations them until the mid-1960s. After Britain placed severe restrictions on emigration and scholarships granted to commonwealth citizens, Canada emerged as a main center for studies among West Indian students and scholars. By 1970

TABLE 14

Bauxite 4–5 tons $40–$80	Alumina 2 tons $200–$350	Primary aluminum 1 ton $700–$800	Sheet, plate bars, rods, etc. 1 ton $1,000–$1,500
MINING Earth-moving process	BENEFICIATION Chemical process	SMELTING Electro-chemical process	SEMIFABRICATION Metallurgical processes

Processes, products, and values in the bauxite-aluminum industry.[7]

Canada's direct investment in the Caribbean was estimated to be $435 million more than in any other developing region.⁸ These investments were concentrated in banking insurance and bauxite-alumina production. Alcan was the main investor in bauxite-alumina production in Guyana, Jamaica and Trinidad.

The traditional friendship between Canada and the West Indies however suffered a severe setback when six Trinidadian students charged a professor at Sir George Williams University with racial discrimination. In protest they and their friends barricaded themselves in the computer building for a few days until their accusations were heard and their demands met. Unfortunately, while there they did a considerable amount of damage to the computer records. The news spread quickly and became the focus of protests all over the Carribbean. In Trinidad demonstrations were held in support of the students. The demonstrations, which continued over a number of days, escalated into mass protest against Canadian racism and economic exploitations. University students and nationalists accused Canada and Canadian business as being the new neo-colonial power in the region contributing to underdevelopment and dependency in the regions.

The accusation was ironic because the Canadian government and the scholars were themselves at that time going through a period of examination and evaluation of foreign (American) investments in their country. In addition, a few Canadian and West Indian scholars had worked closely and shared information and ideas on this subject. The government of Pierre Treadeau, which had pledged itself to adopting a more sympathetic attitude to third world nations, found itself in a dilemma.

In the early sixties the Canadian Government's interest in Guyana was more straightforwardly economic. The bauxite mines in Guyana provided Alcan with about 50 percent of its raw material.⁹ The company's main smelter at Arvida, Quebec, was almost totally dependent upon bauxite from Guyana, and the smelter at Kitimat, British Columbia, received bauxite from Guyana during the winter. The company's operations employed 17,200 people in Canada directly, and had exports of over $227 million. At that time the company was the sixth largest exporter in Canada. As a result of this dependence not only did the company have a political interest in Guyana but the Canadian government did also. As a result when Guyana went through its domestic turmoil in the early sixties, the Canadian government was deeply concerned. Any severe disruption of bauxite supplies in Guyana would have caused a similar problem in Canada. It was because of this concern that the Canadian Government appointed in February 1964 Mr. Milton Gregg as Consul General in Guyana. Significantly, he earlier had been Minister of Labor and was at the time of his appointment an official with the United Nations. Mr. Martin said that "relations were established because of Canadian business, educational and religions links with Guyana; the Canadian government, however, entered Guyana primarily to promote its economic interests, which were related to those of Alcan."[10] This situation of dependence on bauxite from Guyana was due to change. On April 9, 1970, Alcan announced that it expected to use alternative sources of bauxite which were being opened up in Australia, Brazil and Guinea. This increase in bauxite sources gave the Canadian government less cause for concern and the luxury of a more independent foreign policy. Bauxite now could be obtained from many sources and Canadian workers would not be affected by the Government's support or lack of support for the company's policies.

This new position of the company and Canada's low standing in the Caribbean left the Canadian government free to pursue a new policy. As a result it displayed an ambivalent attitude to Guyana's announcement of its invitations to Alcan to discuss new terms of ownership of its subsidiary, Demba. The new situation also put Alcan in a more formidable position.

Two days after the government of Guyana announced its intentions to renegiotate its relationship with Demba, Alcan, its parent, announced in Canada that "if the supplies of alumina and metal grade bauxite from Guyana are affected, Alcan believes that alternative sources of supplies can be arranged."[11] The company's strategy seemed to be indicating to the Government of Guyana that it could not hope for too much since Alcan was not as dependent on Guyana's bauxite as it had been earlier. Alcan had to contend with the possibility that, if Guyana won this battle, its other source of raw material, Jamaica, could ask for the same conditions. Together the two countries supplied most of the bauxite used in Alcan's smelters around the world.

Meanwhile, the strategy and reasoning of the Guyana government reflected its own interests as well. While recognizing the need of the company to make and retain a reasonable profit, it contended that the Demba mines, Alcan's original and main plant for more than fifty years, were the source of the company's eventual global expansion. As a result it felt that the country was entitled to a certain level of reinvestment, which was not taking place. Instead, it contended, many countries around the world which produced no bauxite ore had refining facilities employing thousands of people. Apart from Guyana's lack of employment opportunities within the aluminium manufacturing business, the government felt that the company's failure to expand its refining capacity had kept the economy of the country weak, given the resource it had to work with. Furthermore the government contended that the company, by pursuing such a policy, was wasting the country's non-renewable assets. Prime Minister Forbes Burnham in his address on November 28, 1970, put it this way:

> A nation cannot achieve economic independence unless it owns and controls its resources, unless the decisions with respect to the exploitation, use and disposition of these resources are taken with its own borders.
>
> Otherwise its wealth will continue to be drained away for the benefit of the citizens of other nations while its own economy and people enjoy minimal benefits, its standard of living and growth rate remain low and unemployment rises.
>
> In Guyana, more particularly since the birth of the Co-operative Republic on the 23rd of February of this year, the Government has been set on a policy of owning, controlling and deploying the nation's resources in the national interest.
>
> Mineral resources invariably supply the raw materials for industrial development and are therefore an important base for economic growth and progress. But they are wasting assets and non-renewable.
>
> One can in 1970 plant cane or rice on an acre of land on which cane or rice was planted last year. But one cannot replace a ton of Bauxite once it has been removed from the bowels of the earth and processed into calcined ore or aluminium. Once taken out it is like the neglected opportunity; it comes not back.
>
> If, therefore, Guyana does not get the maximum benefit from its minerals, it has, to this extent, lost part of its wealth forever.[12]

In explaining further his reasons for asking for majority control, Prime Minister Burnham pointed out that the company still used wheat flour from Canada as a flocculent rather than the locally produced cassava starch. He contended that a number of linkage industries like the caustic soda industry which should have developed, never did because of Alcan's policy.

The Negotiations

The contents of Prime Minister Burnham's communications and the conditions set down were made public by Alcan on November 30,

1970. Revealing the contents of the letter detailing Guyana's demands put both the government and the company in a precarious position. It was stupid of the Canadians and must have been done partly out of arrogance. It meant that neither party was in a position to negotiate after that. Now if Burnham settled for anything less there would be major domestic fallout; but Alcan found the terms difficult to meet. Needless to say, the government was shocked when it learned that Alcan had made the contents of the letter public. The conditions set down were as follows:

  (i) Government's participation shall be a majority one;

 (ii) Participation would be by means of purchase of a share of the assets of the company;

(iii) The value of such assets shall be no greater than that given by the company as the written down book value for income tax purposes on the 31st December, 1969, with additions of value during 1970 not by revaluations or reappraisals;

(iv) The Government will pay for its share of the assets out of future profits of the joint undertaking after tax;

 (v) The Government's majority holding shall confer on Government the control which inheres in such majority holding;

(vi) The agreement finally arrived at between the Company and Government shall be deemed to take effect from 1st January, 1971.[13]

Apart from these, all other terms, including the exact size of the majority holding, the government said were negotiable. The stiff terms laid down by the government was an indication of how strong it felt about this subject. But it also meant that the government was pledged publicly on a number of points, and so there could be no compromise.

Negotiations opened on December 7, 1970. On the delegation of the Government of Guyana were Guyanese and West Indian academics who at the time held teaching appointments at the U.W.I. and in Canada, and who had done research on the bauxite industry. After initial presentations, Alcan made a counter proposal on December 15, 1970. It suggested that "the Government of Guyana should raise a loan from the World Bank for expanding the production of calcined ore and put it into the new entity as equity. Alcan would then put all of Demba's assets into that entity, part of these assets to represent Alcan's equity, the rest to be an interest bearing loan to be repaid in installments—presumably annual. These installments were to be chargable against cash generation and before taxes. Alcan desired freedom from exchange control and from withholding tax and proposed that they should appoint the Chief Executive Officer of the new company."[14]

The counter proposal showed the company to be cynical, insensitive and short-sighted. From a domestic standpoint there was no way that the PNC government could accept such a proposal. For a start the PPP would have ridiculed such an agreement and Burnham would have lost his credibility and standing in the Caribbean and in the Non-Aligned movement. Even if he was able to withstand PPP criticism at home, Burnham could not see accepting less than was given to other nations in similar positions. Having portrayed himself as a Caribbean and Third World leader who was merely seeking what was fair, Prime Minister Burnham was shocked that the proposal was rejected.

On February 9, 1971, Alcan put forward another proposal for consideration, which was later summarized by Prime Minister Burnham as:

(i) That a new company would be formed after Government had agreed in advance to commit the new entity to Alcan's scheme for the expansion of calcined bauxite and after Government had undertaken to provide the $50m needed for that scheme.

(ii) That the new company would be capitalised at $100 in $1 shares, 50 to Government and 50 to Alcan. The Company later conceded 51 to Government and 49 to Alcan.

(iii) The existing assets of Demba (approx. $100 m) would be put in as a fully interest bearing loan at current commercial rates.

(iv) The new entity and its shareholders should not be subject to any Income Tax, Corporation Tax, Property Tax, Withholding Tax, Import Duty, Export Duty Royalty, or any Guyana Tax or Impost, nor any Exchange Control restriction with respect to any interest, dividends or fee for its shareholders.

(v) That if Government should sign with any other bauxite producer an agreement containing any single term more favourable than the corresponding term reached with Alcan, the agreement with Alcan would be changed to include the more favourable term.[15]

Again this proposal the government found unacceptable as it proposed to expand the mining operation and made no mention of plans for the manufacture of alumina and aluminum, a move which would have enhanced the country's industrial base. As a result, Burnham

announced on February 23, 1971 that the company would be
nationalized. Burnham himself considered Alcan's counterproposal a
personal affront to him. As he saw it, the company had been less than
candid with him from his first conversation with them while on his tour
of Canada just after independence in 1966. He described Alcan's attitude toward the negotiations in this way:

> Taken as a whole they show a kind of arrogance and lack of concern
> with the realities in Guyana. One wonders that the controllers of such
> vast wealth as Alcan possesses, can be so insensitive to the aspirations of
> developing nations.
>
> What was clear was that Alcan, Demba's parent, was not prepared to
> invest further money in the enterprise; that the much advertised expan-
> sion in alumina production announced on the 21st September, 1969, was
> not to be; that any expansion was to be exclusively in calcined ore
> production financed entirely by Government and that the undertaking
> given by the President of Alcan in July, 1966, to me in Montreal to
> construct an aluminium smelter if reasonably priced power were to be
> available, was never seriously given or intended. [16]

Realizing after six months of talks that both he and Alcan were
stalemated, Prime Minister Burnham sought to resolve it by inviting
ex-U.S. Justice Arthur Goldberg to arbitrate in the dispute. Goldberg,
who at that time was also legal counsel to Reynolds Metal Company,
accepted the invitation. On July 14, 1971, Demba and the Government of Guyana announced that they had reached a final settlement.
The arbitrator, Mr. Goldberg, upheld Guyana's position on sovereignty over its bauxite resources. Alcan was awarded approximately
$45 million in government notes as compensation for Demba, which
would be completely taken over or nationalized by the government.
Payment was secured on the country's general revenues and not on
future profits of the nationalized industry. Both sides seemed pleased
with the outcome as each could declare himself the winner. The selection of Arthur Goldberg as arbitrator was a clever tactic by Forbes
Burnham. Not only had the arbitrator been a labor lawyer and U.S.
Secretary of Labor, but he had also been U.S. Supreme Court Justice
and a U.S. Ambassador to the U.N. Burnham knew then that he would
be familiar with the resolutions passed by that body and the sentiments
of Third World countries. He also knew that because Goldberg was a
lawyer for an American bauxite company, which itself had rather small
installations in Guyana and much larger ones in other parts of the

Caribbean, greater pressure would be upon him to be firm. The agreement was arrived at the day before vesting day, July 14, 1971.

Though Burnham put on a good face, he was surprised and annoyed at the choice he was forced to make. He had gone into the negotiations to try to get 51 percent and control of the company and was instead forced to nationalize. He felt deeply hurt and betrayed by western business interests. He sincerely thought that the terms he had asked for were fair, especially since they had previously been granted to several African countries. In addition the number of successive U.N. resolutions passed on the subject made Burnham feel that he was on firm ground when he presented his terms. When he made his proposal he did so under a belief that this change of outlook had reached the corporate boardrooms of the multinational corporations around the world. But like most Third World nationalists, Forbes Burnham also felt that Guyana had a right to see its industrial base expand proportionately to the minerals which were being extracted. For years the people of the developing countries had felt that the western business and governments had used their countries only as sources of raw materials. Many felt that their resources were being used to support the development and high standards of living that were enjoyed only by the people of the more developed countries. Burnham saw his attempts to get a larger share of the pie as a right, considering the contribution Guyana had already made to the development of Alcan and indirectly to the other countries in which Alcan had installations. Now that Guyana had become more mature the thinking was that the company should have been more sensitive.

In this writers view, Western business seems to expect underdeveloped nations to form strong friendships with companies which would exclude those countries from the fruits of their own development. This expectation has caused much resentment on the part of the people of developing countries toward business. Traditionally, big business has exploited developing countries while refusing to take responsibility for the social and economic shock waves their arrogant exploitation sets off.

Except in a few instances banks have been careful to finance only certain projects, namely those which have had a clear economic benefit to the west. The lack of a proportional reinvestment in these countries could only cause them to become poorer and make them more likely to adopt a more radical position to the west itself. The terms granted for

trade between the developing countries and the West have been severely weighted against the poorer countries and is part of the reason
why these countries cannot be expected to be interested in the stability
the West likes.

Political Power National Policy and Personal Interest

In a speech on February 23, 1971, Prime Minister Burnham announced that the government had decided to nationalize Demba, the
subsidiary of Alcan. Sometime later, after the final negotiations had
been worked out, it was announced that July 15, 1971, would be
vesting day—the day on which the government and people of Guyana
would assume full control of the company's installation at Mackenzie.
During this period, however, a strike occured within the industry
which tested the government's methods and competence and revealed
the anxieties of people, who, even though committed to support a
policy, put their own personal welfare first.

In his speech to the nation announcing the government's decision,
the Prime Minister had a message for the people working at the bauxite mines.

"Comrades at Christianburg-Wismar-Mackenzie you, in particular,
are in the vanguard of our struggle for economic freedom. Be assured
that Guyana recognises with gratitude the part you are called upon to
play. The whole country, the whole world watches your response and
is anxious to learn from you the lessons of heroism, of discipline, of
solidarity, of self-reliance which you are destined to teach. Without
lacking appreciation of the other sections I want to tell the Guyanese
supervisory staff, particularly the foremen and general foremen that all
who work in the industry have paid tribute to your very important role
in management and your mastery through intelligence and experience
of your varied operatio.s and processess. Your country relies on you to
work with a greater sense of purpose in the future for material rewards
that are no less than you now enjoy.

"I want to assure you that the Government will allow all those systems and procedures suitable to the industry and its operations to
continue and will expect them to improve with time. You will continue
to work in a business enterprise using business methods. However, the
change of ownership will mean a change in the social relations of the

industry. Not only will the technical management staff and foremen have the opportunity of using their initiative, of real authority—collective and individual—but all ranks of members through their representatives and through their union will be afforded the opportunity to play a part as of right in the decision making bodies and processes of the enterprise."[17]

The Prime Minister was well aware that the people he was promising job security to had always been staunch supporters of his party in national and local elections. In 1969 almost 88% of Mackenzie voted for the PNC; in 1968, over 93%; in 1970 no other party contested the area.

The Prime Minister himself also enjoyed much personal support in the area and had quite a large practice there as a lawyer. On October 17, 1970, when it was announced that the Guyana Mine Workers Union and the Demerara Bauxite Company (Demba) had failed to reach agreement on a new workers' wage contract, the Prime Minister personally intervened and forced both parties to go to arbitration. The company, which had until then resisted all attempts by the union to go to arbitration, agreed to do so on October 19. On November 18 the arbitration tribunal was appointed. At the time that the tribunal was appointed, the government was a third party. But then came the participation talks and their collapse, and the announcement of nationalization. The government, in a dramatic turn of events, went from being a sympathetic third party to becoming the distrusted employer.

The Tyndall arbitration tribunal, which was set up to arbitrate a wage dispute between the Mine Workers Union and Demba, started its sessions on January 11, 1971. Nothing was heard about the work of the tribunal, even after the government's decision to nationalize the company. The workers became fearful that their own interests were being submerged to that of the government. And with no information or reassurances on the horizon, the workers of Demba staged a wild cat strike on April 20. This strike, coming as it did after the decision to nationalize the company had been announced and before the final settlement had been negotiated, embarrassed the government severely.

Because the strikers had traditionally been staunch party supporters, the government could not explain away the strike as easily as it might have done. The reason given by the workers for the strike was the failure of the tribunal to reach any conclusion about an award after nearly six months. When it was revealed, after the strike had begun, that all of the work of the tribunal was finished except for the union's final presentation the workers became infuriated. The president of the union had been nominated by the government as the worker representative and was serving as a member of the government's team negotiating with Demba. Obviously, the union members felt, he was sacrificing union business in favor of government business. This information immediately destroyed the credibility of the unpopular union president and his executive. The ineptitude of the union's leadership surfaced at a time when the workers needed leadership. No one had bothered to inform them at any stage whatsoever as to what their future situation was going to be when the proposed changes in ownership were finally achieved. Not only were they concerned about the outcome of the wage arbitration, but they now had to contend with a change in ownership and all the uncertainty which having an inexperienced owner implies. And from the beginning, the workers were kept in the dark about the decisions being made affecting their only means of support.

The strikers were particularly insistent that the strike award on wages should be retroactive to the date on which the last agreement between the company and the union had expired. They also insisted that whatever money was awarded should be paid before vesting day, when the government would take over the enterprise, so that there would be no chance that the money would "disappear" in the transition.

The concerns that were voiced and the demands that were made by the strikers showed that they had given careful thought to the ramifications of the proposed changes in the company's structure. All attempts by the union leadership to explain to the rank and file the reason for the delay of the Tyndall Report were abortive and ineffectual. Every meeting ended in disorder. At one meeting union officials had to escape through the windows after being locked in the union hall with hundreds of angry strikers. At other meetings they had to leave under heavy police escort. Attempts by the Minister of Labor Mr. Winslow Carrington (himself a unionist) on the first day of the strike to reassure the workers that their demands would not be neglected fell on deaf ears. He announced that he was prepared to call upon the arbitrator to make the monetary award "now." He also explained that the government had suggested to Demba that an interim payment could be made to the workers, but that Demba had turned it down, saying that it was prepared to await the findings of the tribunal. Carrington stressed that whenever an award was made, the government would see to it that Demba carried out its obligation by a fixed date. Finally he promised to have the results of the tribunal available in three weeks.

The events described show the cat-and-mouse game which was being played by both the government and the company, each trying to get the better of the other, with the workers caught in between. The refusal by the workers to accept Carrington's proposals indicate the degree to which they had come to distrust both the government and their own union leadership. Though they were PNC supporters, they did not view the PNC as a vehicle for solving their industrial relations problems. The party thus found out that the support of the union members could not be taken for granted on bread and butter issues. The workers remained resolved not to return to work without an acceptable answer to their grievance.

On the evening of the first day of the strike, the Workers' Action Committee, the body set up to speak on behalf of the strikers, telephoned the Prime Minister and, it was reported, gave him an ultimatum to travel to the mining city (Mackenzie) by midnight that night.[18] The strikers had called the Prime Minister because they saw him as their political leader. He had come to be perceived as the only man who could get things done. But after receiving the ultimatum, the Prime Minister decided not to go to Mackenzie. Whether his decision not to go was wise is debatable. However, his refusal exacerbated an already embarrassing situation. Following his refusal, the Workers Action Committee sent for Dr. Jagan, the opposition leader. Dr. Jagan seldom visited or even campaigned in the area and was in no position to enlighten or help in solving any of the workers' grievances. His invitation was more an attempt by the strikers to further embarrass the Prime Minister and the PNC government. On this ground Dr. Jagan accepted the invitation and addressed the workers. Jagan had always advocated nationalizing the bauxite industry; however, when he was in office prior to independence from 1957–64 he did not have the power to do so and it is doubtful, given the political climate at the time, whether he could have accomplished that. When the proposal was debated in Parliament he had suggested that the government's attempt to gain 51 percent of the company was too timid an approach. He suggested that they nationalize the industry outright. "Take all," he urged. Dr. Jagan declared his support for the workers. His speech to them gave them renewed confidence to carry on. When the Prime Minister then invited the Workers Action Committee to meet him at his residence they flatly refused. "We want the Prime Minister here" was their reply. Before the meeting finished there was a sharp exchange of words, then a fist fight, resulting in the hospitalization of the messenger.

That these events were taking place within an industry that the government proposed to take over created a problem for the government, especially when the morale of the country as a whole would be significantly affected. The government still had not reached a final agreement with Demba as to how much it would pay for the plant and the terms acceptable for doing so. Time was dragging on and the nation was clearly becoming tired. Dr. Jagan's visit to Mackenzie was the trigger which loosed the panic that swept the PNC government.

On April 24, 1971, the Prime Minister in his first official statement on the strike situation in the mining city accused Demba of "antinational" behavior and of deliberately setting out to confuse the workers on the Tyndall Tribunal Award. He promised to submit to the workers immediately upon their return to work proposals on the establishment of a new pension scheme to be based upon the money contributed to the RILA plan (the company's pension plan). He then went on to recall that it was at his instrumentation that the company had agreed to go to arbitration. He noted further that he was assured by the Chairman of the Arbitration Tribunal that the tribunal would be in a position to make its findings known within three weeks, though it would take longer for the full report to be submitted. He then urged them to return to work. The strikers disregarded the Prime Minister's pledge and continued the strike.

On April 20 the newspapers had given prominence to the fact that some fifty houses in which Demba's expatriate officers lived were then vacant, their occupants having left for Canada. This report only confirmed what was already known in the mining town. Since the announcement of its intention to nationalize the industry, Demba had been relocating its engineers and other senior staff. The company had also extended the offer to some senior Guyanese engineers and staff, who accepted their offer. The comments made by some of the departing personnel ("you Guyanese can never run this industry without us") and the sight of personnel departing with no replacements available combined to make the workers feel very insecure. It appeared that

Demba had its own schedule made up even though so far the government had given no indication to anyone of when it would take full
control. Little supervision was being given by the company personnel
to the few senior workers who continued on the job. There was no
positive effort by the government to cope with the situation.[19]

To what extent the systematic removal of its staff was a deliberate
attempt by the company to undermine the confidence of the ordinary
worker is uncertain. However, from the speed at which it was taking
place, it was clear that the government, having expected to get 51
percent, had made no contingency arrangements for nationalization.
That this situation occurred in an industry which employed 1.8 percent
of Guyana's total labor force and contributed 14 percent of the country's gross domestic product was irresponsible and reckless and the
strikers seemed to be the first to realize this.

The PNC government, embarrassed by these developments sent a
number of politicians into the area to encourage at a party level a
return to work, "because the government was losing much needed
revenue." These politicians had only moderate success in getting their
workers to return to their jobs and this tended to be among the older
group. A committee set up by the PNC to organize a return to work got
many workers out of their homes on April 26, but when the siren
sounded for work to begin, many did not report for duty. Some said
that they had been threatened. Political operatives who cajoled them
were treated with contempt. Meanwhile the Workers Action committee at their daily meeting condemned the few who had returned to
work and voted to remain on strike. In a release they said that they
were seeking a meeting with the Prime Minister so as to obtain an
assurance that they would receive wage increases before vesting day.
They contended that if vesting day passed before they received their
increases, they might never get them.[20] The underlying fear of the
workers was the danger that they might be treated like government
workers after nationalization and therefore receive only a few of the
benefits to which they had become accustomed while working for a
commercial business.

Workers loyal to the party began to trickle back to work as the strike
continued. But when questioned about their attitude upon returning
to work they said that "they had been told that after Demba had been
nationalized the government would freeze the workers' wages, because
it was common talk that the workers of Demba were too highly paid."
Another worker said that he was told that "the government would have

difficulty finding suitable supervisors to take the place of the expatriates who were leaving the country." Yet another worker summed up his feelings thus: "The National Insurance Scheme has people running backward and forwards to draw injury benefits. What can we hope to happen when the government takes over Demba?" Yet another said "we have been told that the government wants our retroactive pay and our RILA plan savings to develop other parts of the country because the administration has no money."[21] A look at the comparative rates paid to different categories of workers shows the basis for their anxiety.

TABLE 15
Comparative Basic Weekly Wages

		1956	1962	1966	1967	1968	1969 (6 mths)
Bauxite:	Labourer	$23.52	40.00	46.00	50.00	50.00	52.00
	Electrician	33.60	60.00	71.20	77.20	77.20	80.40
Sugar:	Labourer	12.48	18.96	21.60	21.60	23.40	23.40
	Electrician	14.50	23.62	26.50	38.40	38.40	38.40
Government:	Labourer	15.12	18.24	24.00	24.00	24.00	24.00
	Electrician	23.52	26.45	32.16	32.16	32.16	32.16

Source: R. E. Rosane, *Bauxite in Guyana*—Extracted from Appendix III.

Many of the fears expressed by the workers were clearly planted by departing expatriates who had an interest in doing so; however this should have been expected by the PNC. Had the PNC itself or the government or the union kept the workers informed about the decisions being taken, decisions which affected their personal future, the workers might have been more sympathetic to the government's plight. To accuse the departing personnel of being "un-Guyanese" just does not answer the more fundamental question of the government's attitude toward workers who were the staunchest of PNC supporters. In their dealings with the workers, the PNC failed to realize the extent to which a disciplined industrial work force comes to respect and appreciate efficiency, characteristics which the government had not shown in dealing with the matters at hand. It was because of this and because of a lack of information that staunch PNC supporters were open to the leadership of others. Until then the government had been accustomed to dealing with civil servants and assorted urban groups who did not have the benefit of organized, large numbers and who had not been accustomed to as high a level of efficiency.

From the time the strike began, the government beefed up the police patrols in the area around Demba and had the Guyana Defense Force maintain sentries there. On April 28, the police used tear gas to disperse angry demonstrators who were proceeding toward the plant, apparently in an attempt to bring out the few who had returned to work. Tear gas was also used against demonstrators who tried to do the same to the office staff. The fumes from the tear gas affected the children in the Mackenzie primary school. In the panic to leave the school some children were injured. The news quickly brought angry and concerned parents and onlookers into the streets in large numbers.

It was reported later in the press that the demonstrations took place because of the frequent visits by the police to the union headquarters (then taken over by the rebel strikers).[22] The day ended with twenty-one people being arrested, including two militant strike leaders. Two persons were hospitalized. Just prior to these demonstrations the strike leaders began losing their grip on the support they once had. The use of tear gas by the security forces against the demonstrators served to consolidate and unite their flagging support. The action of the Army and police reinforced the belief that the government would do anything to coerce the strikers into returning to work without settling what they still considered to be their outstanding problems. Not only was it not good policy to use tear gas on their own supporters, but it was bad for the morale of the entire nation, which was kept well-informed of the events in Mackenzie by the press.

Realizing this, the government sent to Mackenzie on April 29 a team of four Ministers, which included Deputy Prime Minister Dr. P. A. Reid and the Minister of Labor Mr. Carrington. Their efforts to persuade the workers to return to work were not successful. The strikers stuck to the original conditions they had laid down for a resumption of work. Further, they now insisted on the release of all strikers arrested as a result of the illegal demonstration. This added demand gave a new dimension to the strike problem. Later in the day, at another meeting attended by two of the ministers, the strikers passed a number of resolutions. One called upon the government to investigate the financial position of the union, another banned the union's executive and the minister of labor from entering the union hall. The closeness of the union officials to the PNC, which had prevented the union's chairman and some members of the executive from being voted out sometime earlier, had come to haunt the party. The last called upon the government to release those strikers who were in police custody.[23]

In a further attempt to settle what was clearly a very bad situation, the government, which was stalled in its attempts to talk price with Demba, sent a team of Trade Union Council executives to Mackenzie on April 30 to try to defuse the situation. This team got a better reception than any other. Without agreeing to resume work, the strikers agreed to have the TUC negotiate on their behalf the following points with the government: 1. the immediate release of the twenty-five workers charged during the week; 2. to have the Tyndall Tribunal award ready in one week; and 3. payment on the basis of the award made within three weeks from the time of its announcement, and before the government's announcement of vesting day.[24] The workers' insistence that the TUC obtain in writing the government's agreement shows the extent to which the workers distrusted the PNC government at an industrial level.

Again on May 1 the government showed its incompetence in dealing with the situation by refusing to allow the traditional Labor Day parade to take place at Mackenzie. Recent Guyanese political history, in which the PNC played a large part, shows that the surest way of getting a bigger and better demonstration in times of crisis is for the police to disallow it. Despite police disapproval, the strikers went ahead and planned a parade. The police tried to breakup the gathering by using tear gas but the demonstrators ran through alleys and reassembled at different points. Realizing that a parade was going to be held whether or not they gave their permission, the police relented and gave their permission. The news of these happenings reached the main city of Georgetown quickly. The Prime Minister and PNC government were further embarrassed. It was rumored that the Prime Minister was so shaken by the situation that he had allowed the Commissioner of Police, Mr. Carl Austin, to decide whether or not permission for a parade should be granted when asked.

On May 2, the Prime Minister addressed the nation and the strikers at Mackenzie once again. He gave the striking workers an assurance that he intended to visit Mackenzie to discuss their problems with them subsequent to a full resumption of work. His statement was largely a reiteration of the statement he had made a week earlier. However, this time he had a firm proposal for the RILA fund. "As regards the RILA Plan the government would submit for your information, examination and comment firm proposals for the establishment of a new pension scheme."[25] He also reminded them that his government always had a deep interest in their welfare and was still most concerned with their problems.[26] This statement by the Prime Minister seemed enough. On Monday, May 2, after 13 days, the workers returned to work just as suddenly as they had called the strike.

The strike shows that politics in Guyana like other developing countries is not as ideological and dogmatic as some people believe. While groups might support policy at a national level they might not support its implementation at the local level and then turn to other leadership groups to articulate their disagreement. It shows clearly too, the need to have organizational leadership at different levels as people do not always see the dominant political party as the vehicle which could best represent all their interests.

Soon after the company was nationalized on July 15, 1971, the government renamed the mining city "Linden," taking the first name of the Prime Minister, Linden Forbes Sampson Burnham. In place of the old company, Demba, it set up a new one, Guybau.

Nationalization and Aftermath: Few people disagreed that the government had a duty to try to get Alcan to begin some investment in the country after extracting millions of tons of bauxite ore for more than fifty years. Economic sense and political and social pressures made it a logical step for the government to take. The company itself should have been astute enough to realize this, and should have pre-empted the government by itself approaching it, for both sides had much to lose.

The wealth gained from bauxite is considerable, as has been pointed out before. Processing the bauxite through its final stages generates even greater wealth and provides significant employment. Four tons of bauxite make two tons of alumina, and two tons of alumina make one ton of aluminum. "This increased value is paid out in wages and salaries, rents, purchases, interest and profits in the countries where refining is done. At present, 90% of the increases in value of Guyana bauxite goes to the United States and Canada. The fabrication and manufacture of aluminum products bring still higher increases in value."[27]

Even though the economic reasons for the company's expansion or government participation are persuasive, such a policy must be carefully planned. Not only must the strategy for talks be mapped out, but contingency planning must also be made, as the temptation is always there for a multi-national the size of Alcan to feel that it could thwart the policy of a small underdeveloped nation. The rapid extraction of its senior staff, both Guyanese and expatriate, and the comments made by these departing officials to the lower level staff is all part of a war of nerves which a big company is apt to play in such a situation. That the Guyana government did not anticipate the departure of some Guyanese among the Demba Senior staff could only be due to their own lack of understanding of the ambitions and preferences of some professional men.

Once acquired, the successful running and expansion of such an enterprise requires even more careful planning and maneuvering. To operate such an enterprise with purely local staff is a mistake, as one runs the risk of not keeping up with the technology and not having the cross-fertilization which is gained from having a variety of people who have studied and worked in different countries and who have experienced a number of different engineering and management situations. Only some of this could be substituted for by having an ongoing education policy and a ready supply of magazines, research papers, and journals. But for a small nation which does not have a university system with a strong engineering and chemical research capability and which cannot afford the funds for extensive research and development, the cross fertilization of having other nationals engaged at different levels in the local enterprise is invaluable. It is precisely because the multi nationals could and do use this arrangement that they are as successful as they are. Such an arrangement can only work if it fits in with the government's overall plan of running an international business operation, otherwise a nationalized industry loses its competitive position.

Political Fallout

The act of nationalizing Alcan's Demba caused a consequent change within the PNC. Rather than see nationalization as a challenge, many young ambitious political assistants within the party saw it as a glamorous happening. In their speeches they referred to it as part of an overall plan to take control of the "commanding heights of the economy." The new slogans of the ambitious young political assistants and opportunists fitted in quite nicely with the PNC's idea of co-operative socialism. Rather than nip it in the bud the PNC and top leaders also adopted this new rhetoric. It was probably too much to expect the PNC leaders not to embrace the advantage which they could flaunt at

Dr. Jagan and the PPP. For the first time in their history they could whip the PPP with its own rhetoric. But rhetoric continually runs the risk of turning noisy propaganda slogans into basic principles. Everyone knows how to start an action but few people know how to stop it; this was the situation within the PNC after nationalization. Ten years after nationalization, bauxite production has fallen and none of the ancilliary industries the PNC hoped would be developed have been built. Only in one area has some movement been made where cassava starch has replaced some wheaten flour as a flocculent in refining alumina. A policy is a bad policy if it prevents the achievement of formerly set priorities. In that sense, the way nationalization was undertaken must be questioned as it has over the years severely damaged the government's strategy for the political and economic improvement of the nation.

The most notable political development which came about because of nationalization involved two organizations: Ascria and MAO.

By 1970 Ascria had matured and had carved itself a niche as the unofficial cultural arm of the PNC. Though no formal ties were established, this was perceived to be generally so by those seeking favors from the government. The easy access that Eusi Kwayana, the head of Ascria, had to the top levels of the political leadership within the government confirmed peoples' suspicions and caused Ascria to be seen as much more powerful than it was. As has already been pointed out, the two organizations competed for support among the same group of people—the Afro-Guyanese. At Linden, like the PNC, the organization seemed to be particularly strong. Prior to Demba's nationalization, Ascria had been directly involved in the Owen Young affair and in the Demba Nurses strike. Owen Young, a Guyanese engineer employed by Demba, was dismissed according to the company for inefficiency. However, it was well known that the real reason behind his dismissal was both his and his wife's inability to get on with the white senior staff. Ascria accused the company of discrimination and promptly called a 24-hour protest strike after his dismissal. The power of a cultural organization to go over the head of both the union and the government and call such a strike caused the government, the union and the company some concern. Apart from their concern at the loss of production, they were equally amazed at the ability of the organization to translate its cultural hold on the workers into political action.

In the Nurses strike, Ascria charged the company with dragging its feet in disciplining a white staff member who had been caught practically naked in the dormitory of the trainee nurses. Not only did Ascria antagonize the union but it accused the leaders of not representing its members properly, a charge resented by union officials. During the strike prior to nationalization Ascria came into open conflict with the PNC. The strike reflected the sluggish state into which the PNC organization had fallen. On the other hand, it demonstrated the degree of organization within Ascria. Because many of the rebel strike leaders were staunch Ascria members, the organization was looked at with suspicion. As the strike continued and the PNC became frustrated, the younger political organizers and assistants of the PNC began accusing the leadership of Ascria of seeking political power. Because many leading members of Ascria took part in the unauthorized Labor Day demonstration at Linden along with members of the Movement Against Oppression (MAO) and the PPP, groups opposed to the PNC, this was seized upon as further evidence of Ascria's ambition.

But Ascria had never claimed to be part of the PNC. It seemed always careful to give constructive and supportive criticism to the PNC. But to a PNC embarrassed by a strike this was interpreted differently. By the end of the nationalization strike, relations between the two organizations were cold.[28] The first indication of an official break between the organizations came when the newspapers gave prominence to the fact that Ascria executive members were picketing the Ministry of Education with Mrs. Da Scent. She had been picketing the ministry for months trying to draw attention to her dismissal from the ministry. Ascria's involvement in her case marked the beginning of serious and irreconcilable differences with the PNC.

The Movement Against Oppression, MAO, was another group with a presence, albeit a token one, during the nationalization strike. The organization was formed in December 1970 to protect the civil liberties of the poor within the City of Georgetown. It was a coalition of several organizations comprising academics and professional people who commented on government policy or made alternative policy prescriptions from time to time in their publications. Its leading members were drawn from the New World Group, Ratoon and the University of Guyana Staff Association. These groups came together to form the Movement Against Oppression after the police had attacked, beaten and ill-treated several people from the poorer areas around the city, and shot one person from the Tiger Bay Area. Though the leadership was professional, the organization was located in the poor Tiger Bay area where much of its membership was located.

The New World Group was organized in Guyana in the early 1960s. The group put out a quarterly journal which published commentary on social and economic issues in Guyana and the Caribbean. The group was comprised mainly of professionals (mainly lawyers) who worked outside the government and academics from the University. The Ratoon group formed in September 1969 after Clive Thomas was expelled from Jamaica. He was expelled, after criticizing the Jamaican government for banning Walter Rodney from the country, while attending a conference in Canada. The group was formed almost totally by university academics, and published a monthly paper commenting on government policy and making suggestions for economic and political change.

The University of Guyana Staff Association was begun in the early 1960s as a body to represent the academic staff on the University of Guyana campus. However, as the PNC began to influence and control nearly every organization which could provide a forum for alternative political expression, the association reorganized itself in 1968 to incorporate the academic and non-academic staff at the university and registered itself as a union. This organizational change increased its membership and put it in direct contact with the other industrial unions. It was largely the members of these groups and their friends who were the main force behind the formation of the Movement Against Oppression in December 1970. The organization never gained a widespread following but the real significance was that it was the first time that these groups had become involved at the community level with the ordinary citizen. It was against this background that the political parties prepared for the 1973 elections.

The nationalization of Demba did not have an immediate economic effect on the country. The payments made by the government for the company were offset by an increase in the price of sugar paid to the government in 1972 and 1973. As a result there was no noticeable decline in the standard of living of the people.

However, the people had already suffered a marked deterioration in their standard of living when the government set up the External Trade Bureau (ETB) as the sole importing agency for all goods. The agency quickly gained a terrible reputation for incompetence and bungling when it failed to import the goods as fast as private enterprise once did. Soon the people of Guyana became accustomed to shortages and lines. The agency itself was not as incompetent as people imagined; being new to the world of commerce, it did not have the credibility that the private companies did, and as a result its orders were not filled as quickly. In addition several of the large firms with whom they dealt were not willing to do business with a government agency on the same basis as they dealt with private companies, a factor which the government did not anticipate or understand. They apparently thought that government backing was all the credibility another company should need. As a result the Guyanese people suffered while the External Trade Bureau and the foreign companies worked things out between themselves.

Elections 1973

The government announced its intention to hold new general elections on July 16, 1973, a few weeks before the originally scheduled date for elections. A few weeks before the elections were held the government introduced a motion in Parliament to lower the voting age from 21 to 18. This move was surprising in view of the recent history on the subject. When the PPP was in office from 1957 to 1964, they advocated a lowering of the voting age because they thought that this would benefit them at the polls. At that time the PNC and UF, then opposition parties, staunchly opposed the idea. Now the incumbent PNC introduced the motion to parliament. The motion in the house failed by one vote, as both the PPP and the UF opposed it. Though not opposed to the idea in principle, the PPP claimed they were afraid that the PNC would take the opportunity to register more of its supporters while excluding PPP supporters. The PNC accused the PPP of hypocricy and asserted that they were always fair about all aspects of registration and urged the PPP to have no fear. The PNC left the parliament, claiming that it needed a two-thirds majority in order to fully implement its policies.

Because the United Force was never really active apart from election time, it found its ranks substantially depleted in 1973. Its workers had drifted away and its secretariat had all but closed. The resignation of Peter D'Aquiar as the party's leader in 1968 and his subsequent departure from the political scene was a blow to the party and illustrates just how personal Guyanese political parties are. As a result of its disarray the UF joined with a group of conservative Indian professional

men who had earlier formed the Liberator Party to contest the elections. Dr. Kumar, head of the Liberator Party, agreed with the UF
that while he would remain leader of a joint party, the leader of the
UF, Mr. Marcelus Fielding Singh, would be the person designated to
choose from their prepared list those who would go into parliament
based on the votes they received.

The campaign was a rather lackluster one. All of the parties contesting the elections relied on a cadre of activists who were old and tired.
There seemed to be a feeling among some, especially PNC activists,
that general elections were coming too quickly, one after another, with
little space to breathe. The PPP accused the PNC of preparing to rig
the elections by once again preparing packed overseas lists and by
excluding many PPP supporters from registration at home. They accused the government of first taking over the foreign-owned national
press and then turning it into a mouthpiece for the ruling PNC government. It also accused the government of gross mismanagement of the
economy and listed a number of projects which had been undertaken
at great expense but had borne no result. They listed the road to
Brazil, which was not completed or likely to be completed, and the
Global Agri agricultural project, which was rocked by scandal and
which was later renamed by the government. They also accused them
of politicizing the civil service, the police and the army in an effort not
to make them more responsive to the process of modernization but to
make them more sympathetic to the PNC. The PNC, on the other
hand, extolled the virtues of nationalization and of the people owning
and controlling their own resources. They reminded electors that their
party had restored the country to peace and completed projects, which
they rattled off by name. They then outlined their plans for the country
once they won a victory of two-thirds of the seats in parliament.

The election campaign was the most violent ever conducted in the
country. Blatant efforts were made by the PNC to disrupt PPP meet-

TABLE 16

	Seats Won In 1973	Seats Won In 1968
PNC	37	30
PPP	14	19
Guyana Liberator Party	2	0
United Force	0	4
Total	53	53

ings, especially in areas in and around Georgetown. The election followed the pattern set in 1968. On election day 2 people were killed and 17 injured. In the end the result could have been predicted.

The PNC got the two-thirds majority it wanted. The PPP and the Liberator Party were both incensed at the results and declared that there had been "massive electoral fraud." Both parties refused to take up the seats allotted to them under the proportional representation system. In a joint statement issued on July 24, 1973, the parties stated, "the National Assembly has been reduced by the minority PNC regime into a farce and merely serves to rubber-stamp edicts." Burnham declared after the election that the results showed that his party, which had previously been based largely on the support of Afro-Guyanese population, had succeeded in widening its base to include Indians and other races. Most observers agreed that there were many irregularities during the election, but with the election machinery in the hands of people chosen by the PNC no redress could be hoped for. As a result the PPP and the Liberator Party refused to take their seats in parliament and declared a policy of "noncooperation" with the government. This decision by the opposition embarrassed the government, especially since the PNC itself knew that, if anything, its support had shrunk, and it needed the opposition's presence in parliament to lend it some degree of legitimacy.

NOTES

1. Keesing's Contemporary Archives March 1–8, 1969 P. 23227.
2. The Small Man A Real Man. Speeches by the Prime Minister, Mr. Forber Burnham in the National Assembly on the Republic Motion. Guyana Lithographic.
3. Ibid.
4. Ibid.
5. Quoted in A History of Guyana Vol III by Dwarka Nath p. 134.
6. For a different interpretation of these events see Norman Girvan, Corporate Imperialism: Conflict and Expropriation, Monthly Review Press N.Y. 1976.
7. Ibid.
8. Statistics Canada, Canada's International Investment Position, Ottawa, Information Canada 1971, p. 77. Quoted by Isiah Litvak and Christopher Maule-Nationalization in the Carribbean Bauxite Industry—International Affairs R11A London 1975 p. 44.
9. Ibid.
10. Isiah A. Litvak and Christopher J. Maule-Nationalization in the Carribbean Bauxite Industry. International Affairs London January 1975 p. 48.
11. Ibid p. 48. For a complete study of the government's preparations for the Bauxite negotiations see Norman Girvan, Corporate Imperialism: Conflict and Expropriation—Transitional Corporations and Economic Nationalism in the Third World. Monthly Review Press 1976.

12. Guyana's Bauxite-Broadcast Address to the Nation by Prime Minister LFS Burnham Saturday 28 Nov. 1970 p. 6–7.
13. Control our Own Natural Resources. Address by Hon LFS Burnham Republic Day Feb. 23, 1971.
14. Control of Our Natural Resources, Address by Hon LFS Burnham SC Prime Minister of Guyana Republic Day February 23, 1971.
15. Ibid p. 5–6.
16. Ibid p. 17.
17. Ibid p. 9–10.
18. Guyana Graphic, Saturday April 24, 1971.
19. In an interview conducted by the writer, one transmission foreman said that whereas formerly he and his men got over one hundred job cards a month, during the transition period they got as few as thirty.
20. Guyana Graphic April 27, 1971.
21. Guyana Graphic April 26, 1971.
22. Guyana Graphic, April 30, 1971.
23. Guyana Graphic, April 30, 1971.
24. Guyana Graphic May 1, 1971.
25. Press statement by the Office of the Prime Minister May 2, 1971.
26. Ibid.
27. Philip Reno, "The Ordeal of British Guiana," *Monthly Review Press*, New York 1964, p. 102.
28. For a summary of Ascria's view of the strike and its relationship with the PNC see the Bauxite Strike and the Oil Politics, by Eusi Kwayana, Georgetown, Guyana, 1972.

CHAPTER 10

Musical Chairs

BY 1973, after the Prime Minister had been in office for nine continuous years, one would have thought that he would have found a dependable cabinet to work with. This unfortunately was not the case. Forbes Burnham seemed to have a constant need to change and reshuffle his cabinet. Most observers had by this time become accustomed to Prime Minister Burnham's style. Normally a cabinet is reshuffled to bring in new blood or give able men within the cabinet a new challenge; it can also be a power play, to keep those persons off balance, thus strengthening the position of the leader. There is little doubt that the Prime Minister used it to strengthen his position.

As the PNC continued in office, cabinet reshuffles were so common that it became difficult for ministers to establish themselves or to be taken seriously by the civil servants with whom they had to work. During the eighteen-month period prior to the July 1973 election, there were no less than three cabinet reshuffles. The first occurred on December 1970, the second in August 1971, and a third in July 1972, just after the election. The regularity of the reshuffles indicate that either the ministers were incompetent, or that insufficient forethought went into their selection and suitability for the job, or that it was a ploy to keep ministers from building a power base of their own within the bureaucracy. Whatever the intent, it left many of the ministers powerless after a while, as the press, the bureaucrats, the party officials, and the public openly flouted the orders of the ministers, as they were likely to be replaced before anyone else. This style of management increased the Prime Minister's power and visibility; little wonder then that the population at large looked to him when things went right or wrong, no matter which minister was functionally responsible. These power maneuvers increased the power of the civil servants, as they were the only ones with any in-depth knowledge of the departments; but the service itself was so politicized that they could not collectively use the power they possessed to become a strong interest group. The end result was that many of the very qualified government personnel who had returned so eagerly a few years earlier began to look elsewhere in the Caribbean and to North America for jobs. The trickle northwards had begun, just as it had a decade earlier under the PPP. The continuous emphasis on politics to the exclusion of everything else left many people exasperated.

A New Turn

The momentum created by the rhetoric of the PNC to justify its nationalization, and its own euphoria at the opportunity of outdoing the PPP, put the government on what seemed to be an unconsidered path. While there was a certain glamour to be had from making speeches laden with socialist rhetoric, the PNC was beginning to loose its credibility as the economic condition of the country worsened. The government's preoccupation with domestic politics seemed to be in part a response to some economic failures and its inability to redress the situation. The government argued that it was in the process of reordering its economic priorities so as to take on a greater role in developing the country. Perhaps this strategy was devised because of a precipitous decline in foreign and private investment. The government filled the breach, as the tables opposite indicate.

Even if the PNC had given some thought to a shift to a more socialist form of economy and government, their method seemed hurried when events at this time are considered. "The business of the politician is to consider not merely what is morally or theoretically desirable, but also the forces which exist in the world, and how they can be directed or manipulated to probably partial realizations of the ends in view."[3] If the new socialist trust of the PNC represented a change of policy, it did not seem to be producing the desired results. The very people whom these new economic policies were designed to help were constantly feeling the pinch of a sagging economy. The PNC argued that the new economic measures undertaken at this time were necessary to overcome obstacles of a colonial economy. Public support of economic policy is vital in any country with a claim of democracy: the govern-

TABLE 17
Sources of Investment
($ G Millions)
1968–1973

	(1) Public Investment	(2) Private Investment	(3) Of Which Foreign
1968	41.0	62.0	32.4
1969	42.6	62.3	36.4
1970	56.2	67.0	39.0
1971	66.3	39.1	17.3
1972	73.8	47.3	14.7
1973	114.2	43.6	N.A.

Sources: Columns (1) and (2) Bank of Guyana, *Economic Bulletin No. 8*, October 1974 Table XVIII, 6; column (3) *Economic Survey of Guyana*, 1972, Table 9.2.

TABLE 18
Percentage Distribution of Gross Domestic Product
by Sector

	1966	1971	1973
Sugar	12.5	14.8	11.5
Rice	5.7	2.9	2.1
Livestock	2.2	2.3	2.4
Other Agriculture	2.9	2.9	3.0
Fishing	1.4	1.1	1.2
Forestry	1.8	1.0	1.2
Mining and Quarrying	17.2	18.3	15.5
Food and Tobacco	3.9	3.7	3.7
Other Manufacturing	3.7	4.2	4.3
Transportation and Communications	6.8	6.0	6.1
Engineering and Construction	6.4	7.8	9.7
Services	22.6	20.9	19.3
Government	12.8	14.1	20.0

Source: Computed from Bank of Guyana, *Economic Bulletin No. 8*, October 1974, Table VIII, 6. Figures for 1973 are provisional.

ment risks losing professional and skilled personnel necessary for the success of these policies, as they are the very ones who are the first to migrate. Indeed this happened in both Guyana and in Jamaica. No matter what standard of analysis is used, the performance of the Guyanese economy is dismal.

Per capita output in 1973 stood at about $523 G, down from a peak of

$539 G reached in 1971. What is worse is the fact that the 1973 figure is but 4.8 percent higher than the level reached in 1962. Over time the performance of the economy has been erratic, with years of relatively rapid growth alternating with years of relative stagnation or decline. Thus the years 1966, 1968, 1970, 1972, and 1973 all had growth rates of 1.5 percent or less; while the years 1967, 1969, and 1971 saw increments in per capita domestic output ranging from 2.7 percent to 4.3 percent."[4]

The economic policies changed nothing that they had been intended to change.

Most noticeably the export industries, sugar and mining, continue to dominate the economy. Between them these two sectors account for 29.7 percent of output in 1966 as opposed to 33.1 percent in 1971 and 27.0 percent in 1973. At the same time, the domestic-oriented industries continued to lag badly. Combined, the livestock, other agriculture, fishing, forestry, food and tobacco, and other manufacturing sectors contributed only 15.9 percent of output in 1966; in 1973 the percentage 15.8 percent. Thus sugar and bauxite continued to dominate production, while the domestic industries remained relatively insignificant as contributors to the nation's production.

"Post-colonial Guyanese history thus exhibits a profound paradox. Government has shown itself to be innovative and nationalist, especially with regard to reorganizing the ownership structure of the bauxite industry. At the same time, however, production in the economy has remained stable on a per capita basis; and, what is worse, *the old colonial-type dependence on export production has persisted*. There has been, in short, very *little movement toward the convergence of resource use and domestic demands and needs*."[5]

Clearly the government failed to motivate its people in order to translate its policy and institutional change to productive uses. A drop in the production of goods meant that the country earned less, as less was exported. As a result less foreign exchange was earned and the country could import less. Coupled with this the government was making substantial payments for the industry it had nationalized earlier. The steep increase in 1973 of oil prices by OPEC dealt another blow to the government's plans. Even though the balance of payments situation had begun to worsen, the government continued implementing its economic and social welfare programs. A plan to provide free primary, secondary and university education was instituted in 1973.

A New Cartel—Bauxite

The Government of Guyana was one of the main organizers in Conakry, Guinea West Africa, of a meeting of bauxite producing countries from February 28 to March 8, 1974. Seven countries—Australia, Guinea, Guyana, Jamaica, Sierra Leone, Surinam and Yugoslavia, representing some 63 percent of the world bauxite production—attended the meeting. At the meeting these countries set up an International Bauxite Association. The stated aim of the new organization was to "promote the orderly and national development of the bauxite industry" and to "secure fair and reasonable profits for its member-countries in the processing and marketing of bauxite, bearing in mind the interests of the consumer countries."[6] The conference called on countries to process their own bauxite so as to become producers of aluminum and thus to increase their income. It also called on members to provide for the exchange of information, harmonization of decision, joint research, and co-ordinated purchasing of materials required by the bauxite industry.[7] The meeting was a triumph for the Government of Guyana. If successful, the IBA could give the government everything it needed: a steady flow of revenue through a stable price, access to research from countries with this capability, and a vehicle for the purchases of plant equipment for its installation.

However, these plans were being made at precisely the time that the aluminum industry was going through serious problems. The industry, dominated by a few major integrated companies, were all feeling the pressure of rising energy costs. This meant that their newer, more efficient plants had to produce enough to carry the more costly,

TABLE 19
Growth in Total Aluminum Consumption by Region

	Compound Annual Growth 1961–74	Compound Annual Growth 1974–79	Change in Rate of Growth
United States	8.3%	.8%	−90%
Japan	15.4	7.1	−54
Western Europe	7.2	3.3	−54
Rest of World	12.3	4.5	−63
Western World	9.3%	3.0%	−68%

Source: Metallgesellschaft AG

older plants. In addition the companies were beginning to experience a drop in consumption of aluminum around the world. The companies were forced to decide which of their plants were worth keeping and which had become too costly to run.

While the members of the International Bauxite Association realized that bauxite was not nearly as strategic a resource as oil, they felt secure about their future knowing that they had the major producers among their group.

On May 16, 1974, the Jamaican Prime Minister, Mr. Michael Manley, announced a new formula for calculating royalties paid by foreign bauxite mining companies operating in that country. Under this new system it was expected that Jamaican income from this source would go from approximately $30M a year to about $200M a year. The announcement was followed by other measures designed to secure greater physical control of bauxite resources, including the nationalization of bauxite deposits and the land owned by the bauxite mining companies.[8] Shortly after on June 10, 1974, the heads of government of Guyana, Mr. Forbes Burnham, Jamaica, Mr. Michael Manley, and Trinidad, Dr. Eric Williams, held a one-day meeting in Port of Spain. At the conclusion of the conference the three heads of government announced that they had concluded plans for building two aluminum smelters—one in Trinidad to be operational in the late 1970s, and a second in Guyana. The plants were to be owned jointly by the governments of the three countries.[9] Trinidad was included in these plans because it was used by Guyana for stockpiling bauxite so that large ships could be topped off after leaving Guyana's shallow waters, and because as producers of oil and gas they could easily provide the large amounts of energy required for such an operation. Also, by including Trinidad the producers were assured of the financing for the project from that country's oil revenues.

These economic plans, though commendable, seemed to ignore the realities of the marketplace in other parts of the world. Apart from the fact that aluminum consumption was already on the decline, there were new discoveries of bauxite in several countries with both the market and the resources to exploit and refine their discoveries. The most obvious example is Brazil, where the availability of cheap power complemented raw materials. When the Australian Prime Minister, Mr. Whitlam, lost the election later in the year and was replaced by a more conservative business-oriented Mr. Faser, the IBA lost the active interest of one of its largest producers and with it most of the clout it might have been able to wield.

Reynolds Nationalization

In July 1974, the government of Guyana announced that legislation was to be introduced to link taxes levied on the exports of metal grade bauxite of Reynolds Guyana Mines, a subsidiary of Reynolds Aluminum of America, to the world price of primary aluminum.[10] The level of taxation proposed was almost identical to that introduced earlier by Jamaica. Almost as soon as talks between the Guyanese government and the Reynolds Guyana Mines opened, they deadlocked. Despite a lack of agreement, tax legislation was introduced into parliament by the Minister of Energy and Natural Resources, Mr. Hubert O. Jack, and was passed unanimously on September 25, 1974. In the debate Mr. Jack told the parliament that the government had responded to representations from Reynolds Metals by reducing the intended total levy for 1974 to $6.8M from $17M. However, the company had offered to pay only $3M, inclusive of income taxes and other existing taxes. This offer was later increased to a "final" offer of $4M. Mr. Jack further informed the house that, while Reynolds Metals had agreed in principle to the linking of the levy to the current price of aluminum, it had "refused to discuss any reasonable application of such a formula," and had made its final offer conditional on the government agreeing not to nationalize or to acquire a majority share in Reynolds Guyana Mines for at least five years.[11]

Despite the passing of a law by the legislature to enforce the legislation just passed, the company refused to pay for the first half of 1974 when the levy fell due on October 5, 1974. Instead the company initiated legal proceedings to have the levy declared invalid on the grounds that it violated a tax agreement of 1965. The government then placed a total ban on the company's export of the high-priced and profitable calcined and chemical grade bauxite, though the company remained free to export the lower metal grade bauxite, which was not liable to the new tax if mined before October 5. Because of the government's action, the company ceased all exports from Guyana, recalled most of its expatriate staff, and on October 28 laid off one-third of its local work force. The government characterized the company's action as "an attempt to victimize innocent workers and to bring pressure to bear on a dispute with the government which is before the courts and as yet remains unsettled." It further described the company's action as "part of a deliberate maneuver by Reynolds Metals to abandon its operations in Guyana in such a way as to qualify for OPIC (United States Overseas Private Investment Corporation Insurance)."[12]

On December 14, 1974, Prime Minister Burnham announced the government's intention to nationalize Reynolds Guyana Mines Ltd. The announcement fixed the date of nationalization as January 1, 1975. In their subsequent negotiations Reynolds Metals was represented by OPIC. It was agreed that the government would pay $10M compensation to the company out of future profits of the mines in 13 annual installments, less the $6.8M levy claimed by the government. The company also agreed to compensate the government for payments made to workers laid off during the dispute and to transfer to the government the company's pension funds held outside Guyana.[13] Upon taking over the company, the government found that most of the company's plant was old and fully depreciated. This prompted several managers to question the wisdom of the government in nationalizing the company and spending so much political capital.

By contrast the deal Jamaica made with the bauxite companies was more advantageous. After somewhat arduous discussions with the six North American companies which mined bauxite on the island, it was announced on November 21, 1974, that an agreement had been reached between the government and the Kaiser Aluminum and Chemical Corporation.[14] The agreement allowed the government to purchase a 51 percent shareholding in the Jamaican subsidiary. The company also agreed to sell its 40,000 acres of mining land to the government on a "lease back" basis.

Even though the terms of the agreement involved the payment by the government of some $23M (about $15M for the shares and $8M for the land) over a 10-year period, the agreement, it was said, would yield the government a net income of $1.8M per annum, in addition to the company's payments under the bauxite production levy. In turn, the company was guaranteed access to reserves of bauxite sufficient to maintain current rates of extraction for 30 years, with additional reserves sufficient for a further 10 years' extraction to be assigned at a later date. Kaiser Aluminum was also promised that its payments under the bauxite production levy would remain fixed at 7.5 percent of the current aluminum price for the next two years, rather than rising to

8.5 percent as planned, and would therafter remain 1 percent lower than the normal rate.[15]

Upon the conclusion of the participation agreement, Kaiser withdrew its appeal against the levy lodged with the International Centre for Settlement of Investment Disputes.[16]

Later the Jamaican Prime Minister, Mr. Michael Manley, described the agreement as "a significant breakthrough, providing a basis for a stable partnership between a developing country and a large multinational corporation which takes account of the legitimate interests of the developing country while preserving the viability of investment."[17] Subsequently, the other companies also reached similar agreements with the government.

Change in Direction—From Consultative Democracy to Paramountcy

With a substantial sector of the economy in the hands of the government and with a tightening control of the press, the PNC government looked invincible, but was in fact very weak. But for the legal shell which it had built around itself to make it invulnerable to public opinion and the opposition, it would have been voted out of office. Unemployment was rising rapidly, production was slowing. And the rise in oil prices had imposed another burden with which the government could barely cope. Enthusiasm had reached a low point and some type of dramatic action was needed.

The state of the economy and the morale of the people forced the government of Prime Minister Burnham into a defensive position. The government-controlled press poured scurrilous abuse upon his often defenseless opponents. While the government did not stop the opposition and dissident groups from printing newspapers and political tracts, it increased the tax on newsprint to such an astronomical degree that few other groups than the government could afford to communicate in writing. The result was that people began to rely on rumor and other sources for their information even more than usual, an insidious position for any government to put itself into. As a result the Catholic Standard emerged as the only paper independent of a political party in the country. Because it at times questioned government policy and action it too began to be seen as opposed to the government.

On December 14, 1974, Burnham, speaking to a Special Congress of the PNC as its leader, announced a sweeping change in the direction for both the government and the party. The change was designed to give the party and government a socialist character. Burnham began his address by recalling that it had been exactly ten years since the PNC had assumed office. He then went on to say:

"In November of last year (1973) there was held a Special Congress four months after our Party had won a two-thirds majority in Parliament. At this Congress, there were a serious examination and a definition of the role of the Party in the new circumstances.

"It was agreed after lengthy discussion that the emphasis should be on mobilising the nation in every sphere and not merely for periodic elections and in support of specific action and programmes. It was also decided that the Party should assume unapologetically its paramountcy over the Government which is merely one of its executive arms.

"The comrades demanded that the country be given practical and theoretical leadership at all levels-political, economic, social and cultural-by the P.N.C. which had *become the major national institution.*"[18]

The raising of the party to assume what he called "paramountcy" meant that the PNC was prepared to drop whatever trappings of democracy which remained and regarded itself as the sole party, unanimously supported. The very reverse was true at this time. The party was unpopular and its organization sluggish and sometimes nonexistent. Many of its organizers needed favors from the government or felt compelled to be active to preserve their jobs. It was because of this, and to make these new measures palatable that the Prime Minister proposed a code of conduct for all party members and party leaders. Mr. Burnham went on to enunciate the philosophy and goals of the PNC.

That ours is a Socialist Party, committed to practising Co-operative Socialism, is declared, and the objects are fully and clearly set out. Some of these are:

(1) To ensure and maintain through the practice of co-operative socialism, the interest, well-being and prosperity of ALL the people of Guyana.
(2) To pursue a commitment to the Socialist ideal and more particularly to ensure that the people of Guyana own and control for their benefit the natural resources of the country.
(3) To provide every Guyanese the opportunity to work for and share in

the economic well-being of the country and to ensure that there is equality of opportunity in the political, economic and social life of the country.

(4) To motivate the people of Guyana to improve by their own efforts and through the Party, the communities in which they live.

(5) To pursue constantly the goal of national self-reliance.

(6) To work for the closest possible association of Guyana with her Caribbean neighbours and to maintain a link with International Organisations and Agencies whose aims and objectives are consistent with those of the People's National Congress. [19]

Nothing in the declaration was really new, but for the proposed organizational changes. Making the PNC an official arm of the government was a radical departure from the way politics had been conducted and insured that no other political group could compete with it. Many people saw this as a deliberate attempt by the PNC to further limit the activity of the opposition and dissent while making itself the only party people could turn to. After spelling out organizational changes he proposed to make within the party, Burnham came to what many thought to be the diabolical part of his speech.

"As we complete our tenth year in office, and proceed to the country's tenth anniversary of independence, we cannot do so with a Constitution out of step with modern trends, and our own ideas and ideologies; a Constitution which reflects for the most part the beliefs and ideology of our former imperialist masters; a Constitution which was taken out of the drawer, so to speak, as were several others for various ex-British colonies; with the minimun relevancy to the Guyanese peoples' needs, aspirations and thrusts. The Constitution must go and in its place a new and relevant Constitution must be substituted." [20]

The informed electorate was stunned at the proposal. They saw it as a clear attempt by the Prime Minister to fashion a system to suit himself, having lost the goodwill of many of his old and faithful supporters. To these people this bombshell was an affront to their sensibilities and a betrayal of the trust they had put in Prime Minister Burnham. They knew from then on that they had lost even the remaining influence and control they had over him. Burnham was seeing treasonable opposition in well-intentioned criticism, and was harrassing, even prosecuting, his alleged enemies, feeding into the already charged Guyanese political atmosphere.

In the area of foreign trade and private investment, the Prime Minister announced to the Congress his intention of extending his control over the economy:

"As we move to control land in the interest of the nation, *we will also take control over all foreign trade—import and export.* Already, through a marketing committee on which the Sugar Producers are represented, the Government is responsible for sugar exports. Our other major exports—bauxite, rice and forestry products—are already handled by public agencies. This pattern will be extended to all other exports. The object is to ensure quality and reliability, as well as an effective monitoring of the system. In addition, your Government as the agency finally responsible for the whole economy, must be in a position to decide, after consultation, on directions of trade in the general national interest.

"Similarly, import trade cannot continue as it is now, subject to whimsical preferences on the part of private importers, which preferences are frequently dictated by tradition and agency agreements rather than considerations of quality, price and relevancy to Government's international agreements and national policies.

"We are frequently asked about our Policy in relation to foreign private investment. The time has come now to give, indeed to repeat, the answer once and for all. Private investment from abroad is welcome in specific fields in consortium with Government and/or the cooperatives, provided that in each case Government and/or the cooperatives hold majority equity and real control. A Committee of the Party and Government will shortly be appointed to set out clearly the fields and areas contemplated for such joint ventures as well as the attendant terms and conditions, one of which will be a guarantee against confiscation. The work of the Committee will have to be completed by March 31st 1975. When the list is adopted and published there can be absolutely no doubt or grey areas."[21]

To the average Guyanese the prospect of having the government assume further control of foreign trade was not a pleasant one. The first phase of the attempt to control foreign trade through the External Trade Bureau (ETB) had resulted in shortages, long lines, and was recognized as slow and cumbersome by importers. The government had been greatly criticized by its supporters about the inefficiency of the ETB as early as 1970. By 1974 the government needed to institute more revenue-producing controls because it needed the foreign exchange to pay for the nationalized industries, for new development, and further increases in oil prices.

The delay of imports cannot be attributed to the ETB itself. The companies which the ETB had replaced had had a long relationship with their suppliers and had built up a track record which the ETB did not have. As a result orders from overseas companies for the ETB were filled more slowly. Furthermore, the ETB as a government corporation meant something in Guyana where government is the major employer. The government failed to realize the extent to which Western merchants and other businessmen disliked doing business with governments or their agencies. They find them bureaucratic and slow to pay; as a result they usually insist on more careful documentation and absolutely prompt payment. And shipping time to Guyana was not their concern. In periods of shortages, it meant that the ETB, as a new customer, was the last to be supplied. All this made trade difficult for Guyana.

The institutionalization of the PNC as a socialist party, with a record of nationalization, even if they were forced to do so, left the PPP in a predicament. Not only were they outmaneuvered on the ideological front by the PNC, but by not taking up their seats in parliament since the 1973 elections they did not have that forum to voice their view. In addition, Dr. Jagan and the PPP saw Prime Minister Fidel Castro of Cuba fly into Guyana in September 1973 with Prime Minister Michael Manley of Jamaica aboard, pick up Forbes Burnham, then together take off for the Conference of Non-Aligned Heads of State in Algiers. Between 1970 and 1975 a parade of heads of states of non-aligned countries visited Guyana and were hosted by Forbes Burnham. It must have galled Dr. Jagan to see these socialist friends come and go and not be a part of the picture even as opposition leader. It must have been obvious to him that his strategy of non-cooperation, in effect since the 1973 election, had no effect on these men and their dealing with Burnham.

In mid 1975 Dr. Jagan attended a meeting in Cuba of the Communist International to which his party is affiliated. At that meeting the Soviet Union announced a change of strategy to their affiliates. Rather than seeking political power as these parties were trying to do, they suggested that these parties should begin supporting indigenous governments which were moving in a socialist direction. This change of tactic gave Dr. Jagan a way out of his dilemma in Guyana.

In August 1975, Dr. Jagan announced a change of tactics to the PPP Congress. "Our political line" he said "should be changed from non-cooperation and civil resistance to critical support."[22] As he explained later, because the PNC government had begun to institute many socialist policies which the PPP could support, it ought to be support-ing them, not blindly, but as an aid against unfriendly western inter-ests. As a result, after two years of protests, the PPP parliamentarians took their seats in the house.[23]

Obviously Jagan felt he had something to gain by this move; the PNC certainly was relieved. Even though the government had put on a good face over the two years, they were constantly embarrassed at the PPP absence from parliament and Dr. Jagan's constant protest over the 1973 election results. Furthermore, foreign visitors were generally well informed, and aware of the domestic situation and his absence. By entering parliament the PPP did not legitimize the PNC government, but they made them more acceptable.

As has been suggested, one reason for the abrupt change to "critical support" by Dr. Jagan and the PPP was pressure from the Soviet Union. Some argue that the Soviet Union by this time began to see developments in Guyana as taking on a socialist direction and urged Dr. Jagan to support the government in the interest of ideological solidarity. Another school of thought saw Jagan caught in a vise: with Burnham increasingly calling himself a socialist, a move further to the left would have caused him to lose support. So to preserve his credibil-ity and influence, Jagan decided to support the government's economic policies. Four months after his announcement, to the consternation of most observers, the government announced that it had decided to hold elections within the sugar industry for the workers to choose freely the union which they wanted to represent them. It was a momentous announcement of immense proportions. And it was a complete reversal of the government's position of ten years standing. The struggle for recognition by the Guyana Agricultural Workers Union had first brought Dr. Jagan to prominence in 1948, precipitated the formation of the PPP, caused the constitution to be suspended in 1953, and was the source of much violence in 1963–64. Having the union recognized had been a dream of the PPP for many years. No persuasive explana-tion could be found for the government's change of mind except that the PNC needed the PPP and wanted to look magnanimous, knowing full well that it could control the union. When the elections were held between the Man Power Citizens Association (MPCA) and Guyana Agricultural Workers Union (GAWU) in December, 1975, the GAWU won easily with 98 percent of the vote. By winning the elections so overwhelmingly the PPP demonstrated that the base of its support was still intact.

The general state of the economy had stabilized by the end of 1974, after the initial increases in the price of oil. During this time the country was helped by the relatively high and stable price paid for calcined bauxite and because of the high price paid for sugar on the world market. The country's foreign reserves stood at a reasonably high level. The Prime Minister felt that this windfall should be used to purchase and replace capital equipment. His civil service advisers—professional economists—argued strongly against such a policy, but they were overruled. In deciding to go against his advisors, Forbes Burnham knew he was gambling, but went ahead anyway. The government had had an ongoing lobbying campaign at the World Bank for sometime, and the speeches of the bank's head, Mr. McNamara, took a sympathetic view of countries trying to industrialize. This interpretation of the bank's new policy might have led Forbes Burnham to believe that Guyana's Hydro-Electric project would be given the World Bank financing it was counting on. Failing that, he may have thought the Soviets or East Europeans would come to his aid to finance the project, thus providing the stimulus for the country's economic take-off.[24] If this was his analysis, it was a miscalculation on both counts.

By late 1975 it was clear that the government's much publicized campaign to "feed, clothe and house" the nation by 1976 was not going to succeed. While remarkable progress was made in its attempt to house the nation, the other two legs of the policy were less successful. The policy was not ill-conceived; rather it was not properly understood and was badly executed. Instead of cultivating new crops which were unfamiliar to the farmers and for which the soil conditions were not particularly well-suited, the government should have put its efforts into raising production in those areas in which it had a comparative advantage. A greater effort to produce more poultry, hogs, cattle and rice would have been relatively lower in overhead cost, simpler for farmers to learn, and would have provided the protein needed to feed the nation. The planting of cotton, a new crop which required much attention and fertilizer, which had to be bought at steep prices with valuable foreign exchange from abroad, was not advantageous to Guyana at that time.

The government's banning of certain imported foodstuffs in an effort to help domestic substitution brought it further political trouble, as there was very often no substitute to replace the banned items. And in those instances when they could be obtained, only limited amounts were ever on the shelves. The food situation created further problems for the government, which neither it nor anyone else could have foreseen. Among the people, the concern for proper food became such a preoccupation that even top civil servants found themselves devoting part of their working time to assuring and obtaining adequate supplies for their families. The result was that an already weak bureaucracy functioned even less well, and a preoccupation with privilege and material comforts developed. Although humanly understandable, such preoccupation led to bureaucratic lethargy, status consciousness, and neglect of the reforms of privilege in government that Burnham had pledged to effect.

In early 1974 Britain renewed the Commonwealth Sugar Agreement with its former colonies. Under the agreement, Britain contracted to buy sugar at a fixed price for its own refineries to be used for domestic consumption and for commercial use. Under the agreement, Britain had agreed to pay its Commonwealth partners £83 per ton. At the time the agreement was signed the Commonwealth countries were annoyed because Britain had not yet been able to get the EEC to honor its commitment to provide access to Europe for 1.4 million tons of Commonwealth sugar. By mid-year the situation had changed drastically. Because of a disappointing European beet crop and a disastrous British crop, the price of sugar on the open market rose quickly to £355 per ton. Prime Minister Burnham suggested the British Government in turn pay Guyana an amount that reflected the inflated prices Britain commanded for Guyanese sugar. The British government refused to renegotiate the agreement, and Burnham abitrarily suspended all shipments of raw sugar from Guyana to Britain. In the meantime the presence of Emiliano Lezcano of the Cuban Sugar Corporation in Guyana shortly after the Soviet Union had agreed to pay Cuba £182 a ton under a long-term contract, increased the anxiety of the British Government.[25] Burnham's stand caused the British Minister of Agriculture Mr. Fred Peart to fly to Guyana for discussions. But the British government's attitude was constrained by a number of her own domestic problems. The country was facing a projected balance of payments deficit of £4,000 million, and inflation was high and farmers were agitating to have their prices moved up to EEC price levels. At the same time the government was anxious to obtain supplies, "not only to relieve the present scarity but to aid the UK cane refining industry, where jobs were at stake."[26] It also had to face the possibility that any new agreement made with Guyana would be demanded by the other Commonwealth countries as well.

At the end of their talks Mr. Piert and Mr. Burnham agreed that Britain would pay Guyana £140 per ton for 85,000 tons of sugar, as opposed to £83 a ton originally agreed for 136,000 tons. When asked about the further 85,000 tons originally contracted for, Mr. Piert said that "a considerably higher price would have been needed to obtain the full total."[27] He went on however to characterize his discussions as "very reasonable" in view of the present world market price. The added amounts of sugar sold on the world market gave Guyana's foreign exchange position a hefty boost. Burnham's leadership on this issue did much to maintain his prestige both in the Commonwealth and among the non-aligned group.

Jim Jones: Border Outpost

It was about this time that the Reverend Jim Jones of California was given land by the PNC government to build a permanent agricultural community in Guyana. Originally Jim Jones was attracted to the country for a number of reasons. The people spoke English and land could be easily and cheaply obtained. A substantial percentage of the population was black and the government espoused a socialist philosophy not too far from his own.

Guyana had had a long involvement with different American religions and political groups. Beginning in the late 1960s different groups had come and gone, with none ever gaining strength in numbers or developing the large agricultural settlements they promised. The government had no reason to suspect that Jim Jones and his group was any different. Far from that his credentials and references from respected American politicians were good, and he seemed well financed. After having as many setbacks in its agricultural policy as it did, the government was willing to welcome any group possessing money and workers. The government interested them in the Matthews Ridge-Port Kaituma area, an area where it had been trying to develop agriculture for some time. The area was originally one where manganese was mined and so possessed some infrastructure, hence the original reason for creating farming communities in that area. But the government was particularly interested in keeping the area populated and active because of its proximity to Venezuela, with which Guyana has had continuing border problems. The presence of a small town with a thriving population, it was felt, would deter the Venezuelans from making illegal, undercover excursions into the disputed area.

Even though Jones' group decided to begin an "agricultural mission" in 1974, it was not until early 1975 that a skeleton crew arrived to begin work at Jonestown. The mission had varying numbers of persons working at the sight for nearly two years, and it was not until the end of 1977 that Jim Jones and the rest of his congregation arrived to take up permanent residence at the township.[28] Although government officials visited the outpost from time to time no inspection was made of the fledgling town and its facilities. On the other hand the town provided as much produce as possible to convince the authorities that all was well, and to keep them optimistic about future supplies.

Because the residents of Jonestown remained in their hinterland town and only ventured into the city in small groups on occasion few Guyanese knew of their presence in the country. Those who knew about them never knew their number. This was part of the reason why few people paid any attention to opposition charges during the constitutional referendum that the PNC government was allowing new Guyanese to participate in the voting. It came as a great shock to the Guyanese people and the government when reports reached the city on November 19 that 400 residents of Jonestown had committed suicide. The Guyanese people were stunned. Four hundred people. How did four hundred people get into that area, many asked. They were more taken back at the number. This does not mean that they were not saddened by the deaths of innocent people, but events made many realize how much things had slipped beyond their control. The quantity of drugs and ammunition and the freedom to use them that Jim Jones and his people were given would never have been given to a local group. When the final numbers were in, 905 dead, and the extent of the tragedy became known many Guyanese were embarrassed.

Though those who had died were American, that it happened in

Guyana made Guyanese numb. Despite the government's attempts to play the tragedy up as an American affair, most Guyanese felt that the government had not discharged its responsibility properly which in the end contributed to the tragedy. The politicians argued that the government had relinquished its sovereignty over the area it granted to Jim Jones and his followers, and allowed him to run a state within a state.

The End of Bookers Guyana

Prior to 1966, when Guyana was still a British Colony, most people referred to the colony as B.G. (British Guiana). At that time some people cynically referred to the abbreviation B.G. as meaning Bookers' Guyana. What they were referring to was the dominant position the giant British Multi-national Corporation of Bookers McConnel and Company held in the country. Bookers, as it was commonly called, began after the abolition of slavery to consolidate the numerous small estates into a few giant ones. To support these large estates the company became involved in engineering, wholesale and retail, and agriculture. As a result of their vertically integrated operation, British Guiana, up until WW II, was not much more than a number of giant sugar estates separated by a few townships. The whole country was almost one giant company town. [29]

The country's lack of economic development could be traced to a deliberate policy by the British Government to keep the economy straitjacketed. A combination of policies created an economic environment in which profit was gained by the sugar producers at the expense of economic growth for the country. [30] This situation lasted until the early 1950s when the economic environment in the sugar market changed. As a result the companies undertook a policy of mechanization, thus displacing the pool of labor it had had on constant call for seasonal work.

This dynamic of colonial agri-business policy left a bitter taste in the mouths of colonial peoples, for business in general and for the multi-national in particular. It made them suspicious of all business, especially foreign business. It is against this background that a developing country must pursue a strategy of economic development.

Guyana, after independence, was seeking to move away from being just a cog in the wheel of international trade to becoming more involved in international business. The government took a further step in doing so when it sought to expand the power of the ETB from being a mere importer on behalf of the retail companies to taking over the distribution also. This is how the government approached the Bookers Stores, Ltd., part of the Bookers Group in Guyana. The company, after listening to Burnham's request that they relinquish this lucrative part of their business told the government that any talks should involve the whole group of companies, not just the distributive Bookers Stores. Furthermore they informed the government that they had no intention of maintaining their plant since the government had raised the question. The government was surprised at the company's bold response; it had no alternative but to enter negotiations on a price and terms for a government takeover of the enterprise. On May 26, 1976, the Bookers Group of Companies was nationalized by the government of Guyana. The decision was of monumental significance, for with it the government had amassed control of over 80 percent of the national economy. The nationalization raised some basic questions about the government's development strategy.

From the sequence of events beginning with the nationalization of Demba in 1971 to that of Bookers in 1976, the government's strategy seemed unplanned and hurried. If the goal was to get into international business, then not much thought was given to a clear strategy for doing so. Management personnel, where they would come from, what was to be done for their development, and training was all unthought of. With each nationalization the small management pool became further strained.

With the Bookers nationalization, the government seems to have thought it was in a much better position because local managers were in charge of so much of the industry. Upon nationalization, however, much of the management personnel chose to leave rather than work, contrary to the government's expectations, which put a further strain on the limited resources of a small country.

But there are other problems apart from those of personnel inherent in a policy of acquisitions. All business executives know that too rapid an expansion causes a loss of control, and in losing control operating costs go up. In addition it takes time to understand the operational realities of the businesses you are acquiring and, done too rapidly, it can result in severe losses. Knowing this, the quick succession of nationalizations by the government of Guyana seem foolhardy. How much thought was given to the political arguments for nationalization over the economic realities of successfully running the acquisitions? Where did the money come from to purchase so many expensive companies within such a short time? No one can doubt that to own and control one's resources is politically desirable. How well a government is able to effect the transition, though, must also be weighed in the balance.

Estate Manager Politics

The managers of the large sugar estates were very powerful in colonial times. Not only could they fire a person, but they could also order him to vacate his company-owned house as well. If the person came from an outside village he could be ordered not to set foot on the estate again. The estate manager, since he was the only employer, was also the ultimate authority. This rule was only reconfirmed when the government assumed control over 80 percent of the economy. The few people who were not in total agreement with policy or who flouted the government's policy were dismissed, harrassed, and eventually forced to leave the country. For a country with an abundance of professional talent, such a program might not have been so harmful. But for a country like Guyana, with few such people, and given their ready access to jobs in the Caribbean, North America, other developing countries and the UN agencies, such a policy was disastrous. The example made of those who ran afoul of the government caused others to reassess their own positions and to make alternative plans. The constant drain of high-level personnel put a greater and greater strain on those who remained. Together with the other problems of living within the country, it made life very unpleasant. Eventually people began to go to work more out of habit rather than for the satisfaction of growing and developing in their field. As managers were fixed and replaced, some people began to wonder how many layers of managers the government would go through before the system finally broke down.

New Constitution and New Politics

First mention of the government's intention to rewrite the constitution had been made in December 1974. Not much was heard about the idea after it was originally announced. The government itself realized that the decision would be controversial. In 1978 it introduced a bill in Parliament to amend Article 73 of the constitution to make it unnecessary to submit any future amendments of the Articles to a referendum. The bill was another attempt by the government to widen its powers in a legal way. Even though the government had a two-thirds majority, it had to submit to a referendum any changes it proposed to make to the political and electoral provision embodied in Article 73, in addition to having a two-thirds majority. The article was a safeguard to make it difficult for a government to become a dictatorship overnight. The bill would cancel the need for all further referendums in making any future changes, enabling the PNC government to use its two-thirds majority more effectively.

The PNC needed to make this drastic move because it had become tremendously unpopular, and it feared that the members who were always willing to cooperate with it in circumventing the election laws were diminishing and in some cases could no longer be trusted. The government was also aware that their old technique of manipulating the election was being carefully monitored by the PPP and the new, very active Working Peoples Alliance (WPA). The old methods would not suffice if the government were to stay in power and project a degree of respectability. It had to admit in 1976 that it had not been able to feed, clothe, and house the nation as it had promised it would do. Its agricultural policies were not the success it had hoped they would be. The nationalized industries were barely maintaining production levels and had to be paid for out of declining foreign exchange reserves, as the price of sugar had by this time fallen. The expected loan from the World Bank for the hydro-electric project for which the government had made huge cash outlays was still not forthcoming. The general economic conditions within the country were worse than they ever were.

The groups opposed to the bill fell into two broad categories: The first professional and social, the second political.

"The first was the Citizens' Committee opposed to the bill, comprising the following organisations: Lawyers Committee, Architects, Committee of Medical Practitioners, Committee of Concerned Educators, University of Guyana Staff Association, Clerical and Commercial Workers Union and National Agricultural Commercial and Industrial Employees. The Guyana Council of Churches was an observer and attended all meetings in that capacity.

"The second was the Committee in Defence of Democracy, which comprised the Civil Liberties Action Council, The Committee of Concerned Educators, Democratic Teachers' Movement, Guyana Agricultural and General Workers Union, Guyana Hindu D'Harmic Sabha, Guyana Peace Council, Liberator Party, Organisation of Working People, People's Democratic Movement, People's Progressive Party, Progressive Youth Organisation, Rice Producers Association, United Sad'r Islamic Anjuman, Working People's Alliance and Women's Progressive Organisation."[31]

Many of these groups did not meet as a collective; rather they met among themselves to discuss the referendum and the future of the country. The government must have been surprised by the depth of the response by the most dormant groups. But the willingness of such a diverse group to become political once more shows the extent to which they viewed the government with disgust. Two goups, more than any other, emerged at this time as leaders opposed to the referendum: the Working Peoples Alliance (WPA) and COMPASS.

The WPA was a further outgrowth of groups begun sometime earlier—New World, Ratoon, Ascria and IPRA. The group gained greater prominence with the 1974 return to the country of Walter Rodney, the well-known historian and radical professor. The refusal by the government to allow him to take up a teaching post at the University of Guyana after having been offered a job by the academic committee added to his notoriety and probably attracted those looking for a change. Sometime thereafter in 1973, these amorphous discussion groups and committees came together to form the WPA. The organization was successful in attracting a number of young people from both major ethnic groups, a fact which must have disturbed both the PPP and the PNC, and which supports the main thesis of this book.

The other group which emerged at this time was COMPASS. It was made up of top employees in the government corporations, trade unionists, professional men, and a few top ex-civil servants. The group was headed by Pat Thompson, former executive with the Bookers group, former Ambassador to the UN, and at that time, Chairman of Guyana Mines Ltd. That such a top official should head such a group indicated the gravity of the problem and the risks people were prepared to take. The group organized discussions among themselves and put out position papers on differing aspects of the political situations. They published three thought provoking papers which were extremely well-received. They called for a government of national reconstruction to see the country through its economic problems, but the PNC would not hear of this. Rather, the PNC pressured and threatened the executives of several government corporations into withdrawing from the organization.

As the date for the referendum approached concerning Article 73, the PNC regarded every gathering as seditious and sinister. The one point which was being constantly debated by the opposition groups was whether to participate in the referendum or boycott it. The main argument of those who supported a boycott was that voting was irrelevant to the result, as the system of voting had been effectively destroyed. It was thought that it would be undignified to participate in such an obvious farce.[32] Yet some of those who agreed with the arguments felt that they had a civic duty to vote. They felt that a boycott would be defeatist and argued that it was better to get the people out to vote and expose them to the situation on voting day. As a compromise it was agreed that the Secretary of the two groups should write the Minister of Home Affairs to request a meeting to discuss their minimum demands for a referendum. The letter read:

"DEAR SIR,
   With the passage in parliament on April 10th of the Constitution (Amendment) Bill No. 8 of 1978, and even more so after the passage and subsequent enactment of the Referendum (Amendment of the Constitution) Bill No. 12 of 1978, our organisations have been repeatedly asked by members of the public a number of questions about the arrangements for the holding of the Referendum.
   People have asked whether the overall responsibility rests with the Elections Commission and if not, why not. Subsequently, from a full page notice in the GUYANA CHRONICLE of Saturday and Sunday, May 27 and 28, 1978, it appeared that a Mr. R.A. Hammond was in charge subject to your direction.
   Our organisations have become aware of profound public disquiet concerning the question of whether the Referendum will be free or fair. The unavailability of the Electoral List to organisations with the capacity to examine them critically such as the opposition political parties, the extremely short time for claims and objections to the list; the receipt by many persons of notices of objections to their names on the list after the dates for hearing such objections have passed the availability of such lists to P. N. C. activists official statements that votes will be counted centrally yet again without any valid reason, and experience of the 1973 elections, all of these, together with the avoidance of the Elections Commission provide more than sufficient reason for this disquiet.

In the circumstances the organisations mentioned below present eight clear minimum demands, compliance with which we consider absolutely essential to the conduct of a free and fair referendum.

These demands are presented without prejudice to our contention that the unconstitutional avoidance of the supervision and direction of the Elections Commission in the compilation of the present Electoral List, the introduction of overseas votes, and the unusual extension of proxy and postal voting, have already seriously if not fatally impaired the possibility of a free and fair Referendum.

In view of the urgency of this matter, we consider it essential that the above issues should be clarified before the end of this month and request a written response from you by 30th June, 1978."[33]

No reply to the letter was ever received. Despite several official requests by the Secretary of the groups, Mr. Rodrigues, the courtesy of a reply from either the minister or someone designated by him was not granted. This refusal to reply had come to be standard operating procedure used by the government when faced with embarrassing problems.

In the absence of an official reply to discuss their concerns, the groups held a joint meeting on July 1, 1978. It was agreed that the minister's attitude showed an unwillingness to recognize their grievances, and therefore it could be assumed that voting procedures on referendum day would be the same as they had been in the past. It was resolved that the groups boycott the referendum and urge their members and supporters not to vote.[34] Above the protest of these groups, the referendum was held on July 10, 1978. As could have been predicted, the government won, but it was an immoral victory, for it showed the PNC's worst side and showed that it was determined to make the country the personal instrument of its leader. It forced on the opposition parties the realization that there was no way they would be able to replace the PNC in a legal manner. According to opposition groups which monitored the polls, voter turnout was 14 percent. The government, however, put the turnout figure at 71 percent. With the referendum passed, the government went to parliament and voted to extend its mandate for fifteen months. The reason given for the extension was that a new constitution was needed and there was not sufficient time to prepare one before Parliament had to be legally dissolved. The government then set up a Constituent Assembly to discuss a new constitution. The United Force and a few social groups and trade unions gave their input at the public sessions as to what the new constitution should embody. But the most active political groups and professional associations stayed away. Their feeling was that the PNC was going to write a constitution favorable to their own interest anyway and any deposition they gave would only be used by the government as an indication of how much freedom the political groups still enjoyed.

But there was also a general feeling that the PNC was using this interim period to buy time before the anticipated election. The government knew that its support had fallen drastically and perhaps it felt that an expected change in either the domestic or foreign economic situation could help them. But no change occurred. Instead the steady increase in the price of oil and a fall in the world price of sugar put the economy in still further trouble. The WPA, in the meantime, was making good use of the government's bad fortune. The public was forced to view the WPA as a serious alternative to the sectional politics of both PPP and the PNC, and it became quite active holding discussions and public meetings. Vexing as it was to the government and PNC party, a larger number of people were beginning to question PNC directives and defy their instructions.

On the night of July 10, 1979, one year after the referendum had been held, the Ministry of National Development and General Secretary of the PNC was bombed and destroyed by fire. The building had replaced Congress Place, itself destroyed by fire a few years earlier, and under the reorganized PNC the Ministry of National Development was then a ministry of the government responsible for implementing the PNC "Paramountcy" doctrine, a nation which opposition groups found repugnant.

Early the next day of July 11, 1979, five leading members of the Working People's Alliance were arrested. They included Dr. Walter Rodney, Dr. Omawale, and Dr. Rupert Roopnarine. Those arrested were held without any formal charge for three days. When writs of habeas corpus were filed on their behalf, Rodney, Roopnarine and Omawale were charged with arson. In the midst of this the bauxite workers at Kwakwani (the former Reynolds mines) went on strike on July 12 after a wage dispute with the government. On Saturday, July 14, the accused were taken to court. As they arrived they were greeted by a number of WPA supporters and well-wishers. In court, bail was set, after which the accused were hustled by the police back to prison pending lodging of bail. The demonstrators outside the courts marched with their pickets along Brickdam in the direction the police vans had taken. Suddenly in the vicinity of the police station, the demonstrators were charged by a gang wielding sticks and knives. As they were attacked the crowd scattered. The editor of the *Catholic Standard*, Michael James, was badly beaten. As the melee continued, Father Bernard Darke, a Jesuit priest and photographer for the *Standard*, took pictures. Noticing some of the attackers heading toward him, he started running but tripped and fell. The attackers beat him, then one drew a bayonet and stabbed him in the back.

A plainclothes policeman who happened along fired two shots in the air, interrupting the ambush. He arrested one person and further arrests were made later. Father Darke died later that day. His death marked the beginning of a new round of violence in the country. All of those arrested were members of a religious sect located in the city known as the House of Israel and headed by Rabbi Washington.[35] The cult which he led was known to be aligned with the PNC and had a history of breaking up meetings by groups opposed to the PNC. Though Father Darke's death embarrassed the PNC, the party showed no signs of this in its public statements or in its paper. Rather it served notice to its opponents that they intended to stand firm in the face of any and all further opposition.

On July 23 the strike in the bauxite industry spread to the Linden area. The government dubbed the strike as "politically motivated." The atmosphere in the country was charged with political tension. So great was the solidarity and sympathy for the daring of the WPA that on July 27, 1979, the WPA felt confident enough to declare itself a political party. Though it was beginning to attract the support of a great number of people, much of its executive membership were academics and professional.

The government submitted a draft of its new constitution to the constituent assembly on August 1, 1979. The new constitution vested executive power in the office of the President. The office of Prime Minister would become largely administrative. The President would appoint a Prime Minister and Cabinet. The legislature, it was proposed, would be comprised of 53 members as before, but would have 12 nominated members also. The new constitution was a clear throwback to that of colonial times, with Burnham taking the place of the British government. It had been known for sometime that Prime Minister Burnham had become weary of the day-to-day chore of running the government, and wanted some arrangement which would allow him to retain his power while shifting the mundane task of running the country to someone else.

At their public meetings the WPA, now allied with the PPP, and often including speakers from that party, attacked the PNC vehemently. Walter Rodney, the party's main speaker at these meetings, never referred to Prime Minister Burnham by his name or title, instead he called him "fat boy" or "King Kong," a reference to the Prime Minister's physical stature. Needless to say the euphemism angered the Prime Minister. At that time the only paper which printed any type of hard news other than what the government handed out was the *Catholic Standard* and the *Mirror*, the latter being a newspaper. It did not come as a surprise then when on August 9, 1974, the *Mirror* was told that there was no more newsprint available for it. When other Caribbean newspapers heard of its predicament and offered the paper 5 tons of newsprint, the government refused to issue an import license for it.[36] That left only the government-controlled *Chronicle* and the *Catholic Standard*, a thin weekly, to dispense the news. The *Catholic Standard* had survived because it had switched from using newsprint to using a heavy bond paper. Both the *Mirror* and the *Standard* had earlier reduced their size to four and eight pages because the tax had made newsprint too expensive to use.

But the government's problems did not end with trying to stifle the news. A number of unions, including the GAWU (the PPP-controlled sugar union) and the Clerical and Commercial Workers Union (CCWU), representing workers in the government corporations, gave notice to the government that they intended to go on strike in support of the bauxite workers who had by then been on strike for nearly a month. The WPA, in an attempt to get some political mileage out of the strike in the bauxite industry, went to Linden and held a meeting to express its support for the workers on August 15. After the meeting, two bombs exploded at the homes of prominent WPA activists in the area. On that same day, 46 prominent citizens published a statement indicating their support for a broad-base alternative government not dominated by party or ideology. Because many of these men had no prominent association with politics their suggestion attracted a lot of interest, even though most knowledgeable observers did not expect the PNC to take such a suggestion seriously.

The three WPA leaders appeared in court once again on August 17, 1979. As usual their supporters gathered outside the courts with pickets. In a rush similar to the one a month before, the picket lines are attacked by a gang of unidentified persons and chased from the scene. Some were beaten and still others were put on a bus and taken outside the city limits and released. A few blocks away on that day, the CCWU picket lines outside of the government-owned Guyana stores was violently broken up by a group led by a government minister. The next day the picket lines outside the stores were again broken up by a gang. The president of the union, Mr. Gordon Todd, was picked up, and taken outside the city and held for sometime before being released.[37]

The next day, on August 19, 1979, the executive of the Mine Workers Union and the Clerical and Commercial Workers Union called off the strike by their respective unions.

In its attempt to keep up the momemtum it felt it had achieved, the WPA continued to hold political meetings around the country. At one such meeting on August 22, one of the party's executive members, Moses Bhagwan, was beaten and sustained a fractured hand. It was clear by this time that the country was in for a period of sustained, low-level violence.

In an attempt to weaken the CCWU for calling a sympathy strike with the bauxite workers, the government on August 23 fired 80 workers who had participated in that strike. The government said that it was entitled to take such a course of action because the strike was politically motivated. On the same day members of the legal profession in Georgetown staged a one-day boycott of the courts to protest the beating of their colleague, Moses Bhagwan. The strike in the sugar industry, which had continued despite the return to work of the bauxite workers and the clerical and commercial workers, was eventually called off on August 25. When Prime Minister Burnham took off for Cuba on September 2 to attend the non-aligned conference, it was clear that from the government's prospective, the crisis was over. A few weeks earlier the Prime Minister had cancelled his attendance at the Commonwealth Prime Minister's conference scheduled for August 1–7 in Lusaka, Zambia, because of the domestic political situation. But the intimidation and harrassment of WPA supporters and sympathizers continued. A WPA meeting on September 4 at Vreeden-Hoop was broken up. Their public address system was smashed and the platform speaker, Rupert Roopnarine, and others fled in their car. They were pursued and, abandoning their vehicle, fled for safety into the sugar cane fields. When they could not be found, their pursuer set fire to their car.

Because many of the top executives were employed at the University of Guyana, no one was surprised when on September 11 the government announced that the reopening of the University would be delayed until January 1980 due to a lack of funds. No one believed the government. The executive members of the WPA who were charged with burning down the Ministry of National Development appeared in court again on September 14. It was announced that they would be tried under the Administration of Justice Act. The government had pushed through this piece of legislation earlier to strengthen their position to deal with its political dissidents. The Prime Minister went to Linden on September 17 for an extended stay. It was his first extended visit in that area since nationalization, and it was designed to reestablish his party's dominance in that area. But time was passing and the government's hopes for an upturn in the economy or a large infusion of foreign aid did not materialize. In an effort to buy itself some more time, the government on October 22 postponed national elections for another year. The official reason given was that it was taking longer than expected to draft a new constitution. This second postponement of elections further enraged opposition political groups and other social groups alike, but they were not in a position to do much. When the opposition tried to keep up the pressure on the government, to try to make it more accountable, they found that people were tired of the constant political turmoil, and no longer responsive to opposition appeals.

In December 1979, the PPP-affiliated GAWU called another strike in the sugar industry. The union had contended that the workers were entitled to a share of the profits the government was making on the sale of sugar. The government, as employer, saw these profits as returns on their investment, to be used for other industrial expansion. The result was a disastrous three-month strike. The country could not afford such a strike in an industry that was such an important foreign exchange earner. Despite that, both parties settled in to wear each other down.

It was generally known that government policy was to keep key opposition figures under constant surveillance. When in April 1980 security could not account for the whereabouts of Walter Rodney, there was no real cause for alarm. When it was discovered that he was out of the country attending the independence celebrations of Zimbabwe, it became a problem. Strict orders had been issued that he was not to leave the country and his passport had been seized, yet he was able to leave and return undetected. Clearly this budding political upstart was going to be a bigger problem than government and security agencies had imagined. Though the government never made mention of Rodney's departure and return, it soon became widely known: Being able to outwit the security police was a sure pathway to celebrity. In early 1980, a number of people on the West Coast were arrested and charged with treason for plotting the armed overthrow of the government. The trials added to the air of hostility toward the government for the severe way it chose to deal with a dissident group of political activists. Rodney himself had added to the hostilities by comparing the "Treason Trials" with those of the government of South Africa. His comparison further infuriated the government. Then on the evening of Friday, June 13, 1980, Walter Rodney was killed with a hand-made bomb while sitting in his car. His brother Donald was also in the car and was thrown clear by the impact of the explosion. The country was numbed at the implications of this action which had surely been plotted by the PNC government.

On the evening of his death, Walter Rodney had gone to the house of a contact to collect a walkie-talkie. He had planned to use the transmitter to coordinate his political activity. His contact, Mr. Gregory Smith, who had sold himself to Rodney as a sympathizer, had given him a number of instructions to follow, which, given the political climate, seemed sensibly cautious. Rodney was to go to Smith's house at a particular time to pick up the sets Smith was constructing for tests. Instead of going himself, Rodney had his brother drive him to Smith's residence, then sent him in to collect the walkie-talkie while he remained in the car. Smith was adamant that Rodney had contradicted his instructions, but calmed down after being reassured that Walter Rodney was in the car. Smith gave Donald Rodney precise instructions to be followed in testing the transmitter. He stressed that he wanted Walter to walk with the walkie-talkie around the Georgetown prison because he wanted to observe the effect of the expanse of metal on the efficiency of the set. Smith himself would remain at home to operate the companion set. They synchronized watches and Donald left with the carefully wrapped package. Even though instructed to walk with the transmitter, Walter Rodney had his brother drive the route instead. It was only after the explosion that Donald Rodney realized that what they had been given was a sophisticated bomb. Donald ran from the scene. As he was running he noticed a number of unmarked police cars pull up at the site of the explosion. Changing his mind about going to the police station, he went to the home of WPA executive member

Omowale. He told Omowale, Andaye, and Karen deSouza that Walter was seriously injured and that they should go to the scene. Later the WPA put Donald Rodney into a private hospital.

The government in the meantime reacted publicly to the incident by charging that Walter Rodney was on his way to blow up the Georgetown prison when his bomb went off. Shortly after his death, police searched Walter Rodney's house and the house of his mother. The police also desperately wanted to find Donald Rodney, who they knew had been at the scene of the explosion when it happened. But the WPA executed a brilliant maneuver against the government authorities. They kept the surviving Donald Rodney in hiding while they informed the Caribbean and international press of Walter Rodney's death. After the Caribbean press arrived, the WPA arranged for Donald Rodney to make his statement of the incident to them on June 16. By hiding him from the police, the WPA made sure that the press got their side of the incident, and it ensured that the police could not keep him from making a public statement by claiming to be holding him for questioning. It further ensured that having been seen alive by the press, his immediate safety was guaranteed. The flurry of statements which came from PNC politicians and other government organs immediately after Walter Rodney's death denouncing him and warning against the WPA sickened even those still partial to the PNC.

A large bi-partisan crowd turned out for the memorial service for Rodney on Saturday, June 21, 1980, at the Catholic Cathedral. Rodney was not a Catholic, but the *Catholic Standard*, as the only non-political weekly published in the country, had assumed the role of printing news and views which were never seen in the government-owned *Chronicle*. As a result, the Catholic church had grown close to the WPA and to groups opposed to the government.

The funeral itself, which took place two days later, drew a mammoth crowd. The multi-ethnic composition of the crowd was an indication of both the extent to which the WPA had managed to bridge the racial gap, and the frustration others felt with the PNC. After the funeral there was a spate of firings and harrassments by the government against those who had attended. The most notable was the harrassment of Sister Hazel Campayne, the Guyanese nun who was principal of St. Rose's High School. She had preached the sermon at Rodney's memorial service and was known to be sympathetic to the WPA. Eventually she was forced to give up her position and leave the country.

Walter Rodney had succeeded in antagonizing the government more than any other politician had. At his meetings, he often said that when the WPA formed a government, there would be investigations into the money spent on the many incomplete and failed projects of the government. And that, he said, "is the living firing squad." His words must have caused many a government minister to shiver. This was one essential difference between the politics of Dr. Jagan and the PPP and Rodney. The PPP had held office and had had failed projects and scandals, so their position and the PNC's was the same. The WPA had not held office and could afford to make such threatening comments.

The police never found Gregory Smith and never really tried. Though information remains sketchy, it is known that he was a member of the Guyana Defense Force (Marine Branch) who was sent by the GDF to electronics school in London. Whether he was still in the army or not has not been properly established. His disappearance is of course very suspicious. That no investigation was held concerning Rodney's death is indicative of the government's attitude toward the political process in the country.

On October 16, the government announced that elections would be held under the new constitution, and held on December 15, 1980. The opposition parties went through the same arguments, as they had at the time of the referendum, about whether they should or should not contest the elections. The two established parties—the PPP and the UF—decided they would contest the elections.

The PNC scored an important psychological victory against the PPP by procuring the support of PPP executive member Ranji Chandisingh. Mr. Chandisingh, who was known as the foremost PPP theoretician, had resigned from the party in March 1976. He had not been identified with any party since then, and his emergence as a supporter of the PNC was a surprise to many. At the time of his resignation, Mr. Chandisingh had given a very reasoned argument in his letter of departure. It read "As a socialist I functioned in the PPP for 18 years, believing that the leadership for that party was committed to the cause of socialism. To my deep regret and dismay, however, I discovered from bitter experience—at a crucial period in Guyana's history when the PNC had demonstrated its commitment to socialist transformation and development in deeds, not merely in words—that the PPP leaders were less interested in socialism and the unity and well-being of the Guyanese people than in furthering their ambitions for personal power and prestige.

"The PPP nurtured at that stage an almost pathological fear of being rendered irrelevant in a Guyana being led toward socialism by the PNC. Even the attempt to analyze, to work out socialist policies and tactics based on sound political judgement began to give way to sheer obstruction motivated by jealousy and malice. . . ."[38]

Despite this reasonable stand, it cannot be doubted that the knowledge that the PPP seemed to have no reasonable chance of returning to office had taken its toll on the PPP as a whole and made vulnerable to PNC offers. The WPA, still dazed from Walter Rodney's death, did not enter the campaign, partly on principle and partly because they were still a party that was largely urban-based.

Because of past experience in the way the PNC government ran elections, several groups invited international observers to observe the process. The government was not pleased and did its best to hamper the movement of these observers. Whatever tactics the PNC used, they worked. The election results were overwhelming: PNC, 41 seats; PPP, 10; UF, 2

NOTES

1. From Jay R. Mandle—Continuity and Change in Guyanese Underdevelopment. Monthly Review—September, 1976, p. 43.
2. Ibid p. 43
3. Edward Hallett Carr. What is History? Vintage Books, N.Y. 1961, p. 170–171
4. Jay R. Mandle. Continuity and Change in Guyanese Underdevelopment—Monthly Review Press September, 1976, Vol. 28, No. 4, p. 44.
5. Ibid. p. 45–46
6. Keesing's Contemporary archives Sept. 30–Oct. 6, 1974 p. 26745
7. Ibid
8. Ibid
9. Ibid
10. Keesing's Contemporary Archives, March 17–23, 1975, p. 27027
11. Ibid
12. Keesing's Contemporary Archives, March 17–23, 1975, p. 27027
13. Ibid
14. Ibid
15. Ibid
16. Ibid
17. Quoted in Keesing's Contemporary Archives, March 17–23, 1975, p. 27027
18. Declaration of Sophia. Address by the leader of the People's National Congress, Prime Minister Forbes Burnham, December 14, 1974
19. Ibid p. 19
20. Ibid
21. Ibid
22. As quoted in Jay Mandle—Continuity and Change in Guyanese Underdevelopment, p. 48

23. For a different interpretation of these events see Jay R. Mandle, Monthly Review, Vol. 28, No. 4, Sept. 1976, p. 48–49
24. Interview with Senior Civil Servant
25. Financial Times Sept. 9, 1974
26. Financial Times Sept. 11 and 13, 1974
27. Ibid
28. Marshall Kilduff and Roy Javers—The Suicide Cult. The Inside Story of the Peoples Temple and the Massacre in Guyana. Bantham Books 1978. p. 92–97
29. For a good account of the central place sugar played in the economy until then see Jay Mandle, The Plantation Economy: Population and Economic change in Guyana 1938–1969, Temple University Press, 1973
30. Jay Madley, Continuity and Change in Guyana Underdevelopment. Monthly Review Sept. 1976, p. 38
31. Trinidad and Tobago Review August 1979 p. 16
32. Ibid
33. Ibid
34. Ibid
35. Trinidad and Tobago Review, August 1979
36. Trinidad and Tobago Review, August, 1979
37. Trinidad and Tobago Review August 1979
38. Ranji Chandisingh, *Why I Left the PPP*, Guyana National Litographic Co. Ltd. ND.

CHAPTER 11

Continuity through Change

THE most pressing problems of developing countries stem partly from their governments' failure to provide sufficient political stability and to create stable institutions to support development. The political parties that brought independence to the countries which have become independent since WW II have degenerated into the personal instruments of the leaders who created them. These parties—open forums when they opposed the European colonial rule—clam up tight after independence. Rather than remain active centers of debate, they became defenders of their leaders and of government policy. A disproportionate emphasis was placed by these parties on maintaining the government in office, even though the government regularly failed to do the job it was elected to do. In general over the last twenty-five years, these leaders and their governments have survived because they have proved to be more clever at frustrating their opposition, and not because they were successful in anticipating and dealing with their country's economic problems.

The root of the problem in most developing countries lies in the failure of the political parties to impose limits or controls on themselves. Most of the heads in these countries have shown an amazing capacity for clinging to power. In so doing, several of them have raised the political ante in their countries to such a point of brutality that desperate action or total silence is the only refuge of any opposition.

For their part many of these leaders see themselves as irreplaceable, a notion which could only be enforced by developing power. This generally manifests itself through the party or constitutionally. Doing so through the party means raising the party to the level of part of the state apparatus. Doing so constitutionally means changing the constitution to suit the leader in office. The reasons for doing so are born out of a genuine political concern for the preservation and continuance of the established economic and political principles of its founding leaders. However it is this precise point which leads to a stifling of political and economic growth and eventually to high-handed government and dictatorship. What these leaders do not seem to realize is that a political party, like society, is a living organism and must grow and adapt to continually changing situations. This does not necessarily mean that its basic philosophy has to change, but that certain tactical changes may be necessary at times for the survival of the party, changes which are not necessarily opposed to the party's ultimate strategy. To see this is much more a function of leadership; to imbue the party with a philosophy which could serve as its underpinning for decades or its lifetime is more important than to try to be its leader for life.

Now that the founding leaders of these independence parties are too old to continue much longer, or have died, a second opportunity presents itself to their parties and to the new parties that may emerge in the aftermath. The crucial political problem so far has been one of tenure—the period of time the leader of the party serves as head of government before relinquishing his post.

I believe this is the single most important political problem these nations must face. The world today, with its modern communications, has speeded up expectations of people to the point where results are expected faster, and this does not permit a lengthy tenure in office. A leader has to have much more than the confidence of a majority of the voters in order to succeed. The leader must have the support of the civil service and of business: The civil service, because it is the vehicle that executes government policy, and business (whether state-owned or free enterprise) because it is the sector which provides the greatest number of jobs for the people. Of the two, the civil service has gained more attention recently, although the other is equally important. A great amount of money has been spent on educating and training the civil service top-echelon. Like most professionals, these men and women not only want a job and want to be able to serve their country, they want to be challenged, to develop their professional skills and abilities. They want job satisfaction.

This does not necessarily mean being made head of a department or of a particular project, but it means a chance to compete with one's peers, to interact with other professionals. When these professionals are not given an adequate opportunity to develop, they either leave or become apathetic and cease to strive for the excellence which makes them useful to the government.

The story of Guyana during the PPP tenure between 1962 and 1964 is a case in point. During this time many of the senior Guyanese civil servants who should have remained to succeed the departing British themselves migrated to other Caribbean islands or to the U.S., Canada, and Britain. The same thing happened once again between 1975 and 1980 when it became apparent that the PNC was determined to remain in office indefinitely, despite their lack of any clear economic plan. This was true more recently in Jamaica, where there was a wholesale flight of professionals from the Manley government between 1975 and 1980. This drain of skilled manpower means that a country with limited resources will be run by second-rank bureaucrats, who have neither the training nor the experience to do as good a job.

To attempt to run a government without the cooperation of the bureaucrats is difficult. Politicians who do not cultivate some type of working relationship with this group have a troubled tenure in office. In some countries where immigration is not allowed and the relationship is poor, this frustration is evident in the agonizingly slow pace with which the bureaucracy functions.

If these parties are to serve as a vehicle for progress, their new leaders must think foremost of the survival of the party as an institution. It is the institution for debating and adumbrating the political desires of those whom it represents, so it must never be for too long the personal vehicle of a few within the party, no matter how popular they are, no matter how right their ideas. It must be recognized that tenure in office is not a factor in determining greatness, as many leaders seem to think. Seizing opportunity and handling important events in a bold and daring manner are much more important. Here conviction and pragmatism are the qualities needed; conviction for inspiring party and people and pragmatism in operating the government. A prolonged tenure in office begets economic policies which are intended to break the economic potential of political opposition and to give the government more patronage, resources and employment opportunities.

A stifling atmosphere is created in any country when any one person heads a modern government for an unlimited period of time. No matter how great the euphoria at the outset, an unspecified, prolonged tenure in government is not compatible with today's modern society. It leads to exhaustion and frustration. All heads of governments, whether from the military or politicans, have to appeal to the mass of people for support. A modern leader must recognize the need to govern on behalf of the common good. And no one person or group can claim to have a corner on the ideas necessary for governing for a prolonged period without being challenged by others with different ideas or a different style and emphasis. A particular leader may be able to get away with it if the economy is booming. But the leader who is in office over two terms, whatever their duration, begins to tire from the strain of holding office and of political wrangling. The temptation to muzzle opponents is great, as he convinces himself that he needs time and opportunity to complete his plans.

Must dissent always be stifled? Must dissent always be interpreted as a threat to national security? Every country needs to maintain some type of offensive and defensive posture to ensure its security. However, history is laden with examples of those who see themselves as their country's national security. Such power is notoriously seductive, and notoriously destructive, no matter how great the leader. Leaders should see their greatness not in remaining at the helm forever, but in selecting and training other talented persons to continue their policies. If the ideas behind the policies were good, even their opposition would not dare dismantle them. Greatness is not having the ability to survive in office or to implement good ideas, but having lasting ideas which span generations.

Prolonged continuance in office can also be an impediment to the development of alternative ideas. Some people would never work for certain leaders no matter how popular, no matter how sound their policies. Honest men differ on the most elementary subjects. As a result there are always a number of persons who do not support a given government. When the disaffected are added to this number over time, the opposition grows. The mechanics necessary for excluding a popular and growing group from the political process for a long time could, and have, in the heat of political battle, produced rash judgments by some of the ablest persons. To avoid this, there must be a specified term for anyone to remain head of government. Political groups feeling the weight of a prolonged, indefinite wait to be tested at the polls make the system too circumscribed and drain it of vitality.

With a defined term of office imposed for the head of government, even those out of favor within the party will be more willing to wait their turn. The hope offered by regular elections must exist to counterbalance the frustrations of those not in power. It is this limitation—institutionalized change—that Third World parties must impose upon themselves if they are to continue to be in the political forefront in the decades ahead. It is necessary for their survival.

The tenure of the leader of government has occupied the attention of many observers and practitioners for some time. In some countries, because of their history, a system evolved. In others a more tacit agreement was followed, and in still others it had to be mandated. I would like to look at four models in practice—Britain, United States, Mexico, and Japan—and the military for the insight they can provide for Third World countries.

Britain

The British system is an evolutionary one, the whole concept of parliamentary government having evolved over a long period of time. The theoretical underpinnings of this form of government is generally known to all. However, some of the practical manifestations of the system tend to be overlooked. If we agree, as most scholars do, that modern Prime Ministers began with Walpole, we see that he had twenty-one continuous years of service from 1721 to 1742. He provided Britain with a legacy of political stability after a century of division and turmoil. He also, through the appointments he made, built up the Court and Treasury Party that was to be the core of Whig strength for many generations after his death. Since then, no Prime Minister has served as long as Walpole. Only three men have served more than fourteen years as Prime Minister: Pitt, Liverpool, and Salisbury. The system in action has produced an even more interesting result in the present environment. Since the departure of Salisbury in 1905, no one Prime Minister has served as many as ten years in office. The longest serving was Herbert Henry Asquith. He was Prime Minister for eight years and eight months, the longest so far in the twentieth century, topping Winston Churchill by three days. The evidence suggests that in a world of ambiguity and rapid change in which people are seeking answers, we use up our leaders more rapidly than in the past.

While the political parties themselves have at times been in office for longer than ten years, Prime Ministers have found it difficult to retain the confidence of their party and the people for a prolonged period. So that while the Prime Minister and cabinet members might resign, the party remains in office. It is understood that a party's policies may still have the confidence of the people, who disapprove only of the party's Prime Minister. The office has been a barometer of the leader's stature within this party and, as Prime Minister, of his command of both his party and the electorate.

United States

The U.S. presidential system has functioned for nearly 150 years by tacit agreement. The founding fathers, and all who came after, agreed that a president would be limited to two 4-year terms. It is interesting that as far back as 1776, American politicians realized the problems that could spring from having a president elected an indefinite number of times. It was not until Franklin D. Roosevelt became President and was elected four times (due to the exigencies of WW II) that a law was passed, making what was until then an agreement, mandatory.

It is also interesting to note that in its two hundred years of presidential government, the U.S. has had only seven presidents to serve eight continuous years in the White House.

Mexico

Mexico was the first country to go through a major revolution in the twentieth century. The Mexican revolution touched every aspect of Mexican life and institutions, and it was prolonged and bloody. The revolution was the result of public disgust at the long despotic rule of Perfidio Diaz. Each one of the many plans put forward by the revolutionaries and thinkers contained a basic requirement of non-reelection. The Mexican President, it was agreed, would serve one 6-year term. Indeed the revolution itself, which had been incubating for some time, was given urgency when the near senile President Diaz rigged yet another election and declared himself winner. Even though Diaz had provided the country with one of its longest periods of stability, the price of his remaining in office was greater repression.

The result of the adoption of the principle of non-reelection, imperfect as it is, has been that Mexico after the revolution has enjoyed the longest period of political stability in its entire history. Admittedly, one party, the Party for the Institutionalization of the Revolution, has run the government for the past fifty years. The ritual of a new President taking office every six years with his own group of advisers and consultants has survived. (This example, when contrasted with others, suggests that people become disenchanted not necessarily with the party but with the prolonged governance of one particular person or small group within the party.)

Japan

Japan combines both the British Parliamentary and the Mexican system. It is interesting because it is relatively new, not much older than the parties in most Third World countries. The Japanese political process, even though it prescribes no fixed term that a leader can remain head of government, has produced a fair number of Prime Ministers since the Second World War. The regular replacement of men at the top has enabled one party to lead the government since then. The Liberal Democratic Party has been in office continuously and has produced all of these men.

Again, this suggests that the head of the party and his advisers are perceived to be the ones who need to be changed continuously, not necessarily the party. This holds true even if the governing group might be the military.

The Military

The military generally is as great a concern to any government and rival for power as any civilian interest group. Again, sufficient time has elapsed since independence in the Third World to begin to make some general observations. There can be no doubt that the armed forces are part of the elite of a country and an important center of power within a country. They have an interest in maintaining stability and in insuring the general improvement of the state. The difference between them and other interest groups is that they can do something which other interest groups can't do. They can intervene when political disagreement threatens to destroy the society or when political parties have fought so bitterly that they have either destroyed or exhausted each other.

Recent events have shown that the military also intervenes when the government becomes too dependent upon them as a means of staying in power. While the armed forces can be used in a number of ways, to use them for political purposes is a very dangerous business. The military simply concludes that they can do the job themselves. It does not serve any purpose to bring up examples here, but the use of the military to collect information about or to sabotage the opposition is suicidal. The military can in no way replace an efficient party organization. The laziness that sometimes comes from being too long in office or being too far removed from one's political party has driven many a politician to rely too heavily on the military, to his own detriment. The solution to both the party and its leaders is to take the leaders out of this position by limiting the term in office.

While it is true that the military occupies an excellent position from which to assume power, not all military leaders desire to take advantage of the opportunity. Those officers who show themselves less willing to do so seem mostly to be persons who, as in the case of the West Indies, have had some experience in another occupation before joining the army. Many of these officers were civil servants or teachers with part-time commission in the old British Volunteer Force. At independence, these weekend soldiers had the option of joining the military or continuing their regular jobs. Working with politicians in the civil service had given these men an understanding of the need for compromise and the ability to work with politicians. Because the majority of the officer corps was brought in in this manner, those who had gone to officer training school directly after their formal education had to follow the precedent set by the majority who were accustomed to subordinating their own political and social views to those of their political head.

In most developing countries, the army is for defensive rather than offensive purposes, and it would repay politicians to keep it that way. This is no guarantee of nonintervention by the army, but it is a precaution. Maintaining a proportion of the army's officer corps, made-up of former civil servants with at least five years experience and a short officer's course, would go a long way toward ensuring a certain neutrality in the military.

APPENDIX I
House of Assembly—1953

Speaker—Sir Eustace Gordon Woolford, O.B.E., Q.C.

Ex-Officio Members:

The Chief Secretary	—Hon. John Gutch, C.M.G., O.B.E.
The Attorney-General	—Hon. F. W. Holder, Q.C.
Financial Secretary	—Hon. W. O. Fraser, O.B.E.

Elected Members:

People's Progressive Party

The Honourable Dr. C. B. Jagan	—Leader of the House (Minister of Agriculture, Forest, Lands & Mines & Member for the Corentyne Coast)
The Honourable L. F. S., Burnham	—(Minister of Education & Member for Georgetown North-East)
The Honourable A. Chase	—(Minister of Labour, Industry & Commerce & Member for Georgetown South)
The Honourable Dr. J. P. Latchmansingh	—(Minister of Health & Housing & Member for East Bank, Demerara)
The Honorable Jai Narine Singh	—(Minister of Local Government & Social Welfare & Member for West Bank, Demerara)
Mrs. J. Jagan	—(Deputy Speaker & Member for Western Essequibo)
Mr. F. Bowman	—(Member for Demerara-Essequibo)

Miss J. I. S. Burnham	—(Member for Georgetown Central)
Mrs. J. Philips-Gay	—(Member for Central Demerara)
Mr. M. Khan	—(Member for Corentyne River)
Mr. S. M. Latchmansingh	—(Member for Western Berbice)
Mr. C. S. Persaud	—(Member for Mahaica—Mahaicony)
Mr. Ramkarran	—(Member for West Central Demerara)
Mr. Ajodha Singh	—(Member for Eastern Berbice)
Dr. R. S. Hanomansingh	—(Member for Eastern Berbice)
Mr. C. R. Wong	—(Member for Georgetown South Central)
Mr. F. O. Van-Sertima*	—(Member for Georgetown North Central)

National Democratic Party

Mr. W. O. R. Kendall	—(Member for New Amsterdam)
Mr. E. F. Correia	—(Member for Bartica & Interior)

Independents

Mr. T. Lee	—(Member of Essequibo Islands)
Mr. W. A. Pang	—(Member for North West)
Mr. C. A. Carter	—(Member for Upper Demerara River)
Mr. T. S. Wheating	—(Member of Pomeroon)

Total number of elected members—twenty-four

1953—Executive Council

His Excellency The Governor	—Sir Alfred William Langley Savage, K.C.M.G.

Departments

Chief Secretary—Honourable John Gutch C.M.G., O.B.E., M.H.A.	Police (including Immigration) British Guiana Volunteer Force Public Information Bureau Public Service Commission Interior
Attorney-General—Honourable	Legal

---

*Election subsequently declared void as a result of election petition.

F. W. Holder, Q.C., M.H.A.	Crown Solicitor
	Public Trustee and Official Receiver
	Registrar (functions other than those as Registrar of the Supreme Court)
Financial Secretary—Honourable W. O. Fraser, O.B.E., M.H.A.	Treasury
	Customs & Excise
	Income Tax
Honourable Dr. C. B. Jagan, M.H.A.—Minister of Agriculture, Forests, Lands & Mines (Leader of the House of Assembly)	Agriculture
	Forestry
	Lands & Mines
	Geological Survey
Honourable Sir Frank McDavid, C.M.G., C.B.E., M.S.C. (President of the State Council)	Minister without Portfolio
Honourable L. F. S. Burnham, M.H.A., Minister of Education	Education (including Technical Institute), Queens College
	Bishop High School
Honourable Ashton Chase, M.H.A.—Minister of Labour, Industry & Commerce	Labour,
	Supplies & Prices
Honourable S. E. King, M.H.A., Minister of Communications & Works	Public Works
	Post Office (Other than Post Office Savings Bank)
	Transport & Harbours
	Civil Aviation
Honourable Dr. J. P. Latchmansingh M.H.A., Minister of Health & Housing	Medical
	Registrar General
	Government Analyst
	Town Planner
Honourable Jai Narine Singh, M.H.A., Minister of Local Government & Social Welfare	Local Government
	Social Welfare
	Prisons

Interim Government—1954

Legislative Council

Speaker

Sir Eustace Gordon Woolford,
O.B.E., Q.C.

Ex-Officio Members
The Chief Secretary

—Hon. John Gutch, C.M.G.,
O.B.E.

The Attorney-General

—Hon. F. W. Holder, Q.C.

Financial Secretary

—Hon. W. O. Fraser, O.B.E.

Nominated Members of Executive Council

The Honourable Sir Frank McDavid,
C.M.G., C.B.E.

Member for Agriculture, Forest,
Lands & Mines

The Honourable P. A. Cummings

Member for Labour, Health and
Housing

The Honourable W. O. R. Kendall

The Honourable G. A. C. Farnum,
O.B.E.

The Honourable G. H. Smellie

The Honourable R. B. Gajraj

The Honourable R. C. Tello

Deputy Speaker Mr. W. J.
Raatgraver, C.B.E.

NOMINATED OFFICIALS:

1. Mr. W. T. Lord, D.S.O.
2. Mr. J. J. Ramphal

NOMINATED UNOFFICIALS:

1. Mr. T. Lee
2. Mr. W. A. Pang
3. Mr. L. A. Luckhoo
4. Mr. W. A. Macnie, G.M.G., O.B.E.
5. Mr. C. A. Carter
6. Mr. E. F. Correia
7. Rev. D. C. J. Bobb
8. Mr. H. Rahaman
9. Miss Gertie H. Collins
10. Mrs. Esther E. Day
11. Dr. H. A. Fraser
12. Lt. Col. E. J. Haywood, M.B.E., T.D.
13. Mr. R. B. Jailall
14. Mr. Sugrim Singh

Government—1957

1957 Executive Council

His Excellency the Governor—Sir Patrick Muir Renison—Chairman

Departments

Chief Secretary-Honourable F. D. Jakeway, C.M.G., O.B.E.

Police (Inc. Immigration)
British Guiana Volunteer Force
Government Information Service
Public Service Commission

Attorney-General-Honourable A. M. I. Austin

Law Officers
Crown Solicitor, Public Trustee & Official Receiver
Deeds Registry

Financial Secretary-Honourable F. W. Essex

Treasury
Customs & Excise
Post Office Savings Bank
Inland Revenue
Licence Revenue Office
Statistical Bureau

Honourary Dr. C. B. Jagan—Minister of Trade & Industry

Trade & Industry
Supplies & Prices
Cooperative Development

Honourable B. H. Benn
Community Development &
Education

Local Government
Social Welfare
Prisons
Essequibo Boys' School
Education (Inc. Queens College, Bishops High School and Technical Institute)

Honourable E. B.
Beharry—Minister of Natural
Resources

Agriculture
Forestry
Lands & Mines
Drainage & Irrigation
Land Settlement

Honourable J. Jagan—Minister of
Labour, Health & Housing

Labour, Medical, Registrar General
(except as regards electoral
matters)
Government Analyst

Honourable R. Karren
Communications & Works

Public Works; Post Office (other than
P.O. Savings Bank)
Transport & Harbours; civil aviation

NOMINATED MEMBERS OF PPP
   Mr. R. B. Gajraj   —Nominated Member
   Mr. R. C. Tello
   Mr. R. E. Davis
   Mr. A. M. Fredericks
   Mr. H. G. J. Hubbard
   Mr. A. G. Tasker

Total number of elected members—fifteen.

Government and Opposition—1961

1961—Legislative Council
His Honour R. B. Gajraj — Speaker

People's Progressive Party Ministers

Dr. the Honourable C. B. Jagan —Premier & Minister of Development & Planning (Member for Corentyne East)

Honourable B. H. Benn —Minister of Natural Resources (Member for Demerara Coast-West)

Honourable B. S. Rai —Minister of Home Affairs (Member for Demerara Coast-East)

Honourable R. Karran —Minister of Works & Hydraulics (Member for Mahaica)

Honourable R. Chandisingh —Minister of Labour, Health & Housing (Member for Lower Demerara River)

Dr. The Honourable Charles Jacob (JNR) —Minister of Finance (Member for Vreed-en-Hoop)

Dr. the Honourable F. H. W. Ramsahoye —Attorney-General (Member for Canals Polder)

Honourable E. M. G. Wilson —Minister of Communications (Member for Boerasirie)

Parlimentary Secretaries

Mr. G. Bowman —Parliamentary Secretary to the Ministry of Natural Resources (Member for Corentyne Central)

Mr. L. E. McR. Mann —Parliamentary Secretary to the
Ministry of Works & Hydraulics
(Member for Mahaicony)
(Resigned 24.2.64)

Other Members of the PPP
Mr. S. M. Saffee —Member for Berbice-West
Mr. G. L. Robertson —Member for Leonora
Mr. M. Bhagwan —Member for Essequibo Islands
Mr. J. B. Caldeira —Member for Pomeroon
Mr. V. Downer —Member for Berbice-East
Mr. M. Hamid —Member for Demerara-Central
Mr. G. McL. Henry —Member for Houston (election was
declared void on November 27,
1961)
Mr. D. B. Jagan —Member for Suddie
Mr. H. Lall —Member for Corentyne-West
Mr. M. Shakoor —Member for Corentyne River

People's National Congress
Mr. L. F. S. Burnham, Q.C. —Member for Ruimbeldt
Mr. W. O. R. Kendall —Member for New Amsterdam
Mr. J. Carter —Member for Werk-en-Rust
Mr. E. F. Correia —Member for Mazaruni-Potaro
Mr. N. J. Bissember —Member for Campbellville
Mr. W. A. Blair —Member for Berbice River
Mr. R. S. Hugh —Member for Georgetown-South
Mr. J. G. Joquim —Member for Kitty
Mr. R. J. Jordan —Member for Upper Demerara
River
Mr. C. A. Merriman —Member for LaPenitence—Lodge
Mr. H. M. S. Wharton —Member for Abary

United Force
Mr. P. S. D'Aguiar —Member for Georgetown-Central
Mr. S. Campbell —Member for North West
Mr. R. E. Cheeks —Member for Georgetown—North
Mr. E. E. Melville —Member for Rupununi

Total Number of elected members—thirty-five.

Bibliography

PRIMARY SOURCES

Official Reports

British Guiana Commission Report Cmd 2841, 1927.

British Guiana Constitution Commission, Report HMSA 2985, 1927 Memorandum prepared by the Elected Members of the Combined Court of British Guiana to the report of the British Guiana Commission Cmd 2841 HMSO 3047, 1928.

British Guiana Conference 1963 Report Cmd 2203, 1963.

British Guiana Constitutional Commission 1950–1951 Report Col. 280, (Sir E. J. Waddington: Chairman).

British Guiana Constitutional Commission Report Cmd. 9274, 1954 (Sir James Robertson: Chairman).

British Guiana Constitutional Conference Report Cmd 998, 1960.

British Guiana Constitutional Instruments 1961 for British Guiana Government 1961.

British Guiana Development Programme, Report by Kenneth Berrill, British Guiana Sessional Paper 2/1960.

British Guiana Independence Conference Report Cmd 1870, 1962.

British Guiana; Suspension of the Constitution, Report Cmd 8980, 1953.

Commission of Inquiry into Disturbances in British Guiana in February, 1962 Report Col. 354, 1962.

Commission of Inquiry into the Sugar Industry of British Guiana Report Col. No. 249, 1949 (J. A. Venn: Chairman).

Commission to Review Wages, Salaries and Conditions of Service in the Public Services of British Guiana 1958–1959 (L. H. Gorswch) British Guiana Government Publication.

Enmore Commission—Report, Legislative Council No. 10/1948.

Financial Situation in British Guiana, Report Cmd 3938, 1931 Memorandum on the Financial Position of British Guiana 1920–1946 by O. A. Spencer. British Guiana Government publication.

Financial Position Report by K. C. Jacobs Col. 358, 1964.

Local Government in British Guiana, Report by A. A. Marshall, Georgetown Argosy 1955.

Racial Problems in the Public Service, Report of the British Guiana Commission of Inquiry, constituted by the International Commission of Jurists, Geneva 1965.

Report of the British Guiana Independence Conference 1965 Cmd 2849.

Report of the Government of British Guiana on Employment, Unemployment and Underemployment in the Colony in 1956 by E. McGale, I.L.O., Geneva, 1957.

West Indies

Brown, G. St. J. Orde—*Labour Conditions in the West Indies*, London, HMSO Cmd 6070, 1939.

Conference on West Indian Federation, Report Cmd 8837, 1953.

The Plan for British Caribbean Federation Cmd 8895, 1953.

The West Indian Royal Commission (1938–1939) (Lord Moyne: Chairman) Cmd 6607, 1945.

Party Publications

PPP—Constitution, ratified by First Congress. Georgetown Arcade Printery 1951 Amended 1962.

Vanguard, Pamphlet Georgetown Arcade Printery 1953.

The Great Betrayal, Georgetown Arcade Printery—September 1957.

1957 Election Manifesto, Georgetown, 1957.

1961 Election Manifesto, Georgetown, New Guiana Co., 1961.

PP's Fight for Free Elections, Georgetown, New Guiana Co., 1961.

History of the PPP-Georgetown New Guiana Co., Ltd., 1963.

PNC—"We're No Pawn of East or West"—Pamphlet by People's National Congress, 1960.

Legislative Record 1957–1961 (duplicated 1961).

U.F.—Economic Dynamism . . . and you, 1961 Election Manifesto, La Penitence 1961.

Books and Theses

Almond, G. A. and Coleman, J. S. (eds.), *The Politics of Developing Areas*, (Princeton: Princeton University Press, 1960).

Almond, G. A., and Powell, Bingham G., Jr., *Comparative Politics: A Development Approach* (Boston: Little, Brown and Co., 1966).

Almond, G. A. and Verba, Sidney, *The Civic Culture: Political Attitudes and Democracy in Five Nations* (Princeton: Princeton University Press, 1967).

Anderson, Charles W., Vow Der Mahden, Fred R., and Young, Crawford, *Issues of Political Development* (Englewood Cliffs: Prentice-Hall, Inc., 1967).

Apter, David, *The Gold Coast in Transition*, (Princeton: Princeton University Press, 1955).

——————, *The Politics of Moderanization*, (Chicago: University of Chicago Press, 1965).

——————, (ed), *Ideology and Discontent*, (New York: Free Press, 1964).

Austin, Dennis, *Politics in Ghana*, (Oxford University Press, 1964).

Ayearst, Morley, *The British West Indies: The Search for Self-Government*, (London: Allen and Unwin, 1960).

Bahadoorsingh, Krishan, *Trinidad Electoral Politics: The Persistence of the Race Factor,* (Oxford University Press, 1968).

Banfield, E. C., *The Moral Basis of a Backward Society*, (New York: Free Press, 1958).

Beckford, George, *Persistent Poverty*, (Oxford University Press, 1971).

Bell, Wendell (ed.), *The Democratic Revolution in the West Indies*. (Mass Schenkman Publishing Co., 1966).

——————, *Decisions of Nationhood: Political and Social Development in the British Caribbean* (Denver, Colorado: Monograph).

British Guiana Trades Union Council. *The Communist Martyr Makers: An Account of the Struggle for Free Trade Unionism in British Guiana in 1964*, (Georgetown, 1964).

British Guiana Trades Union Council, *The Freedom Strikers: An Account of the 1963 Trades Union Council General Strike*, (Georgetown, 1964).

Burnham, Forbes, *A Destiny to Mould: Selected Discourses by the Prime Minister of Guyana*, (London: Longman Caribbean, 1970).

Butler, David and Stokes, Donald, *Political Change in Britain: Forces Shaping Electoral Choice*, (London: MacMillan & Co., 1969).

Cameron, N. E., *The Evolution of the Negro*, Georgetown Argosy Co., 2 vols., 1934.

Carr, E. H., *The Twenty Years Crisis*, (New York: Harper Torchbooks, first published Macmillan, 1939).

Carter, Martin, *Poems of Resistance from British Guiana*, (London: Lawrence and Dishart, 1954).

Chase, Ashton, *A History of Trade Unionism in Guyana 1900–1961*, (ed. by Audrey Chase), (Georgetown: New Guyana Co., 1966).

Churchill, Winston, *Great Contemporaries*, (London: Fontana Books, 1937).

Clementi, Sir Cecil, *A Constitutional History of British Guiana*, (London: Macmillan, 1937).

—————, *The Chinese in British Guiana*, (Georgetown: Argosy Co., 1915).

Coleman, J. S., *Education and Political Development*, (Princeton: Princeton University Press, 1968).

Dahl, Robert A., *Modern Political Analysis*, (Englewood Cliffs, New Jersey: 1970).

—————, *Who Governs*, (New Haven, Connecticut: Yale University Press, 1962).

Demas, William, *Economics of Small States*, (McGill University Press, 1967).

Despres, Leo, *Cultural Pluralism and Nationalist Politics in British Guiana*, (Chicago: Rand McNally, 1967).

Deutsch, K. W., *The Nerves of Government*, (New York: Free Press, 1963).

Deverger, Maurice, *Political Parties: Their Organization and Activity in a Modern State*, (London: Methuen, 1964).

Edwards, Adolph, *Marcus Garvey*, (London: New Beacon Publications, 1967).

Emerson, Rupert E., *From Empire to Nation*, (Cambridge: Harvard University Press, 1960).

Fanon, Franz, *The Wretched of the Earth*, (New York: Grove Press, 1965).

—————, *The Wretched of the Earth*, (London: Penguin Books, 1969).

Farley, Rawle, "The Rise of the Peasantry," *British Guiana, Social and Economic Studies*, ii/4 (1954).

—————, "The Unification of British Guiana," *Social and Economic Studies*, (1955).

—————, *Trade Unions and Politics in the British Caribbean*, (Georgetown, 1957).

—————, *The Caribbean Trade Unionist*, (Georgetown Daily Chronicle, 1959).

Fried, Morton H., "The Chinese in British Guiana," *Social and Economic Studies*, v (1956).

Geertz, Clifford, *Old Societies and New States: The Quest for Modernity in Asia and Africa*, (New York: Free Press, 1963).

Glasgow, Roy A., *Guyana: Race and Politics Among Africans and East Indians*, (Martinus Nijhoff, The Hague, 1970).

Gravesande, Laurens Storm van's, *The Rise of British Guiana*, compiled from dispatches by C. A. Harris and J. A. J. de Villiers (London: Hakluyt Society, 1911), 2 vols., Nos. 26–27.

Griffith, Robert, *The Politics of Fear, Joseph R. McCarthy and the Senate*, (Lexington: University of Kentucky Press, 1970).

Griffith, William E., *Communist Esoteric Communications Explication de Texte*, Centre for International Studies, (Cambridge, Mass.: MIT Press, 1967).

Halperin, Ernst, *Racism and Communism in British Guiana*, (Cambridge, Mass.: MIT Press, 1964).

Harrod, Jeffrey, *Trade Union Foreign Policy: A Study of British and American Trade Union Activities in Jamaica,* (London: Macmillan, 1972).

Hodgkin, Thomas, *African Political Parties,* (London: Penguin Books, 1961).

Hoetink, H., *Two Variants of Caribbean Race Relations,* (Oxford University Press, 1967).

Horowitz, Irving L., *Three Worlds of Development* (Oxford University Press, 1966).

Hughes, Colin A., *"The British Guiana General Election, 1953." Parliamentary Affairs,* Vol. 11, 1973–1954, pp. 213–220.

International Bank for Reconstruction and Development, *The Economic Development of British Guiana: Report of a Mission Organized by the International Bank* (Baltimore: Johns Hopkins Press, 1953).

Jagan, Cheddi, *Forbidden Freedom: The Story of British Guiana,* (London: Lawrence & Wishart, 1955).

——————, *Bitter Sugar,* (Georgetown, n.d.)

——————, *The West on Trial: My Fight for Guyana's Freedom,* (London: Michael Joseph, 1966).

Jagan, Janet, "What Happened in British Guiana," *Monthly Review,* April 1962.

James C. L. R., *The Case for West Indiana Self-Government,* (London: Hogwarth Press, 1933).

——————, *Party Politics in the West Indies,* (Trinidad Verdic Enterprises, Ltd. 1962).

Jayawardena, C., *Conflict and Solidarity in a Guyanese Plantation,* London School of Economics, Monograph on Social Anthropology (London: Athlone Press, 1963).

King, Sidney, *Next Witness—An Appeal to World Opinion, Labor Advocate,* (Georgetown, 1962).

Kohn, Hans, *The Idea of Nationalism,* (New York: Macmillan, 1951).

Knowles, William H., *Trade Union Development and Industrial Relations in the British West Indies,* (Berkeley: Univ. of California Press, 1959).

Lamming, George and Carter, Martin (eds.), *New World Independence Issue,* (1966).

LaPalombara, Joseph and Weiner, Myron (eds.), *Political Parties and Political Development,* (Princeton: Princeton University Press, 1966).

Learner, Daniel, *The Passing of Traditional Society,* (Glencoe, Ill.: The Free Press, 1958).

Lewis, Gordon K., *The Growth of the Modern West Indies.* (London: MacGibbon and Knee, 1968).

Lipset, Martin S., and Solari, Aldo, *Elites in Latin America,* (Oxford University Press, 1967).

Lutchman, Harold, *Interest Representation in the Public Service.*

Man, James A., *Social Change and Images of the Future*, (Cambridge: Schenkman Publishing Co., Inc., 1967).

McKenzie, R. T., *British Political Parties*, (London: Heineman, 1955).

Michels, Robert, *Political Parties*, (New York: Dover, 1959).

Milbraith, Lester, *Political Participation: How and Why People Get Involved in Politics*, (Chicago: Rand McNally & Co., 1965).

Miller, J. D. B., *The Politics of the Third World*, (London: Oxford University Press, 1967).

Mordecai, Sir John, *The West Indies: The Federal Negotiations*, (London: George Allen and Unwin, Ltd., 1968).

Moskos, Charles C., *The Sociology of Independence*, (Cambridge: Schenkman Publishing Co., Inc., 1968).

Naipaul, V. S., *The Middle Passage*, (London: Andre Deutsch, 1962).

Nath, D., *A History of Indians in British Guiana*, (London: Thomas Nelson and Sons, 1950).

Newman, Peter, *British Guiana, Problems of Cohesion in an Immigrant Society*, (London: Oxford University Press, 1964).

Norris, Katrin, *Jamaica: The Search for an Identity*, (London: Oxford University Press, 1962).

Ogueri, Eze A., II, *Seven Amazing Days*, (Boston, Mass.: House of Edinborough Publishers, 1954).

O'Loughlin, C., "The Economy of British Guiana, 1952–1956: A National Accounts Study," *Social and Economic Studies*, viii/1 (1959).

——————, "The Rice Sector in the Economy of British Guiana," *Social and Economic Studies*, vii (1958).

Oxall, Ivor, *Black Intellectuals Come to Power*, (Cambridge: Schenkman Publishing Co., Inc., 1968).

Parry & Sherlock, *A Short History of the British West Indies*, (London: Macmillan, 1956).

Preiswerk, Roy (ed.), *Documents on International Relations in the Caribbean*, *Rio Piedras, Puerto Rico* (University of Puerto Rico, Institute of Caribbean Studies, 1970).

Pye, Lucien W., *Politics, Personality and Nation Building*, (New Haven: Yale University Press, 1962).

——————, *Aspects of Political Development*, (Boston: Little Brown and Co., 1966).

Pye, Lucien W., and Verba, Sidney (eds.), *Political Culture and Political Development*, (Princeton: Princeton University Press, 1965).

Reno, Philip, *The Ordeal of British Guiana*, (New York Monthly Review Press, 1964).

Rinhoman, Peter, "Centenary History of the East Indians in British Guiana," *The Daily Chronicle*, (Georgetown, Guyana, 1946).

Rodney, Walter, *The Groundings with My Brothers*, (London: The Boyle L'Ouverture Publications, 1969).

Rodway, J., *Guiana: British, Dutch and French,* (London: T. Fisher, Unwin, 1912).

――――――, *History of British Guiana from 1668,* (Georgetown, 1891), 3 vols.

Rostow, W. W., *The Stages of Economic Growth,* (Cambridge University Press, 1960).

Ruhomon, Peter, "*Centenary History of the East Indians in British Guiana, 1838–1938,*" *Georgetown Daily Chronicle*.

Sancho, T. Anson, *Highlights of Guyanese History. A Study Pinpointing Some Signposts in Our History,* (Georgetown, Guyana: Independence Publication, 1966).

Sigmund, Paul E., Jr., *The Ideologies of the Developing Nations,* (New York: Frederick Praeger, 1963).

Simms, Peter, *Trouble in Guyana: An Account of People, Personalities and Politics as They Are in British Guiana,* (London: George Allen and Unwin, Ltd., 1966).

Singer, Marshall R., *Weak States in a World of Powers,* (New York: Free Press, 1972).

Singham, A. W., *The Hero and the Crowd in a Colonial Polity,* (Connecticut: Yale University Press, 1968).

Smith, R. T., *The Negro Family in British Guiana: Family Structure and Social Status in the Village,* (London: Routledge and Kegan Paul in Assoc. with ISER UWI, Jamaica, 1956).

――――――, *British Guiana,* (Oxford University Press, 1962).

Swan, Michael, *British Guiana: Land of Six Peoples,* (London, HMSO, 1957).

The Yearbook of World Affairs 1945–1966.

Thomas, C. Y., *Sugar Economies in a Colonial Situation: A Study of Guyana's Sugar Industry,* (Studies in Exploration No. 1), (Georgetown: Ratoon Group Pub. 1970).

Wallbridge, Rev. E. A., "The Demerara Martyr," *Daily Chronicle,* (Georgetown, Guyana: 1943).

Weber, A. R. F., *Centenary History and Handbook of British Guiana,* (Georgetown, Guyana: Argosy Co., 1931).

Williams, Eric, *Capitalism and Slavery,* (London: Andre Deutsch, 1961).

――――――, *History of the People of Trinidad and Tobago,* (London: Deutsch, 1964).

Young, Allen, *Approaches to Local Self-Government in British Guiana,* (London: Longmans, 1958).

Zolberg, Aristide, *Creating Political Order: The Party States of West Africa,* (Chicago: Rand McNally and Co., 1966).

――――――, *One Party Government in the Ivory Coast,* (Princeton: Princeton University Press, 1964).

Index